The Optimum Utilization
of Knowledge

The Optimum Utilization of Knowledge

Making Knowledge Serve Human Betterment

edited by **Kenneth E. Boulding**
and **Lawrence Senesh**

Westview Press / Boulder, Colorado

Academy of Independent Scholars Forum Series

This book contains position papers presented at a symposium on the optimum utilization of knowledge at the University of Massachusetts, Amherst, November 5–November 8, 1981.

Published in 1983 in the United States of America by
Westview Press, Inc.
5500 Central Avenue
Boulder, Colorado 80301
Frederick A. Praeger, President and Publisher

Library of Congress Cataloging in Publication Data
Main entry under title:
The Optimum utilization of knowledge.
  (Academy of Independent Scholars forum series)
  "Papers presented at a symposium . . . at the University of Massachusetts, Amherst, November 5–November 8, 1981"—Verso t.p.
  Includes index.
  1. Learning and scholarship—Congresses. 2. Knowledge, theory of—Congresses. I. Boulding, Kenneth Ewart, 1910–   . II. Senesh, Lawrence. III. Series.
AZ103.O67   983   001   82-23787
ISBN 0-86531-544-2

Printed and bound in the United States of America

Contents

Foreword

In 1979, a small group of men and women representing the natural sciences, the social sciences, the humanities, government, and other professions established the Academy of Independent Scholars. The academy's primary objective is to stimulate the creative work of those senior members of society who, because of their retirement, have lost their institutional association or those whose lifelong independence in their creative work has isolated them from the traditional network of creative scholars.

The academy is a private, nonprofit organization. Its membership has expanded to almost 400, extending beyond the boundaries of the United States. It is committed to encouraging intergenerational dialogue on national and global topics and to repairing lines of communication between young and old.

The academy also identifies the needs of members who lack institutional affiliation and helps them get support for continuing their creative work. It encourages retrospective writing and provides consultation. An important commitment of the academy is to promote the optimum use of knowledge for human betterment. This volume is an expression of that commitment.

On November 5–8, 1981, the Academy of Independent Scholars held a symposium on the optimum utilization of knowledge on the Amherst campus of the University of Massachusetts. This symposium, supported by grants from the National Institute of Education, the American Association for the Advancement of Science, and the Exxon Education Foundation, brought together thirty internationally known scholars from a wide range of disciplines. Each participant prepared a paper addressing the issue of how his or her discipline and profession can contribute to the utilization of knowledge for human betterment.

The impact of knowledge on human welfare is ambiguous. There is no doubt that human knowledge makes us richer, extends our life span, and gives us both comfort and advice. But it also opens up the probability of nuclear holocaust and environmental disaster. Much existing knowledge is not used in the service of human welfare. Questioning what institutions and which patterns of behavior will improve the utilization of human knowledge and diminish its abuse was one of the basic inquiries of the Amherst symposium. The subject is enormous. The chapters in this volume are witnesses to the fact that the participants rose to the challenge and made a start, however modest, in steering a course for the use of knowledge for human betterment and building a bridge between the frontiers of knowledge and the education system.

Some of the participants felt that the symposium organized by the academy, because it was multidisciplinary and because it was organized with a system vision, offered a rare platform for discussion by frontier thinkers of diverse backgrounds. In contrast, most learned societies usually break down knowledge into academic disciplines and, by doing so, isolate themselves from the real world. Many other participants felt that the greatest contribution of the academy's symposium was in bridging the gap between knowledge and the educational process. Some expressed the feeling that scholarly societies are plagued with an allergy to the education process so there is little effort to put new knowledge into the public domain and to close the gap between frontier thinking and the public schools. Many felt the sciences ignore the humanities at a time when there is an urgent need to link scientific discovery with ethical judgment.

Participants were concerned that the dialogue not end with the symposium and that the theme of the optimum utilization of knowledge become an ongoing commitment of the Academy of Independent Scholars, a responsibility that the academy accepts. As part of this responsibility, the academy proposed that the American Association for the Advancement of Science (AAAS) include in its 1982 annual meeting in Washington, D.C., a report on the findings of the Amherst symposium. The AAAS agreed, and in order to continue the series in 1983, the academy presented another symposium on the optimum utilization of knowledge in service of health at the annual meeting of the AAAS in Detroit, Michigan.

Also as a follow-up, the Academy introduced a one-semester experimental freshman seminar at the University of Colorado, in Boulder, on the optimum utilization of knowledge, from which it hopes to develop curriculum and reading materials for national distribution.

The participants in the Amherst symposium formulated many follow-up suggestions to continue and expand the ideas of the original program, such as:

- Writing teams could be formed to prepare studies on the optimum utilization of knowledge for the K-12 curriculum.
- Projects could be organized to demonstrate how to translate frontier knowledge into the public domain.
- To prevent the loss of historical memory, senior creative scholars could be identified and encouraged to communicate their life experience for future generations.

On behalf of the academy and the participants in the Amherst symposium, we would like to express our appreciation to the professional staff of the academy who worked tirelessly in the preparation of and follow-up to this program. Special mention should be made of Vicki Holzhauer, who was responsible for the coordination of the symposium. We would also like to express our appreciation to Diane Johnson for providing thoughtful editorial assistance. In addition, we would like to thank academy staff member Stephanie Mines for keeping track of the manuscript in its final stages. The editors would like to express their gratitude to our friend and member of the academy Henry Koffler, who at the time of the Amherst meeting was chancellor of the University of Massachusetts. Without his hospitality, this symposium could not have taken place.

Kenneth E. Boulding
Lawrence Senesh
Copresidents,
Academy of Independent Scholars

KENNETH E. BOULDING

1

The Optimum Utilization of Knowledge: Some Central Concepts

The Nature of Knowledge

The problems of the human race do not always originate in deficiencies in human knowledge or its utilization, but the solutions to any of these problems must originate there unless they come by pure luck. If problems that could be solved fail to get solved, or if decisions made with the best of intentions turn out in fact to have been bad decisions, the reasons must lie in the structure of human knowledge and either failure to utilize this knowledge or success in misutilizing it. The search for greater success, therefore, in encouraging processes that lead to bettering rather than worsening the human condition must begin with a consideration of the nature of human knowledge and the processes by which this knowledge is utilized.

All human knowledge consists of some kind of structure in human bodies, mostly in brains. In the first instance it is a structure of information, although exactly what the physical machinery for coding this information is we still do not really know. The knowledge structure in all human bodies around the world is what the great Jesuit philosopher Pierre Teilhard de Chardin called the *noosphere*.[1] This is an essential component of the state of the world at any one moment, and its character and the changes in it profoundly affect future changes in the state of the world as it passes through a succession of states from moment to moment in time.

Knowledge, especially in the form of know-how, is by no means confined to human beings. Conscious human knowledge is only the tip of the iceberg of knowledge-like structures that go very far down the process of evolution. In chemical valences, carbon "knows how" to combine with four hydrogen atoms to form CH_4 (methane) but does not know how to combine with five, and unsatisfied CH_3 is well named a "radical." With the genetic structure coded in DNA, the appropriate genes know how to make an ant or chicken or human being from a fertilized egg. All genetic structures involve know-how of some kind. Just what is included in the noosphere, therefore, is a little arbitrary. The human noosphere is a subset of the larger noosphere that includes all genetic structures and potentialities. The human noosphere, then, consists of images in the minds of all human beings; images, for instance, of physical objects in space and time, of one's own body, even of one's own mind, one's friends, buildings, towns, countries, the geography of the earth, the solar system, the universe, the chemical elements and compounds, patterns of behavior, ideas of cause and effect, the laws and limitations under which one state is transformed into another, and so on. It also goes beyond images of "fact" to those preferences and evaluations by which different images of the world are ordered, which are especially important in making decisions. It also includes emotional states of liking and disliking, hatred, anger, and fear; languages; symbols; and so on.

It is curious that there seems to be no word in the English language to describe simply the actual content of a human mind; the word "knowledge" has the almost implicit assumption that our knowledge is true. We have to admit, however, that the content of the human mind may include both error and ignorance.

Access to human knowledge takes many forms. The physiological probing of the brain gives us very little access simply because at present we cannot identify the coding that goes on within it. Nevertheless, we do have access to our own knowledge through consciousness and introspection. We constantly give ourselves examinations. I can ask myself, for instance, "Do I know the names of my senators?" If my answer is "No," I can ask someone or consult a reference book. Thus, through the instrument of language, we can probe the knowledge structures of others and deposits of knowledge in writing, print, and records. Language, indeed, plays an important part even in the probing of our own knowledge structure, though it is not the only component in this process. I can, for instance, picture the house where I was born in my mind without any words at all attached to this image. Because of language, however, I can have images of places that I have never visited and of times before my birth, as well as some idea of the images, values, and emotions of those around me. No other creature that we know can do this. The study of language, therefore, is a very important clue to the formation of knowledge structures and their transmission from one mind to another.

Knowledge structures are immensely complex and have a great many dimensions and aspects. Perhaps the most elementary is the genetic aspect of know-how, which preceded the human race. It existed long before consciousness, as in the gene or genetic structure of the fertilized egg, which knows how to make an organism. In humans much know-how is also unconscious. We know how to hit a tennis ball without having the slightest understanding of how we really do it, what physical processes are involved, and what differential equations we are solving. A male and a female know how to fertilize an egg, although they may not have the slightest idea what they are really doing or what the results will be in terms of a new organism. We know how to speak or to write a sentence that transmits structures in our minds to the minds of others, though again we do not really know the exact mechanism by which this is done. Of course, we often learn know-how consciously (as when we learn how to drive a car), but once learned, such know-how often slips back into the unconscious.

Beyond know-how is "know-what." This consists of images in our mind of objects in the world outside the mind, which in some sense, oddly enough, include the brain and the mind itself. This also involves images of processes by which objects are transformed in time, space, and structure. Know-what is by no means confined to images of material objects. It includes images of our own thoughts, feelings, and emotions, as well as images of the thoughts, feelings, and emotions of other people. It also includes images of abstractions and ideas that relate to, but do not consist of, images of particular objects. This becomes very complicated in connection with images of taxonomy—that is, classes of objects. Classification is necessary when using language, for we are incapable of accessing more than a limited number of separate words and symbols on the order of some tens of thousands, whereas we are aware of a vastly larger number of individual objects like the grains of sand on the seashore, the leaves on trees in the forests, even the four-and-a-quarter billion other human beings. Identifying a particular object often depends on our ability to place it in a series of diminishing subsets, as in the old "twenty questions" game. This is really what a postal address is: a number on a street, in a town, in a county or state, in a country, in the world.

We also perceive logical and mathematical relationships. They are independent of our experience in the world of objects, but we believe the world of objects must conform to them. Formal logic and mathematics are essentially sets of related truisms—things that cannot be different. Two plus two *must* be the same as three plus one, by the meaning of the words. On the other hand, we also recognize that our logic and mathematics may be a function of the human mind itself. Thus, we seem to have a capacity for transcending the obvious axioms of Euclidean mathematics, as we do, for instance, in Einstein's theory of relativity, which assumes that the larger universe is governed by a geometry and a logic that are repugnant to our common-sense experience.

Another part of our conscious knowledge structure seems to go beyond know-how and know-what into what we might call "know-why." This involves images of purposes, goals, final causes, and patterns in the processes and structures of things that we perceive as having meaning and significance. Three- and four-year-olds are constantly asking "Why?" often to the great frustration of the adults to whom the questions are addressed, perhaps because three- and four-year-olds are so newly conscious of themselves and the world around them that they tend to relate everything in their environment to how it affects them personally. The answers to "Why?" questions often serve to fit immediate experiences into some larger time scheme or framework. "Because Daddy says so" is often a surprisingly satisfactory answer to a child's awkward question. Ask a biologist, "Why is grass green?" and we may get a long disquisition about photosynthesis, chlorophyll, light absorption, and survival value. The purposes of a war—like the "Four Freedoms"—are often thought up long after the war has been started, yet a young man who asks, "Why do we have to go to war?" is often treated like a three-year-old.

As we get older, "know-why" may well diminish in importance, but we never escape having to face "know-whether." This is a structure of evaluation among alternative futures that underlies all decisions. Should I accept a job that I think will increase human misery? Should I have a child that I cannot support? Should I tell a lie to save a friend's life? Moral dilemmas are as much a part of daily living as they are exercises for moral philosophers. All decisions must come from some kind of knowledge of alternative futures and at least a rank ordering of preference for those futures.

A cynic might say that one of the most important parts of knowledge is "know-whom"—that is, two persons having images of each other with some degree of richness and accuracy. The networks of know-whom are an important element in the dynamics of power. One way to get rich and powerful is to know people who are rich and powerful and be known (favorably) by them.

Within the knowledge structure a distinction is frequently drawn between images of fact and images of value. This is important in decision processes, where we distinguish between the agenda of decision (consisting of a range of images of possible expected futures) and the evaluation of these images (which involves ordering them from the most to the least preferred). The theory of maximizing behavior suggests, of course, that we always choose from our agendas the expected future we think is best at the time, but the actual process of forming agendas and evaluating them is complex and often mysterious.

Another important aspect of knowledge structures is their capabilities and reserves. These relate to the process of change in knowledge structures through learning. A fertilized egg has the know-how to produce a brain and higher nervous system by morphogenesis, which may go on to some extent throughout life, although most of it is accomplished before maturity. However, realizing the potential of this genetically produced structure for knowledge in all its forms involves a learning process. Again, we very imperfectly understand that process, but it certainly has two major aspects. One is the internal operation by which the human brain constantly produces an enormous, turbulent succession of images in a great process of mutation and internal selection. The other aspect is the messages from the outside world coming in through the senses. This factor involves both mutation and selection processes. Messages from the senses criticize the images forming in the mind and may also be active in the creation of new images in a mutation process.

The role of language here is very important, as the input of language—and to some extent its output—creates new images and destroys old ones in a never-ending process. I have an image of where my friend lives; I go there and find he has moved. I inquire and learn his new address, go there, and find him. We have a conversation in which I express a certain evaluation. He criticizes this and tells me I am wrong. Because of my respect for him, I believe him and change my evaluation. This process of constant mutation of images and selection by testing is the essence of the human learning process, continually changing the content of individual minds and of the whole noosphere.

A very important concept is that of the "quality" of human knowledge—that is, of cognitive content—both in individual minds and in the whole noosphere. An image in the human mind may be true or it may be in error. The quality of truth is closely related to the concept of mapping the real world. An image is true if there is a one-to-one mapping of its structure with some structure in the real world it is supposed to represent. It is false or in error if the mapping is inaccurate or incomplete. Error is detected through testing by complex and extremely varied sets of processes. When I went to my friend's house and found he had moved, an old image was tested, found to be in error, and abandoned, or at least was perceived as erroneous. An image can be perceived as fantasy; if there is indeed no structure corresponding to it in the real world, this perception is not an error. I have an image of a unicorn, but I do not believe such an animal exists. Negative images can also be true. After I went to my friend's house and found that he did not live there, I added that address to the vast number of places where he does not live.

The problem of what constitutes "truth" in mathematics, in logic, and in deductive processes is surprisingly difficult, especially in the more sophisticated inquiries. Elementary mathematics and logic are true enough for most practical purposes. But we have to go beyond Euclidean geometry in the physical sciences, and we should go beyond Cartesian algebra in the social sciences. For in social systems, minus-minus does not make plus; not doing harm is not the same thing at all as doing good. There is need to go beyond Aristotelian logic when the reality is probabilistic. Gödel's proof that no system of deductive reasoning can be self-sufficient suggests that at least we should not take mathematics and logic for granted. There are problems, too, in quantification, where the reality of which we are trying to form an image is topological rather than quantitative. Used mechanically, without reference to the nature of the field of inquiry, quantification can be quite misleading. For instance, a consumer price index used mechanically can accelerate inflation. A single number that claims to represent multidimensional and structural reality can never be more than an approximation to truth.

"Folk" and "Scholarly" Knowledge

Knowledge structures can be divided rather loosely into "folk" knowledge and "scholarly" knowledge. Folk knowledge is what we acquire in the ordinary business of life. It is universal. It includes the image that I have of my own person, my family, my friends, my house in town, my job, my engagements next week, and so on. Folk knowledge tends to have a high quality of truth, simply because, for the most part, it is easily testable. It can, however, take pathological forms, as in the case of the paranoid or the schizophrenic. In such a case the testing process breaks down and the image within the mind becomes increasingly in error, often to the point at which the decision-making process breaks down and the person becomes incapable of participating in ordinary life. This pathological state may be in part a breakdown in the interpretation of language, as when, for instance, the schizophrenic takes metaphors literally. Part of it may be an inability to change images in the face of testing; in these circumstances a test that fails to produce the expected result is interpreted as showing a change in the real world, not requiring a change in the image. We can learn a good deal about complex systems by studying their extreme positions. A lot can be discovered about normal human learning by studying its failures in pathological cases.

Scholarly knowledge is what is acquired and transmitted by specialists in the acquisition and transmission of knowledge. Adam Smith in *The Wealth of Nations* describes the process delightfully:

> In the progress of society, philosophy or speculation becomes like every employment, the principal or sole trade and occasion of a particular class of citizens. Like every other employment, too, it is subdivided into a great number of different branches, each of which affords occupation to a peculiar tribe or class of philosophers. And this subdivision of employment in philosophy, as well as in every other business, improves dexterity and saves time. Each individual becomes expert in his own peculiar branch, more work is done upon the whole, and the quantity of science is considerably increased by it.[2]

Adam Smith's later denunciation of the division of labor as a destroyer of the overspecialized person might also, however, have some application to "philosophers"!

It is customary to divide the world of scholarship into the sciences and the humanities, but this distinction is rather arbitrary. Acquiring scholarly knowledge follows essentially the same processes as acquiring folk knowledge, but in more refined forms. Thus the use of language may be more important and the languages used more specialized—the most specialized of all, of course, being mathematics. Scholarly knowledge is also distinguished from folk knowledge by the greater complexity of its structures and the correspondingly greater complexity necessitated in the testing process. The famous Michelson-Morley experiment on the velocity of light involved much more complex testing processes and concepts than testing where my friend lives and required much more apparatus than a door knocker. But the essential process of the testing of images is the same in both cases. Images are produced by a combination of internal fantasy and external information. The commonest form of testing is done by devising some kind of projection of the future to predict an event that may be either realized or not realized. Testing can also be done by perceiving patterns in the record of the past, as in planetary astronomy or social and economic statistics.

Scholarly knowledge, like folk knowledge, may be true or false or may have degrees of truth, and its mapping of the real world may be more or less accurate. In all cases, testing must be indirect, for, as David Hume pointed out more than two hundred years ago, we can never directly compare an image with the reality it purports to map. We can only compare one image with another image in our minds.

Testing is largely a process of comparing an image of the future as time goes on with the image of that future when it has become the past.

Scholarly knowledge, like folk knowledge, can exhibit pathologies. The possessors of scholarly knowledge may resist testing because it threatens their status or income. Ideology tends to become a pathology of scholarly knowledge. It is a set of ideas bound up so closely with the image of identity of the people who hold them that testing cannot be permitted. When ideology becomes pathological, the threat system is invoked to destroy or at least silence dissent. We have seen many examples of this in human history, from the Spanish Inquisition to Lysenkoism in the Soviet Union. A rigid ideology, indeed, easily degenerates into schizophrenia of scholarly knowledge.

A very interesting question is whether images of value can also have a quality of truth similar to that attributed to images of fact. It is certainly more difficult to say what in the "real world" corresponds to our images of value than it is to conceive of what reality corresponds to our images of objects. Nevertheless, images of value result from the same kind of process of internal mutation and selection as that by which images of fact are produced. We see this, for instance, in the way every subculture develops an ethos, a set of individual preference structures regarded as appropriate to the subculture. This ethos then is used to criticize the preferences of individuals within the subculture, usually to the point where the individual either leaves the subculture or conforms to its ethos and changes preferences accordingly. A Jesuit who preaches atheism or becomes a thief is likely either to leave the order or to be expelled from it unless he changes his mind and once more conforms to the ethos of the order.

The ethos in each subculture is similarly criticized by the ethos of the larger society in which it finds itself. This criticism may take the form of preaching or of legal sanctions. The drug culture has an ethos of its own that it imposes on its adherents, but in turn it is severely criticized by the ethos of the larger society. We see, therefore, a pattern in the formation of images of value that is in many ways similar to the pattern in the formation of images of fact.

Images of fact are continually tested and challenged by the existence of the real world to which they are supposed to correspond. In the evolution of these images, error is a little less stable than truth. Hence there is a tendency for the noosphere to improve in its truth quality over time, simply because error can be found out and truth cannot. A very similar process occurs in the evolution of images of value. The concept of an external value reality that tests and criticizes our images of value is perhaps harder to sustain than the concept of a real world that tests our image of fact. Nevertheless, there is certainly a sense in which some values are less stable in the long-term evolution of the human race than are others, and it is by no means absurd to call these less stable values more erroneous than those that are more stable.

Instability in values can happen either because the cultures that hold certain values are themselves unstable and disappear (like the child-burning culture of ancient Carthage) or because within a culture there is a constant process of criticism of existing values that changes them. Creating linguistic structures that are powerful in the criticism of values is an important aspect of human history. The creators of evolutionary potential in society, indeed, the founders of religions, ideologies, nations, even corporations are often those who have been skilled in the linguistic formulation of value critique; Moses, Jesus, Mohammed, Marx, Jefferson, perhaps even Henry Ford are historical examples. This is not to deny, however, that short-term changes in values can take place—for instance, through the persuasiveness of leaders like Hitler or Stalin—that are "bad" and that increase human misery and suffering. It is even possible that the whole human race could become extinct through the development of the persuasive values of nationalism and militarism. The classic remark, attributed rather dubiously to Abraham Lincoln, "You can fool some of the people all the time, and all the people some of the time, but you can't fool all of the people all of the time" remains testimony to the principle that human valuations are not arbitrary, meaningless, or random. There is a real distinction between truer and more erroneous values, and there is a long-term tendency to move toward the truer ones.

The problem of the knowledge of values is crucial when we consider the optimum utilization of human knowledge. Any kind of optimum implies human valuation, and an optimum based on erroneous values would clearly be an erroneous optimum. There is no simple litmus paper, however, by which we can test whether values are erroneous or whether an optimum is false. Testing values is a very long, complex, and difficult process, and we can never be quite certain if it is going the right way. Nevertheless, we cannot simply dismiss this problem, and we may have to find many different partial answers to it, especially when we come to consider the real meaning of "optimum."

The Dynamics of the Noosphere

A very important question is that of the dynamics of the "noosphere," that is, of the total quantity and quality of human knowledge. Human knowledge is contained primarily in human minds, which are in turn contained in human beings who are subject to birth, aging, and death.

One year from now everybody who is now alive will be either one year older or dead, and some 100 million new human beings will have come into existence.

Aging has two aspects. Beyond a certain age, which probably occurs even before maturity, the actual number of neurons in the human brain steadily diminishes. We do not know much about how these processes differ from person to person. The number of neurons, however, is so large—between 10 and 100 billion—and the brain seems to be so enormously redundant (I have seen estimates, no doubt rather dubious, that even at best we use barely 10 percent of it) that the capacity for increasing the structure of knowledge continues for many decades beyond maturity. Throughout most of life we are, as it were, increasing the complexity of the arrangement of a constantly diminishing stock of neurons, and with all those billions of marbles to play with, it is not surprising that we make very pretty patterns, even quite late in life. However, DNA eventually catches up with everybody. The human organism is a self-destructing machine, among other things, and eventually all persons die, making the knowledge structures in their brains unavailable.

The noosphere, however, is continually able to expand because the knowledge structure that exists in one brain can be transmitted into another and also can be put into records, which can be transmitted to another brain even after a considerable interval of time. The invention of writing meant that knowledge could be transferred from the dead to the living. Education is essentially the process of transferring knowledge from decaying older minds into decaying younger ones. This means that the noosphere itself, as a total body of knowledge, does not have to decay. In fact, throughout the thousands of years of human history it has almost continuously expanded, despite the facts that individual minds as they get older tend to forget things and that when a person dies the whole content of the brain disappears from the noosphere.

Within the noosphere we must also include what might be called the "prosthetic devices" of the mind, which create records and facilitate the transmission of knowledge from one mind to another. The invention of writing, the first great discovery in this regard, enormously accelerated both the growth and the security of the noosphere. The almost incredibly slow development of the noosphere before writing, for instance, in the paleolithic period, unquestionably resulted from the division of the human race into small noncommunicating bands. Knowledge might grow for several generations, but plagues or battles would periodically wipe out the elders who knew anything. The transmission of knowledge to the younger generations would be broken, and the groups would slip back into earlier states of knowledge. In the more stable societies of the early neolithic, knowledge could be transmitted for many generations by poets and singers, but the oral tradition had sharp limits. It was not until the invention of writing that the noosphere could expand almost indefinitely. The development of specialized institutions for the storing and transmission of knowledge, like libraries and universities, also assisted this process.

Phonograph records, tapes, and other mechanical devices have preserved not only written but spoken language, and computer tapes and memories make it possible to code knowledge in a very small space and on a very large scale. It is not enough, however, to have knowledge stored away. Knowledge must also be accessible to the mind that wants it. When that mind knows exactly what it wants, computer storage seems admirable. Very often, though, the mind that wants knowledge does not know quite what it wants. In this situation the codex or the book turns out to be much more valuable than the scroll, simply because the book can be flipped through while a scroll has to be turned slowly. With microfilm, microfiche, and computer memory, one detects a return to scroll-type access that may interfere with what might be called the "serendipitous search," so characteristic of the book. There is a real dilemma here: Information has to be surprising or it is not information but just a record of what we know already. Consequently, the growth of knowledge has to include a certain randomness. How this is best organized is a very difficult question, far too infrequently asked. Knowledge, furthermore, is by no means the same thing as information, which is only the raw material of knowledge. The process by which information is converted into knowledge involves much more the orderly *loss* of information than its meaningless accumulation. The main object of statistical analysis, for instance, is to condense an unintelligible mass of quantitative information into a much smaller but more comprehensible number of bits.

The Role of Formal Education

The enormous expansion of the noosphere, especially in the last few hundred years, has greatly increased the role of formal education in transmitting knowledge from one generation to the next. Up until a few decades ago, formal education was confined to the lower grades and usually stopped at about age fourteen even in quite developed societies. Today in the United States, for instance, well over 90 percent of the population goes through high school and close to 50 percent goes to college. This is unprecedented in the history of the human race and may have consequences that are now unforeseen, especially as we know so little about the actual dynamics of human learning. Education, it can be said rather unkindly, is still a craft industry. Its first major technical innovation was the classroom, which perhaps goes back to the ancient Greeks. Printing was the next great innovation. There is room for some skepticism as to whether computer-based instruction and other technological developments are any great advance.

There is a difficult psychological problem in the process of transmission of human knowledge from one generation to the next, created by the fact that we learn essentially by failure, for unless a test fails, it merely confirms what we knew already and adds nothing to human knowledge, as in the story of my friend who moved. Failure, however, can have two profound and opposite psychological effects. That we have made a mistake, corrected it, and do not have to make it again can be accepted as a learning process. Or it can be regarded as a threat to our identity as learners, teaching us that we will always make mistakes and that we are no good at learning. The process of learning by failure must, therefore, always be supplemented by positive reinforcement of the learner's identity to prevent the learner's learning that he or she cannot learn.

This problem is taken care of, for the most part, in acquiring folk knowledge. That kind of knowledge is so stable simply because the learning process takes place either within the family, which is supportive of the child who is learning, or in apprenticeship situations, where failure is accepted as part of the learning process and easily corrected without any threat to the identity of the learner (though, of course, there may be exceptions to that principle in practice). Formal education, however, especially in crowded classrooms where there is not much time for personal interaction between a student and the teacher, often creates something of an adversary relationship between the teacher and the learner, in which the learner's identity is not reinforced and thus the failures and mistakes that are an inevitable accompaniment of learning can easily be interpreted as failures of identity. There is a great danger in formal education, therefore, that we will teach people not to learn. There are enough examples of this to cause worry. The problem becomes particularly difficult as formal education becomes virtually universal. When only a select group passed through formal education, as was the case in my own youth, those in high school were very conscious that they were a select minority, so the identity problem was less acute. The student had a secure identity as a member of a select minority, which largely offset the adversary relationship between teacher and student. As education becomes universal this identity no longer holds, and it is not surprising to find increasing alienation, disorder, and crime in high schools, as well as an apparent decrease in the amount of learning. We can argue indeed that the main functions of a teacher are to create motivation, to cheer students up, to bring a certain sense of excitement to the learning process, to guide students toward resources, and then to get out of the way and let students learn for themselves. These functions, however, are too seldom recognized.

A formal education is usually regarded as a means of transmitting scholarly knowledge rather than folk knowledge. Because formal education takes place in schools, colleges, and universities, where young people are segregated, it may interfere with the transmission of folk knowledge from older people to younger ones or may create a folk knowledge of its own. Our own society is particularly vulnerable in this regard because we are the first society in human history to segregate such a large proportion of our adolescents and young adults in institutions of formal education. In all previous societies, young people have lived in the middle of older people as farm children, apprentices, or child laborers of various kinds, growing up largely within the family group and so on. There were many agents for the transmission of adult folk knowledge. Today, these systems may be weakened, and we see a "youth culture" developing that may become quite pathological in its values. This problem deserves much more investigation than we have given it.

The Noosphere and the World System

The next question is, What are the links between the dynamics of the noosphere and the dynamics of the total world system? It is a crucial question in the general theory of evolution, for even before the advent of the human race, know-how in the form of genetic information and instructions was the key to the whole process of biological evolution. The "genosphere"—that is, the sphere of all genetic information embodied in living organisms—is really what evolves. The "phenosphere"— that is, the sphere of all living organisms themselves—is derived essentially from production processes by which the genetic know-how in the undivided cell or the fertilized egg is able to organize the growth of an organism, which in turn is able to transmit its genetic know-how to new cells or eggs before it dies. In biological evolution, mutation takes place primarily in the genosphere, i.e., in DNA in the genes; selection takes place mainly in the phenosphere. There is an exception to this rule, however, in what I call "noogenetic evolution," which is the transmission of learned structures in the phenotype from one generation to the next by a learning process.[3] This permits mutation within the phenosphere, when an organism acquires new knowledge that it then transmits to the next generation, on to the subsequent generations. Some bird songs seem to be an example of this. It becomes quite important in the behavior patterns of higher animals and, of course, overwhelmingly important to the human race. The exact relation between the biogenetic and the noogenetic in humans is still a matter of dispute, but certainly over the fifty thousand years or more of human history, changes in the biogenetic gene pool have been minuscule compared with the vast growth in the noogenetically created and transmitted corpus of human knowledge.

Human history is a continuation of the evolutionary process, mainly in the field of human artifacts. The human noosphere is the genosphere—the know-how that produces the "sociosphere" of human artifacts, which in turn consists of material artifacts, from flint arrowheads to the space shuttle; organizational artifacts, from the hunting band to the World Bank; and persons, who are partly genetic artifacts from the information of their fertilized egg and partly human artifacts in terms of the knowledge structures they have acquired. Production, whether of the chicken from the fertilized egg or of the house or automobile from the blueprint, is essentially a process that originates in the genetic factor of know-how, which knows how to direct energy toward the selection, transportation, and transformation of materials into the shapes of the product or the phenotype in the process of morphogenesis. The genetic factor may be limited in its operation—that is, may be unable to realize the potential it contains—by the constraints imposed by the "limiting factors," mainly various forms of energy, forms of materials, availability of space, and availability of time. The most limiting factor is the one that is most important. This may be energy in the tundra, water in the desert, soil on the rocks, or cultural obstacles to learning in economic development.

An important aspect of evolution is the way in which increased know-how pushes back the limiting factors and permits a larger variety of species and larger populations. This is noticeable even in biological evolution; in human history it is critical. Increases in human knowledge and know-how have permitted a huge expansion of the human race and its artifacts. We have seen this in the rise of agriculture creating civilization and now in the rise of science and science-based technology creating an unprecedented population explosion and arms race that threaten human welfare and even survival. The only answer to these threats, however, seems to be faster learning and more know-how, especially at the level of political and social skills.

The production of human artifacts is strongly affected by the value structure of the noosphere, which creates niches in the social ecosystem for things that people want and have the power to acquire. Goods will be produced for the market if enough people are willing to pay enough for them to motivate their production. Public goods and weapons will be produced if the political process allocates government budgets for their purchase. Underlying both private and public demands is a constant process of preachments and persuasion that changes people's values.

All decision, as we have seen, is a phenomenon within the noosphere. It involves learning agendas on the one hand and learning how to evaluate them on the other—two processes that continually interact. Our evaluation of different agendas and different images of the future will depend on the alternatives that we envisage. Policy is decisions about decisions—that is, decisions that will affect the decisions we make in the future. It is also profoundly affected by the learning process. In the political arena we have a constant interaction between folk knowledge and scholarly knowledge. A perfect example of this was the triumph of scholarly Keynesian ideas in U.S. economic policy in the 1950s and 1960s and the triumph of a much less scholarly, more folksy economics in the Reagan administration.

Normative Science

Human knowledge is going to be utilized no matter what in production, education, decision making, and policy. When we talk about the "optimum" utilization of human knowledge we are really asking ourselves whether we can evaluate changes in the state of the world, particularly in regard to whether things are getting better or getting worse. Improving the utilization of human knowledge would presumably mean directing it toward those uses that will make the state of the world better rather than worse, according to somebody's valuations. This raises a sticky problem, of course, of whose valuations. Everybody values things differently; I may think a certain change is for the better and you may think it is for the worse. Indeed, a change could quite easily be better for me and worse for you. Economists, especially, have shied away from the problem of evaluating the values of different people.

The problem of the optimum utilization of human knowledge, therefore, falls squarely in the field of what can be called "normative science"— the study of human valuations within the ethic and methods of the scientific community. Normative science is not likely to come up with any simple or definitive answers. There are, however, things we need to know and that we can find out in the field of human valuations, even though we may not always get universal agreement on whether the world is getting better or worse, or even on the ultimate effect of particular decisions on the actual state of the world. It may be that optimum utilization is too high an ambition. In many situations there is a wide range of choices and alternatives that, when evaluated, turn out to be about equally valuable and among which, therefore, the search for an optimum is likely to be frustrating—rather like looking for the highest point on a very level plateau. We may find it more useful to concentrate on catastrophe—that is, on the "cliffs" that may surround the plateau—where there would be widespread agreement that things are indeed becoming worse rather than better.

One difficulty here is that we cannot rule out randomness in decision making and even in the dynamics of catastrophe itself. Automobile accidents are a good case in point, with the exception of those that stem from a suicide decision. Automobile accidents are not "planned"; they do, however, result from faulty decisions usually made under stress. A considerable proportion of them arise from the reduced decision-making capacity that follows an excessive use of alcohol or other drugs. Sometimes they reflect a reduction in the decision-making capacity of the driver because of emotional states, such as anger or impatience. Just how we utilize knowledge to prevent automobile accidents is a good question for study, the answer to which is by no means obvious.

A very useful exercise would be to study what utilization of what knowledge might have prevented certain catastrophes in the past. What, for instance, should Herbert Hoover and his congresses have known and done in order to prevent the Great Depression of 1929–1933? Clearly the people in the federal government did *not* know or do the things that they should have. Suppose, however, that they had better national income statistics and had understood the effects of deflation, the collapse of profit relative to interest, and the distortions of the relative price and wage structure, which happened in those years. Could we now write a scenario in which appropriate things were done so that the Great Depression would not have happened? Similar exercises in regard to the two world wars would also be of great interest.

An important question in the utilization of knowledge is that of the resources devoted to research. One of the most important uses of knowledge is to gain more knowledge. The enormous knowledge explosion over the last five hundred years has largely been due to our increasing knowledge of how to get more knowledge in a process of almost exponential, or perhaps even accelerating, growth. Research on knowledge itself—on the processes by which it grows and the processes by which it is utilized—is clearly an important order of business. The question is, What knowledge is it that nobody yet knows that it hurts us not to know? Perhaps the most significant thing that could happen to the human race in the next few decades would be a substantial increase in the knowledge about human learning, which is still very primitive. This might follow from some breakthrough in the neurosciences, uncovering what really goes on in the brain and perhaps even how to intervene in it more directly than we do now. Certainly stranger things have happened.

Then we have the problem of knowledge that somebody knows, that is in somebody's head, but that fails to get transmitted into the head of somebody else who would find it useful. This is a universal problem. We find it, for instance, in the professions, especially the medical profession. The sum of what is known by somebody is enormously larger than what a single person knows. The search for access to existing knowledge by somebody who either wants it or needs it (which is not the same thing) is increasingly difficult. Computers may help, but in their present form, they are incapable of the extraordinary search that goes on in the human brain. There may be a twofold approach to this problem of improving access. One comes from the neurosciences; the other is more traditionally associated with the humanities or psychiatry, which use language to explore inner states and processes.

The Pathology of Organizations

Another problem that needs careful study is the relation of organizational structures to the creation of new knowledge or the transmission of old knowledge. The great dilemma of organizations—especially large ones—is that whereas a hierarchy is necessary to prevent information overload (even a hundred people cannot all talk to each other!), a hierarchy easily perverts both the image of fact and the image of value of the powerful. Why does power corrupt and absolute power corrupt absolutely? Why does influence often corrupt even more than power? Why does impotence corrupt where there is need for empowerment? These are very difficult questions. An organization can almost be defined as a device for preventing information from reaching the powerful. It is, indeed, a hierarchy of wastebaskets; there is always a possibility that what goes into a wastebasket on the way up is what is really needed at the top. The Point Four Program that initiated U.S. foreign aid was literally fished out of a wastebasket in the State Department when President Truman wanted a speech with four points rather than three.

How, then, can we mobilize needed knowledge that already exists? There is, of course, an extensive market in private knowledge, as innumerable consulting and research firms testify. Knowledge is also a public good. It is supposed to be supplied to those in authority by organizations such as the National Academy of Sciences and the National Research Council. The question of how this system might be improved is well worth asking. How far could the professional societies, such as the American Association for the Advancement of Science, be mobilized to improve the transmission of human knowledge to places where it is needed?

The dilemma that besets us in education, however—that learning may threaten the image of personal identity of the student—applies even more to learning on the part of the powerful. It is often hard for those in positions of authority, respect, and prestige to learn—and hence to change—without threat to their very authority, respect, and prestige. How can we develop a culture and perhaps an organizational structure that can overcome this problem? In regard to the long-term survival of humanity, this is perhaps one of the most important questions we can ask.

I have formulated what I have called the "dismal theorem of political science"—that all the skills that enable people to rise to power make them unfit to exercise it. Although there have been some notable exceptions to this theorem, there are certainly enough examples of it to merit the name "dismal." How we protect ourselves against this situation through political institutions like constitutions and political culture is a critical question for social and political research, both of which involve the optimum utilization of human knowledge.

A related question, and one crucial in the utilization of human knowledge, is that of the legitimacy or prestige of those recognized as having superior knowledge. Civilization almost certainly resulted from the fact that certain individuals organized into priesthoods and were able to convince ordinary people that they had unique knowledge necessary for human welfare. Nearly all early civilizations seem to have been ruled by priests who had persuaded the food producers to give them part of the crop in return for priestly services that were supposed to assure that crops would continue. The "knowledge" of the priests may well have been largely error; the Aztecs, for instance, are supposed to have believed that human sacrifice was necessary to make the crops grow. The persuasiveness of priesthoods seems to have been related very loosely to the truth of their beliefs.

In our own day, science has become something of a priesthood. There is a slight feeling of the temple about the laboratory and a certain feeling of mystery about the doctrines, which seem to be understood only by initiates. Scientists are called to testify in court and before congressional committees. The National Academy of Sciences sponsors studies and makes pronouncements almost ex cathedra.

Nevertheless, the legitimacy of science is a little precarious. It can be corrupted by government, especially when government has a monopoly of the funds available, as we have seen in the Soviet Union in the Lysenko case. Science is identified with the military technology that is all too clearly leading us toward destruction. It can be corrupted by the unbridled search for private gain, and even by foundations. Nevertheless, the ethos of science, with its emphasis on curiosity, veracity, testing, and persuasion by evidence rather than threat, is an important value system for the rest of society. The wise utilization of knowledge, especially the prevention of its misutilization, may depend in no small measure on the capacity of the scientific community not only to remain true to its own ethos but to spread that ethos as a larger ideal for society.

There are no simple answers to these problems. We cannot find an optimum utilization of human knowledge by linear programming or marginal analysis, for there is no single "objective function" or measure to be maximized. There are, however, things we can do. We can perhaps identify some of the "cliffs" and the processes that lead to disaster. We can identify some organizational and political structures that favor or hinder human learning and we can help create a culture of learning in political and economic life like the one we experience, however imperfectly, in the scholarly and scientific community. We can study how to ritualize conflict and how to reduce the threats to personal identities, especially those of the powerful, that learning may produce. We can study the subtle processes that make societies relaxed rather than tense. We can study how to turn language into a way to let the real world speak for itself, rather than merely a way to propagate our own images by the arts of misleading metaphor, persuasion, and threat. Most of all, if we can see this larger problem of human learning in all walks of life as the focus of a major intellectual effort in the next decades, we may not optimize, but at least we will be going up rather than down!

Notes

1. Pierre Teilhard de Chardin, *The Phenomenon of Man* (New York: Harper and Row, 1959).

2. Adam Smith, *The Wealth of Nations* (New York: Modern Library Editions), bk. 1, pg. 10.

3. Kenneth E. Boulding, *Ecodynamics: A New Theory of Societal Evolution* (Beverly Hills, California: Sage Publications, revised paperback edition, 1981).

FRITZ MACHLUP

2

What Do We Mean by the Optimum Utilization of Knowledge?

What we mean by optimum utilization of knowledge depends on who "we" are. If we are engineers, we probably think of using technology in productive processes. If we are medical doctors, we may think of diagnostic and surgical skills, of the knowledge of pharmacology and human physiology in the cure and prevention of disease. If we are business managers, we are likely to think of management techniques— the collection and processing of data on market prices and cash flows— to use in running a successful business. Most of these kinds of knowledge are *practical* knowledge of the knowing-how, knowing-what, and knowing-that types but are chiefly related to how-to knowledge and to pieces of information that seem relevant at the moment but may soon become irrelevant.

Practical knowledge, however, is only a small fraction of what we, meaning *all* of us (any one of us), know or believe we know. The largest part of human knowledge is not usable if by "usable" we mean guiding us in practical actions. We have *intellectual* knowledge to satisfy our intellectual curiosity and sometimes also for the pleasure of showing off by displaying our superior erudition; we have *spiritual* knowledge to help us gain salvation and thereby secure peace of mind, sureness of purpose, and perhaps a happier afterlife. We have *pastime* knowledge to satisfy our appetite for fun, gossip, chitchat, and entertainment.

I submit that the question "What Do We Mean by Optimum Utilization of Knowledge?" does not refer to these categories of knowledge. I thus go back to types of knowledge that can be of practical use, either directly or indirectly by aiding the acquisition of applicable knowledge.

How Knowledge Is Used

What can "optimum utilization" mean regarding such actually or potentially "useful" knowledge? Most people think of decisions, action, and performance when they think of "using" knowledge. Using knowledge with a good chance of success presupposes the knowledge is "true," not erroneous or false. Many analytic philosophers embrace a "strong" meaning of knowledge; they want "I know" to mean, first, that what I claim to know is really true; second, that I am sure of it; and, third, that I have a right to be sure of it. I do not take this JTB (Justified True Belief) fanaticism seriously; indeed, I believe it contradicts a genuine scientific attitude, which requires a perennial preparedness to question, modify, and reject what may seem the closest approximation to the truth.

Those who demand more efficient, or even optimal, utilization of knowledge evidently believe that the knowledge "potentially available for use" is *reliable.* This may be unwarranted optimism. Frank Knight was fond of quoting the comedian's dictum, "It ain't ignorance that does the most damage; it's knowing so derned much that ain't so." We act too often on what we *believe* we know, assuming that it is true and reliable; we would be better off if we had more doubts and recognized we do not really know "for sure." We should worry less about obstacles to the utilization of knowledge—about unduly wide gaps between those who presumably know and those who make decisions—and worry more about damming the flow of unreliable knowledge to decision makers. Devices to speed new knowledge to those who take action may be counterproductive if such knowledge is not sufficiently tested and adequately qualified. Perhaps the adjective "optimal" is meant to imply an appropriate skepticism leading to more testing, sifting, risk evaluation, and consequently more decisions *not* to use the knowledge in question.

The Dangers of Ersatz Knowledge

As an economist, I am particularly sensitized to the warning against using what is claimed or pretended to be knowledge. Government actions taken on the basis of overconfident claims to knowledge have done much harm. Such damage might have been prevented by the decision makers' not accepting advice offered by economic advisers or by the failure of advice, or of the knowledge on which it was based, to reach government decision makers.

For example, in the early 1930s two economic statisticians became convinced that the level of commodity prices was a simple function of the price of gold. On the basis of this "knowledge" they recommended a sharp increase in the dollar price of gold. President Roosevelt accepted the advice and asked Congress to raise the price by almost 60 percent. The action did not have the "predicted" result, but instead caused substantial outflows of gold from other countries, severely deflating their money stocks, prices, incomes, and employment.

My skepticism about what is advertised as knowledge refers largely to positive knowledge: knowledge that something *is* really so and not otherwise and that particular courses of action would surely have certain desired effects. It is easier, as a rule, to know that something is *not* so and that specified actions would *not* have the intended effects. The unimpeded and rapid flow of such negative affirmations—knowledge that denies rather than affirms—is of utmost importance. Instead of leading to decisions to act, it results in decisions to desist from acting, which are important because the actions in question might be injurious, perhaps disastrous. The optimal utilization of this kind of knowledge is deliberate inaction.

This is not a general defense of inaction; it refers only to instances where we "know" a proposed action *cannot* achieve the desired results. Action is urgently needed if one learns that past measures, undertaken in the hope of securing desired effects, have proved counterproductive. Action to correct earlier mistakes, say, to repeal bad legislation, is certainly advisable.

What I have said thus far about what we mean by optimum utilization of knowledge has probably disappointed many readers. Those who originally asked the question may have greater confidence in the quality of our useful knowledge, especially in its probability value (to use Reichenbach's term). An information scientist might offer a very different statement, talking chiefly about research and development, storing and retrieving information, data processing, vertical and horizontal dissemination of selected findings, and management procedures designed to channel the right kinds of knowledge to the right kinds of people. To such a specialist, pursuing the optimality goal might mean analyzing benefits and costs for designing and maintaining alternative systems that provide the most significant feedback loops and the most adequate separation of noise from the information essential to the right decisions for action.

Discussions of the problems of dependable communication are highly important; it just happens that I cannot contribute to these aspects of our question about optimum utilization of knowledge. Moreover, I place some weight on the fact that the question refers to knowledge, not to information. Although there are many instances in which these two words are meant to be interchangeable, they may differ in some respects:

for example, when we want to contrast a *flow* of information with a *stock* of knowledge, or when we want to contrast the *timeliness* of information with the *timelessness*, or at least indefinite tenure, of knowledge. Since we are dealing with human learning and utilization of knowledge, I feel justified in deemphasizing information and computer sciences.

Who Is Using Knowledge, and to What End?

I must, however, raise a different and, I think, important issue. I began by saying that what we mean by optimum utilization depends on who "we" are. At that point I was alluding to the bias associated with special interests, particularly with special occupations in special fields. Now I want to refer to larger groups of people—communities, nations, groups of nations, and generations of people.

Let us, to select a timely issue, contrast a national point of view with foreign and cosmopolitan ones. The use of knowledge always complements the use of other resources, such as labor or material or, at least, the user's time. One cannot use knowledge without also using something else, and the complementary input may be scarce and valuable. We have the knowledge to carry out irrigation projects in developing countries in Africa or Asia and the knowledge of how to extend social services in the United States, but each of these programs would require additional scarce resources. Is there a way to decide "rationally" which program would be a better way of using our stock of knowledge? All may be deserving, all sensible, all gratifying to many people; but whether there is a unique answer that can be called "optimal" is highly questionable. Since the examples I selected for the sake of argument are not subject to the norms of a market economy, we face conflicting value judgments based on possibly irreconcilable value structures. One may perhaps agree on what is best for the United States and what is best for a developing country receiving aid, but there is no way to determine a unique optimum for the world as a whole.

This raises some interesting problems of environmental economics. Assume that an industry in country A pollutes the air that blows into the neighboring country B or the water that flows into country B. The knowledge of how to prevent such pollution exists, but actual prevention is very expensive. Where the polluters and the victims of pollution are in the same country, the problem can, in principle, be solved by benefit-and-cost analysis and appropriate schemes of emission and effluent charges and taxes. The problem is much more difficult when the currents of winds and streams disregard the political frontiers that separate beneficiaries and victims. It takes an agreed-upon international ethic to approach an "equitable" solution, but standards of equity are no firm basis for determining optimality. Just visualize the quandary if the polluting industry, the beneficiary, is located in a poor country and the victims of the pollution are in a much richer country.

The optimum use of knowledge for the benefit of different generations is the most problematic case. Assume that we know (or believe we know) how to prevent the excess accumulation of carbon dioxide, and that we know (or believe we know) that such accumulation would have deleterious effects on the fertility of land in fifty or eighty years. If preventive measures are expensive, the real income of the present generation would be reduced in order to increase the real income of future generations. What is the best thing to do? Do we owe anything to our neighbor's great-grandchildren? Why should we accept a heavy sacrifice for the sake of people whom we do not know, whom we might dislike if we did know them, and who may be richer than we are? Most of us have heard the cynical question "Why should we do anything for the benefit of future generations if they do nothing for us?"

Moreover, we have invested in physical and human capital, some of which will be left for future generations, and in the accumulation of knowledge, all of which will be at the disposal of future generations. Why should we go beyond this large estate they will inherit and sacrifice even more to safeguard and maintain some natural resources for them? It is conceivable, or even quite probable, that future generations will learn to clean up the messes that we, in our unconcern, leave to them, that they will find ways to restore, without undue cost, the fertility of the land and the productive capacity of other resources, or that they will discover or develop alternative resources. In these cases our thoughtfulness, solicitude, and generous sacrifice would have been uncalled-for and useless waste. The future may well take care of itself, without any overcautious provisions on our part.

There is a final consideration, one that may justify radically discounting all previously cited chances or odds or even reduce them to irrelevancies. The underutilization of our present (but rather poor) knowledge of how to resolve international conflicts by peaceful means may lead to the active use of the (unfortunate) knowledge of how to destroy life on this earth. This might reduce or remove the chance of there being any future generations. If this were to happen, using our time or our available knowledge of how to preserve a full complement of productive resources for future generations would be an exercise in futility.

In offering all these arguments against using our available knowledge of how to preserve resources for the future, I am not seriously debating such efforts at preservation. My purpose is only to show how difficult it is to agree on what is meant by "optimum" utilization of knowledge. Since knowledge can be used only together with other resources, the question of choosing the best possible trade-offs from among all alternatives is undecidable, given our uncertainty and our ignorance of comparative values and comparative risks. Is it better to use our knowledge to increase the production of rice in Kampuchea or to reduce the production of babies in India or to preserve the fertility of land in Chad or to increase productive investment in the United States? If we should do all of the above, then in what proportions? I cannot see how to determine the optimum.

The essential difficulty with the notion of optimum utilization of knowledge is the lack of specifications concerning its utilization by whom, for whom, for what, for how much, and (most critically) *what* knowledge. Knowledge is not a pile of homogeneous material but a complex structure of heterogeneous thoughts, each available at zero marginal cost but usable only together with resources available only at positive, and often very high, cost.

I confess that I have some misgivings about my conclusions: They are so defeatist that I ought to ask myself whether I cannot find a more helpful way to address the question assigned to me. Perhaps my understanding of the issue of optimum utilization of knowledge is out of line with the ideas of most of my fellow participants in this symposium. Perhaps we can arrive at a less forbidding interpretation if we narrow the focus and address more specific questions.

One such question would be the utilization of patented technological knowledge. The lawmakers have chosen to allow investors of new products and new production techniques to restrict the use of their newly acquired knowledge for seventeen years. The purpose of such temporary monopoly grants was to let monopoly profits act as an incentive to invest in inventive and innovative activities. If new knowledge were fully utilized, there would be no returns to those who have invested in its creation and development. This problem has been discussed for several hundred years; indeed, as early as the fourteenth century grants of privileges to inventors were accompanied by discourses on the conflict between adequate incentives for the creation of new knowledge and adequate utilization of the knowledge thus created. I have written a book and several articles about this dilemma, and I am glad to see Leonid Hurwicz add his contributions to this theme.

Another way to narrow the focus of my discussion would be to shift it from the totality of potentially useful knowledge to some particular, specific batches of knowledge. Instead of asking for the *optimum optimorum*, the very best of all possible alternative actions, social and private, we may, more modestly, resolve that in all actions that we decide to take we try to act intelligently, with full consideration of the pertinent knowledge at hand and of the pertinent knowledge available at reasonable cost.

This rule is quite different from the quest for optimality in using the totality of knowledge. The rule that whatever we choose to do we shall do wisely, not foolishly, requires little philosophical argumentation. The economists may say, in their professional jargon, that our actions should be cost-effective to the best of our knowledge. The economist who wants to go further will enjoin us to be Pareto-efficient. This extension, however, already invites speculation that may again widen the focus to include choices among alternative actions on different fronts, actions for which different batches of knowledge are used; in this case, we may easily slip into the sea of indecision.

Bibliography

Machlup, Fritz. *An Economic Review of the Patent System.* Study no. 15 of the Subcommittee on Patents, Trademarks, and Copyrights of the Committee on the Judiciary, United States Senate, 85th Congress, 2nd Session. Washington: Government Printing Office, 1958.

————. *The Production and Distribution of Knowledge in the United States.* Princeton, N.J.: Princeton University Press, 1962.

————. *Knowledge and Knowledge Production.* Princeton, N.J.: Princeton University Press, 1980.

————. *The Branches of Learning.* Princeton, N.J.: Princeton University Press, 1982.

PART ONE

—————□—————

What Do We Know About Human Learning?

KARL H. PRIBRAM

—— **3** ——

The Brain, Cognitive Commodities, and the Enfolded Order

Introduction

When certain parts of the human brain are damaged, the patient suffers an agnosia, an inability to know. Studying such patients as well as monkeys in whom similar damage is produced experimentally has gained for us considerable insight into how we know.

First, we can distinguish, on the basis of localized brain damage, three distinct types of knowing: knowing what, knowing how, and knowing that. When a patient no longer knows *what* a pencil, key, or toothbrush is he no longer knows the use of such an object. Shown a pencil and asked to demonstrate what it is, the patient may try to brush his teeth with it or try to fit the pencil into a keyhole. Such defects in *knowing what* are called the agnosias.

Deficiencies in *knowing how* are called apraxias. A patient may have no difficulty in moving about yet be extremely awkward in carrying out skilled actions. Such a patient may fumble with a key, hold his pencil in a most unusual fashion, and drop his toothbrush as he begins to brush his teeth. But if he is trying to use the object correctly, he has an apraxia, not an agnosia.

Finally, there is *knowing that*. When there is damage in another brain location the patient may be completely unaware of certain body parts or of parts of the world. Such "neglect," as it is called, may extend to one entire side of the body or may be limited to an extremity. Neglect may also encompass a portion of the visual field, so that it is often difficult to decide whether a patient ran his car into a telephone pole and sustained a brain injury or suffered a stroke that led to visual neglect and so to the accident.

On the basis of evidence from brain-damaged patients, what these cognitive processes appear to have in common is that the knower adds considerably, by means of brain processes, to that which is known. Some of the addition comes by way of inherited brain mechanisms set so that certain events, and not others, arouse interest and certain skills are more easily mastered. Other additions, like the ones that determine the form of linguistic knowledge, musical knowledge, or knowledge about sports, for example, come from experience that alters brain processes in the formation of memory mechanisms. But the additions made to events by the knower's brain are the essence of knowing. Knowing is an active, constructive process.

Representations and Computations

How does the brain operate to make such additions? Recently this question has been addressed in terms of a computer metaphor: Does the brain store representations of knowledge or does the brain compute knowledge anew every time it occurs?[1] At first glance it seems as if the storage of knowledge is uncontestable; after all, we can remember stories, pictures, and feelings, and how could we, were they not stored in the brain? There is additional evidence for this point of view. In 1981 researchers reported on patients who, when recalling scenes, would recall only half of them because their brains were damaged on the side opposite to the missing half.[2]

The issue of brain representation is unfortunately not so clear cut. There can be "memory-without-record," as von Foerster once called it.[3] We can take another technical metaphor, the thermostat. The thermostat "remembers" the temperature at which it has been set and operates a furnace or air conditioner to maintain that temperature. In a sense, the thermostat "computes" in a very simple fashion the difference between its setting and the amount of heat in the surrounding space.

We know from a good deal of research that an essential aspect of brain organization is "homeostatic"; that is, the elementary functions of the brain are carried out in a manner similar to the way thermostats operate.[4] In fact, thermostats were invented by Norbert Wiener based on the experience he had in a physiological laboratory at Harvard where the homeostatic principles of brain function were discovered.

"Memory-without-record" means that a system does not necessarily have to store as a record that which it reproduces. What may be stored is a computation that will construct the reproduction. For example, we do not store the answer to the problem, "What is 1233 divided by 3?"

No. We learn certain operations by which we can compute the answer (411), and thus we can reproduce that answer whenever the problem recurs. There is, moreover, a tremendous gain in power when a computation rather than a record is stored. Now we can divide *any* number by another and obtain a reproducible answer. The savings in storage space of a computational memory-without-record is huge.

By now I may have convinced you that knowledge is stored in the brain as a set of computations somewhat similar to those carried out by thermostats. Brain computations are, of course, more complex than thermostatic ones. Instead of simple set points, a series of computational procedures, such as arithmetical division, must be stored. Often these procedures can be described in terms of mathematical equations; if not, computer simulations allow *in vitro* manipulation and experimentation. ("In vitro" means "in glass"; in biochemistry it indicates an experiment carried out in the test tube rather than in vivo, in the live organism.) Research on "artificial intelligence" has shown the utility of this type of experimentation.

Imaging and Isomorphism

Though you may have become convinced by the arguments for a computational, procedural memory—and rightly so—there is still more to be said regarding the complexity of the brain's knowledge systems. Roger Shepard initiated another line of research by showing that when we imagine a three-dimensional object and rotate it in space, the time it takes to rotate the image of an object is proportional to the time it takes to rotate an actual object.[5] Now if there were no resemblance between the brain procedure and the actual procedure, such proportionality ought not to hold. Shepard therefore reasoned that, in some instances at least, brain procedures and actual procedures were analogous—that whatever is happening in the brain is in some sense a facsimile, a copy or record, of actual occurrences. In the brain/behavioral sciences the idea that a brain copy is made of external actuality is called *isomorphism* ("iso" meaning same, "morphism" meaning form). This geometric definition of isomorphism is, however, not the only one. In mathematics, isomorphism is said to exist whenever the transformations between descriptions are linear, i.e., when the transformations are readily reversible. Shepard, therefore, has distinguished between primary isomorphism of the geometric kind and secondary isomorphism, which is algebraic and transformational.

Which kind of isomorphism between knowledge-in-the-world and knowledge-in-the-brain exists? Many years ago, B. F. Skinner asked me, while I was teaching a class at Harvard, whether I believed in isomorphic brain representations. He meant representations in the geometric sense and I understood his meaning. I answered "Yes" to his question. He then suggested that I imagine some green grass growing. I did this. Next he said, "Now mow the lawn!" I clutched my head in response—and the absurdity of the geometric isomorph position struck me full force.

Why had I then and why do other neuroscientists today still entertain the geometric isomorph or representational (rather than computational) alternative? For two reasons. The first is that the body surface *is* more or less isomorphically represented in the arrangement of connections to the brain cortex. This is true of skin receptors, the receptors of the cochlea of the ear, the receptors in the retina and the muscle system. There *is* an overall topological correspondence between sensory and motor organization in the periphery of the body on the one hand and the overall organization of the sensory and motor "projection" cortex on the other. Thus "knowing where" and "knowing whither" are sketched out within a framework that is characterized by a rough geometric correspondence between body surface and brain. Our phenomenal subjective experience reflects this body-brain geometry in the where and whither dimensions.

But, as the lawn-mowing example portrays so forcefully, there is considerably more to phenomenal experience than can be accounted for by geometrical isomorphy. Constructional procedures *must* be involved. However, as in the Shepard figures, some of these procedures are secondarily, i.e., algebraically isomorphic and described by linear transformations; others, such as the production of languages, seem to involve nonlinearities. As the powers of language and languagelike systems have been universally extolled as *the* unique characterization of mankind, I want to concentrate on the linear operations to show something of the surprising range of human knowledge systems and the cognitive processes that these linearities (secondary isomorphisms) can encompass.

Not long ago—in the 1950s—brain/behavioral scientists had no inkling as to the existence of such linear transformations, which literally make the form of brain processes utterly different from the form we experience while maintaining the proportionality between the forms. Brain/behavioral scientists did know, however, that they were faced with very serious problems for which they had no explanation. One of these problems was imaging, the other memory. I have already discussed both of these problems from a current vantage point, but it is useful to go back a quarter-century to see the importance of the discovery of a specific procedural operation that, at one stroke, resolved the most puzzling aspects of both problems.

Perception and Reality

At first glance, the problem of the brain mechanisms involved in imaging may not be obvious. After all, we image the objects in the "real" world and the imaging is "direct," i.e., we are not aware of any steps intermediate between object and image; the object and image appear to be one. This directness has led scientists such as James Gibson to suggest that all we need to know are the attributes that make objects, objects—the "information" in external stimulation that reaches the senses and so becomes imaged.[6] From a brain scientist's viewpoint this sort of "naive" realism—even when it becomes "critical" in the sense that the "information" may not be what it initially appears to be—begs a number of important questions. Certainly the structure of the ambient array of information is important; but sensory transduction and transformation of this array is not to be ignored. We have already noted that transformations are truly trans-forms, that the form present at any particular stage of processing may not look at all similar to that present at another, even if the transformations are linear and invertible and secondarily "isomorphic" in the algebraic sense. For the brain physiologist the puzzle is *how* image and object correspond despite the *variations* in the ambient array that strike the sensory receptors. Whatever the "information" provided by these variations, it must be computed by correlating across the variations. Thus the "information" is not just a property of the array but is also a function of the transforming and correlating powers of the organism. This is an extremely important point to grasp: In one view (Gibson's) the organism is a passive gatherer in an object world; in the other (the brain scientist's) the organism is actively involved in the construction of this object world.

Those who take the view that perception is direct would argue that a distinction must be made between perception and cognition. In perception (and in action), they would hold, the brain process "complements" the ambient array rather than representing it. The brain scientist, on the basis of considerable evidence, notes that cognitions enter into perceptions by way of preprocessing: The parts of the brain involved in knowing actively alter the functions of the sensory projections at several stages.[7]

Despite this evidence of cognitive preprocessing in sensory channels, there is a hierarchy that can be made out in our perceptual-cognitive processing. There is, first, a level of "complementation" in which images of objects are present in experience. This presentational level appears to be directly related to phenomenal experience. At the other extreme is the linguistic level, which is obviously re-presentational and in which the connection between re-presentation and what is re-presented is largely arbitrary.

Cognitive Commodities

In between, however, is a level of perceiving and knowing that has been almost completely ignored. This aspect of the perceptual-knowledge process can most easily be understood in terms of the construction of environmental representations of the results of brain/behavioral processes. Such "realizations" of brain/behavioral processes in the environment are *cognitive commodities*. It is with these constructions that the active, inventive, and creative aspect of processing becomes especially evident.

Take, for example, your perception of a chair. How do you know that it is a chair? What "information" do you perceive to be the chairness of chairs? What is in the "direct" perception of an array of stimulations coming from a chair that makes it a chair? Is it the flatness of the seat at a certain elevation from another surface, the floor? The chairback? What about Eames chairs, which are highly contoured? Isn't it the use made of particular objects that helps define them as chairs rather than just their physical conformation? And isn't use a cognitive process, one that involves memory? I see the chairness of a chair as "directly" and immediately as I see its shape, texture, and color (unless the chair is something "totally modern"—something out of the world of my experience of chairs).

Realizing the constructive aspect of direct phenomenal experience, of perception, makes explanations of creativity and invention possible. Not only does the cognitive mechanism preprocess the events in sensory channels to construct perceptions, but the same mechanisms have been found to operate in the motor systems.[8] Here the images-of-achievement are constructed that, when they become realized in action, result in *cognitive commodities.* Chairs, computer programs, and the like join what Karl Popper has called World III, the world of cultural inventions and artifacts.[9] Sports equipment, musical instruments, furniture, telecommunication devices, and economic exchange media such as money are all cognitive commodities. Though language and languagelike processes may play a significant role in constructing these cognitive commodities, two at least equally important aspects of their construction are perceptual iconicity (geometric isomorphism) and proportional fittingness (algebraic or secondary isomorphism).

Holography and Brain Theory

The second major seemingly unsolvable problem facing brain scientists in the 1950s was the question of the brain mechanisms responsible for learning and memory storage. Lashley stated the problem succinctly: "After a lifetime of search for an engram [any trace of a specific memory] the only conclusion that I can reach from the evidence is that learning is just not possible."[10] The issue that Lashley and other brain/behavioral scientists faced was that damage to the brain, no matter how extensive, does not impair any memory for a specific event in isolation. A patient having suffered a stroke does not return to his family, recognize his children, but turn to his wife and find her a total stranger. Memory storage appears to be distributed within the brain and at the same time of a piece. No wonder brain/behavioral scientists were puzzled. When disturbances in remembering do occur, they usually involve a time period (the antegrade and retrograde amnesias following head injuries) or a retrieval mode (the aphasias, apraxias, and agnosias described earlier).

Early in the 1960s engineers developed optical information-processing devices based on a mathematical proposal made by Dennis Gabor.[11] Gabor suggested that, instead of being used to make photographs in the ordinary way, film be treated as an interferometer, recording the interference patterns created when two different electromagnetic beams interact.[12] One beam of electrons or photons would reach the film directly from a generating source; the other would be bounced off an object. The wave forms generated on the film would resemble those produced in a calm-surfaced pond when two (or more) pebbles are thrown in. The ripples produced around each pebble spread away from the source, and where they intersect they interfere with or reinforce each other. If one took a movie of the whole process, from pebble to interference patterns, one could show the film in reverse so that the pebbles would seem to be produced from the ripples. Gabor's insight was that the mathematical processes (called spread functions) that describe the "rippling" process of making interference patterns can be applied a second time to reverse the process, creating images of the objects that produced the ripples. Gabor named the new type of photography "holography" because the interference patterns stored on the film displayed novel and interesting properties, among them the fact that the entire image could be reconstructed from any portion of the film. Whole and part were related in a unique fashion, a fashion very like that which appears to relate memory storage in the brain to the recognition and recall of events in phenomenal experience.

In the fifteen or more years since this striking resemblance between holography and certain brain/behavioral processes was noted, much evidence has accumulated to show that what began as a metaphorical simile has been developed into a precise neurological model. Now based on evidence, this holographic brain model continues to be sharpened as relevant results from tests of various hypotheses (only some of which are derived from the model) have accrued. There is little remaining doubt that some brain processes are characterized by holonomic transformations that result in algebraic isomorphisms between the image/object domain on the one hand and the holographic transform domain on the other.

What advantage does this transform domain contribute to processing? One obvious advantage is resistance to damage. Others include enhanced storage capacity and ready associative recall. But perhaps the most relevant to our purpose here is that extensive correlations can be carried out much more simply and rapidly. Since invertibility insures that no information is lost, the steps involved in transforming and retransforming enhance efficiency. This is why statisticians use the FFT program (the Fast Fourier Transform, an invertible spread function) when they use computers to do their calculations, and why image reconstruction by computerized X-ray tomography relies heavily on these computations.

The peculiarity of holograms is that because information becomes stored throughout, each part of the hologram encodes the whole. The relationship between whole and part is therefore both distributed and enfolded. In fact, the holographic representation enfolds the coordinates of space and time as well as the specific images of objects that are extended in space and time. Thus the memory store is organized neither in space (in any place in the brain) nor in time (in a sequence as if it were registered on a tape), though spatial and temporal markers may well accompany any specific to-be-remembered episode. The feasibility of rapid and extensive correlation stems from the distributed nature of the transformed store.

Holonomy and Education

The discovery of the holonomic organization of memory has important consequences. As noted earlier, the brain has mechanisms for organizing retrieval from the distributed store, and we might properly call the operations of these gnostic mechanisms "thinking." According to the holonomic hypothesis, the operations involved in thinking must invert the distributed memory into images—not necessarily visual images but also kinesthetic/tactile, olfactory/gustatory, and auditory/linguistic. An experiment by Wallach and Averbach in 1955 showed that thinking had to be carried out in one or another sensory mode, that there is no such process as "pure" nonmodal thought.[13]

The problem for education is to communicate the enfolded memory store of the educator to the enfolded memory store of the student. Two separate thought processes must be engaged in order to accomplish this. First the educator must be clear in his unfolding, in his thinking, to establish meaningful, useful images. Second, the teacher must engage the student's enfolding/unfolding mechanism, the student's modes of thinking. If the student is primarily a visual imager and the educator is using primarily auditory/verbal thinking processes there is a mismatch. If the student has tactile/kinesthetic mechanical abilities and the educator is highly auditory/verbal there is a mismatch. There is good evidence that as a group males and females differ considerably in their preferred modes of thinking: females are primarily auditory/verbal; males are often visual and kinesthetic.[14] Since much elementary and secondary education is provided by female instructors, there is a considerable opportunity for mismatching with the thinking processes of their male students.

Holonomic storage per se allows myriad novel combinations to be extracted from the brain. Images of unicorns, changes in interpretation of history, departures from accepted theory in science, inventions of new machines and of other *cognitive commodities* become possible. Whether any particular novel combination is useful and viable is another matter. But in the classroom one must not severely prejudge viability lest the creative process become permanently stifled.

You may object that the educator already has enough trouble just transmitting the current culture to the next generation without the distraction of novelties that can lead to classroom anarchy. My own special remedy for this is to distinguish clearly between education and instruction. Education (from the Latin *ex ducere*) means to lead out; instruction (*in structura*) means to put structure in. Education should, in my view, portray the exciting panorama of knowledge humankind has fashioned so students can then fashion their own visions within the framework of that panorama. In contrast, instruction trains in a discipline that preordains how to function within the panorama of knowledge. Without the three Rs, students will become limited because they can't acquire the knowledge stored in books; they can't progress to other portals of the knowledge system if they can't write; they can't take advantage of sales and other accesses to the culture of consumer goods if they can't handle money.

A physican *must* know drug dosages, a dentist *how to* straighten and fill teeth, a physicist *how to* solve equations, a psychologist *how to* use statistics. Ideally, instruction follows the decision to explore one or another vision achieved through education. That decision must of necessity be made by parents and the educational system when the students are younger; but this does not mean that the separate goals of education and instruction cannot be made clear to the student. I believe a great deal of negativity toward schooling would disappear if students were made aware of this distinction by having each classroom exercise clearly labeled as either necessary although perhaps temporarily uncomfortable training or a widening of the horizons of knowing.

Holonomy and Economics

A final point: Are there any cognitive commodities that embody the holonomic transform domain or display an enfolded order? There is a commonly experienced cognitive commodity that operates within an enfolded order—the economy. Hayek pointed out that every transaction in the marketplace contains within it information about what is taking place over the entire reach of that market.[15] What a dollar will buy reflects the skill of the Japanese, the industriousness of the Germans, the availability of a Ford product during a strike, the size and efficiency of the Washington bureaucracy, your and my needs and desires, the monetary policy of the U.S. Treasury, the availability of gold, of Eurodollars, of oil, of grain—one could go on and on. The marketplace is an enfolded order; the value of money encodes and distributes information within that order. Given this insight, the question is whether the economic enfolded order is holonomic: Are the transactions of the marketplace invertible transformations, and if so, what significance does this have for managing our economic cognitive commodities?

With this question I defer to the economists and educators, for, as noted earlier, I believe that the educational as well as the economic establishment can profit from an examination of the enfolded orders that characterize the construction of cognitive commodities.

Conclusion

The problem of representation in the brain/behavioral sciences has no simple solution. Brain research allows us to distinguish (1) receptor-brain geometric isomorphisms within which image/object complementations and iconicity in phenomenal experience become implemented; (2) secondary algebraic isomorphisms that depend on linear invertible (holonomic) transformations that enhance efficient correlations and the constructive aspects of experience; and (3) possibly nonlinear procedures such as language and languagelike operations. These procedures are involved not only in the phenomenal experiences of knowing but in the production of the cognitive commodities that compose our social/ cultural/economic world. The holonomic transformations and their characteristics are the least familiar of these processes. Examining the enfolded orders produced by such transforms and embodied in some of the cognitive commodities could reveal principles interesting and useful in economics and education.

Notes

1. For example, see *The Brain and Behaviorial Sciences*, Spring 1980 (entire issue).
2. Bisiach, E.; E. Capitani; C. Luzzatti; and D. Perani. Brain and conscious representation of outside reality.
3. von Foerster, H. Memory without record. In D. P. Kimble (ed.) *The Anatomy of Memory*.
4. Ashby, W. R. *An Introduction to Cybernetics*; Cannon, W. B. *Bodily Changes in Pain, Hunger, Fear and Rage*; Pribram, K. H. *Languages of the Brain*; Pribram, K. H. The rôle of analogy in transcending limits in the brain sciences.
5. Shepard, R. N. Cognitive processes that resemble perceptual processes. In W. K. Estes (ed.) *Handbook of Learning and Cognitive Processes*.
6. Gibson, J. J. *The Ecological Approach to Visual Perception*.
7. Pribram, K. H. Computations and representations. In T. W. Simon (ed.) *Symposium on Language, Mind and Brain, Gainesville, Florida, April 1978*.
8. Pribram, K. H. *Languages of the Brain*. Chaps. 12, 13, and 14.
9. Popper, K. R., and Eccles, J. C. *The Self and its Brain*.
10. Lashley, K. S. In search of the engram. In *Physiological Mechanisms in Animal Behavior*.
11. Leith, E. Holography's practical dimension; Goodman, J. W. *Introduction to Fourier Optics*; Bracewell, R. *The Fourier Transform and its Applications*.
12. Gabor, D. Information processing with coherent light.
13. Wallach, H., and Averbach, E. On memory modalities.
14. McGuinness, D. Sex differences in the organization of perception and cognition. In J. Archer and B. Lloyd (eds.) *Explorations in Sex Differences*; McGuinness, D., and Pribram, K. H. The origins of sensory bias in the development of gender differences in perception and cognition. In M. Bortner (ed.) *Cognitive Growth and Development: Essays in Memory of Herbert G. Birch*.
15. Hayek, F. A. *Individualism and Economic Order*.

Bibliography

Ashby, W. R. *An Introduction to Cybernetics*. New York: Wiley & Sons, 1963.
Bisiach, E.; Capitani, E.; Luzzatti, C.; and Perani, D. Brain and conscious representation of outside reality. *Neuropsychologia* 1981, 19(4): 543–551.
Bracewell, R. *The Fourier Transform and its Applications*. New York: McGraw-Hill, 1965.

Cannon, W. B. *Bodily Changes in Pain, Hunger, Fear and Rage.* New York: D. Appleton & Co., 1929.

von Foerster, H. Memory without record. In D. P. Kimble (ed.) *The Anatomy of Memory.* Palo Alto, Calif.: Science & Behavior Books, 1965, pp. 388–433.

Gabor, D. Information processing with coherent light. *Optica Acta* 1969, 16: 519–533.

Gibson, J. J. *The Ecological Approach to Visual Perception.* Boston: Houghton Mifflin, 1979.

Goodman, J. W. *Introduction to Fourier Optics.* San Francisco: McGraw-Hill, 1968.

Hayek, F. A. *Individualism and Economic Order.* Boston: Routledge & Kegan Paul, 1977.

Lashley, K. S. In search of the engram. In *Physiological Mechanisms in Animal Behavior.* New York: Academic, 1950, pp. 454–482.

Leith, E. Holography's practical dimension. *Electronics* 1966, 39: 88–94.

McGuinness, D. Sex differences in the organization of perception and cognition. In J. Archer and B. Lloyd (eds.) *Explorations in Sex Differences.* Brighton, England: Harvester Press, 1975.

McGuinness, D., and Pribram, K. H. The origins of sensory bias in the development of gender differences in perception and cognition. In M. Bortner (ed.) *Cognitive Growth and Development: Essays in Memory of Herbert G. Birch.* New York: Bruner/Mazel, 1978, pp. 3–56.

Popper, K. R., and Eccles, J. C. *The Self and its Brain.* New York: Springer International, 1977.

Pribram, K. H. Computations and representations. In T. W. Simon (ed.) *Symposium on Language, Mind and Brain, Gainesville, Florida, April 1978.* New York: Erlbaum, 1981, pp. 213–224.

Pribram, K. H. *Languages of the Brain.* Englewood Cliffs, N.J.: Prentice-Hall, 1971 (2d ed. Monterey, Calif.: Brooks/Cole, 1977).

Pribram, K. H. Localization and distribution of function in the brain. In J. Orbach (ed.) *Neuropsychology Since Lashley.* New York: Erlbaum, 1981.

Pribram, K. H. The role of analogy in transcending limits in the brain sciences. *Daedalus* 1980, 109 (2); 19–38.

Pribram, K. H. Some dimensions of remembering: Steps toward a neuropsychological model of memory. In J. Gaito (ed.) *Macromolecules and Behavior.* New York: Academic Press, 1966, pp. 165–187.

Pribram, K. H.; Nuwer, M.; and Baron, R. The holographic hypothesis of memory structure in brain function and perception. In R. C. Atkinson, D. H. Krantz, R. C. Luce, and P. Suppes (eds.) *Contemporary Developments in Mathematical Psychology.* San Francisco: Freeman, 1974, pp. 416–467.

Shepard, R. N. Cognitive processes that resemble perceptual processes. In W. K. Estes (ed.) *Handbook of Learning and Cognitive Processes.* Hillsdale, N.J.: Erlbaum, 1978.

Wallach, H., and Averbach, E. On memory modalities. *American Journal of Psychology* 1955, 68 (2): 249–257.

DIANE McGUINNESS

——— 4 ———
Males and Females and the Learning Process

Introduction

Individual children pursue different interests, learn about the world in different ways, and exhibit a wide variety of learning styles and levels of achievement. Because educators are committed to a curriculum and believe children cannot be left to their own devices, and also because our culture values the creation and dissemination of knowledge, educators have categorized children into groups. Such categories can merely represent a rough segregation of a classroom: good, medium, poor—often relabeled as bluebirds, robins, and orioles, or whatever. More recently these labels have become increasingly pernicious, not because teachers are nastier but because educational institutions have succumbed to an escalating tendency toward hierarchical organization. Somebody at the top must decide what everyone else is going to do. The someones at the top are the "professionals" who often have never seen a child at close quarters, much less in a classroom. But they know about such things as how to select and construct ineffective reading primers, how to draft inappropriate reading diagnostic batteries, and, more important, how to borrow medical jargon to make a strong argument for the relevance of scores on such batteries. Thus we have seen an explosion in the past decade of such concepts as "minimal brain dysfunction," "dyslexia," "childhood aphasia," "nonspecific CNS syndrome," "hyperactivity," and so on. These adumbrations are the result of having scored below a certain percentile on some test or other designed by someone to test something he or she doesn't understand.

Because of my research on sex differences, I was abruptly hurled into this milieu when someone finally let the cat out of the bag: All (or almost all) of those who are scoring "below" are boys—they make up 75 percent of our reading disability populations and 85 percent of the hyperactive populations. To understand what these high percentages mean it is important to understand how achievement tests are standardized and the meaning of the word "normal."

Normality is a statistical concept that refers to what "most people do." Technically what is "normal" encompasses two standard deviations of the Gaussian distribution or 68 percent of any given population, though this cutoff is arbitrary. Learning-disabled children are defined according to their deviations from age norms; that is, they must fall around or below one standard deviation from the mean.

Two examples will suffice to show the extent of the problem. Satz and Morris revealed nine identifiably distinct categories of children with respect to their scores on reading, spelling, and arithmetic tests.[1] Of the 230 ten-year-olds in the sample, two of the nine groups, representing 89 children (or 39 percent), were classified as clearly retarded when compared to the age norms for all tests. Given that 16 percent will be in the superior range on any given test and 16 percent will be in the inferior range, what can be said about the statement that 39 percent of a population are functioning well below "normal"? It only begins to make sense when one considers that Satz and Morris's entire population consisted of *boys* and that the tests' achievement norms are standardized for both sexes.

Take another example: The estimate for the incidence of hyperactive children in the population is 15 percent, with a male-female ratio of 6 to 1. This means that for every 100 children, 13 of the 15 children diagnosed as hyperactive will be male, indicating that 26 percent of *all males* are hyperactive, way beyond the "abnormal" 16 percent.[2] But hyperactivity is not a superior/inferior dimension. It refers instead to behavioral extremes and ranges from hypoactive (stuporous) to hyperactive (uncontrollable). Both ends of the distribution are equally deviant. If 26 percent is the cutoff for normality at the hyperactive end of the distribution, then it *must also* be the cutoff at the opposite end. This gives us a total of *52 percent of all males being abnormal*!

It seems clear that something is terribly wrong with a society that designates 39 percent or 26 percent (actually 52 percent) of its boys as abnormal, suggests that they all have either brain damage or antisocial tendencies, tars them with inscrutable labels such as dyslexia, minimal brain dysfunction, and aphasia, and forces them to comply with norms established for both sexes by largely female instructors. (The *only* diagnosis for hyperactivity is the teacher's or parent's tolerance for annoying behavior.) Having spent some years studying the reasons that females have difficulty in higher mathematics, I believe that assigning female deficits such as mathphobia to social factors like "male chauvinism" while attributing male deficits to "brain damage" reflects more on current politics than on scientific or intellectual acumen.

There is no question that in two major domains of school difficulties—learning disabilities and hyperactivity—boys are overwhelmingly represented. Various hypotheses have been generated as to why this should be the case, and the data are accumulating. Before setting out to review them in some detail, I would like to dispose of four popular theories.

The Brain-Damage Theory

To adopt the view that over a quarter of all young boys have brain damage is, to say the least, to make an astonishing assertion. In fact, no specific neural anomaly has ever been discovered that correlates with learning disabilities. But a sex effect robust enough to produce a ratio of three to one that holds up across many studies in many countries must have something to do with male and female brains. This is not because the brains of one sex or another are "damaged" but rather because they are structurally *different*. McGuinness and Pribram have reviewed the evidence on sex differences in cerebral organization and brain uptake of hormones.[3] Marion Diamond at the University of California, Berkeley, has recently demonstrated striking differences in cortical thickness of the two hemispheres in male and female rats. Diamond found that the developmental curves for changes in left-right cortical ratios were *completely* different in the two sexes, and there was strong evidence of structural differences in the CNS between males and females reared in identical environments. In addition, she found that the environment operates upon a plastic cellular network, setting up patterns of activity that in turn produce further anatomical changes in the CNS.[4]

Cultural Determinism

Culture-only theorists suffer from the grave misapprehension that blaming the culture explains all, when in fact it explains nothing. It just obscures the problem. We know there are limits to our capacity to learn (a biological bias) but that learning *is* possible. The environment does make a difference, yet teaching cannot produce an Einstein (in his case it was even counterproductive).

Apart from instilling values, passing on knowledge, and developing techniques for training the mind, the culture can also produce labels for certain kinds of behavior it does not admire, wishes to ridicule, or wishes to eradicate. Unfortunately, in the case of young boys with learning problems, it is more often the child who is eradicated than the behavior.

If teachers promote maximum self-respect and self-confidence in children while teaching at a pace and style suited to each student, they can do no more. What goes on in the culture, in this instance, is irrelevant. The problem is really what does suit each student? If we discover boys have trouble with certain tasks and girls do not, then the key question is, "What are the girls *doing* that makes learning more efficient, and what are the boys *doing* that makes it inefficient?"

Developmental Lag

There is no longer any logical or experimental basis for a *global* theory of developmental lag in intellectual function to explain male deficits. Several studies have demonstrated that males are developmentally *accelerated* in tasks requiring three-dimensional visualization. Sophistication in three-D tasks in young males has been found in Scotland, in Ghana, and in the Pakeha of New Zealand. Piagetian conservation tasks, especially those involving quantity and area, are solved at a *higher* developmental age by U.S. white boys and by boys in grades three through six in Papua New Guinea. In the conservation tasks, though Papuan boys were considerably below U.S. and European norms, they were two years ahead of girls. One must ask: What, then, is "lagging"?

Attention

Problems in controlling and focusing attention are at the core of the difficulties exhibited by the hyperactive child. But there are two grave difficulties with the term "attention." The first, and perhaps more crucial, issue deals with the question, "Attention to what?" That is, it *does* matter what you ask a child to pay attention to. In most studies purporting to analyze attentional deficits in hyperactive or learning-disabled children, the tasks in question are utterly boring, repetitive, and monotonous; vigilance tasks are a prime example. The staying power of the child, the ability to maintain attention over time, is considered a major indicator of hyperactivity. Suppose instead, one measured the length of time the child spent kicking a ball against the garage door or the number of attempts made to negotiate a steep slope on a skateboard. How would the criterion of time spent on a task fare?

The second issue is that attention in these studies is often defined *exclusively* in terms of the amount of time one is able to concentrate on a task. But there are other aspects in the regulating of attention. An important factor is the ability to inhibit reactions to distractions.

The problem in studies of attention, therefore, is to disentangle variables about the task from elements reflecting the efficiency, or lack thereof, of the systems controlling attention. As there is not a single study among over one hundred I have reviewed that has successfully accomplished this, and the diagnosis of hyperactivity is completely arbitrary, I conclude there is no such thing as hyperactivity, at least as it is currently defined. Hyperactivity accompanies certain brain lesions. But to assume there is a connection between this form of behavior and naughtiness is to strain the imagination.

Reading Disabilities

The reading disabilities problem is more pertinent, and certainly it is more productive to pursue this issue because of the quality of studies in the literature and the amount of crosscultural research.

Environmental Factors in Reading Difficulties

In school populations, the sex ratio for dyslexia is around three to one. However, in clinical or remedial settings the ratio is as high as five or six to one. These figures strongly suggest there are two factors at work. One, I believe, is a biological factor that is outside culture; the other is *environmental,* proving that males are subject to environmental factors that predispose against acquiring fluent reading skills.

In societies where reading is highly stereotyped as male or highly valued among males, sex differences in reading ability disappear. Other data suggest that almost any aspect of environmental manipulation affects male scores. When the reading material is matched to the interest of individuals, boys do as well as girls on reading tests, but when low-interest material is involved, they do remarkably worse. Testing pro cedures are important. Rowell tested 240 third through fifth graders on oral and silent reading comprehension.[5] Girls did equally well on both tests, but boys did better on oral reading. When emphasis is on vocabulary rather than fluency and comprehension, males are often found to be superior. Training methods also make a difference. In phonics-oriented classrooms females improve significantly over males. Gies found vo cabulary scores were significantly higher for boys in closed classroom environments than for those in open class environments. Girls scored higher than boys on other language abilities regardless of type of classroom.[6]

Lanthier and Deiker's study of 117 adolescent in-patients found that male, but not female, reading and math achievement scores were significantly correlated to parent scores, especially to those of the *mother.* The effect of the sex constitution of families turns out to be an extremely important variable in male reading achievement.[7] Cicirelli studied 600 middle-class white families. In the population as a whole females were superior on various language tests. When Cicirelli looked at the sex of siblings in two-, three-, and four-child families he found the boys' performance on language tests and their IQ scores increased noticeably if they had at least one female sibling, especially in three- and four-child families. Here males had a mean increase in IQ of seven points and one stanine higher on reading scores.[8]

An obvious conclusion from these data is that females are more *spontaneously* gifted in language and reading skills, and their abilities are not diminished by type of instruction or size or sex constitution of the family, whereas male reading ability is affected by these factors.

These data bring us to the crux of the nature-nurture issue. In a constant environment sex differences emerge—a biological program. In extreme environments the performance of males, not females, swings dramatically. Males are at *risk* to many environmental situations, at least in regard to reading.

The remainder of this paper explores the evidence for sex differences in auditory and motor skills and the correlates of language function and reading achievement. A theory is proposed that motor functions develop differently in boys and girls and that it is in sensory-motor integration that the sex differences become most pronounced.[9]

Sex Differences in Auditory and Fine-Motor Skills

The evidence supports the contention that females show greater aptitude in speech development, auditory integration, and fine-motor control. Sensitivity to loudness is significantly greater in female children and young adults.[10] Threshold shift—an effect that shows auditory sensitivity to noise—is greater in females than in males at ages four to eleven. Males over fifty with no known hearing deficit were found to have significantly more hearing loss and poorer speech discrimination scores than females. These findings confirm those in a survey carried out by Corso in which females were found to have superior hearing to much later ages. These data suggest a greater sensitization to auditory signals in females.[11]

However, the auditory system is not a unit exhibiting equal facility in all domains. In one study, males and females had similar performances on the threshold task up to approximately 4,000 Hz and identical ones on a difficult pitch-discrimination task when years of musical training were taken into account.[12] The overwhelming sex difference was in sensitivity to loudness. Should this sex effect be maintained in loudness discrimination, this difference would indicate that females have a considerable advantage in processing information concerning the *dynamics* of speech, which convey emotional quality. In that case females would extract information about the emotional aspects of speech before semantic processing had begun. Support for this view comes from studies showing female musicians have greater awareness of musical dynamics than males and from investigations of mother-infant interactions showing females are more consoled by their mothers' speech and that speech increases their babbling rate. This interaction is of primary interest because it has not been found that mothers speak differently to sons than to daughters.[13]

Auditory sensitivity is accompanied by more precocious speech development in girls. Moore found that scores on the Griffiths Speech Quotient were higher in girls at age six months and that by eighteen months this difference was statistically significant. The speech quotient scores were highly correlated with subsequent language development in girls but not in boys.[14]

By age two to two and a half children are completing their repertoire of consonants. In 90 children Paynter and Petty found no significant difference between boys and girls at age two, but by age two and a half many more girls had added the most complex sounds—s, l, st, and r—to their repertoire. In 90 percent of all cases, boys had five consonants, girls seven.[15] Males consistently have more hesitations and revisions, have considerably more trouble singing in tune, and are subject to speech disorders more often than girls.[16]

Various studies have indicated that the primary female aptitude in both receptive and productive language is the ability to process temporal sequences, suggesting a general *motor* program for language. For example, evidence supporting the idea of a generalized motor capacity underlying language comes from Gattney's study of five- to seven-year-old deaf children investigating receptive language in response to signing. Girls were significantly better overall in processing complex linguistic aspects of syntax, word order, inflection, and interrogation. This superiority was independent of IQ, hearing impairment, and months of schooling.[17]

Females show a greater aptitude in fine-motor sequencing ability but not in tapping speed. Girls' superiority over boys actually increases from ages five to ten. Boys do not improve after age eight.[18] An unpublished study found that teaching a simple sixteen-bar dance sequence to eight novice females required only one or two trials. By contrast, several males of the eight tested were unable to make transitions between movements although they understood the patterns and the sequence.

Some studies investigating sex differences show that the effects are most pronounced when information has to be translated between sensory modes. Majeres concludes from his data on speeded crossmodal tasks that the translation to a *verbal* code is what produces the efficient response in females.[19] In my own study, college-age males and females were asked to search for target letters (A or I) or target sounds (eh or ae) in words presented visually or auditorily. In the visual condition, the sexes did not differ noticeably in reaction time or error scores. However, when asked to identify a sound in a spoken word, males made significantly more errors than females, and they performed *at chance levels* when asked to determine whether a target *letter* was present in a spoken word. These are surprising results for a highly verbal university population in Great Britain; they suggest males have great difficulty translating an auditory phonemic code into its visual counterpart.

A wide range of data shows that naming (semantics, the lexicon, etc.) and syntax (the *rules* of generating linguistic strings) are systems independent of those that receive and generate speech. The skills important to reading are acknowledged to be fluent phonic analysis and auditory comprehension.

Although females are somewhat more advanced in learning letter names, the problem in learning to read is not one of *remembering* which sounds are attached to which letters. It is, rather , the problem of being able to make the letter-sound transform *at sufficient speed* to be able to generate a word. The sex effect appears to be determined in large part by the speed at which these transform operations occur. It is not surprising that if one is efficient in performing faster and with less effort a perceptual-motor skill that underpins a cognitive process, one will favor that cognitive process over others. This reasoning may explain why females persist in adopting verbal strategies when they are inappropriate to a task, such as one requiring spatial reasoning; it also provides a hypothesis about why females do poorly in algebra and even worse in geometry and trigonometry. Mathematics, a language describing objects in space, is more closely related to syntax than to phonics. It is impossible to "talk mathematics" or communicate it verbally, which is why mathematicians inevitably retreat to blackboards or table napkins when asked what they are "talking about."

This has been an attempt to untangle the factors that might underlie sex effects in reading disability out of a maze of snarled threads. So far, many of the studies on auditory processing deficits in poor readers have not reported sex effects except in spelling scores. Often where the sex of the subjects has been reported, subjects were selected because they were "poor readers" or "good readers." For example, one study reported no sex differences, stating only that one child of each sex was selected from both above and below the class median—thus biasing the sample to an excess of poor females and good males. Furthermore, motor sequential fluency has never been tested in conjunction with reading in normal students.

All one can conclude so far is that the strongest predictor of reading ability is phonological encoding and a general "language" facility and that females appear adept in both.

Conclusion: Sex Differences and Knowledge

Where, then, is knowledge, and how is it derived? The main question is how a complex world view can be constructed from a limited subset of energies impinging on our senses; it can be answered in part by noting that the nervous sytem is set to respond to *patterns of regularities* in the external environment. Without these regularities, chaos would ensue. Knowledge begins with the predictability derived from the regularities in the world being mapped onto the regularities in the CNS. This means that knowledge consists of three basic aspects: (1) what exists in the world, (2) what sensitivities we possess inherently, and (3) which of those external signals or patterns we *choose* to monitor.

The world-out-there is in two basic modes: objects or entities that do *not* generate information, and objects or entities that do. An inert object in space does not transmit information about itself; information can be derived only by operating upon the object in a number of ways. By contrast, other human beings transmit information or *believe* they are doing so. In order to "know" people, one must operate upon the *information* they believe they are generating as well as the information actually generated in the listener. Note that "information" is used here in the classic sense: to reduce uncertainty. No static object will reduce any uncertainty unless it is operated upon. An operation may be as primitive or minimal as noting the object's relationship to other objects in space.

In focusing on the differences between the sexes, we see that in boys, at least in the West, the predisposition is to be biased toward the world of objects—where knowledge can only be gleaned by action. In girls the predisposition is a bias toward the world of persons where knowledge is gained from *nonaction*—by tuning in. Nonaction does not mean passivity or *no* action. It is "active suppression of motion," a motor readiness.

These very different modes of generating knowledge lead to further predictions about *what* is learned. First, girls are easier to teach, and they find information about persons in complex social settings easier to process. Second, males know more about the physical properties of objects and object relations. Finally, these differences will be reflected in the nature of thought. If the "regularities" from the world are essentially stable and predictable over time, one's thought will become more and more "homogenistic," that is, schematic, hierarchical, and categorical. If, on the other hand, "regularities" only arise by correlating information (statement), belief (assumption behind the statement), and behavior (outcome), one's thought will become "heterogenistic" and interactive. This kind of thinking is pragmatic, context-dependent, and tolerant of multiple ambiguities.

As one's thought is, so is one's language. A homogenistic thinker uses language as a means for naming objects and events, generating rules, and so on. A semantic language user often comes to believe that the name *defines* the object; for such an individual, as Cassirer has noted, description can become magically synonymous with the thing itself. The name *becomes* the thing. A further stage in this process is to name a name and believe one has the meaning *in* the name. Ultimately this can be elaborated in ritual—for a ritual is nothing more than an extension of naming; a ritual is a "name" to magically create an event. The ritual becomes the event and an end in itself. A ritual is the ultimate in referential naming because it must be carried out in exactly the same way, in the same sense that a name will cease to exist if its phonemes are rearranged.

Contrast the homogenistic thinker to the heterogenistic thinker, who uses language as a means to an end. That end is always the sharing of meaning. Language itself doesn't have meaning, but it is used to generate or refer to meaning outside language. A name will never "define" anything, simply because definitions are not at issue. Nor will language define meaning. Meaning can only be approximated by a variety of linguistic and nonlinguistic expressions. Meaning is superordinate to language, never embedded in it; it refers instead to intentions and feelings.

A homogenistic thinker will make remarks like, "Now that you have defined your terms, I see we are in agreement," or "This afternoon we will discuss the meaning of 'knowledge.'" A heterogenistic thinker in similar settings will note, "Gentlemen, you have been talking for an hour and you have said nothing," or apropos of a whining child, "His cry doesn't *mean* anything. Just leave him alone."

It is of some considerable interest that Western society is moving towards a more heterogenic position, especially in science and philosophy. In this we will begin to approach a balance between the masculine and feminine perspectives.

Notes

1. Satz, P., and Morris, R. The search for subtype classification in learning disabled children. In R. E. Tarter (ed.) *The Child at Risk*. New York: Oxford University Press, 1980.

2. Schrag, P., and Divoky, D. *The Myth of the Hyperactive Child*. New York: Dell Publishing Co., 1975.

3. McGuinness, D., and Pribram, K. H. 1978. The origins of sensory bias in the development of gender differences in perception and cognition. In M. Bortner (ed.) *Cognitive Growth and Development: Essays in Memory of Herbert G. Birch*. New York: Bruner/Mazel, 1978.

4. Diamond, M. C.; Dowling, G. A.; and Johnson, R. E. Morphological cerebral cortical asymmetry in male and female rats. *Experimental Neurology* 1981, 71: 261–268.

5. Rowell, E. H. Do elementary students read better orally or silently? *Reading Teacher* 1976, 29: 367–370.

6. Gies, F. J.; Leonard, B. C.; Madden, J. B.; and Jon, J. Effects of organizational climate and sex on the language arts achievement of disadvantaged sixth graders. *Journal of Educational Research* 1973, 67: 177–181.

7. Lanthier, I. J., and Deiker, T. E. Achievement scores of emotionally disturbed adolescents and parents educational level. *Child Study Journal* 1974, 4: 163–168.

8. Cicirelli, V. G. Sibling constellation, creativity, I.Q. and academic achievement. *Child Development* 1967, 38: 481–490.

9. This theory is more fully elaborated in McGuinness and Pribram. The origins of sensory bias.

10. Elliott, C. C. Noise tolerance and extraversion in children. *British Journal of Psychology* 1971, 52: 375–380; McGuinness, D. Hearing: Individual differences in perceiving. *Perception* 1972, 1: 465–473.

11. McCoy, C. Experimental study of learning in the aged as measured by pure tones, word discrimination and the SSW. *Dissertation Abstracts International*, 1978, 38: 4719.

12. McGuinness. Hearing: Individual differences.

13. Shuter, R. *The Psychology of Music*. London: Methuen, 1968; Lewis, M. State as an infant-environment interaction: An analysis of mother-infant interaction as a function of sex. *Merrill-Palmer Quarterly* 1972, 18: 95–121; Phillips, J. R. Syntax and vocabulary of mother's speech to young children: Age and sex comparisons. *Child Development* 1973, 44: 182–185; Fraser, C., and Roberts, N. Mother's speech to children of four different ages. *Journal of Psychological Research* 1975, 4: 9–16.

14. Moore, T. Language and intelligence: A longitudinal study of the first 8 years. *Human Development* 1967, 10: 88–106.

15. Paynter, E. T., and Petty, N. A. Articulatory sound: Acquisition of two-year-old children. *Perceptual and Motor Skills* 1974, 39: 1079–1085.

16. Bentley, A. *Monotones*. London: Novello and Co., 1968.

17. Gattney, D. W. Assessing receptive language skills of five to seven year old deaf children. *Dissertation Abstracts International* 1977, 38: 1665–1666.

18. Annett, Marion M. The growth of manual preferences and speed. *British Journal of Psychology*, 1970, 61: 545–558; Denckla, M. B. Development of speed in repetitive and successive finger movements in normal children. *Journal of*

Developmental Medical Child Neurology, 1973, 15: 635–645; Denckla, M. B. Development of motor coordination in normal children. *Journal of Developmental Medical Child Neurology*, 1974, 16: 729–741.

19. Majeres, R. L. Sex differences in clerical speed: Perceptual encoding vs. verbal encoding. *Memory and Cognition*, 1977, 5: 468–476.

HERMAN T. EPSTEIN

—————— 5 ——————

Brain Development:
Implications for
Educational Policy
and Practice

Optimization in education requires matching instructional input to at least three main aspects of the learner: (1) the knowledge already acquired, (2) the way in which the individual reasons (i.e., learns), and (3) the ambience—both human and inanimate—of the learning situation. Optimization also requires that we understand and utilize the fact that the functioning of the mind is but an expression of the functioning of the brain; they are just two different manifestations of the same entity. Until now little attention had been paid to the brain-based nature of learning and schooling. Only in recent years has the world of education begun to hark to such words as brain, hemispheres, cortex, and so on. Yet, one cannot affect the mind without affecting the brain, and vice versa.

What features of the brain need to be thought about? Pribram has called attention to the extensive interconnectivity of the modifications of the brain resulting from any and all inputs. The extent of the interconnectivity can be appreciated by expressing the matter quantitatively. First, the typical neuron is no more than five synapses away from every other neuron. Second, on the average, each neuron has synapses with one to ten thousand other neurons. This degree of interconnectivity means that every input acts to modify a very large number of regions in the brain. We have been accustomed to think of the brain as composed of what specialists call *feature detectors*. Simply put, a feature detector is a neuron that only responds to a single very elementary input. For example, there are neurons that seem to be activated by only one frequency of sound (e.g., 345 cycles per second). It may well be that there are such neurons, but the result of that sound input does not necessarily go only or even mainly to that one neuron; many—presumably thousands—of other neurons are also activated and neural networks altered by that input. This was first strongly indicated by the failure of attempts to cut away memory of specific events. Lashley found that very large portions of different parts of the brain could be cut away without much effect on memory of the input being studied. This finding led to what Pribram and others call a *holographic* representation of each input: the input is manifested over many parts of the brain. Holography refers to a particular kind of spreading of the input over the brain; we shall not be concerned with that detail in this discussion.

Another aspect of the brain beginning to receive attention is the gender difference: males and females have anatomically different brains. If we connect these differences with different functioning, we are forced to conclude that males and females will actually behave and think differently for biological reasons, apart from any sociocultural differences. There is simple evidence of the brain differences: between the ages of 10 and 12 years, females have about three times as much brain growth as males, while between the ages of 14 and 16 years, males have appreciably greater brain growth. Males have 7 percent greater brain weights, but have appreciably greater body weights, so the brain/body ratios of females are higher than those of males; presumably it takes more brain power to do all the things normally done by females. Moreover, there are well-established neuropsychological differences, such as the greater sensitivity of females to nonverbal cues: facial expressions, body language, and intonation of voices.

Because of these large anatomical differences it is not unlikely that learning (and schooling) of females could be significantly improved by matching inputs to their particular brain properties. While females and males have different brains, it is a difference of equals. Moreover, the spectrum of abilities within each gender surely overlaps that of the other, so there is absolutely no reason to have "lower" expectations of either gender.

In humans, there are periods of relatively rapid brain growth in the age spans of 2–4, 6–8, 10–12+, and 14–16+ years. It turns out that, although the growth varies from region to region and from growth stage to growth stage, there seems to be a major underlying aspect of the growth: an increase in the length and branching of axons and dendrites, an increase in what is frequently called the *arborization* of the neurons. This increased arborization presumably results from a successful evolutionary mutation affecting brain development after the completion of the preceding brain-growth stage. The mutation probably had two main characteristics: First, it yielded additional network complexity that could be instructed by experience and by direct teaching. (The additional networks had no programmed functions of their own.) Second, the expanded network probably had to receive instruction mainly through language. Together, these constraints allowed humans to gain the ability to reason systematically or syllogistically. We now know that at ages greater than 4 or 5 years, the change in arborization is physically shaped, altered, or "pruned" by experience and instruction. Accordingly, the quality of the added brain functioning depends on the quality and quantity of the instructional input because the very networks are physically altered by that input.

Matching Stages of Growth and Learning

The Piaget stages and levels of reasoning have their earliest onset at the ages of the brain-growth stages. Thus, we can use the entire collection of insights from the Piagetian research to help us detect what kinds of reasoning are in place or will appear next. This knowledge lets us match instructional input in great detail to the receptive abilities of the individual. We are at a turning point in education, in my judgment, because for the first time it is possible to work on the problem of the match in a scientific way. About 5 years ago, quantification was achieved for concepts that can be used to describe *both* the instructional input and the receptive capacities of children. Thus, work could begin on ways of achieving the match of input and reception in education.

Within education, optimization has occasionally been discussed under the title "The Problem of the Match," matching instructional input to the receptive capacity of the child.[1] If the input demands higher cognitive skills than the child possesses, no learning can result. If the input demands far less than the child's skills, no learning can result for lack of any challenge. It is only when input and skills are approximately matched that the child has to stretch its mind, thereby increasing understanding and, presumably at the same time, developing additional cognitive abilities.

Previously, optimization focused mainly on input. Yet we still lack not only a comprehensive theory of education but even an empirical model telling us what to teach, when, to whom, or how. We have an abundance of speculative models, but their values are hardly greater than what would result from a late-night bull session among college sophomores. It is not yet possible to decide if optimizing schooling for, say, women, whites, lower classes, or urbanized people would affect, be affected by, optimize, or deoptimize schooling for men, blacks, middle classes, or people from developing countries. Our understanding of schooling is so very primitive that it does not yet demand consideration of the more complex aspects. Thus, any discussion could involve only the simplest, most superficial aspects of schooling. Therefore, our discussion of optimization within education must proceed without much hard data from education itself. The title of this volume spotlights no dangers of disuse or misuse of knowledge about education, not because the main problems have been solved, but because there is so little hard knowledge.

My approach to education is a holistic one: looking at the overall picture of schooling without specifying details of what takes place in the schooling situation. Thus, it is made to order for the present scene. Since it could not come from education, the data base for my analysis comes from biology and, to a small extent, from psychology, disciplines that *do* have some data bases. Let us ask what we can learn from biology and psychology to give clues about improving school strategies and, perhaps, even some tactics for doing so.

Many, if not most, of the major insights in the natural sciences are grounded in the study of invariances, more commonly called conservation theorems. We can think of the advances triggered by discovery of the conservation of mass, momentum, energy, spin, and other principles in physics and chemistry. In biology, the conservation of DNA and of base sequences in DNA has let us unravel some of the workings of genetics and development. Are there similar fruitful conservations or invariances in the human sciences?

One such invariance—though it is not generally thought of as such—is the sequence in which Piaget's stages of reasoning appear. Related to it is the sequential appearance of individual schemata within each stage. It is but a minor digression to consider briefly how such invariances might affect research in the human sciences. Explanations generally derive either from nature or from nurture. In this instance, the invariant sequences could not be due to nurture since one cannot alter them by altering aspects of nurture (unless nurturing can be shown to have a crosscultural character entirely unknown to us at present). Natural constraints—biophysical or biochemical—on the growth of a brain could make operations appear in a fixed sequence. By this reasoning, the experimentally found sequences might be used to predict the locations and natures of the parts of the brain. A third way to account for the invariant sequences is that they are immanent in the nature of logic itself. In that case, experts in syllogistic logic could help us understand the reasons for the particular sequences.

But my discussion will be based on invariances of the brain growth stages, which appear on a biological (i.e., mainly an age-linked) schedule. This gives brain development an invariance in time and in quality that deserves to be studied in detail. Why did such an invariant set of stages appear? How did they develop? Of what functional use is such a sequence?

Let me first sketch the biological basis of my analysis. All organs of mammals show embryological stages of greater and lesser growth in size and complexity. When an organ is first formed, it is a primitive version of what it will eventually become, and its development parallels its evolution. Thus, when the blob that is to become a kidney has to show a new function (an enzyme or hormone, for example), there is a change in expression of the genes so that the cell becomes able to manufacture the new enzyme. Then, in order to service the whole organ and whole organism, this new kind of cell multiplies rapidly to provide enough of the new substance. This so-called functional differentiation is manifested by an increase in the size of the organ relative to that of the body. This size increase has not previously been important to research, so it has not been stressed, even though embryologists have known about it for decades.

We can now turn the analysis around and observe that, while the body is growing steadily, an increase in the ratio of organ to body weight signifies a change in function of that organ; the growth stages of the organ signal the onsets of new functions. This way of looking at the brain growth stages is important for our study. The brain functions in three main observable ways: sensory, cognitive or learning, and psychological or emotional. The major focus of this discussion will be on the cognitive or learning functions: How can we optimize them on the basis of insights and constraints deriving from biological studies of brain growth stages?

First, I will discuss the brain growth stages, details of which can be found in the references.[2] For our purposes I will focus on four postnatal stages, occurring in the spans 2–4, 6–8, 10–12+, and 14–16+ years. Second, it is important to note two additional facts at this point: (1) the net synthesis of DNA practically stops around age 18–24 months; and (2) there is homology between brain growth stages in rodents and in humans that must be explained in some detail.

What is the significance of the very small amount of net DNA synthesis after 2 years? Since DNA is the main genetic material, there can be little increase in the number of brain cells after about age 2, although the brain increases in weight by some 30 percent after that age. Therefore, we infer that the increase is in weight per cell. Since most of the weight is in the axons and dendrites that send and receive signals to and from other neurons, we must be measuring a substantial increase in the length and branching of axons and dendrites, that is, the arborization of neurons.

This conclusion seems direct, but, like all scientific inferences, it has to be checked. One verification is the increase in thickness of the cortex of the brain precisely at the ages of the brain growth stages.[3] Also, an EEG shows the marked change in electrical properties of the brain that could be expected for markedly changed networks, again precisely at the brain growth stages.[4] Furthermore, the first direct studies of arborization in cat brains showed changes at what is probably a brain growth stage.[5] Therefore, brain growth stages very likely manifest anatomically marked changes in arborization in the brain, though the locations of the changes are not yet known and must differ with each brain growth stage.

Marked changes in the neural networks presumably affect functioning of networks, so we infer that changes in functioning can begin at the ages of brain growth. We have no way of knowing what actually triggers the functional changes or what might affect the networks that were formed and altered on a biological schedule; this point will be taken up a bit later. All we can say about cognitive functioning is that we expect to find the onsets of changes in reasoning strategies around ages 3, 7, 11, and 15 years.

The next point deals with what we can learn from homologies between the brain growth stages of humans and mice. Stages have been discovered in mice between 8 and 12 days and between 17 and 23 days after birth.[6] Are there stages in humans having the same main neurochemical and neuroanatomical events as stages found in mice? This question led to our identifying the mouse's 8–12 days stage with a 3–10 months stage in humans and the 17–23 days mouse stage with the 2–4 years stage in humans.[7] The latter identification seemed likely since DNA synthesis virtually stops in mice around age 15 days, just before the last brain growth stage, corresponding to the cessation in humans at 18–24 months, just before the next growth stage.

Let us focus on the fact that the neural networks altered and created during the 17–23 days period may have functions whose significance for mice is similar to the significance for humans of the functions of the homologous networks in the 2–4 years period. It is then important that although human speech has its onset late in the first year of life, it only begins to be used in a thoughtful way around age 2. Mice don't speak; therefore, the networks already present in humans and mice have purposes other than speech. Thus speech was grafted on to existing networks designed for entirely different functions. Vygotsky has pointed out that at this age the parallel and independent development of language and thought ceases so that, thereafter, children can speak in concepts and think in words.[8] One bit of supporting evidence for this theory is that there is no spontaneous speech and no universal language. Children have to be taught to speak any particular language. The uses of these networks are *instruction-dependent.*

The Relationship Between Teaching and Brain Growth

Our own experiences tell us children have to master almost all reasoning starting at school age; there seem to be few spontaneous (i.e., programmed) reasoning abilities appearing after age 4 years. This doesn't mean there are no constraints (or rules). The actual networks constrain how and what kinds of things can be learned, but the content is mainly, if not entirely, instruction-dependent. Those networks, however, are experientially made by the reasoning strategies being used.

Such a situation requires the input of language and thought to be made with care, for we are pruning networks in the most physical sense. If the pruning is inadequate or incorrect, the functioning may be far from optimal. The human brain's functioning is determined mainly by sociopsychological input that, we expect, shapes the very neural networks we have been describing.

Is there evidence that networks are, indeed, pruned? I have already mentioned the arborization changes in cats around a brain growth stage age. Recently studies of learning in goldfish and mice showed changes in the amount of three different proteins produced.[9] If the learning is incomplete, the newly formed materials are later found diffused in the brain. The inference is that the input of information triggers arborization of the ends of dendrites and axons. If the task is repeated enough to be learned, the newly formed extensions are made permanent; if not, they are dismantled. These are preliminary studies, but they do support the hypothesis of the instruction-dependence of the networks themselves. If preliminary studies had shown no increases in proteins at the ends of axons and dendrites, our picture would be much more cloudy.

Now that we have assembled these facts, inferences, and preliminary models, let us see what consequences there may be for learning and schooling. We expect changes in cognitive functioning to become possible at the ages of the brain growth stages. But we recognize that without "proper" experiential input, the appearance and maturation of the new cognitive functioning may be significantly delayed. Thus, children reaching ages 6–8 years are likely to show new reasoning abilities in that period. As we know, most children are fairly ready for school entry at that age. But if our model holds, the onset of sensitivity to instructional possibilities should be spread over a 2-year span; and this seems to be the situation.

Next, if we look at Piaget's studies of reasoning development, we learn that the *earliest onset age* of the stage of concrete operations is this 6–8 years period. That observation leads to looking at the next brain growth stage, at 10–12 years; we find that that stage marks the earliest onset age of the formal operations stage. In this instance, however, the spread is very broad. This finding is not unexpected, for the spread between 6 and 8 years could well lead to an even greater spread at the next stage.

We now have a correlation between the changes in arborization at the brain growth stages and the possibilities of onset of *changes* in reasoning style discovered by Piaget and his associates. This is not the only correlation between growth stages and mental functioning, for the literature reveals correlated stages in increase of mental age, vocabulary, and reading scores.[10]

Significantly, high IQ children show no earlier onset of Piaget stages, indicating that these very bright children (IQ 140–160) do not have earlier brain growth stages and that their high intelligence does not advance the start of arborization. This finding supports the inference that arborization changes occur on a biological schedule. The role of sociopsychological inputs is to take advantage of the additional reasoning power afforded by the new brain growth. Nurture builds on what nature has created.

If we ask about optimization strategies, we can predict that children's cognitive ability rises mainly at the ages of brain growth stages, so schooling should be structured to take advantage of this situation. Our holistic approach to the educational process does not yet give hints about precisely what to do at the indicated ages.

Cognitive Levels

To take this analysis further, we now turn to the concept of cognitive level. This concept was introduced by Inhelder and Piaget for convenience in discussing the fact that not all children manifested the next Piagetian cognitive stage at the earliest onset age.[11] In essence, they pointed out that the later stages of reasoning (concrete and formal operations) appeared in a culture-bound context so that it would be desirable to look to more elementary functions that make up those operations. They broke up concrete operations and formal operations into two: the onset of the stage and the maturation of the stage. With only one or two of the elementary reasoning operations in place, a person is at the onset of the stage and at cognitive levels 2a or 3a (onset of concrete or formal

TABLE 1. Percentages of Individuals at Various Cognitive Levels at Various Ages

Age (Years)	Cognitive Level				
	1	2A	2B	3A	3B
1	100	0			
2	100	0			
3	98	2			
4	92	8			
5	85	15			
6	60	35	5		
7	35	55	10		
8	25	55	20		
9	15	55	30		
10	12	52	35	1	
11	6	49	40	5	
12	5	32	51	12	
13	2	34	44	14	6
14	1	32	43	15	9
15	1	15	53	19	12
16	1	14	54	18	13

reasoning). If, say, half a dozen elementary reasoning operations are in place, this is a mature expression of the stage, and the levels are called 2b and 3b. Thus, the stage picture is reshuffled into a five-level description.

If the Piaget stages were followed in a lockstep fashion, all children of the same age would be at the same stage and same level. But the newly organized and reorganized neural networks are instruction-dependent, so greater or lesser effectiveness of instruction and learning should result in a developmental diversity in cognitive level. That is one reason (of many) why IQ isn't an especially useful or consistent characterization of children. Unlike IQ, however, cognitive level is a developmental parameter, telling us how many of the child's reasoning abilities are in place at any one age, information clearly related to the instructional and learning properties of schooling.

Numerous investigators have tested children for their cognitive levels. The most thorough of these studies tested 2,000 children at each age from 10 through 14 years and 1,000 each at 15 and 16 years.[12] From these studies, we have learned that there is extensive diversity of level at any one age. Indeed, at most ages, children fall into three different cognitive levels (see Table 1).

Next, we can use the cognitive levels to describe the reasoning demanded by both written and spoken instructional inputs to obtain the cognitive demands of curricula. In this way we learn that there is a very serious mismatch between the cognitive-level demands of schooling in the various grades and the cognitive levels of most of the children in those grades. Therefore, *if the performances on the cognitive level tests really reveal the ways in which children reason in school,* there should be a quantitatively predictable set of failures and successes. If there is a match of demand and ability, children should be able to master the input. If there is a mismatch and the demand exceeds the abilities, children should fail—not because they are stupid, but because they have not yet reached the level needed to handle the input. Therefore, optimization of instructional strategies requires matching cognitive level of instruction to the cognitive levels of the children.

There are many corollaries to such a picture of schooling performance. Some relate to predictions of failure by high IQ children. Others relate to the possibility of success by otherwise low IQ children who are old enough to have had the next arborization stage. In general, then, this picture gives teachers a means of knowing why children fail when they do and, equally important for the teacher's mental health, why they succeed when they do. Teachers who have been instructed in this analysis have remarked that this ability to understand the whys of success and failure may decrease teachers' frustration to the point of reducing burnout. This implies that optimization of teaching conditions includes optimization for the teachers. If they don't understand what is happening, their frustration may produce less effective teaching.

There are still other inferences to be drawn from our holistic study of brain and reasoning development. But the approach should now be clear. The mechanical way of formulating the approach is as follows: (1) The brain growth stages tell us *when* (i.e., at what ages) children may be pushed to rise in cognitive level; (2) the test scores tell us *how* (i.e., in what cognitive levels) the children are to be taught; and (3) the details of the test results tell us *what* elementary reasoning functions are in place, so we know the ones that will appear next and can present material accordingly.

Within that framework of when, how, and what to teach, there is no guidance for the detailed tactics of doing those things; they remain to be discovered by teachers utilizing their own experiences and intuitions. If cognitive-level matching is tried and found to have appreciable achievements, successful teachers should be able to describe a variety of teaching tactics that work well enough to be taught to the next generation of teachers.

The most important caveat is that the entire edifice has been based on the use of mathematical and scientific approaches; it is possible (though I feel it unlikely) that the analysis is valid only or mainly for the study of science. Even so, science education is important enough to justify extensive experimentation along these lines, with the hope that at least some of the results will have wider applications to more general education.

Notes

1. J. M. Hunt, *Intelligence and Experience*. New York: Ronald Press, 1981; M. Shayer and P. Adey, *Toward a Science of Science Teaching*. London: Heinemann, 1981; H. T. Epstein, Learning to learn, *Principal* 60: 25–30, 1981.

2. Epstein, Learning to learn.

3. T. Rabinowicz, The differentiate maturation of the human cerebral cortex. In F. Falkner and J. M. Tanner (eds.), *Human Growth*. New York: Plenum Press, 1979, pp. 97–124.

4. H. T. Epstein, EEG developmental stages, *Developmental Psychobiology* 13: 629–631, 1980.

5. S. LeVay and M. Stryker, The development of ocular dominance columns in the cat. In James A. Ferrendelli and Gerry Gurvitch (eds.), *Aspects of Developmental Neurobiology*. Bethesda, Md.: Society for Neuroscience, 1979, pp. 83–98.

6. A. Gottlieb, Y. Keydar, and H. T. Epstein, Rodent brain growth stages: an analytical review, *Biology of the Neonate* 32: 166–176, 1977.

7. H. T. Epstein and S. A. Miller, The developing brain: a suggestion for making more critical interspecies extrapolation, *Nutrition Reports International* 16: 363–366, 1977.

8. L. Vygotsky, *Thought and Language*. Cambridge, Mass.: MIT Press, 1962.

9. V. Shashoua, Molecular and cell biological aspects of learning. In S. Federoff and L. Hertz (eds.), *Advances in Cellular Neurobiology*, Vol. 3 (Academic Press, in press).

10. H. T. Epstein, Growth spurts during brain development: implications for educational policy and practice. In J. S. Chall and A. Mirsky (eds.), *Education and the Brain*. Chicago: University of Chicago Press, 1977, pp. 343–370.

11. B. Inhelder and J. Piaget, *The Growth of Logical Thinking*. New York: Basic Books, 1958.

12. M. Shayer, D. E. Kuchemann, and H. Wylam, The distribution of Piagetian stages of thinking in British middle and secondary school children, *British Journal of Educational Psychology* 46: 164–173, 1976; M. Shayer and H. Wylam, The distribution of Piagetian stages of thinking in British middle and secondary school children: 14–16 years old and sex differentials, *British Journal of Educational Psychology* 48: 62–70, 1978.

PAUL BOHANNAN

——— 6 ———

The Impact of
Cultural Diversity on
the Spread of Knowledge

It is probably just as well that human beings do not fully realize that they live daily with the most bitter cosmic joke ever played by a natural process. In the course of evolution, the precursors of human beings developed the capacity to speak. With language came the capacity for advanced culture. Each of us is born with our genes intact and ready. At birth, and perhaps even before, we find ourselves in the midst of not merely a natural environment but also a cultural environment. Because we are evolutionarily so well prepared for learning, we start to learn everything we can. But—and here is the joke—the fact that we learn one thing makes it difficult or impossible to learn a lot of other things.

The ancient tradition is to call this situation "Babel," after the city and the tower. All humankind spoke one language, and people were getting above their station in the order of things. They said, "Let us build us a city and a tower, whose top may reach unto Heaven" (Genesis 11:4). The Lord's reaction was, "And *this* they begin to do! And now *nothing* will be restrained from them, which they have imagined to do! Go to, let us go down and there confound their language that they may not understand one another's speech" (Genesis 11:6–7, italics added). The Lord did a thorough job. Not only did He make them speak different languages, He made them speak those languages from different cultural premises, and He made most of the premises appear to be part of the natural world.

Speech is undoubtedly the most vital of our uniquely human acquisitions, but *language* is the basis of our misunderstanding as well as our understanding. We learn our native "language" by processes that are only now beginning to be well understood. What is less often remarked or studied is that as we learn our "native" language—say French—we do *not* learn any of the many other languages—say Kiswahili or Iroquois or Kanada. Linguists are learning a great deal about the way that cutting the field of human sound into one set of phonemes programs the brain so that after about the age of eight or nine it becomes increasingly difficult even to hear a new phonetic system, let alone absorb the more subtle dimensions of a "foreign" language.

A number of other things go along with language in the learning process. They are just as subtle as language, just as much out of our awareness as are the rules of grammar. I am, of course, talking about much of the rest of "culture."

Character and Culture

In the process of learning the environing culture, we form our character structures as we reaffirm and alter the culture. The term "character structure" goes back to Freud and perhaps further, but the concept was central to the work of Erich Fromm. He used it at least as early as 1941, but his clearest statement was made in 1973. Character, he says, "is the specific structure in which human energy is organized in pursuit of man's goals."[1]

Fromm goes on to say that "character structure"—the learned way of organizing perceptions and activities that is based on your genetic endowment and strained through the culture in your environment—this character structure *seems*, as you experience it, to be of exactly the same sort as the wholly biologically based qualities of the self and body. Perceptually, it is (in my terms, now) difficult to tell the difference between what you do because you are genetically human and what you do because your particular character structure developed as it did. Fromm's major statement is that: "These character-conditioned drives and strivings are so strong and unquestionable for the respective persons that they feel that theirs is simply a 'natural' reaction, and find it difficult to really believe that there are other people whose nature is quite different."[2]

Thus, culture is incorporated into the character structure in the natural process of living in the environment. Our ethnicity, our age, our education—all provide environmental niches or contexts in which we get culture into our bodies and minds and brains. Once inside us the cultural experience forms the foundations of the premises by means of which we understand and interact with one another.

Take an example from contemporary American culture. In the course of recent discussions about their study of architects and architecture, Edward and Mildred Hall made some statements that precisely illustrate the difficulty of crossing subcultural lines from the subculture of architects to the many subcultures of the people who live and work in their buildings.

A lot of architects, the Halls said, think they understand human needs. But they fail to question their premises. Most architects have never looked into the physiology of the body, how people use their senses to perceive space, how they experience their environments—let alone the subtleties of cultural difference in these matters. The result is that all but the very best architects work to a formula. Even Mies van der Rohe talked about the "universal space" without considering that it depends on what you're going to do in that space—and who you are.

Architects look at architectural drawings or renderings in aesthetic terms: their question is whether it is good design. Many of them, however, stop with the visual aspects. There are exceptions, but too many architects fail to consider how the building will feel, how it will smell, what its acoustics may be, or what is going on in it. Mildred Hall summed it up: "Ask any American woman about American kitchens. Architects are interested in how it *looks*, not how it works. This is a visual bias. People differ as to which of their senses is most acutely developed—and that difference is both inborn and learned. Most architects are visual, and their training underscores their visual inclinations."

It should, by now, be obvious that differences in cultural environments, including training and education, create different sets of basic premises in different people, each of whom has a character structure—that, indeed, there are "natural" boundaries in the dissemination of knowledge, cultural boundaries and character boundaries. Most people cannot "read" a blueprint or rendering. Lots of architects refuse to believe that such people use their senses differently. At best, they think them untrained; at worst, stupid.

Here we have, within our own culture, an ethnocentric bias among people with special talent and training: If I can see it, they can see it. The unstated premise, "If I see it that way, you must see it that way, or else you are stupid," is an effective communications block.

Some people—architects and musicians—have very special talents for either visualizing or hearing in the absence of the kind of stimulus the rest of us need to see or hear. A musician can hear the sounds in a symphony by examining the notes on paper. He can "hear" the entry of the brass; he can take it out when the score says to do so. He can hear the strings and take them out. Most people can't do that. A few novelists can remember emotions and pain the rest of us blessedly forget and insert them fullblown into the fictional situations they create. All this might be called a special talent for "imaging." It is a matter of training and of culture. The information cannot be transmitted to those who are incapable of performing certain learned cultural tricks.

The special talent—whether it is the character or the culture—is also a boundary; it is difficult for talented people to understand that others lack their talent.

Crossing Cultural Boundaries

Let us now examine what happens to perceptions and understandings at a many-stranded cultural border. During my field work among the Tiv of Nigeria, I spent a morning questioning an old man who was eager to tell me about the political organization of his society. After a couple of hours, he said to me, "I have told you everything. You know all that I know. Now you must tell me how your country is governed." I took a deeep breath and began with what was a true statement at the time: "We have an immensely big country that is divided into forty-eight segments that we call states."

The old man interrupted. "You skipped some generations," he said with total conviction. That is *not* a non sequitur in his culture. His political organization—and therefore his view of political organization in general—is premised on the fact that each geographical segment of his country is occupied by the descendants of one man and that the ancestors of adjacent segments were either brothers or agnatic cousins. That is, the people in the compounds near my own are descended from my father's brothers. All of us are descended from our father's father or *his* brothers. And so it goes, with ever larger groups for seventeen to twenty generations, by which time the map of the entire countryside is coordinated with a single agnatic genealogy that includes a million people. Knowing that premise, you can understand why the old man said "You skipped some generations" when I jumped from one to forty-eight.

My major point is that each of us enters a cultural as well as a physical environment, trailing our special genetic clouds. As we learn, in accordance with the capacities of our species and our own particular versions of them, we ingest whatever culture is in the environment. The language and the material culture and, most important, the cultural *premises* thereafter appear to us to be completely natural, as much a part of the animal as is the need for food or the sex drive.

Because of our character and our culture, it takes special training for us to know that we do *not* know what somebody else's equally basic premises may be. When we human beings were punished for building the tower of Babel, the Lord isolated us behind our own premises as well as our own languages. (I wish some of His most ardent followers could learn that.)

Adamson Hoebel, in a classic in legal anthropology, delineates what he calls the "postulates" (more or less what I here call premises) on the basis of which judges in eight cultures decide disputes. A sample of the premises that underlie the solutions to traditional Eskimo disputes runs: "Spirit beings, and all animals by virtue of possessing souls, have emotional intelligence similar to that of man." "Man in important aspects of life is subordinate to the wills of animal souls and spirit beings." "All natural resources are free or common goods."[3]

Here are two of the postulates of the Comanche, Kiowa, and Cheyenne Indians, whose law Hoebel himself studied in the field: "The individual is supreme in all things." "The strongest tie is that of brother to brother."[4]

One more set, from the traditional Ashanti of Ghana: "All men must be allowed to participate, directly or indirectly, in the formulation of laws." "The ancestors will punish the group as a whole, if the group does not punish a sinner and atone for his misdeed." "Basic property belongs to the ancestors."[5]

Every culture is loaded with this kind of premise. The vital questions are: in the process of communicating knowledge, (1) how can we examine the premises of our target audiences so we can judge how the message will be received? and (2) even more difficult, what are the unknown, unstated premises that we ourselves use when we encode our messages? The questions are just as tricky turned the other way: when I try to get information from somebody else, (1) what are the premises by which that particular somebody has encoded the information, and in what way are they different from mine? and (2) what premises do I store in my unconscious that keep me from understanding what that person is saying?

Here is another example of the problem. A lot of old Tiv "knew"—that is, they had a more or less unconscious premise—that white people did not speak their language. I sometimes had to stand in front of them and say, in their language, "I am speaking Tiv." It might even take several repetitions before their eyes suddenly brightened and they responded. Now, of course neither my command of nor my accent in Tiv was perfect. But they were good enough to communicate—indeed, to communicate with these same old people who could not listen to me until they had got rid of their initial premise that because I was white I could not be speaking their language.

Our Own Cultural Premises

How do we find out what the basic premises of a culture or subculture are? We can *not* do it by asking somebody, "What are your basic premises?" That would be like a psychotherapist's asking a patient, "What is your basic character structure that makes you behave in this unsatisfactory way?" If the patient knew, he wouldn't be in psychotherapy. If we knew each other's premises, there might well be disagreement but there would be no misunderstanding.

My example of how to go about it may not be as trivial as it sounds on the surface. If you ask any group of Americans to name all the crimes they can think of in order of heinousness, they will almost always skip all the crimes against the state and start with murder. They will then proceed to assault, rape, kidnapping, and armed robbery. Only then will they start on the crimes against property. And only after coming up with several of those do they get to such crimes as perjury, if they ever think of it at all. Keeping that list in mind, ask the same group which doors inside an American house have locks. They always start with the bathroom. They may stop there or go on to bedrooms. Occasionally a wisecracker mentions the liquor cabinet.

Now, put these two pieces of information together. What emerges is a basic premise that the body is absolutely private and inviolate. Your reaction is probably that that is trite; you knew it all the time. So what? That is the correct reaction—it assures me that I am right. But I am also right in saying that almost nobody would have made that response if merely asked to name some basic American premises on which our law and ritual are based. It is precisely this kind of premise that underlies all of our thinking and that we call silently into play as we try to learn new information.

But, you may say—again making my point for me—*everybody* has the basic value that the body is inviolable. If you investigate other cultures, however, you will find it is not so. It is panhuman—probably pananimal—to try to preserve one's life and integrity. But that does *not* mean that all humans view their bodies as private and inviolable property. These facts are obvious at the intellectual level, but they are harder to understand at the gut level. And that gut level is exactly where culture-shaped character structure lies and where (metaphorically at least) we all get our premises.

When we try to learn information from a foreign source or try to learn ideas about things that are unfamiliar to us, we have to ask,

"What are the premises that underlie the *way* the information is set forth?" and "What are my premises that keep me from understanding it?"

My next example is the stepfamily. There is a premise in American culture (indeed, in all of Western culture and beyond) that stepmothers are cruel. Most of the women who today find themselves married to men who have children from former marriages are not cruel. Therefore, they do not want to be called stepmothers. They look around for an alternate term, and when they find there isn't one, they decide their husbands' children should call them "Mother." However, the children have a premise that the new wives are interlopers, in no way to be confused with Mother. The battle begins.

Moreover, the stepfamily has to find its own way in a society whose basic premise is that all families are nuclear families. A stepfamily is certainly not a nuclear family—your stepchildren are your in-laws just as surely as your parents-in-law are. You and they are related because of a marriage, not because of kinship. However, because the basic premise about families is that they are nuclear, most stepfamilies struggle to become nuclear families—against almost insuperable odds. Only if they change premises can they become a successful stepfamily.

The family, in fact, suffers just such a fate whenever it is examined by social scientists. No writer on the family, no matter how careful, can expect to communicate more than a fraction of his message, because everybody out there knows what a family is. Everyone will, with a total lack of information and data, tell you that you are wrong if you say anything that goes against their premises, no matter how much data you have or how sound your ratiocination. They are reluctant even to admit that they *have* cultural and experiential premises about the family, let alone change them. People will believe that the Bongo-bongo have strange family patterns—but never that they themselves do. Margaret Mead said somewhere that Americans will believe whatever social scientists tell them as long as they are not asked to apply it to themselves.

All of us know people who have—in order to preserve their own premises—almost willfully misunderstood what another scholar has written or another discipline's position. *Of course* nobody wants to question the premises! Unless you can rigidly partition the information in your mind, everything falls into disarray if a premise turns out to be faulty. Many confine each of the contradictory pieces of information in its own cage so that they need never confront one another. This way out may seem safe and predictable; people may even cheer you on when you do it.

Techniques for questioning our premises are *not* usually intellectual ones. Indeed, questioning one's own premises probably cannot be done successfully by oneself, and it seems to be impossible to question somebody else's premises without examining one's own. Character structure and culture will out—the more unconscious, the more mercilessly.

There are, however, several things we *can* do: first, always ask of any incoming information, "What are the premises of the person who is trying to convince me?" The trap here is, of course, that you will state them in such a way as to hide your own premises from yourself. You can then continue to disagree on the basis of hidden premises— the kind of process that Rollo May, in Chapter 7 of this book, correlates with fear.

Next, if we find the information that emerges from an interchange or from a book distasteful, we have to ask, "Why do I find it distasteful or boring or just plain wrong? Which of my premises make me want to dismiss this material?" Think for a moment about the reception of E. O. Wilson's *Sociobiology*. I am *not* saying he was "right" when I say what we all know, that much of the initial objection to the book was neither rational nor scientific. It was an example of: "My premises are affronted, therefore he is wrong."

Looking at the matter from a broadly crosscultural point of view, we can see that we have in the past often been unwilling to learn from some people—the "I would rather be wrong than agree with *him*" syndrome. For instance, until recently we were unwilling to learn from the Japanese; they were supposed to learn from us. Yet today we are eager to assimilate their "better" methods of industrial production.

In recent issues of several national magazines, the Motorola Company asked in a two-page ad, "Is Japan's challenge to American industry going unanswered?" The ad goes on, " 'What are you going to do about Japan?' . . . This is a subject on which many companies can speak out and should. We are doing so because we believe it will be good for our country, good for Japan, and good for Motorola."

The ad then goes through a series of statements that cast some doubt on their claim that "Motorola understands the challenge from Japan." They are trying to get some principles of Japanese production methods and organizations into American premises. I cannot believe that they would have placed that ad if they did not somehow *think* that they did indeed understand Japanese industry and the way it works. And that is the danger—not to know that you do not know. At very best it can lead to what I once, in talking about the traps of colonialism, called a "working misunderstanding."[6]

Obviously, Americans can't understand the organization of Japanese industry *unless they examine the social and psychological premises of the two cultures before they begin the analysis and explanation.* I hope the Motorola adwriters will not take even deeper offense when I suggest that they do not know their own premises any better than they know the Japanese ones. Obviously, they do indeed know—far better than I do—the principles of American economics and business. They have not, on the testimony of the ad, questioned in any way the morass of premises that lies beneath their knowledge.

Given what I have been preaching, I had better state my own premises. I shall put them in the form of hypotheses in hopes that they may be falsifiable (it is a premise of Western sciences that hypotheses are by definition testable and therefore falsifiable). However, not *all* of my premises—or yours—*can* be scientific. It is just here, on my premises, that I should be attacked—but only after you understand and state *your* premises clearly.

Premise 1. Human beings, through their senses, receive impressions, including cultural impressions, from the environment.

Premise 2. A human being must, when encountering new information from the environment, first evaluate it in terms of existing premises and information.

Premise 3. As human beings behave on the basis of information, both cultural and "natural," from their environment, they build their own character structures at the same time that they reaffirm or alter culture.

Premise 4. Premises are difficult to question for several reasons, some of them psychological in nature, some cultural:

Premise 4.1. Many premises are out of awareness (not to say "unconscious," an idea that people's premises distort seriously).

Premise 4.2. If premises are found faulty, everything that is based on them may seem suddenly to crumble, leaving chaos.

Premise 5. There are cultural boundaries in the dissemination of knowledge that are recognizable points at which both stated and unstated premises change. Such boundaries appear between nations, between ethnic groups, between disciplines, and even between individuals.

Premise 6. Ethnocentrism is the practice of evaluating another culture's activities or products by the premises of one's own culture without bothering to see whether they fit.

Premise 7. Different people, by a combination of genetic and cultural pathways, use their senses differently. Such differences, if not understood, are roadblocks in the dissemination of knowledge.

Premise 8. Every culture has its own premises about the nature of the universe, about what are normal human relationships, and about the principles (most of them infracultural) of social organization.

A final statement: If, when you are learning something, you are uncomfortable, that is a signal not necessarily that the new information is wrong, but that it endangers one of your premises. Of course, the new information may in fact be wrong—but it is *not* wrong *because* your premises are endangered. The discomfort is a signal to be read initially as, "Why do I find this information unpalatable?" not "This information is wrong!" If you can figure out your own premises *and* the premises of the person who reports the information, and still find it wrong, you may be right—but you are right only insofar as your own ultimate cultural premises, changed or unchanged, will allow you to be.

Therefore, what we all need is greater insight into our own cultural premises. When we get that, if we do, we will have taken the first step toward more effective communication and use of new knowledge.

Notes

1. Fromm, Erich. *The Anatomy of Human Destructiveness,* p. 251.
2. Ibid., p. 252.
3. Hoebel, E. Adamson. *The Law of Primitive Man,* p. 69.
4. Ibid., pp. 142–143.
5. Ibid., p. 253.
6. Bohannan, Paul. *Africa and Africans.*

Bibliography

Bohannan, Paul. 1964. *Africa and Africans.* New York: Natural History Press.
Fromm, Erich. 1973. *The Anatomy of Human Destructiveness.* New York: Holt, Rinehart and Winston.
Hall, Mildred and Edward. 1975. *The Fourth Dimension in Architecture.* Santa Fe: Sunstone Press.
Hoebel, E. Adamson. 1954. *The Law of Primitive Man.* Cambridge, Mass.: Harvard University Press.

ROLLO MAY

— 7 —
The Fear of Knowledge

Besides its many positive qualities, knowledge brings fear and anxiety. We will not understand the opposition to knowledge in our society until we accept the fact that people have a fear of knowledge that is partially conscious but mostly unconscious. Since unconscious fear can be defined as anxiety, I shall be discussing both fear and anxiety. My thesis is that fear and anxiety of knowledge are not simply senseless prejudice or mere primitive thinking but have a rational basis. More than that, this fear and this anxiety have deep experiential roots in our relation to ourselves and to our world.

The splitting of the atom and the construction of the hydrogen bomb made multitudes of people genuinely aware of the dangers of knowledge. The splicing of genes and cloning may give rise to even deeper fears. Billy Graham has said he wishes we had never learned how to split the atom. But this attempt to avoid fear is not a constructive way to deal with it; we cannot give up our curiosity and our endless quest for knowledge if we are to remain human.

Knowledge is, of course, praised in many different ways. Knowledge is power, as Bacon put it. It is a source of personal pleasure. It enables us to live with some confidence because it gives us a basis for predicting the future. College students are told that knowledge will increase their earning ability after graduation, but I have never heard it said in college or graduate school that knowledge is also dangerous and the source of anxiety, and therefore rightly to be feared.

I propose that the anxiety of knowledge is why so many of our most valued people have trouble in their college studies. Students may, as a result of anxiety connected with knowledge, resort to becoming bookworms—defined by Webster's dictionaries as readers of many books without profit to themselves. They hold off the anxiety of knowledge by garnering mere facts. They can also avoid the anxiety by becoming antiquarians, those who pursue interests as dilettantes and acquire a host of facts that never upset anyone. But to seek genuine knowledge—to be like the scholars and scientists who are open to new ideas that may rock the foundations of society as the atom bomb now rocks our planet—this, indeed, requires a vaster courage and, as I will indicate later, a vaster capacity to rebel. The awe with which people regard the authentic scientist (and the awe that used to be associated with the genuine scholar) are proof of this. Goethe's drama, *Faust,* is a graphic picture of the dangerous qualities of knowledge; the medieval tales of the alchemists are another illustration.

It is not irrelevant that I am a psychoanalyst who has spent most of his working hours for the last forty years listening to people's conflicts and struggles. These conflicts generally come out in the form of so-called unconscious material and in irrational form, as in dreams. We soon learn in psychoanalysis that knowledge drives us and our society out of old grooves, requiring a reforming of ourselves and our society. Hence in psychoanalysis new knowledge—and I am using the term here as a synonym for insight—requires changing the individual's customary patterns. Thus it is understandably met with resistance that is often very powerful indeed. It is surely possible for a person to have self-knowledge without changing himself and his behavior—a point Freud never understood. But to do this you cannot let the knowledge seep into your feelings, your imagination, your right brain as well as the left; you must keep it in special compartments, as do the bookworm and the antiquarian. It is significant that Freud's patients were almost exclusively hysterics, with whom the mechanisms of abreaction, repression, and so on, do actually work. But in our day the kind of neurotics we increasingly see are the compulsive-obsessionals, those who keep their insights (knowledge) separated from their emotions. These people, who compartmentalize themselves so their knowledge never communicates with their feelings, can escape the anxiety of knowledge; compartmentalization is an effective, and deadening, way to do so.

A Clinical Example

The anxiety that comes with knowledge can be illustrated by a patient of mine. He was a research scientist who had been working for many months on a crucial and important problem without any breakthrough. He had read and pondered at length, week in and week out, but the solution to the problem always eluded him.

One morning, before going to his study, he went out to get the newspaper. In this relaxed, early-morning mood, the answer to this problem suddenly dawned, as the phrase has it, in his consciousness.

A mass of demonstrations of proof came along with this answer, all of his previously subconscious material pouring into his conscious mind in a matter of two or three seconds. Elated, he picked up the newspaper and started back into the house. But after about ten steps toward the door he heard a voice in his mind saying,

> Other friends have flown before
> On the morrow he will leave me.

This was accompanied by a powerful wave of anxiety, and he became aware that all the bright ideas he had just been receiving in the last minute were beginning to fade away. He did not know what the couplet meant or where it had come from. But he knew himself well enough to run into the house and quickly write down his insights. All that morning he was filled with great anxiety.

When he got to his hour with me, we traced this couplet to Edgar Allan Poe's poem, *The Raven*, where Poe is describing his fear that the black bird on his window sill will leave him and the whole experience will be phantasmagoric.

I proposed that my patient's anxiety was based on reality. He knew that if his solution was correct, it would upset innumerable colleagues. There would be jealousy, professors would have to rewrite their lecture notes, and heaven knows what other disruptions would occur. All of us have heard about the Inquisition that awaited Copernicus and Galileo. Some form of this stiff examination awaits most such new discoveries, even if of lesser moment. We have our own inquisitions in the McCarthy and Dies committees, and at present in the Moral Majority. New knowledge—now defined as discovery—forces changes in the status quo and causes disruptions in ourselves and in society. In this sense, anxiety is indeed rational. This anxiety is also why, I believe, most people block off the new creative insights at the unconscious level; they repress and forget their new ideas before those ideas even see the light of day.

The Heritage of Myth: Adam and Eve

I shall lean heavily on myth in this paper because this truth—that new knowledge brings with it fear and anxiety—requires something deeper than empirical proof for its demonstration. The myths furnish this since they reflect, in dramatic form, the perdurable images and patterns of our minds and our society. Empirical truth may be changed by new revelations in tomorrow's newspaper, whereas myth is, in Thomas Mann's words, an "eternal truth."

One myth about the origin of knowledge in our Western mythology is that of Adam and Eve in the Garden of Eden. Their act of eating the fruit of the tree of knowledge of good and evil is portrayed in the myth as rebellion against God, which already indicates the danger of knowledge. Their act resulted in the punishment, the introduction of the two most painful and intractable emotions, anxiety and guilt, both associated with estrangement from God, from their own bodies, and from each other through the lies they tell in the drama. The experience of Eden changed the condition of Adam and Eve from the innocence of childhood to adulthood; they not only experienced anxiety and guilt but lived with the other emotions that make us genuinely human: loneliness, estrangement, the sense of responsibility, and love. They left the Garden of Eden, hand in hand, lonely and anxious, but also with the capacity for love. As Milton puts it in the last sentences of *Paradise Lost*:

Some matural tears they dropped, but wiped them soon;
The world was all before them, where to choose
The place of rest, and Providence their guide.
They, hand in hand, with wandering steps and slow,
Through Eden took their solitary way.

If we put aside for a moment the antifeminist form in which this myth is cast, we can see that its real meaning is that knowledge comes to human beings by an act of *rebellion*. The birth of the consciousness of good and evil is an act of knowledge acquired by disobeying the commandment of God.

We then are faced with the curious conclusion that acquiring knowledge has to be done in the spirit of the rebel. Theologically speaking, we see this clearly enough in the myth, when Adam and Eve disobey the commandment and in defiance eat of the tree of the knowledge of good and evil. Sociologically speaking, we see it in the fact that new knowledge drives our society out of its old grooves, requires a reforming of our culture, and frightens everyone in the process. No wonder it brings with it, as it did in the Adam and Eve myth, dire consequences.

If one wished to take a literalistic view of God in the account of Adam and Eve in Genesis, one could well argue that the goodness of God is shown in his participating in the situation in which there *must* be a rebellion with its accompaniment of human consciousness. In any case, the "fall" was necessary and inevitable if we are to have human consciousness and ethical judgment. As Hegel put it, it was a fall upward rather than down. If we still take a literalistic view, the goodness of God seems to me involved in the fact that human freedom, which occurs only after the fall, is such a profound and paradoxical thing that we cannot escape the feelings of continuous adventure in life marked by sorrow and joy, grief and pleasure.

Breaking Away from Conformity

We may summarize our thesis at this point: Human beings fear knowledge because it upsets their homeostasis. Hannah Arendt has said one function of any group is to keep its members in conformity to the group. This conformity is broken down by new knowledge; it rocks people out of their grooves and upsets the balance between themselves and their groups. New knowledge has always the potential of acting like an earthquake: As Copernicus, Galileo, and the line of scholars demonstrate, the quaking of the earth breaks down old forms, temporarily leaving anarchy.

The same thing happens to the individual. If we look at the matter from a Freudian point of view, we see that each person has invested his or her libido in a certain pattern. The new knowledge upsets this pattern or may turn it topsy-turvy in neurotic or psychotic breakdown. If we take a neurological view, the pattern of reactions is thrown into disruption, and time and support are often needed for the person's pattern to reform. If we think of the brain as analogous to the computer, the whole must be reprogrammed. It is these disruptions that the profession I am a part of—psychoanalysis, psychotherapy in all its myriad forms—was devised to minister to.

The Lessons from Oedipus Rex

The most profound account of the danger, fear, and anxiety of knowledge is, to my mind, the two dramas of Oedipus. I would like to hang my thoughts on the trellis of these dramas.

King Oedipus is presented as a person of great intelligence "who knew the famous riddles and was a man most masterful," as the chorus of *Oedipus Rex* puts it. In the drama he is devoted not only to his queen, Jocasta, and the city of Thebes, but with his whole heart and soul to his quest for knowledge: "I must find out who I am and where I came from."

The knowledge he seeks is of course self-knowledge. But every form of knowledge is to some extent self-knowledge. Even in physics, which would seem farthest from self-knowledge, the quest is for the knowledge not of *any* world but of the particular world you and I live in. Heisenberg has said in many different ways that there is no such thing as a truth of nature that is purely objective; the experimenter in physics must be counted as part of the problem. This is true even in mathematics, when we realize that mathematics is in us, the way our heart beats and our blood flows. Especially we see this in Pythagoras, one of the geniuses of mathematical knowledge, as he points out the relations of mathematics to music; music is surely an art very personal to ourselves. It is repressing the awareness of this immediate relationship between knowledge and self-knowledge that makes the bookworm, the antiquarian, and other forms of the compulsive-obsessional.

The main issue in *Oedipus Rex* is whether Oedipus will know himself. It is the tragic drama of the passionate relation to truth. Oedipus' tragic flaw is his wrath against his own reality. When Oedipus calls the old blind seer, Tiresias, there proceeds a gripping and powerful unfolding of Oedipus' self-knowledge step by step, replete with rage and anger at the truth and those who are its bearers. Tiresias' blindness symbolizes the fact that one can more insightfully grasp *inner* reality about human beings—gain *in*-sight—if one is not distracted by external details.

Tiresias at first refuses to answer Oedipus' questioning as to who is the murderer of King Laius:

How terrible it is to know . . .
Where no good comes from knowing! Of these matters
I was full well aware, but let them slip me . . .[1]

In response to Oedipus' new demands and threats, he continues,

Let me go home; . . .
So shalt thou bear thy load most easily. . . .
Ye
Are all unknowing; my say, in any sort,
I will not say, lest I display my sorrow.

The drama that unfolds as progressive self-knowledge has its source really in Tiresias, not Oedipus, and in this sense Tiresias holds the role of psychoanalyst. We can understand Freud's exclamation, on seeing this drama, "But it is a psychoanalysis!" Oedipus exhibits the whole gamut of psychoanalytic reactions, and the closer he gets to the truth, the more violently he fights against it. He accuses Tiresias of planning to betray the city; is this why he will not speak? The blind seer replies,

I will not bring remorse upon myself
And upon you. Why do you search these matters?

Then in a burst of angry projection Oedipus accuses Tiresias of having killed Laius himself. And when Oedipus finally goads the seer into telling him the truth, that he himself is his father's murderer, Oedipus turns upon Tiresias and Creon with the charge that these words are part of their strategy to take over the state. These forms of behavior, termed "resistance" and "projection," are an understandable part of every person's bitter struggle against the impossibly heavy and painful burden of responsibility in self-knowledge and the revolutionary impact of self-knowledge on one's self-image and identity. Resistance is an acting out of the conviction, "I cannot bear to admit it is I, so I will not *see* it!" Projection is a way of crying out, "If it is true, it is somebody else; not I! not I!"

Jocasta tries to persuade Oedipus to blot out the knowledge in the seer's accusation,

> Listen and learn, nothing in human life
> Turns on the soothsayer's art.
>
> . . . but why should men be fearful,
> O'er whom Fortune is mistress, and foreknowledge
> Of nothing sure? Best take life easily,
> As a man may. For that maternal wedding,
> Have no fear; for many men ere now
> Have dreamed as much; but he who by such dreams
> Sets nothing, has the easiest time of it.

But, as Oedipus begins to sense that some portentous mystery surrounds his birth, she, the mother whom he has married, now herself becomes aware of the terrible knowledge that awaits him. She tries desperately to dissuade him:

> Don't seek it! I am sick, and that's enough . . .
> Wretch, what thou art O mightst thou never know!

Oedipus is not dissuaded but insists he must know who he is and where he came from. He must know and accept his own reality.

> I will not hearken—not to know the whole,
> Break out what will, I shall not hesitate . . .

The old shepherd who rescued the infant Oedipus from death on the mountainside is finally brought, the one man who can provide the final link in the fateful story. "O, I am at the horror, now, to speak!" the shepherd cries. And Oedipus answers, "And I to hear. But I must hear—no less."

The Ultimate Punishment: Ostracism

When Oedipus does learn the final, tragic truth, he pulls out his eyes. It is significant that he is not *castrated* nor does he castrate himself; he cuts out his eyes, the organ of *seeing*. (The tendency to call this a "symbolic castration" misses the whole point and is an example of using a theory, e.g., the primacy of the sexual prototype, as a procrustean bed into which to force the data.) His punishment is then *exile*, first self-imposed but later, as pictured in *Oedipus at Colonus*, imposed by Creon and the state. The tragedy has now come full circle: Oedipus was originally exiled when he was a few days old on his father's order, and his life ends in exile. The exile is a fascinating symbolic act from our modern psychoanalytic viewpoint, for we have much data to indicate that the greatest threat and greatest cause of anxiety for Western man in the middle of the twentieth century is not castration but *ostracism*, the terrible situation of being thrown out of the group. This ostracism is a vivid symbol of what makes the anxiety of knowledge so powerful.

Ostracism is what we confront as the various inquisitions—in McCarthyism, the Moral Majority, etc.—that continuously spring up throughout the ages, capitalizing on the fear of the masses that is projected on the scientists and the scholars. Ostracism, or exile, is not at all a simple matter: In primitive tribes it meant certain death. In my book *The Meaning of Anxiety* I refer to studies of natives who were tabooed by their communities, believed they were going to die, and lay down and actually did expire in a few hours. Ostracism was one of the fears of the young scientist in the psychoanalytic case I presented at the beginning of this chapter.

The facts that one can resist knowledge, that knowledge is dangerous, and that it begins in the spirit of rebellion are also what make the pursuit of knowledge so fascinating and give it occasional ecstasy. The more we understand about it, in my judgment, the more we will see that knowledge is an exciting exploration as well as fearful and anxiety-creating; it is a far cry from the mere acquisition of dead facts.

Oedipus at Colonus

In the second drama, *Oedipus at Colonus*, the old Oedipus ponders the deeper implications of his previous actions. This drama has never, as far as I know, been mentioned in psychoanalytic literature, which is a surprising phenomenon. If you are only concerned with the act of sex with one's mother and the killing of one's father, your concern ends with the conclusion of *Oedipus Rex*. But Sophocles was by no means content to stop at that point. And *Oedipus at Colonus*, written in his last years and played on the stage after his death at ninety, ponders these deeper implications.

Oedipus asks, for example, "If I did not know, if I had no knowledge of what I was doing [killing his father], then am I innocent?"

> If then I came into the world—as I did come—
> In wretchedness, and met my father in a fight,
> And knocked him down, not knowing that I killed him
> Nor whom I killed—again, how could you find
> Guilt in that unmeditated act?[2]

And then about his mother,

> But neither of us knew the truth; and she
> Bore my children also— . . .
> While I would not have married her willingly
> Nor willingly would I ever speak of it.
>
> Before the law—before God—I am innocent!

Our society does not accept the lack of knowledge as a guarantee of innocence. But we do have a less severe censure for unpremeditated crime. The problem of *guilt* is obviously a paradox that cannot be simplistically solved but must be confronted as a paradox. Do we share the guilt, in the form of anxiety, for the upsets created by our knowledge?

Responsibility, in Oedipus, is treated similarly. If one does something without knowledge, does ignorance relieve one of responsibility? This is a complex paradox. I recall Werner Heisenberg's saying that the scientist qua scientist cannot be held guilty or responsible for discovering new knowledge but is responsible as a *citizen* for the use of this knowledge.

Though the problems of guilt and anxiety cannot be solved, we can take them into our consciousness and be aware of them as Oedipus was. Living with the paradoxes leads one into accepting the universal human condition and recognizing how each of us participates in "man's inhumanity to man." A deepening awareness of the human condition is brought out in *Oedipus at Colonus* in lines spoken, strangely enough, not by Oedipus but by Theseus, the ruler of Athens, who comes out of the city to talk with Oedipus. After listening to Oedipus' account of the disastrous events in his life, Theseus says:

. . . for I
Too was an exile . . .
I know I am only a man; I have no more
To hope for in the end than you have.

Here we hear a reexpression of the universal motto at Delphi, "know that thou art only a man."

I believe these considerations imply that we can meet the fear and danger of knowledge by means of a new stance toward the human condition, a stance characterized by compassion, mercy, and forgiveness (even though Oedipus would probably have scorned the last). I took this attitude with my patient, the young scientist of whom I spoke. Surely, you are anxious; we all would be in such a situation. But does not the challenge consist of going ahead *despite* the fear and the anxiety? The values that *Oedipus at Colonus* concludes with are *love* and *grace*.

. . . and yet one word
Frees us of all the weight and pain of life:
That word is love.

This is similar to the love in the new Adam and Eve after the fall, now admitting their guilt and responsibility, experiencing the need for each other and walking "hand in hand."

The other value mentioned in the conclusion of *Oedipus at Colonus* is grace. When Oedipus says,

For I come here as one endowed with grace,
By those who are over Nature; and I bring
Advantage to this race . . .

One soul, I think, often can make atonement
For many others, if it be devoted . . .

Transcending fear and anxiety, even while one experiences and accepts those feelings, leads to special grace, which Oedipus now has.

Fear and Anxiety: Prometheus

I cannot leave the Greeks and their struggle over the anxiety and fear of knowledge without referring to Aeschylus and his *Prometheus Bound*. Even more profoundly than Sophocles, Aeschylus presented the danger and the fear and anxiety that accompany knowledge. In the sublime poetry of *Prometheus Bound*, he presents for all time the transformation that occurs when one has confronted this fear and anxiety.

The drama parallels the myth of Adam and Eve in that its theme is the origin of civilization as Adam and Eve's theme is the origin of humankind as we know it. It is similar also in its presentation of gaining knowledge through rebellion, which brings anxiety and punishment.

In the battle between Zeus and Prometheus' brother Titans, Prometheus sided with Zeus because he believed knowledge in the long run would overcome brute force; the Titans in their "savage arrogance of spirit" (as Aeschylus phrases it) resorted only to brute force. But after Zeus' victory, when Prometheus saw that Zeus was set to exterminate the human race, he experienced pity for humankind. (The word "pity," which Aeschylus uses often, can better be translated as "compassion.") He then became the "bringer of light to suffering mankind," as Werner Jaeger expresses it; "the divine power of fire is for him the concrete image of civilization."

Prometheus recounts his gifts to human beings, which relate directly to the scholarly vocation in its highest sense. All of us who teach would like to emulate Prometheus as he describes his calling and his success:

> I found them [humankind] witless and gave them the use of their wits
> and made them masters of their minds. . . .³

> For men at first had eyes but saw to no purpose;
> they had ears but did not hear. Like the shapes
> of dreams, they dragged through their long lives
> and handled all things in bewilderment and confusion. . . .

> They lived like swarming ants in holes in the ground,
> and in the sunless caves of the earth. . . . all their
> doings were indeed without intelligent calculation
> until I showed them the rising of the stars, and the
> settings, hard to observe. And further I discovered
> to them numbering, pre-eminent among the subtle devices,
> and the combining of letters as a means of remembering
> all things. . . .

> I first adjudged what things come verily true
> from dreams; and to men I gave meaning to the
> ominous cries, hard to interpret. [This seems
> to be a direct prediction of modern psychoanalysis!]

> . . . all arts that mortals have come from Prometheus.

All this is done in the continuous fight against tyranny over the minds of human beings. One of the central paradoxes is that this tyranny not only is asserted by tyrannical powers like Zeus, but is even invited and longed for by human beings themselves, as the Grand

Inquisitor in Dostoyevsky tells us. Again, we see that the pursuit of knowledge always contains its element of rebellion, and we can also see why we human beings not only seek knowledge and love it but experience anxiety about it at the same time.

In his struggle against the tyranny of Zeus, Prometheus is supported to an extent by the chorus: "Your mind was yours, not his"; but then the chorus adds, "and at its bidding you regarded mortal man too highly, Prometheus." This is, of course, the eternally arguable question.

Aeschylus' central theme is that "highest knowledge can only be reached through suffering," as Werner Jaeger states. This concept runs as a kind of obbligato through the whole of Aeschylus' writing. In our day when one talks about knowledge coming from suffering, we immediately think of masochism: that someone who values suffering must be an angry necrophiliac or in some other way neurotic. But Aeschylus was obviously none of these things. He foresaw these objections, however, and in the drama he has Prometheus explicitly take his stand "not by pride or stubbornness"; it comes rather from compassion for humankind.

Aeschylus wrote with great objectivity as well as subjectivity and possessed a magnificent poetic comprehension of the world and our human struggles in it. He described the human condition as profoundly, and I believe as insightfully, as anyone ever has. He calls upon God or Zeus, "whatever he may be . . . to cast this dead weight of ignorance finally from out my brain."

Aeschylus also proclaims that order reestablishes itself sooner or later over chaos. Through suffering and through tragedy, he argues, human beings rise to new heights, which the amazing explosion of creativity in classic Greece demonstrates to us. His statement that the highest knowledge can only come through suffering reminds us of the beautiful description by the second Isaiah in the Bible of the "suffering servant," which was written in Israel at about the same time that Aeschylus was writing his plays. Both Aeschylus and the second Isaiah see the great gifts of those who suffer, i.e., those who confront the anxiety of knowledge for the sake of humankind.

These paradoxes hinge upon the age-old search for the "God beyond God," in Tillich's words. The paradox that concerns us is seen in Aeschylus' description of knowledge: goodness that causes such suffering at the same time. It is suffering that comes partly from upsetting the homeostasis of nature and partly from confronting the chaos that exists before order is born. It includes the ostracism, or exile, that we have seen occurring in the radical upsets of our society caused by new knowledge. But it is an exile from one's own nature, most of all, which we in psychotherapy deal with all of the time.

Notes

1. Quotations are from Sophocles, "Oedipus Tyrannus," *Dramas*, trans. by Sir George Young (New York: E.P. Dutton, Everyman's Library, 1906.)
2. Quotations are from Sophocles, "Oedipus at Colonus," *The Oedipus Cycle*, trans. by Dudly Fitts and Robert Fitzgerald (New York: Harcourt, Brace, 1949).
3. Quotations are from Aeschylus, *Prometheus Bound*, trans. by Warren D. Anderson (Indianapolis: Bobbs-Merrill, 1963).

Bibliography

Martin Buber. *I and Thou*. Translated by Ronald Gregor Smith. Edinburgh: T. and T. Clark; New York: Charles Scribner's Sons, 1937.

Soren Kierkegaard. *The Concept of Anxiety*. Translated by Walter Lowrie. Princeton, N.J.: Princeton University Press, 1944; Edited and translated by Howard V. Hong and Edna V. Hong. Northfield, Minn.; St. Olaf College Press, 1976. (Originally published in Danish, 1844.)

Soren Kierkegaard. *Sickness Unto Death*. Translated by Walter Lowrie. Princeton, N.J.: Princeton University Press, 1944. (Originally published in Danish, 1849.)

Rollo May, Ernest Angel, and Henri F. Ellenberger, eds. *Existence: A New Dimension in Psychiatry and Psychology*. New York: Basic Books, Inc., 1958.

Rollo May. *Freedom and Destiny*. New York: W. W. Norton & Company, Inc., 1981.

Rollo May. *Love and Will*. New York: W. W. Norton & Company, Inc., 1969.

Rollo May. *The Meaning of Anxiety*. Revised Edition. New York: W. W. Norton & Company, Inc., 1977.

Harry Stack Sullivan. *Conceptions of Modern Psychiatry*. New York: W. W. Norton, 1953.

Paul Tillich. *The Courage To Be*. New Haven, Connecticut: Yale University Press, 1952.

PART TWO

How to Apply the Knowledge of Learning to Education

—— **8** ——

Formal and Informal
Systems of Knowledge

There used to be many apocryphal anecdotes told in Cambridge about Norbert Wiener, many of which revolved around the contrast between the most sophisticated levels of abstract thinking and knowledge and the kinds of knowledge all of us use to get through the day. One of these stories tells that Wiener was being driven by a young doctoral student to speak at a seminar, and as the car passed through some narrow street, a little girl pursuing a ball ran out from between the parked cars, was struck a glancing blow by the car, and fell down. The student pulled over to the curb and ran out to comfort the crying child. He retrieved her ball and took her into a small pharmacy on a corner (there were such things in those days) where he bought some kind of antiseptic to clean her scraped knee, put a band-aid on it, gave her a lollipop, and, having gotten her name from her, telephoned to her mother and sent her, comforted, on her way home. He got back in the car heaving a deep sigh of relief and resumed the trip.

While all this happened, the story goes, Norbert Wiener sat unmoving in his seat. He remained silent for another ten minutes or so after they resumed their trip. Then he turned to the driver and said, "You have hit a little girl with your car before?" The student gasped, "My God, no, and I hope I never do again, that was awful!" After a few more minutes of silence, Wiener said, "In that case, how did you know what to do?"

I have often used this story as a way of opening introductory courses in anthropology. I then list the types of knowledge the doctoral student used in meeting what was, for him, a novel situation. He knew how to drive, stop, and park the car; he knew the nature of the corner drugstore and what could be found there; he knew something about the conventional way of handling minor wounds in our society and our beliefs about how children can be comforted; he knew how to work the telephone; and he knew how to use the English language. Today he would certainly ask himself questions about legal liability, but even at that time he was surely aware of laws concerning the obligation to stop in case of an accident. And lastly, he knew what was right in that situation, he knew how a good person should feel and act, including the knowledge that the safety and comfort of an unknown child, regardless of class or sex, were valuable. It is worth noticing that none of that knowledge is universal, even the knowledge of how a grown person should comfort a child. There are places in the world where children are better comforted with salt things than with sweet things and places where a crying child would be yelled at rather than addressed softly, and certainly there are places and times in which the value of the child's feelings would have been seen differently.

Informal Knowledge

Although it would take a truly extensive educational program to impart the knowledge used in those few minutes of behavior to someone from a totally different context, very little of the student's behavior was based on school-learning. It is possible he had taken driving lessons, but probably, like most Americans, he had most of the skills needed for driving before he sat behind the wheel. A succession of earnest English teachers had no doubt labored to make some small impact on his verbal use of the language, but most of that was learned before he arrived at school, as were his fundamental values.

This story raises issues that surely should enter into a consideration of the optimum utilization of knowledge, even if our primary focus is on the kind of knowledge found in books and imparted through formal educational systems, or if not through formal educational systems then at least by professional communicators or in systems designed by professional communicators. I am here using the word "informal" as a loose heuristic term that allows us to focus on a range of types of knowledge that share, to varying degrees, a set of characteristics that lead educators to take them for granted or disparage them; this disparagement is sometimes expressed in the term "folk knowledge." Most of the knowledge the student used was held in common within his community and, although it could be codified and systematized (and sometimes is by linguists or anthropologists), it had largely been passed to him in contexts in which neither learner nor teacher/model were dealing with it or aware of it as systematic. The informal nature of the contexts in which he had acquired his knowledge is related to a lack of codification in his manner of knowing, and although knowledge must be organized in some way, this knowledge that he drew on so readily was not presented to him as a systematized structure.

It may be helpful here to draw a distinction between this and current discussions of *nonformal education* by such writers as Ivan Illich and Paulo Freire, which differ from my remarks in two important ways. First, these educators are concerned with *restructuring* educational contexts so that bodies of knowledge that have been systematized and transmitted in the past through formal school systems may be transmitted in other ways and access to knowledge may be democratized. Second, they are concerned with transmitting knowledge across cultural and subcultural lines—with social change. Even though much of their fervor is to define ways of transmission that minimize alienation so as to put new learning in a cultural context, they are concerned with social change and with empowering new kinds of social participation.

Whatever social group we are discussing, it is important to notice that formally systematized and transmitted knowledge, if it is present at all, is only a fraction of the total knowledge of any adequately enculturated individual. Knowledge of other types is present in every person, beginning in earliest infancy, both as a resource and as an impediment, and is certainly the basis on which more formal types of transmission must be built. The corpus of Wiener anecdotes deals with variations on the theme that Wiener, educated as a prodigy, had gaps in his informal knowledge and in his sense of how different kinds of knowledge fit together. This anecdote supplies an example of the transfer of informal knowledge from one situation to another and what linguists refer to as the generation of a novel performance from underlying competences. The "utilization of knowledge" in this case means, among other things, the capacity to apply grammatical rules, legal constraints on the behavior of drivers, and folk-psychological theories about the griefs and comforts of little girls, in a novel and stressful situation requiring a complex performance mobilizing and integrating knowledge in many different areas. It seems probable that many features in the transmission of formal systems of knowledge, particularly in schools, work against such utilization.

Here it is worth remembering the famous story of the centipede who asked himself which foot he moved first and then found himself unable to walk. Using the story as a metaphor of human knowledge, not a discourse on the neurophysiology of centipedes, we can say that the rule for initiating locomotion the centipede knew was a learned rule but one the centipede did not know he knew. His attempt to make this knowledge explicit made him unable to function. Although my primary concern is to call attention to the possibilities of improved learning and utilization of knowledge through a systematic awareness of informal knowledge, it seems important to emphasize that it is strictly impossible for anyone to achieve and maintain a sustained knowledge and awareness of what they know. Nonetheless, effective utilization of very complex kinds and combinations of informal knowledge is something that those who work with formal systems must often sigh after.

Informal knowledge comes first. It is within the context of informal knowledge systems that individuals learn to learn and learn to transfer knowledge, and these vital skills mostly remain out of awareness. A greater awareness of informal systems of knowledge can have a salutary effect on how we approach the formal systems. What would it mean for teachers to approach their classes with a full appreciation of the extent *and complexity* of the previous knowledge with which their students approach them and the relatively small increment that they will be able to make? They could greatly increase their teaching efficiency by bringing some aspects of informal knowledge into consciousness so that students needing to learn additional material of the same sort would realize the extent to which they are on familiar ground, already knowing much about how to know. At the same time, this suggests a profound modification of the teacher-student relationship: both children and illiterate peasants, who may regard themselves as profoundly ignorant and inferior to the urban bureaucrats who run their lives, in fact possess vast amounts of such knowledge before teachers and social reformers ever get to them. An awareness of the complexity of the knowledge they already possess might in itself be a revolutionary force.

Transmitting Knowledge Without Teaching

The pattern whereby certain bodies of knowledge that are not self-consciously transmitted are built on and embedded in informal knowledge is characteristic of all human groups, whether or not they are literate. So far as we know, all human groups have extensive systems of knowledge that are not formally taught or explicitly codified and that are shared, more or less equally, through the community. All cultures impart complex systems of ideas about the nature of the universe, the nature of interpersonal relations, and adaptation to the environment. These must be learned, whether by letting a little boy take his own dugout canoe out on the reef at the age of three or four or by letting him watch the adults operate the elevator in an apartment building. So far as we know, all stable human groups have spoken languages of roughly comparable levels of complexity, and all normally maturing human beings master one of these at an early age, in addition to learning a considerable amount about contextual and stylistic variation.

Knowledge of this sort is built up and integrated in many different ways, some active and some passive, involving experience and observation, play, practice, experimentation, adult examples, and adult responses of approval or disapproval. In all human groups there is some explicit instruction, correction, and admonition by people, particularly parents and peers, who are not specialists in teaching and who do not have an explicitly systematized knowledge of the material they are passing on. There is tremendous cultural variation in the explicitness with which this knowledge is taught, the relative importance of structuring the learning situation so that a performance is correct the first time as opposed to correcting a faulty performance, and the list of individuals who are allowed to play an active role. (In America, the person who scolds a strange child for picking his nose is a busybody, and there are aspects of socialization that "even your best friend won't tell you.")

In our society, we overestimate the importance of explicit teaching. Educated parents put considerable effort into persuading children not to make certain errors of grammar that could be regarded as classic errors ("It's me"), while blithely ignoring highly complex syntactic processes that children succeed in learning without ever having them explained. Similarly, parents spend considerable time telling children to say "please" and "thank you" but do not instruct them in the complex gestural courtesies and alternative forms they will eventually master. Thus, we *instruct* our children to say "Please pass the butter," and they *learn* to say "Would you pass me the butter?" in a tone that makes it accepted as equivalent to the sentence containing "please."

The same is true on matters of values. We instruct our children not to hit, not to make another child cry, and to be nice to a poor little girl, but by example and other subtler clues we also instruct them that in some cases they should hit back and that they should be nicer to some people than to other people. As the song goes, "You've got to be taught to hate." Complex lessons about how social structures *really* work are taught to children before they go to school, often before they are exposed to more presentable but often contradictory verbalized values. These values may then prove to be extremely difficult to teach.

In other words, children growing up in all societies, literate or preliterate, are taught a great amount of cultural knowledge primarily by parents and peers, with a method of teaching that involves occasional corrections and instructions that represent only a fraction (and often a highly inconsistent or nonrepresentative fraction) of the whole.

Given this striking fact, it seems clear that explicit teaching must have functions that go far beyond the knowledge explicitly imparted. Thus, when we teach "Don't say 'its's me,' say 'it's I'" or "Say 'thank you'" or "Don't pick your nose in public," we are using relatively trivial explicit teaching as part of the process of imparting informal knowledge of a highly abstract kind about the nature of correctness, the difference between public and private spaces, and the nature of authority. Much of the kind of learning that Basil Bernstein studies involves the learning of informal knowledge about cultural premises in different subcultural groups, including premises that concern the nature of knowledge and the learning process.

In addition to the vast amount of learning that characterizes all human maturation, much of which is done without formal teaching, a characteristic of all human groups is some more extensive elaboration of identifiable activities that may be regarded as teaching, where the teacher has a sense of an interlocking body of knowledge, usually only slightly codified. We are the animal that relies most on learning in our adaptation, and even more distinctively the animal that relies most on teaching to bring about learning. There are always skills that are not picked up by imitation, trial and error, and occasional correction but that are learned when some older person sets out to teach a child. An American father may take his son out to the park to learn to hit a baseball, and in another context, a father might take his son out on the trail with a spear to learn to track wild animals. A parent may teach a child the words of the Lord's Prayer, presenting it line by line for memorization. A mother may give a lesson before a son or daughter is allowed to use a complex and fragile piece of equipment like a loom or a sewing machine, or expensive materials like wool or butter, or dangerous objects like knives or fire.

Taboos on Learning

Since all human cultures have some degree of role differentiation and division of labor based on age and gender and at least some small degree of differentiation beyond that, one thing that all children must learn is that not everyone is an appropriate model for imitation, at least not in all of their activities. It is not accidental that so many examples of explicit parental teaching are gender-linked. On the other hand, the knowledge of every individual in a culture includes behaviors and skills that it is not permissible to display. Eskimo women know how to build snow houses, but don't.

The whole question of knowledge subject to taboos on utilization (which may be related to other factors as well as gender) can perhaps be explored profitably to understand how knowledge might more effectively be utilized. In this context, one should also look at the case of children reared by servants of another class, for whom the main caretaker is disallowed as an immediate model for imitation. If you speak like the gardener or nursemaid, you will not be a gentleman. If you, as a male child, go too far in imitating your mother, who is likely to be the person with whom you spend the most time and who does the most informal teaching, you will be a sissy. Surely, imposing filters of this sort on the capacity to learn must have wider inhibiting effects.

When the most easily available model for imitation is disallowed, we often see the contextualization of the learning process and begin to find some situations marked as ones in which learning is appropriate, in contrast to situations that may take up a great deal of an individual's time but are inappropriate for certain types of learning. The most drastic case of this kind in preliterate societies occurs in initiation rites. There is a correlation between intense and severe male initiation rites at puberty and childhoods in which males are reared primarily in the company of women and must learn a strikingly different kind of behavior as they mature. The rites contain various forms of instructions to unlearn as well as instructions to withdraw from relationships of intimacy and dependency. In our own society, of course, part of the message of school is that teachers know better than parents; children must be handed over to educators partly because what they learn from their parents is likely to be faulty. This idea, which is implied in any radical contextualization of the learning process, is accentuated in the United States by the immigrant tradition in which children could not learn how to be members of American society by imitating their parents.

Context and Ritual

In examining any contextualization of learning, it is worth considering the way in which cultures exploit or create variable readiness to learn. Everywhere in the world, the contextualization of learning is related to maturation, not simply because one must acquire knowledge before one can use it but also because biological readiness to learn varies in relation to the life cycle, following an epigenetic groundplan through childhood, increasing at puberty and at other life crises such as childbirth. (Postpartum readiness to learn is sometimes referred to as "suggestibility.") The ordeals that often form part of initiation rites, as well as the ritual solemnity or intensity, create a psychological readiness to learn as well as contextualizing the periods of formal tuition that often ensue; formal education has often conformed to this model in both solemnity and unpleasantness. Initiation rites in different societies that are used as contexts for learning may vary from a few days to months or years and share with formal Western systems of education the abstract message that there is a time and a place for learning and other times and places not intended for learning that may indeed be unsuitable for learning. Secret or esoteric knowledge clearly underlines this contrast.

Very often the knowledge transmitted within a ritual context, whether it be a technical skill or a mythological tradition, is highly codified, but it is worth noting that neither the contextualization of learning nor the codification of the knowledge to be transmitted requires specialists in teaching. Specialists of all sorts are likely to be involved in training their successors, and this process is usually more explicit and the knowledge more codified when their successors are not lineal descendents. Most specialists are also called upon to instruct others who are not being trained as specialists: for example, midwives train future midwives (either their own daughters or apprentices), instruct other women during childbirth, and may play some role in the initiation of girls at menarche. But in none of these teaching activities are the specialists defined primarily as teachers. Teaching, as a specialization rather than an aspect of some other role, seems to be rather a late development, accompanied by more formal structures of knowledge as well as more formal contexts of learning and teacher-learner relationships. In our own society at least, the formal contexts of learning are often defined as places where people are taught things they do not already know, while the process of bringing certain kinds of knowledge into awareness is associated with various kinds of psychotherapy. It will be increasingly important to define contexts and processes for transferring or translating one type of knowledge into another and constructing sequences that suit individual learners. For some learners it is easier to move from a rule to an example; for others it is easier to handle examples without an articulated rule. If teachers take the nonverbal knowledge that makes this process possible for granted, they will fail repeatedly in the attempt to teach those in whom this nonverbal knowledge is absent. The overwhelming emphasis in Western education has been on inculcating verbal knowledge. Fortunately, we are increasingly sensitive to the potential for learning of planned movement between visual, kinesthetic, verbal, and other types of learning, as when sign language is used with children who are not deaf but are having difficulty learning language.

It might be protested here that while we have been drawing examples from preliterate societies, not all of what was learned was really knowledge. According to Boulding, knowledge consists of some kind of structure in nervous systems which codes information, contains images of the world which have at least a rough one-to-one mapping of a "real-world," and contains instructions for structural growth and behavior. The real world includes the community in which one lives. Learning a language certainly involves acquiring instructions for behavior and a way of mapping behavior and images of the world. Mythology contains metaphorical statements about the structures of the real and the social worlds, often statements coding vast stores of images and information. In addition, of course, it is important to include here the extremely detailed knowledge that preliterate people tend to have of relevant aspects of their natural environment.

What Are the Advantages of Literate Societies?

Given all these types of knowledge, it's not clear to me at what point individuals in a literate society begin to have *as individuals* significantly greater knowledge than they would have had under preliterate conditions. There is of course no way of making a direct comparison, since we cannot quantify knowledge of these very diverse types. Under some circumstances, children may learn less in the classroom than they would from participating and imitating a wider range of activities. Certainly levels of retention must be higher when learning is structured by the demands of everyday life, while much of what is learned during the process we call education can be forgotten and perhaps should be. On the other hand, formal contexts for learning involve the systematic exposure of the learner to a changing series of experiences and the presentation of new knowledge in a manner related to the structure of what is to be learned. The episodic structure of everyday life certainly does not preclude learning, but eventually the process must slow down as experience becomes increasingly repetitive.

In any case, a comparison of knowledge between societies is not based on what individuals know. The most important expansion of the resources of knowledge we have in a literate, complex society like this one is the knowledge we can "have" without knowing it, the knowledge we do not carry in our heads but have access to in the minds of our colleagues and in libraries and other forms of storage. To utilize this knowledge as individuals we need to know a great deal about how knowledge is acquired and organized. We may think first of skills that are explicitly taught, but even these skills are the tip of an iceberg whose base is formed when children learn to distinguish between fiction and news on television, to formulate questions, to choose an adult likely to give intelligible answers, and to understand why some people are annoyed by questions and others pleased. Very few people know how they approach the problem of learning their way around a strange city, though they may know how to construct a bibliography in a technical field.

First Learning as a Pattern for Future Learning

As we look at the different kinds of learning in societies of increasing complexity (and, incidentally, at the sequence of learning up to adulthood), we see a pattern in which an increasing contextualization of the learning process parallels an increasing specialization and division of labor. The more highly contextualized and specialized a body of knowledge, the more likely it is to be presented as an explicitly codified system, and the more discontinuous it is likely to be from everyday informal systems. The classic example of discontinuity is second-language learning in school. Whereas you use your native language almost without consideration to generate an infinite variety of novel utterances, you struggle to produce any result outside the classroom after two or three years of high school French. Interestingly enough, attempts to reduce discontinuity and improve language learning often involve making the teaching of grammar less explicit.

These processes of contextualization and embedding mean that virtually every bit of formal education involves learning about the nature of the knowledge and how it fits in, which is nowhere made explicit. It seems to me the challenge to educators is to mine this knowledge and use it to facilitate the acquisition and transfer of learning. It seems absurd to teach a second language to people who have already learned one language in great detail without taking advantage of what they know about *how* to learn a language and what knowing a language means. Other kinds of informal knowledge represent a similar resource. Using them means giving people a sense of the order and pattern in their own behavior.

When we look at the differences between the structure of knowledge in our society and that in smaller and simpler societies, we see that one of the fundamental differences is in the degree of integration. Nowhere are individuals able to bring all of their knowledge into awareness; in every society there are variations and overlap so not all knowledge is shared by all members or known in the same way. In our society, however, we have such a complex system of contexts of learning that in areas where there is not a systematic attempt at consistency there is likely to be an extraordinarily high degree of inconsistency—students studying physics in college ask each other their astrological signs, and our mythologies contain statements about the world that no longer parallel other available ways of synthesizing information. It will be increasingly necessary to focus on relationships between different systems of knowledge that in a simpler and more stable society could be taken for granted. Learning is undoubtedly often blocked by unstated premises that contradict what is being taught, but learning may also appear to take place and yet be held insulated from other ideas as necessary connections and transfers are not made. The mind may protect itself from new and disquieting knowledge as an oyster protects itself from a bit of grit.

Because informal learning is not transmitted in an explicitly systematized form, people are extraordinarily unaware of the intricate structure of their own learned behavior, of the intellectual complexity of common sense or the unstated pattern of courtesies that makes Emily Post and Amy Vanderbilt sound like primers, of the ontological and epistemological assumptions on which their lives are premised. It is not sufficient to try and disassemble false premises and persuade people to replace them; people need to be aware of what it means to operate, as everyone does, on learned premises of considerable complexity and up and down a highly abstract scale of logical types. This awareness would increase the acquisition and utilization of knowledge and enable learners to transcend the barriers and discontinuities created by the contextualization of learning. "Conscientization" or "consciousness raising" are terms used for the empowering growth of various kinds of awareness of how society functions. They might equally be used of the intellectually empowering process of becoming aware of one's own informal knowledge.

Bibliography

Bateson, Gregory. *Steps to an Ecology of Mind.* New York: Ballantine Books, 1976

Bateson, Mary Catherine. "The Epigenesis of Conversational Interaction: A Personal Account of Research Development." In *Before Speech.* Margaret Bullowa (ed.). Cambridge: Cambridge University Press, 1979.

Bernstein, Basil. "Elaborated and Restricted Codes: Their Social Origins and Some Consequences." In *The Ethnography of Communication,* American Anthropologist, special publication, 66, no. 6, pt. 2. J. J. Gumperz and D. H. Hymes (eds.). Washington, D.C.: American Anthropological Association, 1966.

Frank, Jerome David. *Persuasion and Healing: A Comparative Study of Psychotherapy* (Rev. ed.). New York: Schocken Books, 1963.

Freire, Paulo. *Pedagogy of the Oppressed.* New York: Herder and Herder, 1972.

Illich, Ivan. *Deschooling Society.* New York: Harper and Row, 1971.

Kindervatter, Suzanne. *Nonformal Education as an Empowering Process.* Amherst, Mass.: Center for International Education and University of Massachusetts Press, 1979.

Mead, Margaret. *Culture and Commitment: The New Relationships Between the Generations in the 1970's.* New York: Columbia University Press, 1978.

Mead, Margaret, and Wolfenstein, Martha. *Childhood in Contemporary Cultures.* Chicago: University of Chicago Press, 1955.

JOSEPH D. NOVAK

——— **9** ———

Concept-Based Learning

The Construction of Meaning

Human beings are unique in their ability to construct meanings from their experience and to code these meanings symbolically. Although other animals have innate or developed signal systems or may be taught to use sign language to signal desires, there is no convincing evidence that these signals have *meanings* similar to those coded by humans in language. In fact, the ability to code and express psychological meanings symbolically is almost synonymous with being human. All normal humans develop spoken language through interaction with their environment involving thinking, feeling, and acting. Although each of these processes contributes to the acquisition and use of knowledge, I will argue that our growing understanding of thinking and the role that concepts play in thinking can make a fundamental new contribution to the production and use of knowledge.

Concepts are what we think with. Gowin defined concepts as *perceived regularities in events or objects as designated by a sign or symbol.*[1] It is possible, of course, to perceive a regularity in events or objects and not have a symbolic label for it (as is common with very young children) or to acquire and use labels but not recognize the regularity they designate (as is common in too much of school learning). Some concept regularities such as love or electron spin are not observed directly but are rather inferred from events and are sometimes considered "abstract," but all concepts represent abstractions from relevant events or objects. Most of the half-million words in the English language were invented to designate some perceived regularity, and many designate two or more different regularities. When I asked a fourth-grade class in Melbourne how many concept labels we have, one bright student said, "You can't tell because people keep making up new concepts." This child not only got the idea that words are used to code or signal

100

regularities but realized that people keep finding new regularities and making up new words for them. This child's understanding of epistemology was centuries ahead of some philosophers and closely in line with contemporary ideas about the nature of knowledge and knowledge production that I will discuss here.[2]

What apparently is "hard wired" into human brains is the extraordinary capacity to *perceive* regularities in events or objects *and* the ability to code these regularities symbolically. All normal children have this capacity and do it without schooling by age two or three. The incredible feat of acquiring spoken language occurs as naturally as growth, and the acquisition of concept meanings accelerates, at least until the child begins school. Unfortunately, by age ten or eleven, the natural capacity of many children for acquiring meanings (perceived regularities) and appropriate language labels is so severely damaged through ego assaults by deleterious school and home practices that they become "learning disabled." But even under the "best" practices in today's schools, only a fraction of human capability for gaining concept meanings is achieved. Thus begins a fundamental problem in the production, acquisition, and use of knowledge.

For two decades we have applied our growing understanding of the role concepts play to designing methods of instruction and to related educational research that has led to some demonstrated improvements in learning. More recently, we have begun to teach students from grade one through university what we know about how they learn and how knowledge is constructed, as well as continually improving the curriculum. Concept mapping is a strategy we have developed to illustrate the role that concepts play in constructing meaning. Figure 1 shows a concept map constructed by a first-grade student who was given a list of words previously introduced in class discussions. With students seventh grade and up we have used another heuristic device to illustrate knowledge construction; Figure 2 shows the generalized form of Gowin's Epistemological Vee. We believe concept mapping and Vee mapping show promise in helping students "learn how to learn," although more experimentation is needed.

Attempting to learn in schools can be dismal. In his 1964 *How Children Fail,* Holt described students' "strategies for failure" with which they preserve self-image. In my view, the root cause for what Rollo May aptly describes as "fear of knowledge" is the ego-assaulting experiences people have had in maleducative practices in schools and other settings. I doubt that this fear can be ameliorated or transformed into a thirst for knowledge unless we can learn more about how people learn and succeed in transmitting this knowledge to future generations. This paper will describe briefly some efforts in this direction.

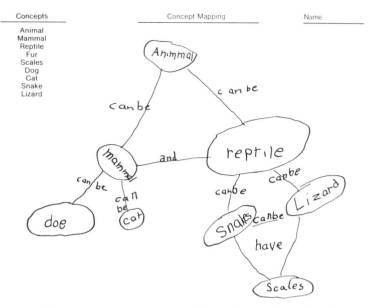

FIGURE 1. A concept map produced by a first-grade student from a list of words provided. The meanings of the words had been discussed previously in class. This was the third twenty-minute session with the class on concepts and concept maps and the student's first effort to make a concept map.

Since 1964, research and teaching innovations have been guided by the cognitive learning theory of David Ausubel.[3] *Cognitive* learning refers to acquisition of knowledge, as distinguished from acquisition of skills or *psychomotor* learning and acquisition of feelings or *affective* learning. Cognitive learning results in further development of *cognitive structure*, the structure of knowledge possessed by an individual. Development of cognitive structure takes place from birth to senescence, with the "log phase" occurring between two and twenty years for most people. Ausubel's work has not been widely accepted in the United States; it is much better known in Germany and many other countries. Over the years, we have made some modifications to the theory.[4] Ausubel's theory of cognitive learning interrelates seven basic concepts; I believe Americans have difficulty with the theory partly because each concept derives some meaning from each of the other concepts. It is a challenging task to understand the theory as a whole until the meaning of each key concept is grasped and integrated. Nevertheless, the theory can account for all aspects of cognitive learning and development, which comprise an exceedingly complex and varied set of events. No other current theory has this comprehensiveness.

GOWIN'S EPISTEMOLOGICAL V

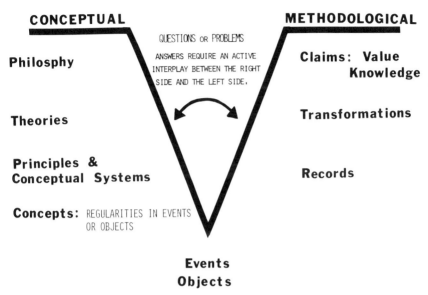

CONCEPTUAL

Philosphy

Theories

Principles &
Conceptual Systems

Concepts: REGULARITIES IN EVENTS
OR OBJECTS

QUESTIONS OR PROBLEMS

ANSWERS REQUIRE AN ACTIVE
INTERPLAY BETWEEN THE RIGHT
SIDE AND THE LEFT SIDE.

METHODOLOGICAL

Claims: Value
Knowledge

Transformations

Records

Events
Objects

FIGURE 2. Gowin's Vee heuristic showing the key elements involved in the construction of knowledge. In the process of knowledge construction, every element interacts with every other element, although much research and routine scholarship does not consciously involve conceptual-theoretical elements in the process of knowledge construction.

Ausubel's central concept is the idea of meaningful learning, which requires (1) that the material to be learned has inherent meaning (which excludes such things as nonsense syllables or arbitrarily linked word pairs, now commonly used in early laboratory studies of human learning; and (2) that the learner make a deliberate effort to relate the new material to relevant concepts he or she already has. Meaningful learning involves *subsuming* new knowledge into existing relevant concepts and propositions,[5] a process that leads to some modifications of both the existing knowledge structures and the newly learned material. The process is somewhat akin to Piaget's developmental ideas of assimilation and accommodation, except that meaningful learning involves *specifically relevant* concepts and propositions, not generic cognitive structures, and results in the alteration of the acquired knowledge. Ausubel describes meaningful learning as involving the incorporation of new knowledge into cognitive structure in a nonarbitrary, substantive, nonverbatim manner; he contrasts this with rote learning, which is arbitrary, non-substantive, and verbatim. When a student learns multiplication tables by relating each product to corresponding addition ideas and/or to base ten, meaningful learning results. If, for example, the product of 9 × 7 is forgotten, the student can reconstruct the product through corresponding arithmetic operations, e.g., 10 × 7 = 70 − 7 = 63. The student who learns by rote can only guess at the product.

The rote-meaningful distinction is a continuum, not a dichotomy; the degree of meaningfulness depends in part on the inherent meaning in the material to be learned and on the extent of *relevant* concepts and propositions the learner has. At one extreme is a telephone number, which has limited meaning, (although even it is not totally arbitrary, since all numbers in the United States and Canada have seven digits). At the other end of the continuum, a scientist or historian interpreting the meaning of new data will bring into play an incredibly large set of relevant concepts and propositions in attempting to grasp the meaning of the new data. Those who make the best synthesis of the new data with existing knowledge may win a Nobel or Pulitzer prize. Grasping the meaning of new knowledge is an *idiosyncratic* process, since every individual has a unique framework of concepts and propositions. However, there is enough commonality among individual cognitive structures that we can successfully communicate to each other using concept symbols. Constructing meaning depends on the framework of concepts and principles we hold but also on our affective experiences that influence what we see as salient or related in a manner Polanyi has described as using *tacit* knowledge.[6] The important role of culture in shaping an individual's concepts is stressed by Bohannan and by Bateson in this volume. They also contrast the rich integrated meanings of "folk" knowledge with the more rigid, conceptually isolated "formal" knowledge acquired in schools. We see this difference in the concept maps children produce to describe a knowledge area they know well from their hobbies and common experiences (such as sports) in contrast with maps they make to describe school learning tasks.

It is important to recognize that there must be a close link between the processes by which an individual grasps meaning and the processes by which scholars create new knowledge in their disciplines, or, more succinctly, we must link our psychology of learning with our epistemology.

Concept Mapping

In our research program with children and adults we have questioned how the framework of concepts individuals apply to observed events changes over time. The usual paper-and-pencil tests are almost useless

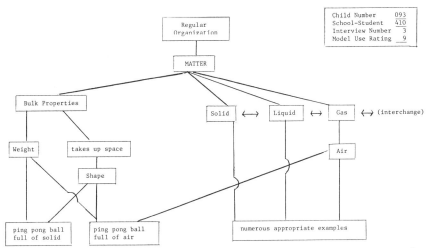

FIGURE 3. An example of an early concept map constructed in our research program to illustrate the concepts expressed by a first-grade student during an interview, as judged by a researcher. This child knew that matter can be a solid, liquid, or gas (and gave appropriate examples) and recognized certain bulk properties of matter (from Rowell 1978).

in addressing this question: too often when students are asked how or why they selected a response, their reasons say less about the concepts they were applying than about their test-taking strategies. Moreover, even when this is not the case, test responses do not reveal the explicit concepts used to select a response. Clinical interviews modified from Piaget's technique have been more revealing, but we struggled with the problem of data reduction when faced with hundreds of recorded or transcribed interviews. We began to use *concept mapping* to represent the set of concepts necessary for properly interpreting phenomena presented to students, as judged by our research staff, and also to represent the concepts utilized by a student, as constructed from an interview transcript. Figure 3 shows an example of one of these early concept maps.

As our experience with concept mapping increased, we began using concept maps as instructional tools.[7] We recognized the importance of specifying the relationship between any two concepts on our maps that formed a specific proposition. In retrospect, we should have recognized this necessity from Ausubelian theory, which says the meaning of a concept is acquired through increasing numbers of successively more precise learned propositions that include the concept. Recent work with students from age six through adulthood has shown that concept mapping

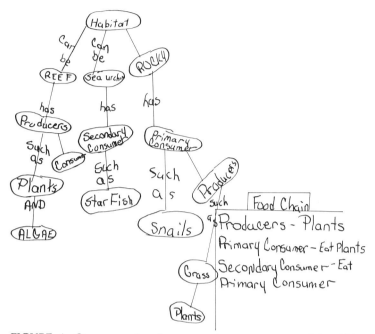

FIGURE 4. One example of a concept map constructed by fifth-grade students who were provided a list of concepts dealing with habitat. This map shows confusion between concepts of producers and consumers and habitat types.

can be taught to students in an hour or two of class time and then used as an evaluation strategy. Of course, proficiency in concept-map construction takes practice, as does taking multiple-choice tests, and we should expect that maps constructed early will be less adequate representations of the framework of concepts students possess than maps constructed after more experience with the technique. In addition, we have found first and second graders catch on to the technique more readily than high school or college students, some of whom are very unhappy when asked to organize ideas into a concept map. The validity of concept maps as representations of students' operative cognitive structures relating to a given task is still in need of much research. However, our work to date suggests that concept maps may have much higher validity than conventional evaluations of student achievement and/or readiness. Scoring keys have been developed that are reliable and easy to use.

We have used concept maps to assess student readiness for learning. The students are given key concept words and asked to construct concept maps from them. Figure 4 shows a concept map constructed by a fifth-grade student in North Carolina. From the twenty-two maps prepared by students in this class, we have a relatively good representation of what they know about one area of ecology and also what faulty propositions or missing concept meanings need to be considered. Seventeen misconceptions or missing concept meanings were identified from the maps of this group of students. It would take numerous clinical interviews to identify a comparable set of misconceptions or "missing links," and obviously classroom teachers cannot find time to conduct and interpret dozens of clinical interviews, even if they possess the necessary skills.

Concept mapping is a practicable strategy for teachers. In the epigraph to his book, Ausubel writes, "If I had to reduce all of educational psychology to just one principle, I would say this: The most important single factor influencing learning is what the learner already knows. Ascertain this and teach him accordingly."[8] Concept mapping can become a powerful tool for both teachers and students to ascertain what they already know that is relevant to a new area of study. Students are often surprised that they do know much relevant material that can be used to anchor new meaningful learning. Teachers are often surprised by how many misconceptions or faulty conceptions students possess. We have only begun to develop strategies to help students recognize and overcome the interfering influence of misconceptions in new learning, and recent research is showing that even A students have numerous misconceptions.[9] Concept mapping will not automatically eliminate students' misconceptions, but it can help students to identify them and deal with them explicitly. Some of the fear of knowledge we have undoubtedly derives from distrusting our ability to use what we know, to make sense out of new knowledge; this source of fear should be dealt with explicitly.

The Construction of Knowledge

Public misunderstanding of the nature of knowledge production is a major obstacle to the optimal utilization of knowledge. The average person on the street believes "smart" people discover new knowledge in much the same way that the skillful prospector discovers gold. One source of this misunderstanding is that most school learning, especially in Third World countries, presents knowledge as facts to be memorized. The implicit view is that knowledge is truth and that to become educated one must gather pearls of wisdom. What is not understood is the central role that concepts play in what we choose to observe, how we observe, how we organize our observations, and what claims we construct from the observations. The roots of this misunderstanding go back to Bacon, who admonished his readers to rid themselves of preconceived notions and be unfettered in observing nature. This admonition was perhaps appropriate in 1620, when notions of gods and demons still dominated thinking about the workings of the universe. Unfortunately, the view persisted and was honed even further by writers such as Karl Pearson, who wrote at the beginning of this century:

> The civil law is valid only for a *special* community at a *special* time; the scientific law is valid for *all* normal human beings, and is unchanging.
>
> The right of science to deal with the beyond of sense-impressions is not the subject of contest, for science confessedly claims no such right.
>
> Science, as I have so often reiterated, takes the universe of perceptions as it finds it, and endeavors briefly to describe it. It asserts no perceptual reality for its own shorthand.[10]

This Pearsonian dogma, entrenched in most school science textbooks, helps foster the fallacy that science discovers truth. When new concepts and new observational tools lead to changed views of how the world works, the public is confused, which contributes subtly to the public's "fear of knowledge." The same unchanging view of knowledge is conveyed in history, grammar, and other areas of school studies. And, as Senesh points out, too much of the school curriculum is obsolete and emotionally "dead."

In recent years as we have used Gowin's Vee heuristic with students and faculties, we have become increasingly conscious of the pervasive nature of Baconian-Pearsonian "positivistic" epistemology in people's thinking. This view seems almost rooted in their bone marrow, and though some may come to recognize the contemporary views of the evolutionary, conceptual nature of knowledge construction, teachers and students continue to behave as though knowledge came in neat, self-contained, hermetically sealed packets. We are largely failing to win people over to the view that knowledge is tentative, constructed, interdependent on other knowledge, but also the unique, powerful construction of humankind, an issue Boulding addresses explicitly in Chapter 1. I believe we must be more explicit, more deliberate in our efforts to achieve the latter view. To this end we have begun to use the Vee heuristic directly with students.

Gowin's Vee, shown in Figure 2, has at the "point" of the Vee the primary source of knowledge, i.e., events or objects we choose to observe. Of course, even the selection of what we observe is influenced by our concepts, principles, and theories, which, one could argue, are thus more "basic" to the construction of knowledge than are events or objects. One might argue with the form of the heuristic, but we believe all of the elements shown on the Vee must be accounted for in any schema of the construction of knowledge.

When we began using the Vee heuristic in a college setting, students and professors commonly remarked that something like this should have been presented to them much earlier. We subsequently conducted a study with junior high school students to ascertain whether or not concept mapping and Vee mapping strategies could be learned at this level. The results showed that seventh- and eighth-grade students could use the strategies.[11] There was also some evidence that these strategies improved their ability to apply knowledge learned to novel problem-solving questions. Several related studies were completed or are in progress;[12] a handbook to instruct teachers on the use of these strategies is also available.[13]

We found seventh-grade students were very successful in constructing Vee maps to show how laboratory activities in science could be viewed as "knowledge construction" activities, albeit the students recognized they were not constructing original knowledge claims. Figure 5 shows two examples constructed by junior high school science students. Subsequent work with students in junior high school and secondary school has been even more encouraging relative to *students'* receptivity to and growing understanding of the epistemology presented. However, we have found only about one in fifty science teachers to be receptive to these strategies. Raised on an intellectual diet of subtle "positivistic" epistemology, teachers are not easily converted to educational practices that view knowledge as a construction. In defense of teachers subject to economic and social pressures, I feel somewhat sympathetic to their concerns and apprehensions about education strategies that might undermine their authority. The "back to basics" movement is antithetical to introducing pedagogical strategies that view knowledge as tentative, constructed, and evolutionary in character. These are indeed bad times to introduce contemporary epistemology directly and explicitly into schools.

Hundreds of research questions emerge from our work: To what extent do concept maps represent actual relationships between concepts in a person's mind? Is knowledge stored hierarchically? Are there better forms to represent students' concepts than the present forms of concept maps? Are the scoring keys we are using valid? Do Vee maps include all crucial elements in knowledge construction? Where do emotions or "tacit knowledge" fit into the heuristics? Our research will continue, but we welcome others interested in studying how to teach students to "learn how to learn."

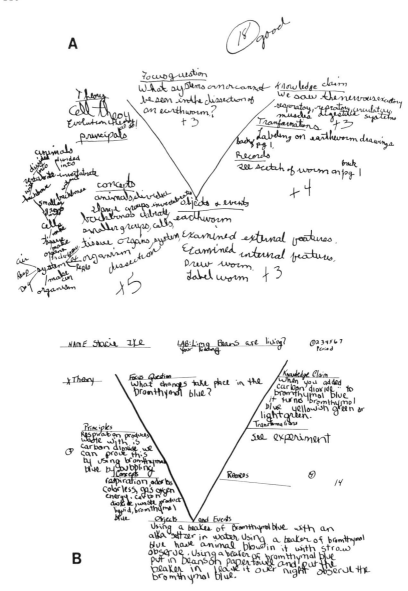

FIGURE 5. Two examples of Vee maps constructed by seventh-grade science students. Figure 5a shows a concept map organized for the "left side" of the Vee and also scoring applied by the teacher (eighteen out of a possible twenty-two points). Some records were placed on lab study guide pages (Novak and staff, 1981).

Learning to Learn

I believe we must help people explicitly to *learn how to learn*. We must also find ways to help people feel learning is worthwhile and valuable. My contention is that much of the fear of or even antipathy to learning comes from the ineffectiveness and negative feelings associated with most school learning. There are no simple solutions to the problems with both massive public misunderstanding of the nature of knowledge and the maleducative practices of most schools. It will be decades before we see significant results from our work, but we must begin.

Learning based on explicit consideration of the key concepts that make sense in any area of human concern will differ dramatically from rote learning of facts and procedures. In any discipline, learning that includes consideration of how knowledge is constructed in that discipline and of the central role of invented concepts in the construction of knowledge will be more than a new educational gimmick. This type of learning, however, rarely occurs in most educational settings today.

In summary, I am suggesting a new hope and also noting a serious dilemma regarding the optimum utilization of knowledge. Although many difficulties must be resolved, I believe that helping students to understand knowledge construction and meaningful learning shows promise. Explicit instruction on the interplay between thinking and feeling should also be of value. But how do we attract the brightest minds to the desperate needs of education? This question has no easy answer. It is my hope that this volume can lead to a great step forward.

Notes

1. Gowin, D. Bob. 1981. *Educating;* Gowin, D. Bob. 1970. "The Structure of Knowledge." *Educational Theory,* Vol. 20, Fall, 1970, No. 4.

2. Toulmin, Stephen. 1972. *Human Understanding.* Vol 1: *The Collective Use and Evolution of Concepts.*

3. Ausubel, D. P. 1963. *The Psychology of Meaningful Verbal Learning;* Ausubel, D. P. 1968. *Educational Psychology: A Cognitive View.*

4. Ausubel, D. P.; J. D. Novak; and H. Hanesian. 1978. *Educational Psychology: A Cognitive View.*

5. Propositions are two or more concepts linked semantically to indicate some specific relationship between component concepts, e.g., sons are male offspring. Cognitive structure is the total available set of propositional meanings an individual has; even for young children this is an exceedingly large number.

6. Polanyi, Michael. 1956. "Passion and Controversy in Science."

7. Bogden, Christopher A. 1977. "The Use of Concept Mapping as a Possible Strategy for Instructional Design and Evaluation in College Genetics"; Moreira,

Marco. 1977. "An Ausubelian Approach to Physics Instruction: An Experiment in Introductory College Course in Electromagnetism"; Stewart, James; Judith VanKirk; and Richard Rowell. 1979. "Concept Maps: A Tool for Use in Biology Teaching"; Novak, Joseph D. 1981. "Applying Learning Psychology and Philosophy of Science to Biology Teaching"; Novak, Joseph D., and staff. 1981. *Teachers Handbook for the Learning How To Learn Program.*

8. Ausubel, D. P. 1968. Op. cit.; Ausubel, D. P.; J. D. Novak; and H. Hanesian. 1978. Op. cit.

9. Nussbaum, Joseph, and Shimson, Novick. "Creating Cognitive Dissonance Between Student's Preconceptions to Encourage Individual Cognitive Accommodations and a Group Cooperative Construction of a Scientific Model."

10. Pearson, Karl. 1900. *The Grammar of Science*, pp. 87, 110, and 181.

11. Novak, Joseph D., and staff. 1981. "The Use of Concept Mapping and Gowin's "V" Mapping Instructional Strategies in Junior High School Science."

12. Buchweitz, Bernardo. 1981. "An Epistemological Analysis of Curriculum and an Assessment of Concept Learning In Physics Laboratory"; Levandowski, Carlos E. 1981. "Epistemology of a Physics Laboratory on Electricity and Magnetism"; Gurley, 'Laine. "The Use of Concept Mapping and Vee Mapping Strategies in High School Biology."

13. Novak and staff. 1981. "The Use of Concept Mapping."

Bibliography

Ausubel, D. P. 1968. *Educational Psychology: A Cognitive View*. New York: Holt, Rinehart, and Winston.

Ausubel, D. 1963. *The Psychology of Meaningful Verbal Learning*. New York: Grune and Stratton.

Ausubel, D. P.; J. D. Novak; and H. Hanesian. 1978. *Educational Psychology: A Cognitive View*. (2nd edition.) New York: Holt, Rinehart, and Winston.

Bogden, Christopher A. 1977. "The Use of Concept Mapping as a Possible Strategy for Instructional Design and Evaluation in College Genetics." M.S. Thesis, Cornell University.

Buchweitz, Bernardo. 1981. "An Epistemological Analysis of Curriculum and an Assessment of Concept Learning In Physics Laboratory." Ph.D. Thesis, Cornell University.

Gowin, D. Bob. 1981. *Educating*. Ithaca, New York: Cornell University Press.

Gowin, D. Bob. 1970. "The Structure of Knowledge." *Educational Theory* 20, no. 4 (Fall 1970) pp. 319–328.

Gurley, 'Laine. "The Use of Concept Mapping and Vee Mapping Strategies in High School Biology." Ph.D. Thesis, Cornell University (in preparation).

Holt, John. 1964. *How Children Fail*. New York: Pitman Publishing Corporation.

Levandowski, Carlos E. 1981. "Epistemology of a Physics Laboratory on Electricity and Magnetism." Ph.D. Thesis, Cornell University.

Moreira, Marco. 1977. "An Ausubelian Approach to Physics Instruction: An Experiment in Introductory College Course in Electromagnetism." Ph.D. Thesis, Cornell University.

Novak, Joseph D. 1981. "Applying Learning Psychology and Philosophy of Science to Biology Teaching." *The American Biology Teacher* 43, no. 1 (January): 12–20.

Novak, Joseph D. 1977. *A Theory of Education.* Ithaca, New York: Cornell University Press.

Novak, Joseph D., and staff. 1981. *Teachers Handbook for the Learning How To Learn Program.* Ithaca, New York: Cornell University.

Novak, Joseph D., and staff. 1981. "The Use of Concept Mapping and Gowin's "V" Mapping Instructional Strategies in Junior High School Science." Ithaca, New York: Cornell University.

Nussbaum, Joseph, and Shimshon, Novick. "Creating Cognitive Dissonance Between Student's Preconceptions to Encourage Individual Cognitive Accommodations and a Group Cooperative Construction of a Scientific Model." *Science Education* (in press).

Pearson, Karl. 1900. *The Grammar of Science.* (2nd edition.) London: Adam and Charles Black.

Polanyi, Michael. 1956. "Passion and Controversy in Science." *The Lancet* 270 (June 16, 1956): 921–925.

Rowell, Richard. 1978. "Concept Mapping: Evaluation of Children's Social Concepts Following Audio-Tutorial Instruction." Ph.D. thesis, Cornell University.

Stewart, James; Judith VanKirk; and Richard Rowell. 1979. "Concept Maps: A Tool for Use in Biology Teaching." *The American Biology Teacher* 41, no. 3: 171–175.

Toulmin, Stephen. 1972. *Human Understanding.* Vol 1: *The Collective Use and Evolution of Concepts.* Princeton, New Jersey: Princeton University Press.

ALBERT L. AYARS

10
Strategies in Transmitting Knowledge in the School System

Purpose and Definitions

Not all knowledge needed for successful learning experiences finds its way to teachers and students. Few possess the knowledge needed to comprehend the world's cumulative advance in knowledge, the meaning and consequence of our complex human relationships, and ways to tap their own resources of vision and creativity. Few of us have the knowledge for understanding and coping with a future that remains largely unknown. This poses the challenge of (1) pinpointing reasons for the blockages in knowledge transmission and application, (2) identifying exceptions to such stifling conditions, and (3) making suggestions as to ways knowledge can and does flow into the schools.

Since the topic is "knowledge," let's define the concept. My definition includes (1) facts, truths, principles, and values, and (2) practical understandings and skills in anything. Schools must be concerned with both kinds of knowledge and with favorable learning conditions. We recognize also the need for a better understanding of the nature of knowledge and how we come to possess and use it. Advances are being made on these fronts. We can all agree that knowledge is important, that it is useful to gain and spread more knowledge to inform our choices or reform our environments. These are sufficient reasons for making knowledge the stock in trade of public education.

Knowledge is unique to each individual and comes from directly experiencing one's environment. Knowledge is employed by the individual to help each adapt to and work out a continuing relevance to a changing environment. A given content item of knowledge has enduring value when students can place it within the context and perspective of their existing knowledge, their own "personhood," and can use it in helping fit into their environment. One of the main tasks of both teacher and students is to organize accumulated knowledge so that additions relate to possessed knowledge, take on relevance, and can be applied with practicality or creativity or satisfaction. Knowledge gleaned today for its own sake may support good judgment or lead to discovery or invention tomorrow.

The Scope of Knowledge to Be Incorporated into American Public School Curriculum

The problems of the intelligence-gathering function of education are changing and will change even more abruptly during the years ahead. In the past, the problem has been gaining knowledge. The knowledge explosion and modern technology have created a different difficulty. Enormous volumes of knowledge have engulfed us. During the past twenty years man has acquired more scientific information than in all previous history. Enough new information to fill a twenty-four-volume encyclopedia is added to the world's libraries every forty minutes. The challenge is to analyze, process, make sense out of, and use it. We face a staggering task.[1]

Educators must weigh carefully the ramifications of the fact that people learn very complex kinds and combinations of knowledge through informal experiences and relationships. The street-wise ghetto youth and the work-wise farm lad are familiar examples. Only a fraction of a person's total knowledge was formally systematized and transmitted.

We should be concerned with whether the school's mechanisms for transmitting formal knowledge may in some contexts inhibit effective utilization and transfer of informal knowledge from one situation to another. It is equally important to detect the individual's gaps in informal knowledge and in sensing how different kinds of knowledge fit together.

The educational task is made more clear and challenging when a teacher is able to determine what of the child's informal knowledge is an impediment rather than a resource and what knowledge is rooted in socially negative values.

Informal knowledge is the base on which more formal types must build. Benefits may be derived from finding informal ways to transmit knowledge previously systematized and formalized. Moral, spiritual, and social values and concepts, along with informal and practical knowledge, may be gleaned through informal activities and relationships fostered by the schools. The work ethic, active concern for the economically deprived, and occupational skills are examples of kinds of learning the student may glean informally from the school, neighborhood, and community. The need for an enlarged learning environment is obvious.

Classroom curricula should not remain one of the culprits hindering the optimum utilization of knowledge. To overcome such stigma requires, as Lawrence Senesh and others have shown, more analytical depth in the learning experience in science, economics, and other fields. Children understand complex adult concepts and societal values when these values are related to their daily experiences. The concepts of risk, price, profit, and competition can easily be related to the transactions of the familiar grocery store. That the bank is an instrument of capital formation and not just a safekeeping place for money is not beyond the understanding of an elementary school child.

To base curriculum practices on minimum understandings blights the potential of our students and creates a society open to exploitation in its ignorance. The challenge is to close the knowledge gap between the general population and frontier thinkers in science, technology, and the social sciences. Even if humanity's problems aren't all caused by a lack of knowledge, their solutions must come from knowledge.

To perform the function assigned them, the schools emphasize learning to develop wholesome interpersonal relationships; respect for and the tools of continuous, lifelong learning; an effective value system; vocational and academic skills; challenging expectation levels; and communications, computation, and citizenship skills. It's a big order. Schools are the testing and training grounds where students learn to function in society and assume the duties of citizenship.

Kinds of Obstacles and Problems

Admittedly there are some obstacles to the transmittal of knowledge, which give rise to the accusation that our elementary and secondary schools are a "closed system." One is a preoccupation with minimal competencies and "basics" as the primary requisites to graduation. Such preoccupation may preclude concentrating attention on the whole curriculum; the pursuit of special interests, experimentation, discovery, and invention; and the development of special talents, skills, and literacy in the broadest sense.[2] It can cause achievement scores to rise as the quality of comprehensive education declines. But it is a natural product of a society that emphasizes conformity, certainties, and self-limiting behavior.

There is no doubt that basic competencies are required, but we must use these as the floor. For about 70 percent of the students, the floor is easily installed. Mastering the basics is a fleeting issue with them. The greatest weakness of the basics movement is that it doesn't tell us what to do with this 70 percent. We need to recognize also that what is "basic" changes with the increasing sophistication and complexity of our society and its technology. Whatever the basic skills may be, we should devote systematic attention to elaborating the comprehensive education of those who have mastered them.

There are other factors. One is the tendency of some school systems to "track" students or select, segregate, and cultivate the so-called gifted, bright, creative, and talented students to the exclusion of those considered average. There is little evidence by which to select certain students to lavish attention on in separate special schools or programs.[3] Average children have untold potential for achievement and creativity; their "giftedness" should not be overlooked. Heterogeneous grouping can provide interest- and knowledge-building experiences for all students. There are times when homogeneous groupings are needed and valuable, but we need to know when grouping is useful and when it is inhibiting. Rather than becoming rigidly committed or opposed to grouping, we in education should devote time and energy to learn when students benefit from such grouping and when they don't.

Some schools' attention to the "minimals" and "basics" has pushed science, social science, esthetics, and the arts off center stage of the elementary curriculum.[4] And some high schools, in attempting to hold and interest all students, have provided options, choices, and alternatives to the extent that students are able to evade what they perceive as difficult and boring courses in the sciences, mathematics, and the languages. Students with high motivation continue to take advanced college-preparatory courses, but many students navigate around challenging courses unless provided persuasive guidance.[5]

Public expectations also tend to undercut the academic menu. The schools are asked to feed, inoculate, integrate, and babysit. They are asked to teach driver education, sex education, special education, physical education, marriage education, child care, and values education and still have time for "regular" education.[6]

Also, staff development has come in for the criticism that not enough attention is given to improving subject-matter competence, updating knowledge and skill, and developing intuitive faculties and research resourcefulness. Staff members must also be helped to organize their knowledge and add to it with understanding and meaningfulness. Staff development should not be an add-on but a built-in fixture for staff members.

It is important to note that today's education establishment deals, on a daily basis, with "all the children of all the people." The proportion of youth attending secondary schools jumped from 12 percent in 1900 to about 50 percent by World War II to about 94 percent by the mid-1970s. In earlier days, students who did not succeed academically could still find employment and move ahead in fields requiring little advanced preparation. A relatively select group went on through high school. In today's scientific, technological age, with virtually all jobs requiring education and skill, students with deficiencies are obvious, standing on the corner watching the jobs go by. With the vast cross section of aptitudes and abilities represented by students, schools are expected to do for all what they previously did for a relatively select few. The educational system, despite temporary population changes, will have to deal with even larger numbers in the future. Developing the technical skills that society requires will demand that high percentages of the growing population stay in school for longer periods of time.[7]

Another serious obstacle is the lack, in some schools, of continuity from early childhood programs through grade twelve. Because it is important for the child to relate the knowledge gained by instruction, experience, observation, play, listening, experimenting, feeling, and in other ways, the teacher must have the know-how and alertness to help the child link formal and informal knowledge and knowledge gained in different disciplinary contexts. A planned progression in instructional content and method is important to the child's relating new information, ideas, and experiences with increasing analytical depth and complexity. A part of such planning should be the reintroduction of important concepts in succeeding years with increasing depth.

The fragmentation of knowledge poses another problem. Effective education requires bridging the gaps between various disciplines and exploring their interconnections and ramifications. Value analysis is essential. Teaching subject matter without considering values involved deters the student's judgmental development and ability to make knowledge operational. It is a job of the schools to discuss the social consequences of advancements made or advocated and possible problems and ethical implications. We don't do enough of this.

Formal education also tends to be isolated from the community and the rest of the world. Segregating young people obstructs the natural flow of informal and folk knowledge from one generation to another. This fact poses another argument for expanding the classroom into the community.

There is considerable evidence that the quality of teaching and the achievements of students of like abilities have improved.[8] But that is not enough to meet today's needs, where even the reluctant, slow, and not academically inclined student must be helped to learn. The problem in American education is not that education itself has deteriorated.

Rather, the adverse consequences of deficient education have expanded. Sophisticated machines will replace the semiskilled worker as the unskilled worker was replaced by general industrialization. Current vocational education skills such as metalworking and welding will likely be outmoded within two decades. We need to get ready for the emerging shift in employment patterns. We must prepare to cope with the trauma of shifts to be made.

Everybody must be equipped with survival skills. Emphasis on the basics *is* a priority task, but we cannot permit that emphasis to upstage our responsibility to creative thinking and sophisticated knowledge that can contribute to the advancement of society. Nor can we forget that our list of basic skills needs constant updating.

Introduction of Strategies

I will not lay out a panacea for all of education's problems. Rather, I will outline a few strategies that have worked and some that hold promise for bringing knowledge into the school. They are not revolutionary—only worth recommending even though current worldwide challenges may call for a profound restructuring of education. I'm aware also of the frustrations of piecemeal innovations and their history of volatility.

Assuring a Strong Instructional Framework for the Transmission of Knowledge

It is important to keep the teaching staff alert to the positive effects of high expectations. The students who feel the teacher cares, expects them to learn, and is confident of their ability to do so, usually do learn. Setting high expectations for teachers and students pays off.

Learning occurs best when:

- It is goal oriented; it serves a purpose
- Students desire to remember what is learned; it relates to their lives
- Students participate in the learning process, goal setting, and choice of materials and activities
- New material relates to previous learning
- Students are aware of their progress
- New knowledge is repeated or practiced in meaningful situations
- Students use different senses
- Students learn by doing

Teachers consistently helping children relate classroom learning to their own experiences should be encouraged. Linking formal and informal learning provides momentum for learning.

Retraining Principals and Supervisors

Convincing research shows the most crucial actor in the educational system is the principal, with more influence on student achievement and the general climate of education than anyone else. With the same staff and resources but a different principal, the results are different. It is vital to give more time and attention to the role of the principal and how he or she functions, since improving the principal's skills will affect the teaching-learning process.

That process involves both the teachers' preparation and the relationship of the teacher and the student. Pupil receptivity, enthusiasm, and motivation are stimulated through the art of teaching. There is a creative, sensitive, almost intuitive element of the teacher able to respond to and unite the student with the subject. This highly individualized characteristic of good teaching should hold a featured spot on our mental list of ways to transmit knowledge.

But teaching skill is not inborn; it can be learned. Talent can be elicited, developed, and made more effective. The sustained growth of knowledge of subject matter and teaching method is best achieved in an orderly fashion, with incentives provided for teachers to participate in staff development programs. Careful analysis of teaching, learning, and observing pupil growth and change have added to our knowledge of effective ways to assist learning. Advancing the art and science of teaching depends on transmitting this knowledge. The school system has a responsibility to provide staff development opportunities, and the principal should take the lead.

Learning style variations among students are infinite. Some learn best by listening, some by discussion, some by reading, and some by working on their own. Matching teaching and learning styles is important.[9] Helping teachers master the components of thinking skills has also become a priority objective.[10] Likewise, finding effective ways to organize content to make it more meaningful and easier to learn is an important educational concern.[11]

Recent research indicates that students differ much more in the *rate* at which they learn than in their basic capacity to learn. The studies show that 90 percent of students can learn up to the levels previously achieved by only the top 10 percent, with motivation and time. What we have termed *individual differences in school learning* may be largely the effect of school conditions rather than basic differences in students' capabilities.

Four years ago, the Norfolk, Virginia, public schools implemented a system to retrain principals and supervisors in effective strategies for instructional supervision. Based on the work of educational researchers Benjamin Bloom, Barak Rosenshine, Madeline Hunter, and others, the model combines a scientific approach to teaching with the "artistry" of teaching—both factors being critical to success. Additional emphasis is given to observation and conference techniques.[12]

The Norfolk public schools department of staff development trained all administrators and supervisors directly involved in the instruction process, including the superintendent and his immediate staff, all principals, assistant principals, and department chairmen. Since, in Norfolk, instructional leadership is greatly emphasized, principals were responsible for orienting their faculties to the process.

Administrators and supervisors were taught skills in analyzing the process of teaching. This involved observing classes, compiling an anecdotal record of what actually occurred in the classroom, and conducting an effective conference with the teacher observed. On the basis of this information, the principals conduct in-service sessions in their schools to promote continuous professional growth for the teachers.

Two-year evaluation results indicate marked achievement gains of students and continued support from principals. As well, the Norfolk model has been recognized nationally, and school divisions from across the United States and Canada have contracted with Norfolk school administrators to train their personnel in the use of this model.

Upgrading School Environment and Staff

Success in assuring teacher competence generally is accompanied by a conscious administrative effort to provide a creative environment and to forge close links between school and community. Demonstrations by master teachers, the use of innovative teaching teams, and exhibitions in schools and in the community help to keep communication channels open.

Elements shared by successful schools generally are a principal with an effective leadership style, an emphasis on staff development, lower student-teacher ratios, emphasis on basic skills, funding for instructional support, and parental involvement.[13]

The effort to improve schools includes finding ways to help teachers contend more successfully with the tremendous demands of today's classrooms, which include:

1. keeping abreast of the outcomes and impact of the communications revolution and instantaneous worldwide contacts, using new communications technologies and competing with them for students' interests and attention;
2. becoming familiar with other new technologies, such as robotics and automation, that are transforming society and may displace half the work force in twenty years;[14]
3. confronting and digesting changes required by completely new, revolutionary scientific understandings;
4. holding in school millions of youth who would have dropped out in earlier decades;
5. dealing with concerns about equality of the sexes and building educational strength on racial and ethnic diversity;
6. coping constructively with outcomes of the civil rights revolution, freedom of expression, demands of due process, affirmative action, and lack of consensus on values;
7. teaching the handicapped in regular and in special classes;
8. adjusting to and reacting constructively to the changes in U.S. life-style, permissiveness, self-image, and attitudes toward traditional institutions;
9. staying up to date on the manifold growth and changes in the knowledge of and thought about every subject taught and learned in the schools; and
10. meeting the educational needs resulting from the growth of specialized knowledge and interest and encouraging students to access educational resources of the community.

Handling Conflict: A Learning Model

The schools are the constant targets of pressure groups with a variety of causes: the Moral Majority, the Right to Life groups, ethnic groups, the back-to-basics people, the environmentalists, the sex education proponents and opponents, the peace advocates, the pro–arms race people, and many others.

Once school policy is established and administrative procedures and regulations set to carry out policy, the administration should be able to deal with special-interest groups. Teachers must be free to teach, within the context of existing policy and regulations. Making this policy known and implementing it is an important strategy in handling conflict.

Authority implies an unequal set of responsibilities, roles, and privileges. Status, the visible aspect of authority and power, generates conflicts in every institution, including the school system. As individuals acquire more status, and as they become more visible, the separation between them and coworkers increases and the potential for conflict increases.

Conflict management is an art that can be learned. The skills, tactics, and strategies effective in managing various types of conflicts can be identified and used effectively. They include listening, observing, conceptualizing, paraphrasing, giving positive and negative feedback, understanding nonverbal behaviors, taking risks, demonstrating flexibility, being authentic, caring, withholding judgment, accepting, being self-disclosing, being self-understanding, communicating effectively, acquiring a sense of timing, and responding creatively. These skills, tactics, and strategies facilitate the kind of human interactions that lead to adjustment, accommodation, understanding, and either acceptance or rejection of differences and similarities that lie at the heart of much conflict. These skills provide the means for identifying the roots of a conflict. They help ascertain acceptable courses of action for ameliorating or sustaining the conflict as needed and for developing a climate within which the agreed-upon course of action can take place and in which knowledge can be transmitted or possessed.

If school administration, staff, and teachers employ these skills they transmit a model of conflict management to the students. The students can then garner these skills from the model and use them in their own human relations. Their success in handling conflict will stimulate their initiative and motivate learning as they become more and more aware of the possibilities for managing conflicts peaceably. When external conflicts are manageable, internal conflicts can be similarly approached, adapting the same learned tools, thereby expanding further individual growth.

Broadening the Concept of Staff and Freeing Teachers to Teach

We need to broaden our view of who has responsibility for education and who can be of help in keeping our educational program current and effective. Some school systems are breaking down the barriers between school and community. The schools are gaining access to the private sector in many ways. Staff members from banks, accounting firms, law offices, retail establishments, media operations, hospitals, and manufacturing plants can and do contribute to the cause. The use in schools of part-time staff members from the community becomes increasingly practical as greater specialization develops in society and in student interests and demands.

It takes extended community effort to break down the artificial barriers among "educational" institutions such as schools, libraries, museums, zoos, planetariums, colleges, and other repositories of special information.[15]

Improvements can come rapidly if staff members of each school are led to consider:

1. what requirements of the school system tend to impede teaching and learning;
2. how to meet each teacher's *needs* for greater knowledge of subject matter and improved teaching techniques;
3. how to improve released time arrangements for staff development;
4. how best to keep people of the community informed of school objectives, programs, and accomplishments and to secure suggestions and advice of community people, thus building understanding and decreasing estrangement;
5. how to strengthen available services of the school system for improving the individual school;
6. how to use current resources and what additional resources are needed;
7. how to draw on the community to strengthen what is done for students;
8. how best to tap the special skills, talents, and knowledge of staff members and community people;
9. how to involve students in learning through active participation in community affairs and pursuits;
10. how teachers convey to students a great sense of commitment, excitement, and involvement with subject matter; and
11. how educators can develop in students interest in learning and "learning to learn," including skills in the use of libraries and in independent learning from books and "real" situations.[16]

Giving serious cooperative thought to these matters can be the first step in the process of involving teachers in the cause of more successful teaching and learning. The process can also play a major role in bolstering sagging public confidence and support for public schools.

Establishing Productive Human Relations

The school system must emphasize human relations in its teaching and in its staff-student-community relationships. Harmonious interactions among students, between teachers and students, and among members of different racial and socioeconomic groups must be a major concern of school systems. Breaking down barriers and establishing true integration are vital to sharing experiences, resources, and ideas. One of the greatest problems of our society has been the isolation of groups with the resultant harvest of distrust, fear, ignorance, and lack of concern.[17]

Parent programs should provide for conferences to encourage and train parents to become involved in school activities and in assisting their children in learning activities.[18] There is also a vital need for active and continuing student involvement in leadership programs and open discussion and for attention to student concerns, with provisions for sharing feelings, information, and concepts. Student participation in student government and due process and students' feedback and reaction to school programs and operations are essential ingredients of a climate conducive to the transmission of knowledge.

At the high school level, substantial student dropout rates continue— about 23 percent overall, higher among black and Hispanic youth.[19] The human relations climate is of special significance in inner-city school systems challenged to educate a high percentage of young people with economic, cultural, physical, and mental handicaps.

It is important that school personnel be sensitized to and preoccupied with human relations. This involves putting the students first, concentrating more on their needs than on the school system's convenience or tradition, encouraging individual participation to the extent of the capabilities and expectations of all students. High expectation, the affirmation of individual importance, a general "inviting in" attitude, and emphasis on the desirability of diversity and options go hand in hand with the teacher's acceptance of the role of adviser, consultant, mentor or tutor, and facilitator rather than lecturer and quiz giver.

Many strategies, or combinations of them, have contributed to the improvement of human relations in school systems. The Norfolk schools began with a top-down approach, placing high-level administrators in charge of human relations, making them responsible for developing workshops on intercultural relations and conflict resolution and addressing conflicts between racial and age groups for students, parents, and community people.

A student ombudsman assumed responsibility for occupational counseling, helping students identify their own life goals and encouraging their involvement in a variety of activities from the traditional extracurricular ones to competitive academic high school "bowls."

Black ministers took the leadership in developing a community program to help the schools meet the challenge of a new minimum competency law. The school district provided the materials and tutor-trainers, while the ministers and their churches determined how to distribute them effectively. The result: no student has been denied a diploma for failing competency tests, and as many as 97 percent have passed the test the first time. Before the new program began, only 60 percent of the black students and 80 percent of the white students had passed the test. While the black ministerial association took the lead for the program, it ultimately involved thousands of students—and tutors—of both races.

A number of mechanisms channel creative ideas from the rank and file to the top administration in the school system. These include a "professional senate" with members elected from each school building, a superintendent's council, and a student senate. In addition, the superintendent informally visits schools, sitting in the library to talk casually with teachers and students. The underlying philosophy is that the strength of public education is in its diversity.

School activities stress this diversity: there is a district-wide drama program so well regarded that professional directors volunteer their guidance, a school camp that offers overnight outdoor experiences, and a program to teach every fourth grader in the system how to swim.

A clear, concise system of developing goals for the entire district spells out the teaching approaches and goals. The school system has already met one goal: making certain every kid is either qualified to go to college or ready to go to work. This choice is one each student makes, but the schools make certain there are no nonreversible decisions as the student moves through the system.

Using Community Resources in Teaching:
Enlarging the Learning Environment

Every school has around it a veritable fountain of knowledge available to administrators and teachers who tap the resources available.[20] People knowledgeable in many fields are available as speakers and consultants in classes and on field trips for classes and teacher groups.

Many school systems utilize businesses, offices, shops, factories, laboratories, and organizations for job and career exploration and on-the-job training or for first-hand subject matter to supplement classroom theory.[21] Such community usage, however, need not be limited to vocational areas. In Norfolk public schools, we provide secondary students the opportunity to learn, perform, and work at the elbows of professionals in the local medical school, opera, symphony, ballet, radio and television stations, newspapers, the National Aeronautics and Space Administration, museums, law and accounting offices, jazz and modern dance groups, and the legitimate theater as well as to study with individual artists and musicians. These extensions of the schools are available inexpensively, with the school system providing the contacts, liaison, coordination, and some student transportation. Our arts and sciences program currently enlists nearly three thousand secondary students out of a total K-12 student body of under fifty thousand, who receive knowledge, experience, and talent and skill development at levels unachievable through the resources of the schools alone. These students are in addition to about one thousand junior and senior high students involved in vocational work study and work experience programs of various types.

During recent years, we've heard a great deal about how the shortage of technically skilled workers in the United States has reached critical proportions. Industry cries out for "high-tech" technicians, and the educational system has not produced enough for them. One reason for the lack of technically skilled labor is the historical stigma placed on vocational and technical education.

More and more of the jobs available require postsecondary training of some kind; within ten years the figure may be 80 percent. An effort is being extended to change attitudes. Also, the fear of unemployment after graduation is causing more high school students to consider technical schools as alternatives to college or university training.

Secondary school educators have a major job showing students the importance of technical jobs and providing the great knowledge and skill needed to carry them out successfully. Cooperative education programs that combine study with learning experiences and improved communication between business and industry can ease the problem. Advanced placement offerings in academic science, computer use, engineering drawing, electronics, creative design, and related fields also contribute.

In Houston, a magnet high school for the engineering professions has strong drawing power. Open to students from all over the city, this school attracts a diversity of students. All the graduates thus far have gone to college. Many are from minority and low-income families. Several major corporations have provided funds, equipment, technical expertise, and subject-matter knowledge. Experts from industry advise regarding curriculum changes and equipment purchases. Working engineers assist teachers and students with projects. College recruiters stand in line to offer scholarships. Academically talented ninth and tenth graders are recruited from all parts of the city.

There are, in every community, people who, with invitation and encouragement, will become involved in planning, implementing, and evaluating school programs. In Norfolk, a city of some three hundred thousand people, we have over eleven thousand unpaid volunteers working in our schools, helping to prepare teaching materials, acting as tutors, and assisting in the offices and lunchrooms, on the playfields, and on bus loading docks. Another two thousand are involved on advisory committees. Such resources are invaluable. They contribute to knowledge, skill, and learning while strengthening public interest and support.

Many of the resources used directly in the education of children are also resources for teacher training and upgrading. Teachers can gain from taking advantage of the resources of industrial and business shops and laboratories, science and art museums, planetariums, aquariums, workshops, lectures, demonstrations, and exhibits available on myriad subjects—from art techniques to space science to sensory perception to environmental improvement to anthropological exploration to the processes of light and sound and seeing and hearing. Teachers glean much that can be applied in their classrooms, in terms of both subject-matter knowledge and teaching principle and technique.

Colleges and universities offer resources of great value.[22] In our own instance, a local university with a special strength in urban education has cooperated by providing a pilot urban education center in unused classrooms of a high school building. Personnel act as student advisers, run workshops and seminars for teachers, introduce teachers to a variety of teaching materials, help test commercial materials and make new teaching aids, introduce teachers to community resources, help teachers reorganize teaching patterns to accommodate diverse student groups, advise on instructional activities, and provide a forum for the exchange of ideas and experiences. The program has been evaluated by participating teachers as outstandingly helpful.

The teacher center idea is, of course, a tested one with a record of success in many communities.[23] These centers have often been established through the cooperation of school systems, teacher organizations, and local universities with financial help under the Education Amendments of 1976. The Ford Foundation has also assisted in establishing and operating teacher centers[24] that provide opportunities for teachers to work together on common classroom problems and for teachers to create materials and experiment with instructional approaches.

Another device to improve knowledge dissemination is using experienced teachers specially trained as advisers to colleagues in the classroom. This idea has been applied extensively in Britain, and the Ford Foundation has helped to develop such programs in the United States.[25] It is psychologically preferable to similar school-system programs, whose value is often undermined by teachers' perception that they may be connected with evaluations and ratings. Advisers and consultants not imposed on anyone or looked upon as part of the administrative hierarchy are less suspect. The City University of New York and the University of Massachusetts (Boston) Institute of Learning and Teaching have been leaders in training teachers to become advisers.

Again, the Ford Foundation has helped to support pioneering efforts in this approach.[26]

Quite a number of school systems have developed programs through which businesses, industries, institutions, and organizations "adopt" individual schools. The "adopters" serve many useful purposes, fostering community support and stimulating learning through a variety of incentives. They are also sources of learning experiences in the classrooms and in the offices, shops, plants, and laboratories.

In Norfolk, the Chamber of Commerce helped organize the adopt-a-school program and to see that no school remained an "orphan." Key figures in the adopt-a-school programs are the adopting agencies' liaison designees. These people are invaluable in enlisting the resources of their institutions that can be of the most value in encouraging curiosity and discovery, awakening interest in learning, revealing sources of knowledge, and opening new and different approaches to teaching and learning.

Using Modern Technology

The educational system has to prepare to cope with increased amounts of information. The explosion of knowledge in almost all fields of human endeavor requires new ways to collect, process, store, and disseminate mountains of information.[27] Technological advances have multiplied spectacularly our capacity for conveying and accumulating knowledge and information. The computer in its various applications and forms, radio, television, sound and picture recording devices, and electronic instruments provide ways of transmitting and storing knowledge not dreamed of by most people a few decades ago.[28] The accumulated knowledge of the generations, as revealed through research, experimentation, discovery, and demonstration, is auditorially and visually at the command of each teacher. Microcomputers available to the individual student provide engaging and developmental learning in mathematics, reading, the social sciences, grammar, the hard sciences, and other disciplines into which programming capabilities can lead. The microcomputer makes possible an information revolution of the magnitude of the industrial revolution that enhanced people's ability to do physical labor.[29]

The technological devices for communicating knowledge, linked with work-doing devices stemming from robotics—all of which will likely be broadly applied in the twenty-first century—pose a real challenge for back-to-basics thinking. Computer skills, keyboard skills, ability to work with statistics, and skills relating to the quality of life may become the basic skills of the decades ahead.

Providing background for students to avoid being frightened and mystified by technology is another challenge. There are many macro-issues to be sorted out and understood, including the specter of nuclear confrontation, concerns for the environment, and water and energy problems.

Far-reaching implications of scientific experimentation that is now under way are bound to have a profound influence on the structure and configuration of schooling in the future. We cannot afford to disregard them. One example is left brain–right brain research and the kinds of learning related to left and right brain functions. The left brain apparently deals with cognitive matters, analysis, and understanding what *is* and the right brain with innovation, sensing, and dreaming up. The development of both is needed in coping with the present and inventing the future. There is some evidence indicating that the right-brain skills of pattern recognition, esthetics, and creativity, vital to many kinds of information and knowledge acquisition, may actually be inhibited by current educational practices.[30]

However the basic skills may be defined at any given time, they are only part of the educational program. And we must continue to devote our attention to the comprehensive education of those who have mastered the basic skills. We cannot omit this consideration from our fundamental strategy.

The complexities of the skills required in the United States and other highly developed nations mean that we can no longer assume that secondary and advanced education is for the few. The development of a complex society demands effective mastery of skills gained through advanced education.[31] Modern technology can be helpful in the task.

Student Exchange and Travel Programs:
Including the World in the Learning Environment

Concurrent with technological advance have come enhanced opportunities for students to increase their knowledge through a variety of travel and exchange programs. Little need be said for the obvious value of combining planned educational experiences and a sense of purpose with entertainment, excitement, and adventure. A planned experiencing of the history, nostalgia, customs, cultures, languages, traditions, arts, crafts, climate, economy, science, technologies, and aspirations of other countries can turn learning into a special, insightful event of lasting impression and value. Both teachers and students can be recipients and beneficiaries.

Imaginative educators may enlarge the learning environment to include the world. Advancements in travel and communications make the most remote areas of the world virtual next-door neighbors.

Stressing Knowledge for a Better Future

Part of an educator's responsibility is evaluating changes in the world and projecting them into the future to provide students with the background for adjusting to rapid social changes and coping with the emerging unknown. One way the Norfolk schools have dealt with this responsibility is to integrate the latest technology into the classroom, making certain students will be familiar with it, not intimidated by it. Our program includes computer-assisted education, microcomputers in the classroom, and a planned school-by-school link to a central computer. In addition, a school channel on cable television and a tie-in with a public TV station allow two-way broadcasting in the schools. The district is now exploring laser disks as another means of hooking into available knowledge and the technologies for accessing it.

Optimists assume there will be no Armageddon and that there will be societies with national identification and independence . . . and the need for extended uses of foreign languages. Solving society's scientific and technical problems will require creativity. Education must recognize that both the direction of technology and sagging productivity imply the need for employing brain instead of muscle power and language and communication over physical skills. In so many ways, the future depends on the leadership taken in education.

The Current Situation

I have alluded to the sagging public confidence in the schools. The crisis in confidence applies most crucially to the core cities, which have suffered from an outflow of industry, leadership, and middle-class population and a shrinking tax base while taking on increasing responsibility in educating children with physical, mental, emotional, economic, and cultural handicaps and deprivation. The public has been disappointed that public school graduates don't measure up to the more select clientele of private schools.

A close look at the record reveals some positive achievements. Many city school systems have, over the past half-decade, brought basic student achievement levels up to or near national norms. A high percentage of high school graduates possess job entry skills and/or qualifications for entering postsecondary education. City school systems have extended a valiant effort to cope with the educational needs of the unprecedented influx of non-English-speaking refugee children.

There is still much justifiable concern about the future of public education in the United States. The challenges emerging from this country's social revolution of the past thirty years have been knee-buckling to our educational system.

There are those, such as Mortimer J. Adler through the Paideia Project, who contend that the force of history and events, particularly in complex cities, is such that a transformation of the educational system is required. We are admittedly in a period of flux, but it is difficult for me to envision the timing of such a transformation or the accumulation of the critical mass that would require it to happen. The schools are bombarded with so many different influences from so many different sources that the required fervency to move in one transforming direction is not likely to arise. It is yet to be seen whether the theory of dissipative structures will hold sway. The system will likely continue to incorporate small changes and go on as before. But, after the system becomes saturated, a major transformation may happen.

We have to recognize that changes and improvements must be made. We're in much the position of the Stanford dean of medicine who informed his students, "Half of what you learned in medical school is already known to be false. Unfortunately, we don't know which half."

Changes in education will come. But the public should be assured that the leadership of the schools welcomes change rather than looking on it as threatening to the system.

We have to overcome the paradoxical directives to respect students' individual differences while maintaining uniform standards and developing specified skills in all—the opposing pressures of uniformity and diversity.[32]

The future is not stable or accurately predictable. The increasing pace of change may require that most people prepare for three or four careers in a lifetime. There is no curriculum for everyone. Problem solving, values, and lifelong education have become important areas of school teaching and learning.[33] The schools must go beyond their current accomplishments in educating more people than ever before, in improving reading scores and literacy, and in setting higher standards.[34]

We can change society only if we change education, but society shapes education. It's a situation similar to that of the job seeker who can't get a job without experience and can't get experience without a job. We can't continue to lean on certainties and tradition. We must become a party to speculation, breakthroughs, and active research.[35]

The job can be done. I am confident that it will be, with the reinforcement of public confidence, expectation, and support. Practices such as those described here can help to bring the necessary knowledge into the schools.

Teachers who expect little of the individual child generally get little. Those who expect a lot get a lot. A society that expects little of its schools is likely to experience the same self-fulfilling prophecy. From high expectation and strong support will come high achievement.[36]

Notes

1. John D. Garwood, "The Wrong Premise in General Education," *Intellect,* (October 1973): 43.

2. Samuel Strauss, *The Gifted and Non-Gifted* (Skokie, Ill.: Saturn Press, 1981), pp. 7–11, 156, 157.

3. Ibid., p. 159.

4. June West, "Arts and the Schools, Executive Summary," *New Ways,* Winter 1981: 2.

5. Diane Ravitch, "The Schools We Deserve," *New Republic,* 184 (April 18, 1981): 26.

6. Dennis A. Williams et al., "Why Public Schools Fail," *Newsweek,* 97 (April 20, 1981): 63.

7. David J. Irvine, "Specifications for an Educational System of the Future," *Foundations of Futurology in Education,* ed. Richard W. Hostrop (Palm Springs: ETC Publications, 1973), pp. 75–76.

8. Roger Farr and Leo Fay, *Then and Now: Reading Achievement in Indiana* (1944–45 and 1976) (Indianapolis: Indiana Department of Public Instruction, 1977).

9. David E. Hunt, *Student Learning Styles: Designing and Prescribing Programs* (Reston, Va.: National Association of Secondary School Principals, 1979), pp. 27–38.

10. Leonard Popp, Floyd Robinson, and J. Paul Robinson, *The Basic Thinking Skills* (St. Catherine's, Ontario: Niagara Center, O.I.S.E., July 1974).

11. John B. Carroll, "A Model of School Learning," *Teachers College Record,* 64 (May 1963): 723–733.

12. Benjamin S. Bloom, *All Our Children Learning* (New York: McGraw-Hill Book Company, 1981), p. 18.

13. Cindy Tursman, *Good Schools: What Makes Them Work* (Arlington, Va.: National School Public Relations Association, 1981), p. 10.

14. "The Speedup of Automation," *Business Week,* 2699 (August 3, 1981): 58–67.

15. Irvine, "Specifications for an Educational System," p. 78.

16. Bloom, *All Our Children Learning,* p. 148.

17. Wilbur J. Cohen, "Changing Influences in American Education," *Foundations of Futurology in Education,* ed. Richard W. Hostrop (Palm Springs: ETC Publications, 1973), p. 99; Bloom, *All Our Children Learning,* pp. 147–148.

18. Bloom, *All Our Children Learning,* pp. 26, 89; R. H. Dave, "The Identification and Measurement of Environmental Process Variables That Are Related to Educational Achievement" (Ph.D. dissertation, University of Chicago, Chicago, 1963); K. Marjoribanks, ed., *Environments for Learning* (London: National Foundation for Educational Research Publishing Company, Ltd., 1974); and R. Wolf, "The Measurement of Environments," *Testing Problems in Perspective,* ed. A. Anastasi (Washington, D.C.: American Council on Education, 1966).

19. Carnegie Council on Policy Studies in Higher Education, *Giving Youth a Better Chance* (San Francisco: Jossey-Bass, Inc., 1979), p. 1.

20. Tursman, *Good Schools*, p. 23.

21. Daniel C. Neale, William J. Bailey, and Billy E. Ross, *Strategies for School Improvement* (Boston: Allyn and Bacon, Inc., 1981), p. 158; Alvin Eurich, Harold B. Gores, and Ole Sand, "High School, 1980," *Education . . . beyond tomorrow*, ed. Richard W. Hostrop (Homewood, Ill.: ETC Publications, 1975), p. 35; Michael Marien, "Space-Free/Time-Free Higher Learning: New Programs, New Institutions, and New Questions," *Education . . . beyond tomorrow*, ed. Richard W. Hostrop (Homewood, Ill.: ETC Publications, 1975), pp. 106–107; and Alvin Toffler, "Toffler: Learning to Live With Future Shock," *Foundations of Futurology in Education*, ed. Richard W. Hostrop (Palm Springs: ETC Publications, 1973), pp. 7–8.

22. Neale et al., *Strategies for School Improvement*, pp. 33, 230.

23. Neale et al., *Strategies for School Improvement*, pp. 220–221.

24. Harold Howe II, *Pedagogy for the Chiefs* (New York: Ford Foundation, 1980), p. 17.

25. Ibid., p. 18.

26. Ibid., pp. 18–19.

27. Irvine, "Specifications for an Educational System," p. 79.

28. Ibid., p. 77.

29. S. D. Milner, "Teaching Teachers About Computers: A Necessity for Education," *Phi Delta Kappan*, 61 (April 1980): 544–546.

30. Marilyn Ferguson, *The Aquarian Conspiracy* (Los Angeles: J. P. Tarcher, Inc., 1980), pp. 279–321.

31. Bloom, *All Our Children Learning*, p. 154.

32. Roland Barth, *Run School Run* (Cambridge, Mass.: Harvard University Press, 1980).

33. Arthur W. Combs, "What the Future Demands of Education," *Phi Delta Kappan*, 62 (January 1981): 369–372.

34. Stephen K. Bailey, "What's Right With What's Left of Public Education," *The Council Journal*, 1, no. 2 (January 1981): 1–18.

35. Ferguson, *The Aquarian Conspiracy*, pp. 279–321.

36. Tursman, *Good Schools*, pp. 5–6, 7, 8, 11, 80, 87.

DAVID HAWKINS

———— **11** ————

The Laboratory of
Archimedes

Two uses of knowledge are preeminent in importance, though un-
equally recognized in different times and places and in different societies.
One is using knowledge to gain more knowledge; the other is using
knowledge not only to pass knowledge on but to spread it more widely.
We of the university world have long been committed to a belief in
some vital coupling of these uses. I believe that we can and should
both increase our knowledge of their coupling and extend it more
widely.

Neither of these preeminent uses can be talked about, except thinly,
apart from specific historical contexts. At one extreme we can see a
kind of stationary state in which knowledge is transmitted, without
either much loss or much growth, across many generations. There has
sometimes been a refinement in cultural adaptation, which in accommodating to a constant environment has approached an almost unchanging asymptote, like the long unchanging biological history of the
opossum or even the oyster.

Indeed, most uses of knowledge are not intended for either growth
or spreading. For the most part, such changes have occurred as historical
byproducts, unintended and often unnoticed except in retrospect. As
long as we've been human, we've known about the rudiments of
cookery, clothing, and shelter; about life and death; about the cycles
of the stars, moon, sun, and other planets. We've known something
about young love and the properties of fiber, mud, and fire; about
midwifery and the instruction of the young. Throughout most of this
history the apprentice has acquired what the master knew—whether
midwife, metallurgist, or story-teller—and has been unconscious of or
too timid to acknowledge what his or her fresh discernment contributed

to tradition. In such circumstances the cognitive egg seems only to recreate the maternal chicken that laid it, and we manage to overlook the little increments or decrements that have in fact made history, however slowly. The main uses of knowledge are not to contribute to its own growth or dispersal, but simply to inform our techniques and shape our ends, to maintain the life and keep the law.

For contrast with all such unreflexive uses of knowledge we must examine the histories and contexts of the institutions that have more lately evolved around the uses I have called preeminent. These involve what Karl Pribram called a reversal of ends and means, of context and content.[1] Thus the arts of inquiry transform the practical life into means, with new knowledge as the end. Practice is reshaped, not to provide food and shelter, not for transmission, but to sustain inquiry beyond practical need; to sustain curiosities and explorations and sometimes, as Kant put it, to force nature to answer questions that reason has chosen.

The Reversal of Ends and Means

As a paradigm of this reversal of ends and means I choose the image of the laboratory of Archimedes. Both history and historical gossip give us a list of the tools and equipment that furnished the laboratory of this great mathematician and physicist, things he did indeed use and investigate. The term *laboratory* itself is merely a pleasant fantasy; there was, I imagine, a large workroom in the house of that illustrious man, and I have taken the liberty of equipping it for him. He was at work there one day in 212 B.C., ignoring the capture of his native city, Syracuse, by the Roman Marcellus, when an overzealous soldier ran him through. That story mentions only his sand table, but I shall list the rest of the equipment so you will see that this laboratory miniaturized and internalized the whole practical world of Hellenistic technology and commerce, reducing it, so far as possible, to its essentials—not for production and transport, but for learning.

One of the categories of equipment was simple machines. Thus, Archimedes had the screw, the wedge and inclined plane, the unequal arm balance, and the lever. I have mentioned the sand table, which was partly a graphic device for drawing figures and erasing them, as well as a challenge for enumeration. How many grains to fill a table? To fill the known universe? Surely no question can be more idle than that one. To think about absurdly large numbers is to get nowhere near infinity, which Archimedes had other reasons to think about. But in coping with the problems of notation for large numbers you must grapple with the far more important matter of extending experience and intuition beyond the ordinary everyday ranges of size and scale. There was also in the lab a variety of balances, some, like the steel yard, borrowed from the marketplace. Some were for measuring weight and torque but also for comparing the volumes of cones, cylinders, and spheres. There was a water table—a miniature of the sea—for floating and sinking and, on occasion, for assaying the royal crown. Finally, there were mirrors of polished bronze, plane, concave, and convex. There was an armillary sphere and finally, gossip says, a scaled-down working model of the known planetary universe, which I assume was geared together by small ropes and pulleys. I may even conjecture it was of a heliocentric design, one that had been posited by Archimedes' near-contemporary, Aristarchus of Samos.[2]

The Laboratory Miniaturizes and Transforms

What is critical here, what was new about the laboratory, is not to be defined by any misleading contrast between pure and applied science. The laboratory was a mirror of the practical Hellenistic life of trade and manufacturing. But it was miniaturized, transformed into an instrument of curiosity, no longer only of the common life. That the outcome of such an interest should also ultimately transform the technology it made use of was still only a premonition, as was the further realization that a transformed technology would again transform the patterns of investigation, and so on. For many reasons, that revolution didn't get started in the age of Archimedes. His age gave only a promise of the revolution that we date from the age of Galileo and his contemporary, Stevin of Bruges. But such spirits as these could reach back to Archimedes in only a few moments of retrospective time.

We can extend the image of the laboratory beyond this world of Archimedes and Galileo to include the beginnings of chemistry and of biology; but even so the image must change. From agriculture and medicine and cookery you can indeed import and even miniaturize a lot; that process, following upon and using the fruits of the physical sciences, has transformed our understanding of biological mechanisms and powers. But you can't bring a tropical ecosystem into the laboratory, or much of biohistory, so you must redescribe the lab in another way, as a kind of base camp.

To Archimedes add, then, not only Robert Hooke and Robert Boyle but also Aristotle and Theophrastus, Lyell and Darwin. Though today there are still frontiers for physics, the historical sciences (including cosmogony as background) increasingly dominate the scientific imagination. The greatest prestige used to go with the discoveries of uniformity, of "laws." Now the laws are taken for granted and the sense of excitement goes, increasingly, with reconstructing histories that explain diversity. After a few billion years, this diversity has become so great that we will no longer seek to comprehend it by any system of formulas. Histories are never twice the same, and the aim of science, increasingly, is not to predict things but to enlarge and sharpen our sense of possibility, to understand how all of nature's variety can have come about in the fullness of time.

The Human Sciences

In human affairs, finally—those human affairs beyond the range of our mammalian biology: affairs of persons, of moral agents, and of associations among these—the tableau is far more diverse still. It includes not only the anthropological sciences but the arts and humanities. The diversity of possible human lives and histories is vastly greater than the variety that even biology requires. The search for causal law and irreducible units fails in the face of this human diversity even more than it does in biology. The detailed study of the particular that is typical or exemplary, and also of the particular that stretches our sense of the possible, is close to the heart of the anthropological sciences, as it is to the arts and humanities. The laboratory is now further extended, reaching out to the theater, the atelier, and—most especially—the library.

Through all such extensions, the human sciences have been increasingly caught up in the knowledge revolution; our grasp of the human condition has been vastly enlarged—in its spatiotemporal extent, its adaptation and speciations, and in the stockpiles and flows of our material existence, our ecologies and economies. Like that in every field, new knowledge of human affairs may be more important for the problems it challenges us to become aware of than for those it can solve. One part of the extension of knowledge is to find new phenomena and reduce them to familiarity; another and sometimes more dramatic part is to make phenomena that have been routinely familiar seem strange and problematic. I believe we have nearly achieved this in our perception of the oldest and most familiar process of our existence, that of cultural transmission, of education. And this is where I have been heading, toward the second of my two priorities: the use of knowledge to spread knowledge more widely, and the possibility of its radical improvement.

I wish, more explicitly, to argue that this second priority requires its own reversal of ends and means, a reversal that has hardly yet begun to occur and that we will be unable to nurture and spread without a full panoply of relevant acquaintance and knowledge. A part of that needed knowledge, I shall also argue, will bring us back to the laboratory of Archimedes and its extensions with a fresh perception of its catalytic importance.

Using Knowledge to Spread Knowledge

Let me start, therefore, with what I call the background process of transmission, the spontaneous educational potential resident in any social context at any time. This potential is quite analogous to the gene pool of the species. Robust cultures, like robust species, are internally diverse, and, as with species, this diversity may lead to incipient speciation in which each subspecies becomes part of the ecological niche of the others, related by cooperation or competition, predation, or even warfare.

Cultural evolution is often said to be Lamarckian. Individually acquired characteristics can indeed be transmitted culturally—with luck. The evolutionary formula is still that of variation and selection, but the variation can be learned rather than blindly random, as in the neo-Darwinian account. This difference leads, in part, to the difference in tempo between these two modalities of evolutionary change, a thousand or ten thousandfold. But the Lamarckian account is too glib by far. What intelligence has thought to change has often reappeared unchanged, as though to spite us. Human habit can be stubbornly persistent, a second nature diffusely and unconsciously transmitted, relatively insensitive to conscious learning and choice. And when cultures do change, in part as a result of conscious redirective effort, the outcomes may be radically different from those of changes intended and worked for. Let us, for instance, consider the history of the industrial and scientific revolution and compute for it the high ratio of unintended consequences to those intended. Indeed, it seems safe to say that through all history this ratio has averaged high. Thus benign outcomes are called providential, the result of a natural order, the work of an invisible hand, or in Hegel's words the Cunning of Reason. When the accrual is less happy it is Satanic, the law of the jungle, or Marx's anarchy of production. But in most cases of either kind, outcomes have been poorly foreseen. Kant was a historical optimist who believed in the reality of progress. But he believed this progress stemmed not from any power of intelligence or the moral law but only from a "conspiracy of nature."[3]

In spite of all these qualifications upon the role of intelligence in directing our history, I wish to argue that this role can be greatly increased under certain conditions and through education. Such a belief is not new; it is even quaint, smacking of an optimism no longer easy to voice in our contemporary world. But this old belief becomes more interesting if we commit ourselves seriously to an analysis of the kinds of education that can begin to exercise this transforming influence. I propose to carry this analysis as far as I know or can guess and urge its importance for continued investigation. If I am at all right in this analysis, then the practical tasks of educational reform that it implies are both possible and difficult, unlikely today to be recognized or in any degree adequately supported. If the manners of our time require a convincing show of pessimism, I can easily oblige. Nevertheless, it is easier and more promising to take on the central problems of education than to tackle those of mankind overall. My examination supports the claim of preeminence in the use of knowledge to extend knowledge more widely and aims at understanding the reversal of ends and means this commitment will entail. So my job is to make this utterly familiar process of learning and teaching seem as strange as possible.

Spontaneous Education

The first step is to describe the educative process in its full breadth and power, as involving all the means of culture transmission and cultural innovation, including all its relevant material and human ambience. When so conceived, the study of education is the counterpart, for human history, of population genetics and of adaptation and speciation in biology.

The more spontaneous processes of cultural transmission have long been ignored or have been treated very superficially in the learned world. The vital mother-infant interaction has until recently been ignored or taken for granted—except, of course, by devoted and intellectually curious mothers, always rated low in the academic dominance order, mute and inglorious. Childhood play and culture have also been taken for granted, except when they were deemed idle. Apprenticeship in work has likewise never been adequately investigated. Indeed, most of the attention we have paid to the processes of education has been concentrated on one atypical, narrow, late-stage aspect of it: schooling. But we should never forget the far deeper beginnings and wider context, the spontaneous potentials and processes.

Structured Education

In all the big societies and some of the small ones the spontaneous educational process is inadequate for reproducing special components of the culture. Schooling has therefore evolved as a new division of labor, a formal education to contrast with, though never to do more than supplement, spontaneous education. Prestigious, marked by credentials and class affiliations, schooling has been a minority affair even for the ages of childhood and early youth until recently. Even in Europe and the United States, universal primary and secondary schooling is only five or six generations old; it is still new and problematic. It came into a world that increasingly demanded the sorts of knowledge not transmitted with the mother's milk or through play and work. With formal schooling, we again begin to approach a reversal of content and context, a reversal socially acknowledged and institutionalized. The spread of knowledge is, for the first time, set apart as a separate goal, dissociated from the common life. It creates a system of customs and traditions, a life of its own, its potential still largely unrealized and ignored.

Now, a century away from the beginnings of such institutionalized schooling, we are in a good position to take a long view of it, though a view still conspicuously absent from most of today's debates. I want to lay down two long-view propositions.

Traditional and Historic Assumptions

The first proposition is that the essential style and content of our early schooling have changed very little in the last century, although many breezes (one can hardly say winds) of doctrine have blown over them. As Marx once said, we change the descriptions but not the things described.[4] These essentials are in turn relatively minor adaptations from still older traditions of the schooling intended for the children of the already well educated. Such schooling, linked to a church or ethnic community, often has been powerful in limited contexts and just as often has provided models that, when followed in wider contexts, fail dismally. The cultural background of children of privileged status implies that the spontaneous educational potential, for the three R's and much else, is usually high. Ninety percent of the relevant learning is already in place when these children start school, and the school exists only to do the easy part—its teachers supposing all the time that they do it all. For children from other sorts of backgrounds, for many poor rural or urban children for example, the learning schools typically value and support may be radically inaccessible. But for neither group of children are the schools teaching very much.

Because of this continuity with an older tradition of relatively superficial early education—superficial because presupposing a high spontaneous potential—early-nineteenth-century hopes for achieving universal public education are now largely deprecated. There is, to be sure, a minority tradition in early education that has probed far more deeply and taught more effectively and within which one can still find that early optimism about educational possibilities; but it is an optimism mixed with pessimism—in which I join—that our society will soon understand or seek to realize these possibilities. This minority craft tradition got its first major recognition in the aftermath of the eighteenth-century philosophers and of such practical followers as Friedrich Froebel.

Its best theoretical analysis to date occurs in the writings of John Dewey, and its most concentrated and adequate reduction to practice in recent decades has taken place in some English and Welsh infant and junior schools. I shall return to it.

The Emerging Role of Research

My second long-view proposition is that the invention and increasing institutional expansion of the scientific research traditions have steadily increased the gap between folk cultures and the cultures of the sciences. This gap creates new educational needs that, on the one hand, are rarely satisfied spontaneously but that, on the other hand, our still-dominant school traditions and routines are rarely appropriate to satisfy. We should not blame the present schools for failing to meet these needs, for they were never designed to meet them. Our schools reflect a conception of the aims and means of education that has become increasingly inappropriate to our needs, and thus they are increasingly demoralized and enfeebled.

The Laboratory of Archimedes in Today's Education

It is in light of these two long-view propositions that I now wish to braid together the lines of my argument. This is my thesis: What our early formal education needs is a reconstruction, a central commitment to carry through in children's education the same reversal of ends and means, of context and content, that historically marked the institutionalization of the search for knowledge. The laboratory of Archimedes is genuine enough historically, but I have summoned it up for quite another reason, to serve as an image, no more. As I have sketched it, the extended laboratory of Archimedes is close in style, in spirit, *and even in detailed content* to a good, lively classroom for children in what Froebel was the first to call the kindergarten—the child-garden.

I believe I could trace the evolution of this child-level Archimedes' laboratory, its enrichment through generations of devoted, perceptive teachers, from the time of Froebel and other pioneers. Today, its tradition is strongest for the earliest years of schooling, though it is not negligible for the rest of the first eight or ten. The laboratory has indeed been extended to include the garden, the seashore and mountainside, the studio, and the library; but in some ways the Archimedean component remains central. Life and mind are most fruitfully understood as linking us together in our working relation to the material world.

This laboratory is still properly called a school. In it, the authority and resources of adults are devoted to realizing those learning potentials of children that Karl H. Pribram has called *readiness, competence,* and *transfer.*[5]

Avoiding the Failure of the Past

These terms—*readiness, competence, transfer*—have long been familiar from the textbooks of educational psychology. Using them, therefore, may be dangerous. *Readiness,* for example, is typically discussed only in terms of developmental status and level of subject matter. But it is far more specific and individual than that.

Consider learning to read. Here, readiness is typically and quite erroneously thought of as related mainly to developmental status and level of subject matter. The score on a test will indicate how *ready* a child is—ready to move along at some acceptable rate through some standard reading program. But this notion is grossly inadequate; for any one child there are many roads into reading, standard or nonstandard, in which what Pribram calls the novelty/familiarity ratio will vary enormously, as will the child's corresponding rates of learning.

If children are learning well in the laboratory of Archimedes, diverse roads will be readily available. As investigators, children will have much to tell and to be told, some verbally, some in their own writing, some from books. With ample choices of tempo and mode, they will virtually teach themselves, somewhere along the road, to read and write. For most of them and most of the time, the mechanics of coding and decoding, of which our schooling makes so much, will be of only minor, occasional importance. As a result of misplaced emphasis on these mechanics and of narrowed expectations, we cause most of the reading failure we seek to cure. The failure is, if I may coin a term, *pedagogenic.*

As one examines the diversity and individuality of successful learning patterns, of ways into and around common subject matter, one is led to see that an individual's *readiness* to learn X is not a single measure, high, middle, or low. It is a function of the alternative access routes and differs, often crucially, for each individual. When one examines the nature of these different functions in terms of concrete examples, one sees that all the concepts in the triad—readiness, competence, and transfer—are essentially involved. A child's (or an adult's) readiness to become seriously involved with subject matter can only be characterized as competence. The individual has become, in this context, "resistant to consequences which earlier on would have been discouraging."[6] This condition of competence and confidence can also be described as one of autonomy; when the condition obtains, the teacher is not the sole agent of learning but a coagent. (One of the best treatments of this matter of agency, by a psychologist who was ahead of his time but whom later times have not yet adequately followed, is John Dewey's *Interest and Effort in Education.*) As autonomy increases, the adult authority is not diminished but transformed. The means-end reversal in children's experience creates some common ground that children, however young they are, can share with wise adults. It gives them some essential equality as a basis for testing and assimilating adult authority.

Pribram's third conceptual key to the potential for learning, transfer, is again, I believe, inseparable from the others. Competent learners are using what they have already learned and consolidated in order to extend their experience and to find new order in it. Problems are resolved by finding and reconstructing connections to what is already known. Sometimes the novelty is marginal, and a new situation is not easy to classify or analyze successfully. We may try this or that account of it, attempting to build bridges of analogy, then return over these bridges for fresh perception or discrimination to the novelty that refused to fit our established taxonomies. There is thus a bipolar tension between a novel situation and the fund of knowledge, a subject-pole and a predicate-pole that cannot be brought together until each has provided a basis for reexamining and redefining the other. The learner must be able to scrutinize novelties, to summon up from a store of knowledge that which may be relevant, to use the relevant knowledge to reinspect the novelty, and then, through fresh perception, to search more widely in the store again.

It is through repeating this kind of interaction that transfer and creativity arise; and in essence they are indistinguishable from each other. Educational research has often split learning and transfer apart, taking a narrow criterion for each. In the laboratory of Archimedes, or in any efficient, educationally significant learning, there is no learning *except* through transfer and no transfer except as part of learning. Many college students have, by one criterion, long since learned multiplication and division, but they still confuse and interchange them even in simple applications. The criterion by which they are said to have learned them, however, is a bad one. The most transferable knowledge is that which has been learned across diverse situations in the first place, so that what is being learned is being abstracted from a wide range of experience. In this sense, transfer *precedes* knowledge—another aspect of the reversal of ends and means.

Curing Education's Pathology

My aim is to present a diagnosis of educational pathology while examining the nature and difficulty of the cure. The cure has several components, intellectual and practical. It ultimately depends, as Kenneth

Boulding has said, upon both the investment in further knowledge and the transmission of knowledge from those who have it to important decision makers who ought to have it.[7]

But in the present case, this research and transmission is powerfully determined by the fact that the essential knowledge, by its nature, is a sort of craft knowledge—practical, reflective, constantly experimental. It is supported, and sometimes illustrated, by writing—by philosophical and theoretical writing, by therapeutic investigation, by examples and case histories, by good stories. But most important, knowledge in practice is transmitted through internship.

If we enlarge our resources for efficient early schooling it must therefore be by steps, to achieve growth, not merely transmission. Such growth can for a time be exponential, provided support grows equally and research keeps pace. This is a major and, in the short term, expensive undertaking. We need to persuade important decision makers that it is based on firm knowledge. How do we persuade? What are the indexes of this firmness?

These questions involve us in value commitments and conflicts deeply embedded in our culture, though open to ethical inquiry and eventual resolution. The invitation to such inquiry must go along with the knowledge we would transmit. Our communication is, therefore, essentially political. It implies that in preparing to modify older and ineffectual patterns of schooling we must also learn to modify now-established criteria of success. The values that surround the existing school establishment are largely incommensurate with those that would be accepted within a new, widespread education. The aim of the debate is to bring alternatives closer together, to find some agreed-upon value commitments and to achieve others.

The other aspect involved in remedying educational pathology is a commitment to increased research. One area of research that I think is vital is neurobiology. If I may make a brash prediction, neurobiologists are more likely to evolve informed views consonant with those of my minority educational tradition than are psychologists, whose tradition says that knowledge of what goes on in organisms has nothing to contribute to the sciences of behavior. On the contrary, not only does such knowledge agree with the best phenomenology of teaching-learning, it can surely advance it.

That is one field of vitally needed research. There are other fields evolving that we should watch closely, in many cases the work of invaders from outside the academic field of psychology. I refer particularly to several aspects of what has come to be called cognitive science, which spans a range from extensions of Piagetian epistemology to schemes of computer modeling. All these efforts have gone beyond the stimulus-response paradigms that the psychologist Dewey so long ago gave good reasons to reject.[8]

There is one more kind of research that I believe still goes unrecognized and with which I finish my discussion. Again, its first recognition comes in the writings of Dewey and is expressed in his use of a Deweyan magic word, *reconstruction*, in several of his early writings on education and later, in his 1899 *Lectures*, in *The Child and The Curriculum*, and most adequately in *Experience and Education*. Dewey recognizes a need for the radical reconstruction of systems of knowledge to make them optimally accessible to new learners; to invite those who are *ready* from their past learning and can *competently transfer* and assimilate new phenomena and new ideas.[9]

The traditional organization of any subject matter follows a formal, logical pattern that is useful to professionals who have mastered a discipline but that for beginners is usually a bottle with a very narrow neck. What is needed is a reconstruction. The alternative image is the Klein bottle, the three-dimensional analogue of the Möbius strip in which the inside is everywhere continuous with the outside. This pattern no longer contains knowledge but invites it, unbottles it, makes it accessible from many starting points in the common experience. Dewey recognized and emphasized this need for reconstruction. Excellent teachers who have mastered subject matter and value it deeply can often achieve it ad hoc, whether to catch kindergarteners or graduate students.

Such ad hoc reconstruction seems to be what Dewey counted on. But it is by itself radically inadequate to any serious educational reform. I see this reconstruction as a research commitment badly needed for all levels, one that involves the working collaboration of persons deeply versed in subject matter and those skilled in the teaching arts. Each initially lacks the mastery that the other can supply, but both are committed, from different backgrounds, to the principles of the laboratory of Archimedes.

Notes

1. The papers in this symposium were written by a group of people each of whom had access, *mirabile visu*, to each other's productions, a condition approximating the economists' miracle of perfect information. The miracle was accomplished in this case by the insistence of our indefatigable editor, who required that we each write first what we were going to write later. The ability to do this is prized in academic circles, and we almost all obeyed. Thus I was able to make reference to a paper by Karl Pribram, and I have depended, rather centrally, on some very specific and precise references to a paper that does not exist. This eminent neurobiologist, and rare disobedient, in the end did not tell

us what he had told us he would tell us but wrote quite another paper, one that opens quite other vistas, which I have shared elsewhere but not here. So readers will understand my reference to a paper that does not exist, I have appealed to our editor to append here Pribram's initial statement of what he later would have, but as yet has not, stated.

Pribram's statement "Neurobiological Limitations in Learning" is as follows:

> The problem of neurobiological limits on the potential of learning is revealed in three issues: readiness, competence, and transfer. Neuropsychological investigations of readiness have shown the importance of "novelty/familiarity" in engaging the student's attention and of movement in making the results of stimulation objective. Competence develops through reinforcement. The consequences of behavior enhance or diminish confidence in similar subsequent behavior, and when a certain level of confidence is achieved, a means-end reversal takes place, with the competent organism becoming resistant to consequences that earlier would have been discouraging. Transfer of learning from one situation to another is the basis of creativity. Neuropsychological research has shown a relationship between the mechanisms involved in processing the "novelty/familiarity" dimension and transfer. Both novelty and transfer depend on the global context within which they operate: the familiarity of well-learned neural mnemonic structures that guide experience and behavior. When such structures become the focus of orderly change, transfer and creativity result.
>
> A myth often repeated by educators is that we use only part of our endowed brain capacity. This is probably not true. Just as a computer can be programmed efficiently or inefficiently, so the contextual competences within which we operate can lead to efficient or inefficient processing. It is the job of educators to provide efficient programs. As this paper suggests, perhaps these new insights into the learning process from neurobiology can be of some help.

2. The heliocentric system is referred to quite casually in Archimedes' essay, "The Sand Reckoner." See Sir T. L. Heath, *Aristarchus of Samos, the Ancient Copernicus, a History of Greek Astronomy to Aristarchus*, Greek text and translation, Oxford, Clarendon Press, 1913.

3. See Kant's essay *Perpetual Peace* (*Zum ewigen Frieden*), tr. Lewis W. Beck, New York, Bobbs Merrill, 1957.

4. In Marx's marvelously promissory "These on Feuerbach." *Opposition of the Materialist and Idealist Outlooks*, London, Lawrence & Wishart, 1973.

5. See note 1.

6. Ibid.

7. I am referring to Boulding's introductory paper in this volume.

8. For Dewey's analysis and restatement of the reflex arc concept, which has finally become fairly fashionable 120 years after his birth, see his essay "The Unit of Behavior" in *Philosophy and Civilization*, pp. 233–248; New York, Capricorn Books, 1963.

9. John Dewey, *Lectures in the Philosophy of Education*, 1899, ed. R. Archimbault, New York, Random House 1966; *The Child and the Curriculum*, Chicago, University of Chicago Press, 1908, 1956; *Experience and Education*, New York, Macmillan 1938, Collier Books 1963; *Interest and Effort in Education*, Boston, Houghton Mifflin, 1938. The last three books are available in current paperback editions.

ELIZABETH WRIGHT INGRAHAM

———— **12** ————

Knowledge as a Manageable Resource in Educational Systems

We have seen disturbing trends toward uniformity in our institutions, growing bureaucracy, overemphasis on academic credentials, isolation of students and faculty from the world—a growing rigidity and uniformity of structure that makes higher education reflect less and less the interests of society. Rather than allow these trends to continue, means must be found to create a diverse and responsive system. . . . We need many alternative paths to education.
The Newman Report on Higher Education 1971

In 1970, the United States was yet again in transition. A decade had passed during which public reaction had moved rapidly from protesting an unpopular war to remonstrating against the institutions that formed American society. It was the end of a decade that had encompassed everything from the Vietnam War to anarchy on college campuses, and it signalled the end of a certain type of thinking—the naivete of believing in endless resources to fuel endless growth was shattered. The idea that war had a workable place in a technologically advanced society was questioned.

At this time the country saw the blossoming of a number of innovative educational arrangements. They included an expansion of the national scientific laboratories, new directions on old campuses, the idea of the

---

I would like to acknowledge and thank Catherine Ingraham for the insights and ideas she contributed to this paper and to the model itself.

free university, and the growth of special centers and institutes. Some innovations repudiated conventional educational structures, some simply addressed the pathologies of the existing system, others looked at institutional structure and the future needs of science, and still others were responding to the challenge for a more humane society. Principles like "freedom of choice" and "the right to know," sloganized under fire in the sixties, were undergoing the long and complicated process of articulation and reappraisal in a new scientific age. Education was *the* field for positive action. As both a testing ground and a training ground, education was where the student learned formally and informally to be a member of society. Despite upheaval on American campuses, the country would still look for leadership in the halls of academia where sufficient leisure and latitude exist for experiencing the paradoxes and permutations of the social process.

In 1970, a small group of people of differing ages, professions, and responsibilities found their interests turning to what the years had meant in terms of attaining and using knowledge. The group founded a nonprofit educational institution to promote, direct, encourage, and develop opportunities for the use, conservation, and preservation of human and natural resources. A positive approach to education, one that increasingly leaned toward the practical task of building a new educational institution, was perhaps evidence of an essential optimism.

This new institution was conceived of as a hybrid of conventional university structures and unconventional institutional arrangements. It was not meant to repeat, in a slightly different way, the purposes of the university, but was rather to be supplemental and complementary to the university. The group's decision to form an adjunct institution, amplifying and examining certain features of the learning process itself, proved to be farsighted—a choice that allowed enormous flexibility while keeping alive the initial experimental impulse. The position of a supplementary institution is both precarious and strong—precarious because it cannot be easily categorized in a specialized society, thus making it both vulnerable and dispensable; strong because it can form symbiotic relationships with the individual, the university, the business community, and the scientific community.

The primary objective of the innovative model was to keep an open and imaginative institutional structure while drafting a mission dedicated to implementing the complex, integrative nature of knowledge, i.e., making knowledge work. It was a statement against the adverse effects of specialization of knowledge in the university. Although specialization was not antithetical to integration, it appeared to stifle creativity, advocating a narrow single-mindedness while allowing the learning process to be channeled for economic advantage. Further, specialization tended to limit the choice of learning methods as the educational system closed around an influx of students seeking credentials. As a result, pressing issues were being ignored.

For example, "environment" was an early concern of many of the innovative institutions. Environment as a concept has a very broad range of meanings, some more manageable than others. The more persuasive meanings have political resonances, challenging this country's ideas of a manifest destiny. One purpose of the model was to develop an environmental sense that was not merely an adversarial conservationist strategy but one that also evaluated the balanced use and management of natural and human resources. In this context, the most difficult single resource to manage and the one that governed the use and conservation of all other resources was human knowledge.

The term "management" may seem mechanistic, unsuited to that variable "thing" we call knowledge. However, when one perceives the environment in its largest sense, that perception raises basic questions about the quality and quantity of our knowledge, its transmission and communication, the fundamental interdependencies of information—all questions about directing and using knowledge. The example of the interconnected physical world leads the observer to consider the manner in which those interconnections are perceived, made understandable, and acted upon. An institution that concerns itself with a scientific understanding of the physical environment and its interdependencies in order to learn and teach principles of energy, or human and natural resource use and conservation, inevitably concerns itself with knowledge management. Such institutions are also engaged in what might be viewed as a paradoxical enterprise, although one in keeping with the nature of knowledge management. On the one hand, these institutions shape a "discipline" of interdisciplinary science and thought; on the other hand, they maintain a nondisciplinary freedom of observation based on the never-ending reciprocity between the physical and the human-built environment. The process of learning and knowing what shapes our very perception of the physical world is a model for freeing the imagination. In essence, as we read the world, we author it.

Free observation and the opportunities for a free exchange of ideas have an adumbrated existence in the university, overshadowed by the demands of a society that wants people with accumulated skills and information that may be put directly to use in the marketplace. The free exchange of ideas also threatens the functional hierarchy of professor to student upon which universities depend. Knowledge is thus construed as a cumulative quantity of discrete information that is communicable; learning is the process of efficiently transmitting this information from one who has it to one who doesn't. In an experiment with the "discipline" of interdisciplinariness—an experiment that resulted in a core course in integrative studies—the innovative model, in a sense, conformed to this functional hierarchy. However, the hierarchy was tempered by the absence of grades and the opportunity for teachers and students to come together for the free exchange of ideas, not as a token dialogue tacked on to a program of lectures but as the key method by which knowledge comes alive for the student, the teacher, the scientist, the planner, the politician. . . .

Establishing a Learning Community

Practically, it was necessary to develop a "learning community" able to embrace both interdisciplinariness and the free exchange of ideas. The institutional "physical plant" was to serve not only as a support structure for educational activities but also as a reference point for the educational experiment. This resulted in the choice and purchase of a 640-acre grasslands field laboratory in a semiarid environment at the nexus of mountains and plains. A slow-moving plains stream tied the section of land to a larger river basin. The campus underwent seasonal extremes of weather. The 12 to 18 inches of annual precipitation defined the terrestrial and aquatic vegetation communities, which included agricultural grazing land. The presence of various soil-holding grasses raised important issues of human impact. The proliferation of resident and migratory wildlife evidenced the abundance of habitats. The accelerated growth of nearby metropolitan areas emphasized contemporary problems. It was a place where the linkages and interfaces of natural and human-built systems could be clearly observed and studied, limits could be explored, and questions could be formed.

The land, designated as a preserve and a significant natural area, is an environmental unit in both the strictest and the broadest sense. By studying the 640-acre campus as if the land were both the object of scientific inquiry and the living laboratory within which other programs were being carried out, the learner is taken into such diverse areas of study as land use, philosophy, economics, business, history, geography, biology, language, politics, sociology, anthropology, and architecture. Environment proves to be an excellent paradigm for integrative study. For ten years, the discovery that studying an environmental unit could in fact instruct one in fundamental ways about the workings and interconnection of all knowledge—a grandiose and very complex discovery—has been at the heart of the educational innovation. Developing the vocabulary of integrative studies is a never-ending language task that attempts to describe both the experience and theory of the educational methods at the field laboratory. The vocabulary needed to manage knowledge in the model forces the integration of a number of disciplines and challenges the compartmentalized mind-set of the typical student. Everyone knows that all knowledge is interconnected to a degree. Certainly the bottom line is not to melt all disciplines into one grand discipline to express this interconnectedness. It is to understand how essential interdependence is to learning; the dynamic interplay between bodies of information leads to responsible problem finding and problem solving. The systems approach used in the model counterbalanced certain diffusive tendencies of integrative studies. This systems approach does not freeze facts into codified systems but provides a way of controlling areas of interpretation so one can examine problems moment by moment, piece by piece. Precisely as one hypothesizes a series of points on a line in order to measure the line, although one knows the line itself has no part or an infinite number of parts, so systems thinking is a way of making knowledge momentarily discrete. This is what the model defined as the "discipline" of interdisciplinary learning. There is no question that the degree of control simulated by systems thinking is constantly mitigated by integrative thinking. The idea of a strong reference point acts as a foundation for new knowledge; in the model, the field laboratory served as the primary reference point.

Integrating Knowledge in Action

By way of illustration, a faculty member wrote about a philosophy student at the field laboratory. The student called the attention of his colleagues, who were peering into a rainwater pool on an outcrop of rock at the edge of the plains, to a swarm of fairy shrimp gliding about the pool in miraculous exploitation of the life supports provided by a recent thunderstorm. Without the living evidence before them, it would have been difficult for the group members to imagine that evolution had converted a marine organism into a creature capable of reproducing itself in the transient fresh water puddles of the semiarid plains. A biologist with the group described what the area must have been like when it formed the bottom of a shallow sea millions of years ago, at which time the remote antecedents of the fairy shrimp were making their contribution to what are now coal beds and oil fields. The sun beating down overhead emphasized the energy that sustained the algae and shrimp in the water so recently sucked up from the ocean and deposited at the pool. All these speculations were interrupted by the thunder of a jet liner above. A chemistry student offered a wry comment about the aircraft's instantaneous conversion of kerosene into four rapidly vanishing white plumes of a condensation trail, the remnants of the hydrocarbons the ancient algae and shrimp had created millennia ago.

A visiting meteorologist explained that the disappearance of the vapor trails was caused by their dispersion and absorption into an air mass that was degraded in the process. A psychology professor noted that the students would soon occupy jet liners returning to distant corners of the country and that, as they passed over the plains, they would remember the fairy shrimp in the pools twenty thousand feet below. He pointed out that the critical characteristic of humans that gives room for optimism is that they can respond to the marshalling of evidence.

In this illustration, a variety of learning methods are obvious: the direct experience of seeing the fairy shrimp, the contextual explanation by the experts, the formation of an image of the site's history and verbalization of an aspect of the future; the collection of facts through inference or analogy could easily be added. This kind of interaction involves students in the integrative process.

The Faculty

Visiting professors from universities across the country and a variety of professionals are invited by the administrative staff to stay from two to five days at the field laboratory "teaching" the fundamental principles of their specialty. Care is exercised in finding those who are interested in the integrative approach and who enjoy teaching. A broad and diverse body of fine professors have welcomed the opportunities to participate. Faculty prepare their own course plan but are asked to relate their session, if possible, to the 640-acre campus or the immediate region. They review field research projects that can be useful in explaining principles. An effort to bring faculty members together to "teach" each other and to replicate the student's schedule has proved valuable. A formal association for visiting professors is presently being reviewed.

The Students

Students live at the field laboratory for a nine-week core course, a reversal of the typical order in which the students move from class to class or school to school and the experts are the permanent residents. Students have six to eight hours of intensive seminars each day with two to four hours of field study or research. Groups of 5 to 11 meet with professors; the ratio of professors to students averages 3 to 1 with students being exposed to as many as 20 different visiting experts. Various days are set aside for independent study and public forums. When a permanent laboratory facility is completed, there can be a total of 180 students, scholars, interns, and staff at any one time. Each person typically stays nine weeks, but interns who wish to continue integrative research or students who move into staff positions stay longer. Plans envisage four nine-week courses per year. Upper-level undergraduate and graduate students apply through their universities; applicants with no institutional affiliation are also considered. Originally, students were selected and financed by a cooperating university or college. Although some universities that have been impressed with student response to the course still finance students, financial priorities in many institutions have shifted, and students are now less frequently funded by their own institutions. Credit for up to one semester of independent work or special subject recognition is given to students in the core course. One dean from a major university wrote, "We have been greatly impressed by the in-depth approach to study at the sessions—the quality of our students' work has been significantly advanced and in each case we have granted ten credits for the core course. We highly recommend this program. . . ." Students come from diverse backgrounds and disciplines, selected largely by cooperating universities and colleges. The only restriction on inclusion in the core course is that applicants be upper-level undergraduate or graduate students or have equivalent training or experience.

The Curriculum

The schedule for the nine-week core course is built around seven teaching blocks, a course that evolved over five years with input from a number of academics and professionals. During the first days, students become oriented to the field laboratory, learning to use sky charts, telescopes, and laboratory and surveying equipment and being trained in fire fighting and first aid. They are introduced to the scientific land inventory and monitoring programs. Different sequences of the teaching blocks have been tried over the years. In general, during the second week a physicist conveys basic principles of energy and entropy, and the students set up energy models for the site, work with weather balloons, make astronomical observations, and so on. The chemistry of air, water, and soil is explored. During the third and fourth weeks, the students move into earth and life sciences with emphasis on under-standing the geologic structures of the region, grasslands and stream ecology, and various identification methods. Work with a plant herbarium and vegetation transects leads into ecosystem modeling. The study of the stream and a tour of the region off-site broadens the data base. From this grounding, students guided by different experts move into the human role in the life processes, including an intensive study of economics, law, and politics. Regional and global case studies in problems of food production, labor and management, and political systems are introduced. At the end of this teaching block, a public forum on a current "hot" topic emphasizes trade-offs used in making decisions. During the sixth week, an anthropologist introduces a broad evolutionary perspective and gives training in methods used to interpret culture. Then the students move into the fields of planning, engineering, and architecture, using local and regional forms to gain some historical perspective and explore modern settlements and concepts of design. Another public forum on an aspect of cities expands the discussions. The eighth week deals with language and linguistics as vehicles for synthesis. The format of the nine weeks varies as the faculty improvises and experiments with new methods of teaching fundamental principles. A biologist has said it takes three months in a classroom to teach what he can do in the field in three days. In the humanities the reference point is not so visible, but there is an accumulation of tools and language as the course progresses that aids in communicating more abstract principles. The faculty finds that the students' ability to build a framework to handle new knowledge improves exponentially during the nine weeks. How long such an ability endures has not been evaluated, but as a student learns the languages of various disciplines, there is a parallel development involving connections and interactions among the disciplines. Discussion and activities involving paleontology, geography, mathematics, art, and philosophy bridge disciplines between the teaching blocks.

Using the Campus as a Text

The students engage in a continuing debate; the campus is the unifying "text." For the graduate student the core course acts as a magnifying lens; for the uncommitted student the course acts as a reducing lens, allowing the student to find a special interest. The task of integrating the different kinds of knowledge presented is placed on the student. The practical introduction of heuristic tools like key words, matrix guides, simulation exercises, and research projects enhances the student's ability to absorb, abstract, and store the diverse information.

On one occasion faculty members gathered in a field to discuss what appeared to be a trivial topic: the meaning of a barbed-wire fence. A philosopher saw the fence as a way of including or excluding involvement; a biologist saw it as a roosting place for birds, observing how nonindigenous plants had been introduced to the area by seeds dropped by birds perched on the fence; a lawyer saw ownership defined; a physicist illustrated the short span of human civilization by using the barbs on the wire to simulate segments of historic time; a hydrologist saw the fence as a barrier to the flow of water, noting that vegetation on one side was more diverse; a historian explained how the invention of barbed wire had revolutionized land use in the West. Students entered the discussion with comments that the change in the different intellectual positions was similar to the idea of parallax in the environment, i.e., the different physical positions that give different orientation. They noted that mere observation fails to relay the truth of a situation.

Students in the core course were responsible for the functional tasks of the field laboratory with as little supervision as possible. These tasks include maintaining shelters, preparing food, organizing special seminars, monitoring the various scientific apparatus, compiling accurate data, and hosting the visiting faculty and public forums. Interestingly, the responsibility of planning so that twenty people could sit down to lunch on time in the middle of an isolated grasslands preserve often proved more taxing than that of organizing an intricate study of nesting birds. Both tasks were essential and each task involved ordering a disorderly set of components, but there were questions about the relative importance of each activity. In the model, the idea that knowledge was to be tapped in all its forms, even the mundane, was seen as paramount to developing a sense of personal worth and human potential.

Students are asked to keep a daily journal to give themselves a written record useful in checking retention and recall of information and in ordering, selecting, and filtering information. One student wrote, "The journal may also be the tool that ultimately facilitates integration. If, for example, I sought to establish some connections between biological principles and various societal issues I could well use my journal as a first reference. Scanning through my notes, I found that no one felt that any one proposal would offer a solution to the current energy dilemma and that a wide variety of energy sources should be developed. Anyone visiting this field laboratory three years ago would have noticed the sunflower population in the north quarter. Today, that mono-culture has totally disappeared. Throughout the biological world the principle that diversity leads to stability generally applies. From this I could begin to establish a link between an environmental condition and our dependence on fossil fuels. Granted that this is somewhat simplistic but I have found that, given a large quantity of data and ideas, the journal has helped me select and synthesize information."

Students are also asked to carry out an independent project to be presented at the end of the session to the student and faculty body, a notion consistent with recognizing the student as the primary integrator and one that gives the student perspective on his or her own expertise. To lose for a time the sense of one's own field and to see the expansion and modification of one's own knowledge into the sometimes unfamiliar freedom of integrative studies can be threatening. The need to integrate a body of information that can be called one's own improves perception while at the same time demanding that the individual present a package of knowledge to validate his or her existence. The integration enhances the "manageability" of knowledge. Quantitative systems of measurement such as grades often serve this end by placing a value on the package; in our model, the value of the product was measured by the student.

Staff members are drawn, wherever possible, from graduate students, volunteers, and interns. The staff coordinates the schedules and the core course. Staff members initiate research projects and handle grants and contracts under the guidance of a principal executive in charge, while policy is set by a corporate administrative board that includes a percentage of former students. Staff positions become a logical extension of the core course for those students who wish to continue exploring the integrative approach. Staff positions, however, are seen as transitional to either further graduate study or professional practice rather than permanent. The innovative model includes only the permanent executive and legal administration. The idea of a permanent research staff is being reviewed.

The Lessons of Experience

Ten years' experience with programs at the field laboratory has produced some interesting insights into "learning." Because most students are taken from the university system and exposed to a short but intense study in a variety of fields, it is important to experiment with optimizing the effects on students from diverse backgrounds. For example, it was deemed important to emphasize utilizing some of the student's acquired knowledge and skills, putting into new use what was already known. This use is an affirmation and reinforcement of the student as the primary interpreter and integrator, providing an automatic participatory responsibility in the student's ability to learn. Ultimately, it may be that this responsibility is what makes knowledge work for the maximum benefit of the learner. In addition, effectively transmitting knowledge may hinge on exchanging or delegating this responsibility. Thus, the intensive nine-week core course encourages students to use their knowledge base as another reference point for understanding alien information and for interpreting and translating their own discoveries. This aspect of the model works better for students who have made some professional commitment.

The field laboratory enlivens the educational process not simply because its pristine setting is free from certain distractions but because the physical setting and the continual process of exchange between different methods of knowing and learning and the teacher/student relationship can be used as a mirror for reflecting on the learning process itself. It brings into consciousness the awareness that one learns not only about natural and human-built systems but equally about the human condition through the dynamics of complex relationships. Through this awareness, the management of knowledge becomes tied to a sense of the future, for almost certainly, as Alfred North Whitehead stated in 1916,

> The race which does not value trained intelligence is doomed. Not all your heroism, not all your social charm, not all your wit, not all your victories on land or sea, can move back the finger of fate. Today we maintain ourselves. Tomorrow science will have moved forward yet one more step, and there will be no appeal from the judgment which will be pronounced on the uneducated.

It has been my intent to outline a working model in knowledge management. This innovative model, in attempting to simulate on a small scale the diversity of a multiversity and the devotion to knowledge found in the guilds, is a vehicle for encouraging a qualitative use of knowledge. Evaluation of the model has been limited to annual student and faculty questionnaires. The majority of the alumni are in advanced study or professionally active. The problems and challenges involved in structuring such innovations so that their discoveries can find a way into the mainstream has not been discussed here.

In closing, I would like to present a brief case for innovative educative models. History tells us that established educational institutions do not change from within. Nevitt Sanford observed that while there have been many reformers associated with the university, there have been few innovations offered by the university itself and even fewer initiated by faculties. Institutions are organized to protect the freedom of those within, and, while this structure creates an atmosphere in which the discoveries of a Galileo can evolve, it also maintains the status quo. The university was generally allied against the Reformation; the Renaissance occurred completely outside the university walls, and the French and Russian revolutions placed universities fully under state control. As educator Clark Kerr has noted, "Change comes more through spawning the new than reforming the old."

In the past decade many educational innovations, excused from formal accountability, defined their missions under the scrutiny of a system already committed to the status quo. While the exercise undoubtedly tightened the reins on spurious operations, it guaranteed the collapse of many genuine efforts to contribute to social change. Educational innovations such as the model described in this paper are not intended to replace mainstream institutions. Many of them act, consciously or unconsciously, as a stabilizing force in a time of change as they mediate issues, experiment with knowledge transfer, and keep creative options open.

Bibliography

Bacon, Francis, *The Advancement of Learning and New Atlantis*, Oxford University Press, London, 1966.

Birkhead, Gene; Ragsdale, John; and Torborg, John, *The Running Creek Field Station Report*, Wright-Ingraham Institute, Johnson Publishing, Boulder, Colo., 1976.

Bronowski, J., *A Sense of the Future: Essays in Natural Philosophy*, MIT Press, Cambridge, Mass., 1977.

Darky, William A., *Three Dialogues on Liberal Education*, St. John's College Press, Annapolis, 1979.

Dewey, John, *Logic, The Theory of Inquiry*, Holt & Co., New York, 1949.

Kerr, Clark, *The Uses of the University: The Godkin Lectures at Harvard University, 1963*, Harvard University Press, Cambridge, Mass., 1964.

Leopold, Aldo, *A Sand County Almanac*, Oxford University Press, New York, 1966.

Newman, Frank, *The 2nd Newman Report: National Policy & Higher Education*, MIT Press, Cambridge, Mass., 1973 (1st Report 1971).

Reisman, David, *Constraint and Variety in American Education*, University of Nebraska Press, Inc., Lincoln, 1958.

Sanford, Nevitt, ed., *The American College: a psychological and social interpretation of the higher learning*, prepared for the Psychological Study of Social Issues, Edit. Comm., Christian Bay, Wiley, New York 1962.

Wright-Ingraham Institute, *Integrative Studies: Seminar Proceedings, August 18, 1978*, University of Colorado Publications Office, Boulder, Colo., 1979.

ROBERT D. BEAM

— 13 —

Fragmentation of Knowledge: An Obstacle to Its Full Utilization

The Problems of Fragmentation

The narrow compartmentalization of knowledge occurs as human beings, in their quest for expertise, differentiate their special talents into finer and finer fragments of learning. To illustrate: The discipline of economics is narrowed to the study of microeconomics and further narrowed to the study of micro-microeconomics.[1] Limiting the scope of inquiry achieves a more efficient production of new knowledge. However, a limited scope easily results in nearsightedness; the specialist is less likely to see the forest for the *leaf*. Such fragmentation promotes inadequate access to knowledge and wasteful duplication of effort through inefficient classification and inadequate understanding.[2]

Fragmentation impedes the crossfertilization of ideas across disciplinary boundaries and prevents the emergence of more general and parsimonious conceptual structures. According to the second law of thermodynamics, all closed systems are subject to increasing entropy, or a loss of differentiation. When the law is applied in a social context, closed societies (those societies whose members have no communications or transactions with members of other societies) display less variety of behavior and belief, less innovation, and greater homogeneity of attitudes and values than societies with an open social environment.

Emergence, the opposite of entropy, occurs only in open societies. The crossfertilization of ideas between open societies, including academic societies, promotes emergent structural development and increased creativity.

Fragmentation also has a negative influence on education. Educators find it difficult to stay abreast of the latest developments in their areas, and narrowed inquiry funnels students into fragmented specialties at earlier and earlier stages in their academic careers. As a result, education neglects continuity and integration of knowledge, thus preventing the development of a "holistic" vision, which is needed if society is to solve its most perilous social and technological problems.

Fragmentation Is a Behavioral Phenomenon

Knowledge is information, or a pattern coded in a human brain. Information is not knowledge if no one knows it; it might as well not exist. Social science knowledge is transmitted by human interaction and cultural diversity. And cultural diversity, cultural ethos, and cultural ethnocentrism engender fragmentation.[3]

Cultural Diversity

The social science disciplines are themselves societies, each with its own unique cultural content and linguistic code of signs (terminology), symbols (concepts), and syntax (theory). Scientific disciplines differ in that they use a formally created code rather than natural languages. Nevertheless, cultural content is communicated to newcomers and members of an academic society, as in all cultures. Reliable communication requires sender and receiver to possess the same linguistic code, so those who do not have the code cannot extract meaning from their communications. For efficiency's sake, members of each disciplinary culture prefer to communicate with and read the literature of those who share the same code—members of the same academic culture. The diversity of linguistic codes and premises of each academic society limits crosscultural communication.

At the intrasystem level, within a society whose members share the same code, internal patterns and judgments become more similar as communications become more accurate. The more accurately members communicate, the more similar their internal patterns become. This sets up a positive feedback process—more interaction brings more similarity, more similarity brings more interaction—that is also known as the normative process.

The intersystem level, among members of different societies is also subject to feedback—less similarity in the code used brings less interaction, and less interaction means less similarity. Accurate communication across disciplines declines, and diffusing cultural content becomes more difficult. Cultural diversity impedes cultural diffusion and is therefore one obstacle to the full utilization of social science knowledge.

Cultural Ethos

The fragmentation of social science knowledge is transactional as well as communicational. Although scientific cultures differ in their formal languages, they are surprisingly similar in other respects. Each disciplinary culture possesses a hierarchy of roles differentiated by title, e.g., instructor, assistant professor, associate professor, each of which encompasses role prescriptions and a specified financial and professional status level. An implicit exchange is established between a society and each new entrant: membership in exchange for conforming to prevailing social (research) norms. Research norms include attitudes about performance, with emphasis on what is expected and approved of by other society members. Conforming to the "ethos of the order" in exchange for acceptance (tenure) and praise (promotion) is a transactional phenomenon. The society's "instructions" concerning approved role performances consist of its norms and expectations, and the society's authority to induce conformity is exercised through social pressures. Members whose research behavior violates established disciplinary norms experience verbal and nonverbal communications of disapproval (colder conversation, fewer smiles, etc.), all of which are transactional. The threat of ostracism, or denial of tenure, is the ultimate social pressure.

Decisions about research interests are made within constraints imposed by preference structures, that is, by the discipline's cultural ethos. In each of the social sciences, academic competence is achieved through disciplinary centrality as faculty, particularly untenured faculty, move their careers to safety within traditional disciplinary (and departmental) bounds. The subsequent decline in interdisciplinary collaboration reflects, in part, the influence of research decisions of each academic society's specialists.

Cultural Ethnocentrism

Both cultural diversity and cultural ethos contribute to cultural ethnocentrism. Symptoms of ethnocentrism include nationalistic attitudes and in-group partisanship among university departments, national scientific organizations, and academic disciplines. Evidence that social science knowledge is organized along disciplinary boundaries is apparent from inspecting almost any university or college catalog. In political science, economics, sociology, anthropology, history, and human geography, course offerings begin at the broad, introductory level and progress to intermediate and advanced courses of narrower and more rigorous focus. As the course number increases, the course itself bears increasingly less relevance to upper-level courses in other fields. Any attempt at integration is left for the student to perform individually. This pattern is the product of disciplinary ethnocentrism combined with specialties organized into autonomous decision-making units. It helps produce vast interdisciplinary gaps in curricula, gaps that result from ethnocentric attitudes about interdisciplinary education.

There is a skepticism toward interdisciplinary learning, a feeling that it results in a student's conceptual confusion by not defining itself or its goals clearly enough to be of lasting value. Introductory interdisciplinary courses are often expected to serve as prerequisites for advanced courses in each separate discipline; in an effort to preserve their respective integrity, departments discourage using the common core concepts and vocabulary necessary to integrate social science knowledge. Thus many interdisciplinary courses remain multidisciplinary hodgepodges of elementary courses, mixed at random. Such courses are rarely successful, and they foster the belief that interdisciplinary programs are a diluted and shallow form of general education in which scholarly rigor is traded for intellectual excitement.

There is also the widespread feeling that without sufficient grounding in a single discipline, students will be both cheated of valuable background skills and mentally unprepared for the challenges of more advanced disciplinary learning. There is also a concern that interdisciplinary programs do not adequately prepare students to enter the job market. Without a certified disciplinary base, students risk disqualification from entry-level positions in industry and graduate schools. Also, in the pragmatic vein, there is concern that interdisciplinary courses and programs are extravagantly expensive in terms of faculty and resources in the face of declining enrollments and dwindling university budgets.

Organizing university departments along disciplinary lines encourages disciplinary discreteness while deterring specialized interdisciplinary research and development. Within university departments, group decisions are achieved through majority vote. The dominant coalition will likely include those from the central specialties of the discipline, since they make up a larger fraction of department members. The nondominant coalition will most likely include "marginal specialists" whose natural allies are peripheral specialists in other departments. As department budgets tighten, increasing the competition for limited funds, space, and personnel, peripheral specialties are the first to be eliminated from the curriculum primarily because peripheral specialists lack bargaining power in the group decision process. As peripheral specialties are eliminated, crossdepartmental communications atrophy and interdisciplinary gaps widen.

Fragmentation Is Offset Through Unification

Knowledge grows by accumulation and by integration. To the extent that fragmentation prevents this integration, it also prevents full utilization of knowledge. With the recent rapid accumulation of knowledge, it has become evident that no one or two specialties are capable of successfully dealing with any one phenomenon. A total understanding of environment, for example, requires an interdisciplinary team of specialists in geology, geography, meteorology, and other subjects. In the traditional sense, interdisciplinary studies will always perform an indispensable role in building bridges by grouping multiple specialists around a single analytic problem.

But there is another way disciplines can be interrelated in the integrative, or system-based, unified approach.[4] The unified approach combines, synthesizes, and simplifies conventional disciplines into one set of analytical relationships. It provides greater common knowledge and technique, permitting students and scholars to move more easily among different specialties, making greater use of the special contributions of each. In particular, this approach seeks analogies, common principles, and formal identities that hold across the conventional disciplines of social science. In contrast to the interdisciplinary approach, which looks at one thing through many conceptual sets, the unified approach looks at many things through one conceptual set. It provides a skeleton on which the subject matters of sociology, economics, and political science can be hung.[5]

Natural laws explaining the behavior of the physical universe are the foundations for physical science. Social scientists assume that human behavior can be explained scientifically through a logical set of nomothetic principles similar to natural laws. All of the separate social science disciplines deal with types of social systems, yet their specialized concepts bear little resemblance to each other. The unified approach sets forth basic concepts underlying all social systems: social, political, or economic. This unified approach gives specialized disciplines a common analytic base.[6]

Despite the proliferation of information, multitudes of decisions—often the most important ones—require human judgment. We are not interested in the number of messages that can be transmitted but in the number that can be meaningfully conceptualized. Compared to computers, the conceptual processes of the human brain can be distressingly slow. Developing more efficient conceptual structures enables the brain to deal with larger amounts of information with a smaller number of concepts, providing greater potential for the brain's utilization of knowledge. Efficient conceptual structures require a high degree of generality and parsimony. Its ability to deal with many specialized disciplines through a single conceptual lens makes the unified approach general, parsimonious, and highly efficient.

Unified Social Science

Given that propositions about social behavior are interrelated, and that it is universities, not nature, that are organized into disciplines, a unified science of human behavior and interaction allows for increased communication and crossfertilization of ideas across boundaries.[7] Unified social science, a discipline in its own right, integrates social science knowledge by reformulating social theory on a simpler, more efficient structure of interlocking system-based concepts. In its view, the basic social science disciplines are not economics, sociology, and political science, but communication, transaction, and organization. More advanced subject areas such as normative processes, comparative advantage, or coalition formation are also only specialized configurations of communications, transactions, and organization among humans.[8]

Unified social science is based on a cybernetic approach to the study of behavioral science with special reference to three irreducible components of goal-oriented behavior: detector, selector, and effector, or DSE. Coordinated action among humans is possible only through a linking together of their control mechanisms. This can be accomplished via their detectors (through communication), their selectors (through transaction), or their effectors (through organization), or through some combination. If used as modular units, these general-purpose conceptual basics can be assembled into a vast variety of special purpose configurations to handle many areas of the social and behavioral sciences on an analytic-deductive basis. As illustrated in Figure 1, the three intrasystem DSE concepts, their intersystem (CTO) parallels, and their interrelations are considered the basic building blocks of the unified social science discipline.

The Unified Lens: Intrasystem and Intersystem Axis of Controlled Systems

System theory has the broad capacity for integrating widely discrepant phenomena into a single coherent whole. The unified framework is based on the premise that man, like all other organisms, is a goal-oriented (controlled) adaptive system. A system is controlled if it "prefers" one system state to another and has some capacity to return itself to, or move toward, that preferred state if it is pushed away. The goals of the human system, along with other details of its control mechanism,

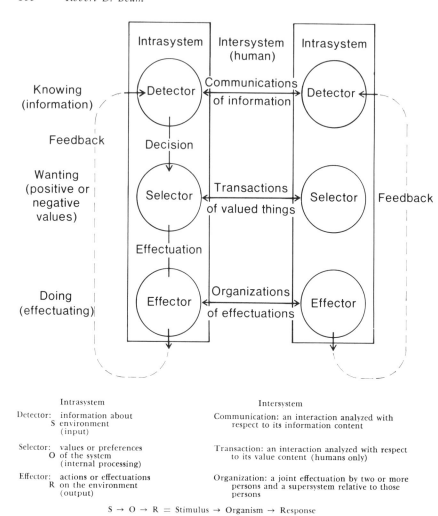

FIGURE 1. The intrasystem-intersystem axis of controlled systems (from Kuhn 1974).

are internal to its behavioral (as opposed to its biological) subsystem. Internal goals are not to be confused with external constraints, which are imposed upon the system by its environment. Although no adaptive system can respond to changes in its environment until it has been modified by that environment, in the strict sense, the system responds adaptively only to these modifications, not to the environment as such. This is the same as saying that humans respond adaptively to their information *about* reality rather than *to* reality as it actually exists.

Viewed from an intrasystem perspective, the adaptive mechanisms of any goal-oriented system include three logically distinct subsystem components: *detector, selector,* and *effector.* The system acquires information about itself or its environment through its detector. It "selects" its own behavior on the basis of its goals and value structures through its selector, and it executes this selected behavior through its effector. Thus the intrasystem analysis of adaptive behavior in any controlled system focuses on the detector, selector, effector (DSE) processes by which its behavioral (or decider) subsystem produces a learned response to environmental stimuli.

For human beings, the DSE functions represent the concept-perception function, the value function, and the effectuation (motor) function, respectively. Briefly, the decision process of adaptive behavior selection is divided into two analytically distinct stages: a performance or action stage and a feedback or learning stage. During the performance stage the system's detector provides information about the system's environment, and then the selector compares this information with the goal state of the system and selects the appropriate response. The effector receives and carries out the instructions from the selector. Once the response has been carried out, a learning stage occurs in which the detector receives feedback information about the state of the environment following the previous behavior. The selector compares this new state with the goal state, and the effector receives and carries out new, possibly corrective, instructions from the selector. A single stream of behavior is manifested in which the feedback stage of a previous action melds imperceptively with the performance stage of the next. Learning occurs when, through experience or a change of goals, a given stimulus input of information elicits a different response (output) than it did before. The human system is the most versatile and adaptive system known and is capable of modifying both its behavior and its goals over broad ranges of environmental conditions.

More complex behavior in humans involving conscious awareness relies on subsystem level controls, or sub-DSEs, for each of the main system functions. It is therefore necessary to shift focus to this sub-DSE level when analysis centers around one's conscious awareness of one's own states of information, values, and performance capabilities. In addition, mutual modifications of one subsystem by another can occur when we see what we want to see (detector modified by selector) or when we enjoy participating in sports at which we excel (selector modified by effector). Regardless of the complexity of the components' interrelations, this system model of human behavior requires only that all three DSE functions be completed before behavior is effectuated. These same three functions correspond closely to the "cognitive, affective, motor" or "stimulus, organism, response" relationships of behaviorist psychology.

For those who feel this approach is too mechanistic and neglects the human factor, please bear in mind that the terms "detector," "selector," and "effector" are conceptual bins only, not descriptions of their content. The detector subsystem encompasses all sensory, cognitive, and intuitive processes by which humans form and test both real and imaginary concepts about themselves and their environment. The selector subsystem encompasses the entire spectrum of emotions, hopes, impulses—all things to which positive or negative valuations can be attached. The effector subsystem is not confined strictly to the bones and muscles but also includes all neural motor connections that direct behaviors as diverse as mowing the lawn, juggling bean bags, or running a mile.

Intersystem Analysis

An individual's behavior is guided toward his or her goals by decisions, which reflect interrelations among the detector, selector, and effector states of his or her behavioral (decider) subsystem. Social behavior is therefore a function of the interrelated behavioral systems of two or more interacting individuals, operating within parametric environmental constraints. Each subsystem component of the DSE trio within the human system is tied logically to its intersystem parallel between human systems. The detector processes information within a given system, and the transfer of information between humans is *communication.* Communications between individuals both reflect and affect the states of their detector subsystems toward the information transferred. The selector deals with values generated within a given system, and transfers of valued things between humans are diagnosed as *transaction.* Transactions between individuals both reflect and affect the states of their selector subsystems toward the goods or services exchanged, including intangible and personal goods such as praise, trust, and respect that have no matter-energy base. Transactions between humans are oriented around power (which is the ability of one party to get what he or she wants from another party) and bargaining power (which is the ability to get it on good terms). Transactions reflect cooperative relations among humans, however their terms of trade may conflict, in that better terms for one party mean worse terms for the other(s). The effector effectuates overt behavior within a given system, and the coordination of effectuated behaviors between humans is diagnosed as *organization.* Organization is an emergent social phenomenon in which attention is shifted from the interacting parties to the overall effects of their joint actions.

In the unified model, social organizations are of three main types. The first type, formal organization, is a controlled system in which multiple human subsystems consciously coordinate their behaviors to achieve well-specified organization goals. Governments, university departments, and business enterprises are all examples of formal organization. By contrast, informal organization is a totally unplanned and undirected social organization in which subsystem individuals pursue their own self-oriented goals while remaining completely indifferent to (and possibly unaware of) the effects of their behavior on the organization as a whole. A pure market economy is an example of informal organization in which firms and households are concerned solely with their own individual welfare and whose interactions are subject to no controls at the whole-system level. The organization has no goals and does not behave as a unit. Its structure results from the interactions of its subsystems and is totally uncontrolled, i.e., is produced without conscious coordination. Intermediate states between formal and informal organization include (1) the informal aspects of formal organization in which members of formal organizations pursue their own goals, and (2) the formal aspects of informal organizations in which individuals, while mainly pursuing their own goals, modify their own behavior while they exert social pressures to modify the behavior of others in ways they feel are better for "society" as a whole.

The intrasystem-intersystem axis of controlled systems is a flexible analytic tool of social analysis. For example, the behavior of an individual is diagnosed with the intrasystem concepts of each individual's detector, selector, and effector processes. Interactions involving two or more individuals are diagnosed with the intersystem tools of communication and transaction theory. If they form an organization such as a family, a government, or a business, their interactions continue to be analyzed with communication and transaction theory; but if their organization acts as a unit, *its* behavior is analyzed with respect to *its* detector, selector, and effector processes. If the organization interacts as a unit with any other outside organization, the interaction is diagnosed through communication and transaction analysis. In short, whenever a controlled system is viewed as a unit, intrasystem analysis is used to describe its behavior. Whenever two or more controlled human systems interact, the analysis shifts to the intersystem aspects of their communications, transactions, and organizations. Real world complications may increase the complexity of analysis but do not require additional analytic tools. For example, a competitive market economy is a kind of informal organization of the whole society. Political science deals with government—a formal organization of the whole society—while sociology studies the social system—a semiformal organization of the whole society. The same basic theory of organization encompasses all three.

Just as all "machines" as diverse as automobiles and bicycles are specialized combinations of the same mechanical basics of lever, pulley, and inclined plane, so all social, political, and economic systems are specialized combinations of the same social science basics of decision, communication, transaction, and organization regardless of size and complexity. Social science concepts such as culture, society, conflict, cooperation, authority, status, competition, and sovereignty can be defined in terms of communication and transactions. One reason why the fragmentation of social science knowledge allows for relatively little crossdisciplinary dialogue is because these concepts are parts of different specialties: markets are the province of economists, elections of political scientists, and normative processes of sociologists. Specialists pay relatively little attention to the influence of cultural norms on market forces of supply and demand or on political elections for the same reason that bicycle mechanics rarely study automotive transmissions and auto mechanics do not examine bicycle chain drives, even though technological advances in each might significantly improve the other.

Social sciences remain the insular "territories" of specialists, separated by large gaps in communication and organization. The common metaphor of building bridges between disciplines by interdisciplinary studies evokes images of islands cleanly separated by expanses of water. Instead, Alfred Kuhn suggests that

> what appear to be islands are really adjacent peninsulas jutting out from the same main body of land. But the mainland has perpetually been shrouded in a fog so dense that no one knows it is there. A steady fresh breeze of unifying concepts can dispel the fog and reveal a terrain that requires only a little bulldozing to lay the base for a magnificent highway system connecting all main parts.[9]

Knowledge of mechanics does not make one a specialist in automobiles or bicycles. But knowledge of the basic principles *does* enable one to comprehend any particular automobile or bicycle as merely a specialized configuration of the same basics. If introductory social science students are acquainted with the basics of social mechanics before they specialize in a particular configuration, they can acquire a more holistic insight into the workings of society. A holistic vision of how societies function cannot be achieved through a large number of different concepts, but rather through a small number that allow for broad and deep understanding.

The central objective of unified social science is not new knowledge but more efficient knowledge. Since a large number of organization concepts, such as conflict, cooperation, authority, leadership, legitimacy, and conformity, can be diagnosed as special-purpose phases of trans-action, a basic transaction theory is a general yet parsimonious tool of social analysis. All interpersonal relationships between humans are aspects of communications, transactions, and organizations. This approach unifies the many different terms and concepts—some parallel, some overlapping, and a few even contradictory—the conventional disciplines offer to describe human social behavior.

The Advantage of Unified Social Science in Education, Scholarship, and the Utilization of Knowledge

Unified social science concepts can be introduced into the early educational curriculum to teach children the basic ideas that underlie all social processes.[10] In fact, the same structure of unified concepts can be taught at each grade level with increasing depth and complexity. Children develop an intuitive understanding of decisions, communications, transactions, and organizations at an early age since they participate in them each day of their lives. For example, the transactional logic of the class bully who seeks to extort lunch money by twisting his classmate's arm is the same as that of the Iranian zealot who seeks the return of the shah by taking over the U.S. Embassy in Tehran. The teacher who understands the unified conceptual set can teach the logic of stress transactions in ways young children can readily comprehend, without teaching the conceptual set itself. Sophisticated analysis of the same logic justifies graduate study, with many possible levels in between. Properly geared to age, the same unified basics can be profitably "orchestrated" throughout the entire educational curriculum.[11] Because communications, transactions, and organizations are the core of social analysis, the unified conceptual set can also be particularly useful in business administration and public policy.

Decision, communication, transaction, and organization are not to be seen as distinct from scholarly research in the conventional social science disciplines. Decision theory is the common property of each discipline: economists pursue its special applications to households, firms, and other economic units; political scientists use decision theory to study government, coalitions, and the political community at large; sociologists use it to study the formation of values or norms that shape social institutions; human geographers use it to study the impact of a region on the mutually contingent social, political, and economic decisions of its inhabitants; anthropologists use it to study the impact of culture on the social, political, and economic decisions of its members; and historians use it to study the decisions of humanity, regardless of culture or region, throughout space and time.

Each discipline is concerned with reaching decisions among conflicting interests with different types and amounts of power in the communicational, transactional, and coalitional processes of deciding. As a discipline in its own right, the unified approach includes all of the foregoing specialized variations. It does not compete with or substitute for the conventional disciplines, nor is it "a little bit of each." Instead, it abstracts their common ingredients and analytic underpinnings into a parsimonious set of interdisciplinary relationships with a common core of basic concepts. It can serve as a solid foundation for the fundamental ideas of each of the specialized social science disciplines.

The question is whether specialists are willing to view their efforts as part of a larger, unified whole. If a comprehensive science of the social system is to be achieved, the separate behavioral and social science disciplines must converge into one comprehensive explanation, expressed in a common scientific language.[12] The widespread use of unifying concepts would allow specialists in different social science disciplines to share common cultural premises and a common linguistic code. Common concepts and code are steps toward overcoming fragmentation and increasing coordination of social science knowledge. These objectives, in turn, will allow society to more fully utilize the knowledge of its social scientists, knowledge that is sorely needed if society is to deal successfully with the social problems it faces in coming decades.

Notes

1. See Harvey Leibenstein, "A Branch of Economics is Missing: Micro-Micro Theory," *Journal of Economic Literature*, vol. 17, no. 2 (June 1979):477–502.

2. See Alfred Kuhn's "Response to 'The Disciplines as a Differentiating Force,' " by Norman W. Storer and Talcott Parsons, in *The Foundations of Access To Knowledge*, ed. Edward B. Montgomery, (Syracuse, N.Y.: Syracuse University Press, 1968), pp. 122–127.

3. See Donald Campbell, "Ethnocentrism of Disciplines and the Fish Scale Model of Omniscience," in *Interdisciplinary Relationships in the Social Sciences*, ed. Muzafer Sherif and Carolyn W. Sherif (Chicago: Aldine Publishing Co., 1969), p. 327; and Robert Ardrey, *The Territorial Imperative* (New York: Dell Publishing Co., Inc., 1966).

4. A system-based unified approach to social science has been developed by Alfred Kuhn. See his *The Logic of Social Systems* (San Francisco: Jossey-Bass Publishers Inc., 1974) and *Unified Social Science* (Homewood, Ill.: Dorsey Press, 1975).

5. K. E. Boulding "General Systems Theory—The Skeleton of Science" (1956), in *Modern Systems Research for the Behavioral Scientist*, ed. W. Buckley (Chicago: Aldine Publishing Co., 1968).

6. This approach can serve as a useful analytic tool in building a fishscale model of omnisocial science. See Campbell, "Ethnocentrism of Disciplines."

7. See Russell L. Ackoff, "Systems, Organizations, and Interdisciplinary Research," *General Systems,* vol. 5 (1960):6.

8. See Alfred Kuhn, "System-based, Unified Social Science," *Social Science Education Consortium Newsletter,* no. 22 (April 1975):2.

9. Alfred Kuhn, from an address to the Association For Integrative Studies, Washington, D.C., March 4, 1980.

10. See K. E. Boulding, A. Kuhn and L. Senesh, *System Analysis and Its Use in the Classroom* (Boulder, Colo.: Publication #157 of the Social Science Education Consortium, 1973).

11. See Lawrence Senesh, "Organizing a Curriculum Around Social Science Concepts," in *Concepts and Structure in the New Social Science Curricula,* ed. Irving Morrissett, (West Lafayette, Ind.: Social Science Education Consortium, 1966) p. 24.

12. See G. J. Direnzo ed., *Concepts, Theory, and Explanation in the Behavioral Sciences* (New York: Random House, 1966) pp. 285–288.)

Bibliography

Ardrey, Robert. *The Territorial Imperative.* New York: Dell Publishing Co., Inc., 1966.

Berelson, B., and Steiner, G. A. *Human Behavior: An Inventory of Scientific Findings.* New York: Harcourt Brace Jovanovich, 1964.

Bertalanffy, L. Von. *General System Theory.* New York: Braziller, 1968.

Boulding, K. E. "General Systems Theory—The Skeleton of Science" (1956). Reprinted in W. Buckley (ed.), *Modern Systems Research for the Behavioral Scientist.* Chicago: Aldine, 1968.

Boulding, K. E.; Kuhn, A.; and Senesh, L. *System Analysis and Its Use in the Classroom.* Boulder, Colo.: Publication #157 of the Social Science Education Consortium, Inc., 1973.

Campbell, D. T. "Ethnocentrism of Disciplines and the Fish Scale Model of Omniscience." In M. Sherif and C. Sherif (eds.), *Interdisciplinary Relationships in the Social Sciences.* Chicago: Aldine, 1969.

Direnzo, G. J. (ed.). *Concepts, Theory, and Explanation in the Behavioral Sciences.* New York: Random House, 1966.

Firestone, F. N. "Academic Structures and the Integration of the Social Sciences." In M. Rubin (ed.), *Man In Systems.* Gordon and Breach Science Publishers, 1971.

Handy, R., and Harwood, E. C. *A Current Appraisal of the Behavioral Sciences.* Rev. ed. Great Barrington, Mass.: Behavioral Research Council, 1973.

Kuhn, A. *The Study of Society: A Unified Approach.* Homewood, Ill.: Richard D. Irwin, Inc., and the Dorsey Press, 1963.

―――――. *The Logic of Social Systems.* San Francisco: Jossey-Bass Publishers, Inc., 1974.

―――――. *Unified Social Science.* Homewood, Ill.: The Dorsey Press, 1975.

Kuhn, A., and Beam, R. *The Logic of Organization.* San Francisco: Jossey-Bass Publishers, Inc., 1982.

Lasker, G. E. (ed.). *Applied Systems and Cybernetics.* International Congress on Applied Systems Research and Cybernetics, Proceedings, Vol. 2., New York: Pergamon Press, Inc., 1981.

Leibenstein, Harvey. "A Branch of Economics Is Missing: Micro-Micro Theory." *Journal of Economic Literature* 17, no. 2 (June 1979): 477–502.

Melcher, A. (ed.). *General Systems and Organization Theory: Methodological Aspects.* Kent, Ohio: Kent State University, Center for Business and Economic Research, 1975.

Morrissett, I. (ed.). *Concepts and Structure in the New Social Science Curricula.* West Lafayette, Ind.: Social Science Education Consortium, Inc., 1966.

Moss, N. H. "Super-Specialization: The Trend and Its Impact in American Medicine." In M. Rubin (ed.), *Man In Systems.* New York: Gordon and Breach Science Publishers, 1971.

Rubin, M. (ed.). *Man In Systems.* New York: Gordon and Breach Science Publishers, 1971.

Senesh, L. "Organizing a Curriculum Around Social Science Concepts." In Irving Morrissett (ed.) *Concepts and Structure in the New Social Science Curricula.* West Lafayette, Ind.: Social Science Education Consortium, Inc., 1966.

Storer, N., and Parson, T. "The Disciplines as a Differentiating Force." In Arlyn J. Melcher (ed.). *General Systems and Organization Theory: Methodological Aspects.* Kent, Ohio: Kent State University, Center for Business and Economic Research, 1975.

LAWRENCE SENESH

————— **14** —————

Closing the Gap Between Frontier Thinking and the Curriculum

On the walls of many libraries and educational institutions is the motto, "Know the truth, and the truth will make you free." This motto, which inspired me for a long time, has taken on a frightening aspect as scientists have penetrated the nucleus of the atom, built the hydrogen bomb, and discovered cloning. I have become aware of the dangers of knowledge and have seen that knowledge without wisdom leads to the misuse of knowledge. These dangers are aggravated by the widening gap between the frontiers of knowledge and society.

The reasons for this gap have been identified by some of the writers in this volume. According to Rollo May, the creation of new knowledge is met with fear. He argues that human beings fear new knowledge because it creates uncertainty and anxiety about the future. This is why most people unconsciously avoid new and creative insights, repressing and forgetting new ideas before they ever come to light.

New knowledge, in May's view, is feared because it may drive society out of its old grooves, requiring the reform of a culture—a process that frightens everyone. Thus, in order to gain and use new knowledge, human beings must overcome this fear.

This fear is only one cause for the underutilization of knowledge. James N. Danziger finds the creation and utilization of knowledge inextricably bound up with the values and biases of the politically relevant members of society. The political system encourages us to withdraw from the frontiers of knowledge because applying new knowledge would upset the bureaucracy and challenge the interests of some powerful political figures. New knowledge raises new issues, stimulates debate, and multiplies the complexities of the social problems at hand. The application of new knowledge to a policy decision may also produce undesirable side effects, such as with urban renewal, public works, compulsory housing, or health insurance. Unwittingly, the political system may underutilize knowledge because of defective communication between knowledge producer and potential user, caused by the knowledge producer's technical language and frame of reference. Knowingly, the political system may suppress the creation and diffusion of new knowledge if such knowledge could expose the failings of current policy and practice.

Robert D. Beam attributes the underutilization of knowledge to its fragmentation. Knowledge advances by dividing labor with ever-increasing specialization. The more atomized the knowledge, the more difficult it is to put it into a context relevant to private and public decision makers. Fragmentation of knowledge and the isolation of academic disciplines destroy the vital sense that everything is related to everything else.

Leo Bogart says that in every mass medium the secret of success generally lies in entertaining a mass audience rather than in meeting the more rigorous standards of the information-seeking elite. Hence, he argues that the mass media are not disseminating new knowledge but serving the interests of the commercial culture.

Herbert Steinhouse blames the mass media for reducing public taste in the United States to the lowest common denominator. The U.S. public is not the initiator but the victim of its mass media. He contrasts this with the Canadian Broadcasting Corporation's official mandate, which declares that the state has an absolute right to request that those who use the radio frequencies or television channels program their broadcasting imaginatively and with regard for the public interest.

Arthur R. Kantrowitz reasons that the underutilization and misuse of knowledge are the result of the insularity of the technical experts. This insularity may be caused by specialized training and its terminology and reinforced by military and industrial secrecy and the conflict of economic interests. Today two establishments confront each other: the "progress establishment," dedicated to technological progress, and the "critical establishment," dedicated to implementing social goals by regulating technology. Both establishments feed on the public's ignorance. Where the progress establishment implies some social benefits from progress, the critical establishment utilizes scientific uncertainty to arouse fear of the unknown. According to Kantrowitz, the polarization of these two groups has resulted in declining U.S. technological leadership.

Paul Bohannan blames God for the underutilization of knowledge. The story goes that the Babylonian architects wanted to build a high rise that violated the heavenly building code. God, not wanting to take a chance with the real estate interests, separated people linguistically, and by so doing also separated them culturally. When the cultures became incorporated into the character structures of the people, this combination produced cultural premises. People with the same premises are drawn together, keeping out people with different cultural premises. People with different premises frequently have difficulty understanding each other. They find the foreigners' ideas distasteful, boring, or just plain wrong. Bohannan asks: How can a free flow of ideas take place between individuals and societies endowed with different cultural premises? How can the educational process make them aware of these differences?

The Gap Between New Knowledge and the Curriculum

In my view, one of the biggest culprits hindering the optimum utilization of knowledge is the U.S. curriculum, which lacks analytical depth and underutilizes available knowledge. There is a general belief that teaching social science concepts has no place in the elementary grades: For example, young children play grocery store with no reference to the concepts of risk, price, costs, profit, loss, or competition. Children visit the bank and "discover" that the purpose of banks is safekeeping of money. Much later they may discover that banks are the source of capital formation. Curriculum builders are preoccupied with teaching minimum understanding for minimum citizenship. Because of the "minimum syndrome" in practically every grade, teachers are preoccupied with unteaching what has been taught in the previous grades. Probably this is the reason why the curriculum in the first year of college is made up mostly of introductory courses, as if the students have learned nothing in the preceding eighteen years.

Instructional Framework: The Organic Curriculum

To help close the gap between the frontiers of knowledge in the social sciences and the curriculum, I developed the concept of the *organic curriculum*. It is based on the hypothesis that children's experiences are potentially so meaningful that the fundamental ideas of all social science disciplines can be related to their experiences, with increasing depth and complexity as the children mature.

Mary Catherine Bateson calls the totality of a person's daily experiences the "informal system of knowledge." This knowledge may be acquired through experience, observation, play, practice, listening, feeling, and experimenting. In the organic curriculum, the informal system of knowledge plays a very important role. The teacher must have the intellectual capacity and alertness to link the formal system of knowledge to the informal. The informal system of knowledge, if properly utilized by the teachers, gives momentum to learning. Informal learning represents a storehouse of latent knowledge that can be brought to awareness. A student is like an airplane taxiing down the runway, gaining momentum for a takeoff. The teacher must sense when to link the informal system to the concepts and ideas of the formal system of knowledge. When they connect the student is airborne.

Informal knowledge is acquired and used when the child is making decisions on how to spend an allowance (underlying concept: scarcity) or on how to make choices between work and play (underlying concept: opportunity cost). Informal knowledge is acquired when the child notices that father stays home one morning because he has lost his job (underlying concept: employment theory) or when the child reads the fairy tale about the three wishes (underlying concept: scarcity and allocation problem). Informal knowledge is acquired when there is ill feeling or open conflict between members of the family and when the family attempts to resolve it (underlying concept: conflict management).

With the help of Kenneth E. Boulding, I adapted his conflict model for the primary grades in a children's story entitled, "How Scientists Study 'Getting Along.' " This story dramatizes three causes of conflict: conflict because people misunderstand each other, conflict because people want the same thing, and conflict because people are not willing to give in. The story ends with the following:

> Scientists who study conflicts want to keep them under control. They think there should be specialists who keep an eye out for conflict among countries, the way forest rangers keep an eye out for fires.
> In the same way, specialists from different countries could work together. They could carefully watch for any signs of conflicts among people. If they thought a conflict could become dangerous, they could try to settle it immediately. In this way we can hope that our future world will be a peaceful world.[1]

These models, together with other social science concepts, can be related to the children's experiences with increasing depth and complexity, growing to match the child's development like an organism. This is the reason for naming my approach the *organic* curriculum.

It is important that the teacher know the accumulated informal knowledge of the students, which may vary among income classes, ethnic groups, cultural groups, and regions. The teacher must also know the premises underlying this informal knowledge. If the teacher neglects the premises of the students that differ from the teacher's premises, the teacher may experience something like what happened to me in the Cardozo School in Washington, D.C., years ago. I was teaching a second-grade class on the concepts of producer and consumer, using the family as a model. We agreed that members of the family who do useful work are producers and those who use or use up something are consumers. We also discovered, through a lively and humorous simulation, that while everyone is a consumer, not everyone is a producer, e.g., the baby, the very old, the sick, and the unemployed are not producers. I asked the children, "Do you know someone who does not work?" Dead silence. I looked at the teacher who came up to me and said quietly, "With black children you never ask, 'Who does not work in your family?' They think you are a spy from the welfare office."

The organic curriculum gains support from Herman T. Epstein's study, which offers four additional building blocks: (1) Information put into the brain triggers the arborization of dendrites and axons, and if the information is repeated often enough to be learned, the new extensions become permanent. (2) Since the forming of neural networks depends upon information, one should expect to find a developmental diversity in cognitive levels. (3) Most children, by the age of 10, are capable of intuitive, systematic, and formal reasoning. (4) In about 95 percent of children, there are brain growth stages at 2–4 years, 6–8 years, 10–12 years, and 14–16 years. For the organic curriculum, this means that those years when the brain is not growing could best be used reinforcing or enriching previous learning.

Epstein's study affirms that there should be a progression of ideas between grades 1 and 12, rather than having teachers unteach what children have learned in earlier grades.

Value Awareness and the Curriculum

Development of value awareness is necessary in order for students to identify goals for themselves and for society. Unfortunately, values are almost ignored in our schools. Some teachers argue that they have no time to deal with values since they are buried in teaching skills and disciplines. Some parents protest the teaching of values in the schools since they believe values are the responsibility of home and church. So, teaching values in the schools is a no-man's-land with few advocates, and youth are deprived of the ability to learn to set meaningful goals for themselves and society. In colleges, the situation is hardly better. Science courses teach that value judgments lie outside the realm of science. Moral issues are shunted to philosophy courses, which usually are not taken by the students who need them the most.

The almost universal neglect of values is producing a society guided, by default, by the reigning value of self-interest. Self-interest is contributing to the destruction of the global environment. Making self-interest the dominant value unleashes conflict, widens the gap between rich and poor, threatens to exhaust the earth's nonrenewable natural resources, and encourages polluting the air, water, and soil. Most professions contribute to these conditions because their primary interest is solving technical problems while ignoring the ethical dimensions of their work.

Modern society is under pressure to choose value guidelines with a new kind of care and wisdom that goes far beyond simple self-preservation or an improved standard of living. The welfare of the planet is at stake.

The educational system must deal with two sets of values. The first set is the scientific component, which is the commitment to the search for truth. Students should be aware that the search for truth requires the complementary value commitments to freedom, justice, and integrity. The other value component is the ethical dimension, which articulates the idea that other people matter. The ethical component requires the complementary commitments to charity, kindness, and beauty (which includes harmony between the natural and manmade environments).

The need for including some value components in the curriculum is reinforced by the increasing recognition of the varied dimensions of learning necessary to gain and make full use of knowledge. The cognitive aspect of knowing is acquired through analyzing, reasoning, and conceptualizing, and the affective aspect is gained through the intuitive, the creative, the imaginative, the emotional, the spiritual, and the esthetic. Both the cognitive and affective dimensions are equal parts of the whole person, and both are necessary for the optimum use of knowledge.

In the classroom, students should be helped to discover social standards of behavior to guide them through a world of diminishing resources, group conflict, threatening military technology, increasing urbanization, and diminishing contact with nature. Some of these standards of behavior may be:

1. Concern for the environment. Students should appraise the costs and benefits of their choices in terms of the impact on their fellow human beings and on nature.
2. Recognition of what is beautiful and condemnation of what is ugly in the environment.
3. Respect for fellow human beings.

4. Respect for freedom of speech and the right to assemble. Teachers should encourage a climate in which students can discuss their ideas freely, even if their ideas are unpopular.
5. Encouragement to work for perfection. Students should receive positive reinforcement for their work instead of emphasis on their failures.
6. Promotion of social justice by reporting and analyzing current social issues.
7. Emphasis on domestic and international tranquility. The class might study throughout the year the causes and prevention of conflict in the family, the neighborhood, the region, the nation, and between nations.
8. Emphasis on the importance of setting goals. Students should discuss what they want out of life and how a career choice is only one of the goals of life.
9. Respect for the general welfare. Students should understand that general welfare means providing food, clothing, shelter, public health, good education, gainful employment, freedom of choice, and a wholesome environment.

Many of the chapters in this book present new dimensions for developing value awareness in our society that should be reflected in the curriculum.

Vernon Ruttan presents two case studies that offer students the opportunity to discuss the ethical dimensions of government-supported programs. The first case study deals with a tomato harvester invented by mechanical engineers and plant scientists in a state university with taxpayers' money. The results of the invention were increased productivity that benefited agribusiness, the canning industry, consumers, and the inventors; it also caused unemployment for farm workers and loss of a market for small tomato growers. The students might discuss the following ethical questions: Should government fund research that puts farm workers out of work? Do farm workers displaced by labor-saving machinery deserve protection from unemployment? Do the small tomato farmers who lost their market deserve protection?

The second case study raises questions about tobacco research supported by taxpayers' money. What are the moral responsibilities of agricultural researchers and research administrators regarding a crop that not only induces chemical dependency but also has the potential to kill people?

Ruttan offers some guidelines for moral responsibility. He thinks agricultural science must show some concern for the effects of agricultural technology on the health and safety of agricultural producers, the nutrition and health of consumers, the impact of agricultural practices on the quality of the natural and manmade environment, and the quality of life in rural communities.

Edmund D. Pellegrino is another strong proponent of the role of values in society. He believes that the technically correct medical decision should be in harmony with the patient's outlook on life, suffering, and death. If the medical practitioner is to adjust the technically correct medical decision to the philosophical outlook of the patient, the practitioner must draw from all academic disciplines.

Teachers, lawyers, engineers, architects, and other professionals should also be able to combine their technical ability with insight into ethical dimensions. The ability to combine the technical and moral dimensions should be encouraged in early as well as in professional education. For example, a class might invite thoughtful lawyers, doctors, city planners, or teachers to discuss the dilemmas they face in their occupations. It might be pointed out that a moral dilemma frequently springs from a conflict between the values of the individual client or practitioner and the dominant values of society. Following such a discussion, younger children might prepare a display on who is a good teacher or what makes a good doctor. In the upper grades, the students might prepare a term paper on such topics as the moral dimensions of urban renewal, the moral dilemma in fighting inflation, or the moral dilemma of decreasing infant mortality: hunger.

Kenneth E. Boulding refers to each individual's images of values, which may be in harmony or in conflict with the outside world. To become aware of this relationship, students might write an essay on their goals in life. The class might discuss the goals of society, and each student could compare his or her life goals with those of society. A second essay could be written about how to reconcile the differences between the student's goals and society's goals.

Boulding states that "in the long run the social process eliminates erroneous values and strengthens the true ones." The class might organize a debate on the validity of this statement. Both sides might relate their arguments to the values of freedom, justice, peace, and beauty.

To understand the relationship between societal values and the use or misuse of knowledge, the class might be divided into five committees. Each committee could prepare a report on such topics as toxic wastes, deregulation of the airlines, the tobacco subsidy, racial prejudice, or mining on public land.

System Awareness and the Curriculum

Fragmentation of knowledge is a serious obstacle to the optimum utilization of knowledge. The late Alfred Kuhn and his associate, Robert

D. Beam, urged the unification of knowledge through the general system vision, which states that everything is related to everything else.

The development of a system vision should also be an important commitment in the school curriculum. Children picked up the phrase "All systems go!" which the Houston space center used as the astronauts were launched into space. Watching part of the space program on television has helped children in the United States gain informal knowledge about the concept of "system." The space age has given us the opportunity to link system vision to the child's experience.

One summer, Alfred Kuhn, Kenneth Boulding, and I worked on this linkage. Boulding and Kuhn represented frontier thinkers and I represented a first grader. My job was to relate concepts to children's experiences. From this effort I made a great discovery: Knowing and ways of knowing are inseparable. The more one internalizes an idea, the more eloquent and clear the communication of the idea becomes. The primary secret of pedagogical success is clarity of thinking, from which clarity of communication emerges. The frontier thinker and educator both seek this clarity. I took some of the concepts of frontier knowledge one by one and attempted to relate them to a child's experience in the form of classroom exercises. Here are a few examples:

Concept 1: A system is made up of two or more parts that interact. *Classroom Application:* To help young people discover systems, students should collect objects or cut out pictures of things such as a vacuum cleaner, a dishwasher, an anthill, a refrigerator, a clock, a family, a tree, a church, the Salvation Army, a school, a post office, a pond, a TV, a telephone, a furnace, a wilderness, a farm, a dog, a human being, and an air conditioning unit. All of these living and nonliving things are made up of parts that interact to do a job. The class will discover that some systems are simple (e.g., a clock), while others are complicated and made up of many subsystems. Such complicated systems include an anthill, a family, and a television set that functions only when linked with other systems.

Concept 2: Systems may be goal oriented or not goal oriented. *Classroom Application:* Students will select from the examples of systems those that are goal oriented: a human being, a church, a school, the Salvation Army, a plant, a cat, a dog, the post office, a family, a refrigerator, an air conditioning unit, etc. Then the students will explain, one by one, the goals of each system and how the system corrects itself if some disturbance obstructs the achievement of its goals.

Concept 3: Some systems are capable of learning, while others are not. *Classroom Application:* The class may discuss the following questions: Are human beings a part of nature? (Yes.) Are human beings a system? (Yes, human beings' organs interact with each other.) Is a human being a goal-oriented system? (Yes.) What are the goals of a human being?

(To change the natural environment or to build an environment to improve the human condition.) What is the difference between the beaver and the human being as a goal-oriented system? (Human beings, through learning, develop many different organizations and life-styles in their settlements, which they can improve through invention and innovation. The beaver's ability to learn is limited; therefore, the life-styles and organization of the beaver colony are static.)

Concept 4: In a social system, inertia plays an important role in keeping the system in equilibrium. *Classroom Application:* The students should try to find examples of how customs keep a system in equilibrium, for example, how the habit of drinking coffee in the United States assures the stability of income of coffee producers and the coffee industry.

Concept 5: Science and technology and changing value preferences perpetually challenge the equilibrium of the economic system. Some systems make adjustments quickly; others do not. *Classroom Application:* The students may discuss how the following forces affect the equilibrium of systems:

1. The invention of the automobile and its impact on the urban system.
2. The expanded welfare system and its impact on charitable organizations.
3. The impact of longevity on the family system.
4. The impact of the assembly line on the design and location of factories.
5. The impact of robots on factories.

Concept 6: Changes in a system create costs or benefits to the society. *Classroom Application:* The class may collect newspaper articles illustrating such relationships. The headlines might be: "Oil Leaks Off California Coast," "Billboards Approved in Yellowstone National Park," "Grand Canyon Slated for Power Generation." After discussing what social costs or benefits are brought about by these changes, the students should consider who ought to pay the costs and who should enjoy the benefits of these changes.

Concept 7: The U.S. economic system is a goal-oriented learning system. During the more than 200 years of its history, six national goals have emerged: economic growth, economic stability, economic security, economic freedom, economic justice, and quality of life. *Classroom Application:* The class might be divided into six committees. For a whole semester, each committee could study and report on the role of its chosen goal in the history of the United States. Each committee should try to answer the following questions: What were the historical forces that caused the recognition of this goal or value? What dislocation of goals was caused by the recognition of the new goal? How did this goal reinforce or conflict with the other five goals? How successful were public policies in achieving this goal? To which of these six goals does the present administration give high priority? Do you agree or disagree with this priority? Why?

Problem Awareness and the Curriculum

The curriculum must develop problem awareness, which means the students should learn that there is a social problem when there is a gap between the ideals or goals of a society and social reality. The students should be able to apply the scientific method to examining a social problem. They should recognize:

1. Symptoms of the problem: Students should be able to deduce from an outward manifestation that something is wrong. Examples: riots, soup kitchens, rising cost of living.
2. Aspects of the problem: This step should reveal the consequences if the problem is ignored or if knowledge is misused in solving the problem. Example: Ignoring the problem of unemployment creates a political polarization in society.
3. Definition of the problem: This step reflects the gap between goals and social reality. Example: How can we provide employment for all who are able and willing to work?
4. Scope of the problem: Students can use statistical data to measure the magnitude of the problem. Example: Historical trend of unemployment according to age, sex, level of education, ethnicity, region, or type of work.
5. Causes of the problem: As a test, students apply a hypothesis exploring what contributed to the cause. Example: Employment theory and supply-side economics.
6. Solution of the problem: This step describes what individuals, volunteers, and government can do to find solutions to the problem. Example: Description and analysis of the present public policy.
7. The dislocation caused by private and public policy measures. Example: Environmental impact of the solution.

Applying the Problem Approach to the Question of Professional Competence

There is an increasing mistrust of the professions in the United States, from medical practitioners to public servants, and since so many college students plan to be trained for professional careers, it is imperative that they should know the nature of the problem. Below, I present five steps through which the problem of professional competence may be studied, based upon Donald A. Schön's "Crisis of Confidence in Professional Knowledge."

Symptoms of the problem: Headlines, public dialogues, and protests reflect a lack of confidence in professional standards and decisions. In 1963, the editor of *Daedalus* characterized the image of the professions by saying that "everywhere in American life, the professions are triumphant." Headlines such as these are in sharp contrast with that statement: "Scandals of Medicare and Medicaid Tarnish Medical Professions"; "Science Enslaved by the Military-Industrial Complex"; "Professional Services: the Privilege of the Rich"; "Pollution: the Achievement of Science and Technology"; "Technically Efficient Solutions Undermine General Welfare"; "Sociologists Arouse Protest by Claiming Differences in Mental Abilities of Whites and Blacks"; "Laymen Turn to the Court for Defense against Professional Incompetence and Venality"; "Consumer Groups Demand External Regulation of Professional Practices."

Aspects of the problem: This step describes the possible consequences of inadequate professional practices, such as: (1) loss of public faith in professional judgment; (2) possible loss of professional freedom; (3) unbalanced professional judgment, which may have severe unforeseen consequences; and (4) the fast application of new professional knowledge, which may create anxiety and fear.

Definition of the problem: This step presents the gap between goals or ideals and social reality. In light of current professional practices, how can professional standards be improved so as to assure optimum utilization of specialized professional knowledge for human betterment?

Scope of the problem: This step presents the statistical data, measuring the magnitude of the problem. Examples of such data are (1) unequal distribution of services among regions and income groups; (2) distribution of scientific and technological professions among the military, the nonmilitary, and research and development; (3) statistics on legal and medical malpractice suits; and (4) the extent of environment destruction caused by highly specialized professional decisions.

Causes of the problem: This step presents the multidisciplinary forces that contribute to the underutilization or misuse of knowledge in the professions, such as:

1. Professional decisions are lacking system vision, namely, the recognition that everything is related to everything else.
2. Social movements of the 1960s began to see the professions as servants of vested interests.

3. The public feels that professionals are powerless to cope with the many crucial problems necessitating political and social skills, such as poverty, pollution, crime, and conflict.
4. Professional inertia prevents the discovery of problems before they reach a crisis stage.
5. Social reality creates problems so complex that even the highly specialized professions are unable to discover solutions.
6. There is an inherent conflict between creation of new knowledge, which requires the reductionist method, and the process of applying knowledge to problem solving, which requires comprehensive methods.
7. Lack of artfulness in professional practice hurts valuable professional-client relationships.
8. The professional practitioner frequently adjusts the problem to fit prevailing models of technical rationality.
9. The positivist ideas that dominate our universities emphasize that human progress can be achieved by a science that creates a technology. The positivist approach may achieve rigor in terms of technical rationality, but it does so at the price of neglecting the complex network of reality, which gives rise to a multitude of interrelationships. After World War II, specialists developed many theoretical models for solving real world problems (e.g., the Club of Rome). In subsequent decades, however, there has been a growing recognition of the limits of these computer techniques, especially in situations of high complexity and uncertainty.
10. The emphasis of professional education is on technical rationality, which excludes as nonrigorous much of what competent practitioners actually do.

Solution of the Problem: There are three steps to the solution:

1. Professional training must be conducted in relation to the larger social network and to the value systems and practices of the individual and society.
2. Professional commitment must be related not only to problem solving but also to problem finding before the problem reaches a crisis stage.
3. Many professional practice situations are complex and uncertain, and training must recognize that science-based models must be complemented by intuitive and reflective knowing-in-action. This means the practitioner cannot always depend on the categories of established theories and techniques but must be able to construct

new theories to fit unique circumstances. This reflective and intuitive knowing-in-action is particularly relevant to the teaching profession, since the teacher's job is to find out what a learner already knows and to connect that with the learning process. Also, teachers should be able to approach a teaching situation in a variety of ways in order to cope with the many difficulties encountered by the students.

To put it in simple terms, professionals have to learn how to think on their feet, a whole way of knowing possible only when the professional can (1) act spontaneously as a result of something learned earlier and (2) reflect on problems that are not in the book.

Knowledge Awareness and the Curriculum

Many chapters in this volume deal with the theory and classification of knowledge, the reasons that knowledge is misused or underutilized, and the conditions that are necessary for the optimum utilization of knowledge. All these dimensions have important curriculum applications.

Fritz Machlup tells us that there is conventional and nonconventional knowledge. The nonconventional knowledge may be divided into three categories: (1) negative knowledge, such as astrology; (2) controversial knowledge, such as parapsychology; and (3) explosive knowledge, such as sociobiology, which investigates race differences as they correlate with mental abilities; genetic engineering, which can lead to the deliberate modification of genes; and nuclear technology, which threatens to destroy all living creatures.

Students in the classroom might discuss the validity and significance of this classification. They might prepare a sociodrama to explain why there is a popular upsurge of interest in negative knowledge such as astrology. Students might organize a panel to discuss whether there is a clear and present danger implicit in genetic research, genetic engineering, and nuclear technology. The class might discuss how the governmental allocation of funds affects what knowledge is created and what knowledge is not created and how the government affects the diffusion of knowledge. The students might discuss the consequences of the government's priorities as it allocates funds for research and dissemination of knowledge.

According to Machlup, a long-debated issue is the optimum use of knowledge for the benefit of future generations. The students might select for discussion an environmental issue or the exhaustion of a nonrenewable resource and discuss the following questions: Does the older generation owe anything to its grandchildren? On the one hand, the older generation may exhaust an important resource, but, on the other hand, it may leave the younger generation a large reservoir of knowledge to help it develop substitutes which are better than the exhausted resource. On the one hand, the older generation may exercise all thoughtfulness in conserving resources, but, on the other hand, the younger generation may develop the scientific and technological knowledge that will make such self-sacrifice unnecessary. On the one hand, in the long run the future generation may have the technological know-how and wisdom to cope with such issues as nuclear fallout or the accumulation of dioxin or acid rain, but, on the other hand, in the short run, the older generation will have died from the pollution. If we owe anything to future generations, do we have to change our values to establish harmony between human action and the environment?

The chapters in this volume challenge the conventional approaches to transmitting knowledge in the classroom. For example, James N. Danziger shows that the holders of political authority frequently stimulate the creation and dissemination of knowledge to their own advantage. Danziger's presentation of the drama of the political process challenges the conventional civics courses and invites a general systems approach in the study of political systems. This approach has been developed by David Easton, visiting professor of political science at the University of California, Irvine, and I have adapted it for use in grades 1-12 by relating these ideas to children's experiences with increasing depth and complexity.

Fundamental Ideas of Political Science

1. The political system is an open system because it interacts with the natural, national, and international societal environment.
2. The purpose of interaction is to meet authoritatively the demands of the people.
3. The political authority responds to the demands of the people; therefore, the political system is a goal-oriented system, and because it responds to the changing demands of the people, it is also a learning system.
4. The political demands are generated by the Congress, by members of the executive branch of the government, by public opinion, and by lobbyists.
5. Political demands create stress because of the scarcity of resources, the unresponsiveness of the government, an overload of the political system, the complexity of demands, and the value conflicts generated by these demands.

6. Political demands may die or may become binding decisions (i.e., laws and regulations), depending on the distribution of political power.
7. Binding decisions generate new demands. They may strengthen or weaken the ties of citizens to the political community, to the constitutional order (the regime), and to those who occupy positions of authority.
8. The political system may be held together through the quantity and quality of binding decisions, which are favored by those who benefit from them, through the people's belief that the occupants of positions of authority exercise their power legitimately, and through the political socialization of symbols, such as flags, anthems, and holidays.

These dynamics of the political system can be introduced to children in the first grade when they study the family and its rules, in the third grade when they study the city, and in the fifth grade when they study the country.

The main theme of Arthur R. Kantrowitz's paper is the exploitation of ignorance by two groups in the political system. As I mentioned earlier, one group is the progress establishment, dedicated to technological progress, and the other group is the critical establishment, dedicated to applying ethical standards to the use of technology. Both establishments, according to Kantrowitz, exploit voter ignorance. He recommends a science court to promote rational public decision making on the costs and benefits of scientific and technological progress.

The class might enact a science court in science and social science classes, with a cast of four case managers, two for the progress establishment and two for the critical establishment. Four judges for the court could examine the statements of the parties for their scientific relevance. At the opening session of the court, the case managers for the two sides would present their cases to the judges. At the second session of the court, they would present the points of agreement. At the third session, they would present their points of disagreement and try to narrow the areas of disagreement through mediation, with the help of the judges. At the fourth session, the case managers would present their statements and arguments on issues of disagreement. Case managers and judges would have a chance to cross-examine each party. If the disagreement was not resolved at the final session, the judges would announce their opinions.

Topics for the courtroom dramas may be obtained from the National Research Council's *Issues and Current Studies* (an annual publication) and from *Science* magazine.

Kenneth E. Boulding's chapter is a rich source for curriculum builders. The following activities illustrate how some of Boulding's concepts can be translated into the classroom.

Beginning in kindergarten, people should attempt to answer these five questions:

1. How do we know? To answer this question, teachers should help children discover that they are learning a lot in informal situations, without realizing they have learned. This informal learning should be an important take-off point for formal learning.
2. What should we know? To answer this question, teachers should emphasize the multi-disciplinary dimensions of life so the child does not see the world through the narrow vision of a specialist. The multidisciplinary dimensions of life are necessary to pursue work and leisure.
3. Why should we know? To answer this question, teachers should stimulate children's natural intellectual curiosity. Children in kindergarten barrage teachers with "why" questions. The classroom should establish an atmosphere that encourages such questions and makes full use of the questioning to motivate this curiosity still further.
4. How do I use knowing to make choices? To answer this question, teachers can help students evaluate alternative futures, a particularly relevant process to students both as individuals and as citizens. An example of decision making would be to ask, "What do I have to know to vote for or against death penalty legislation?" Or another example might be, "What must I know to decide whether or not I want to serve in the army?" Or, "What must I know to render justice to a thief?"
5. Whom should I know? To answer this question, teachers should emphasize the importance of choosing friends and models because such choices effect one's development, one's options, and one's personality over a lifetime.

The students could review each day's events (local, national, or international), using optimum utilization of knowledge as a frame of reference. The optimum use of knowledge makes the world better rather than worse. Misuse of knowledge is one indication that things are getting worse rather than better. The class members may discover some disagreements among themselves due to differences in their values and the extent of their knowledge.

The students may identify national or global problems and then investigate why society is unsuccessful in solving these problems. Possible reasons could be:

1. Physical, cultural, and political limitations may impede the search for a solution.
2. There may be a lack of verifiable knowledge.
3. Misuse of knowledge may occur.
4. Society's values and premises stimulate the production of private and public artifacts that threaten human welfare and even survival.
5. Spokespeople for the frontiers of knowledge may be subdued because they threaten the status or income of the powerful members of society.
6. The organizational structure of bureaucracy may hinder the creation of new knowledge or the use of old knowledge.
7. The problem may not be considered a problem by the politically powerful groups.
8. Decision makers may be uninformed about how to solve the problem.
9. The solution of the problem may threaten the image the authorities want to maintain of themselves.

Students may write a paper on ideals and social reality in the United States. The purpose would be to identify the ideals of the founding fathers, to check the contemporary social scene against these ideals, and to conclude whether in the long run humankind is moving toward values of truth and justice or away from these values.

To learn that the images they form about the world determine the way they act, the students may each read a news report or watch a certain TV program and present a substantive report about their impressions to the class. The class can then discuss the reasons for the differences in their reports and how these differences may affect their possible actions.

To help students discover that the powerful frequently resist testing the validity of their knowledge, the students may search in history for what happened to independent thinkers who challenged the prevailing image of the world and the knowledge of those with political powers.

The class may invite a Marxist to explain the reasons for his or her belief in the scientific interpretation of history. The class may study the ideology of the Soviet Union and determine how the threat system perpetuates this ideology.

So that students may understand that knowledge is made up of images of facts and images of values, the students may write an essay on their goals in life and in the class discuss the goals of society. Comparing them, they can try to discover harmony or conflict between their personal goals and society's goals. Students may discuss how their goals might change if they moved to a commune committed to mutual aid or to a high-income suburban community or to an Amish community or to a community prejudiced against certain minorities.

To help students discover that seeing through the eyes of a specialist distorts social reality, a student panel may be organized in which each student takes a role, such as an economist, a political scientist, a theologian, an engineer, a businessman, or a military expert. Each can bring a specialized point of view to such problems as increasing military expenditures, decreasing aid to the poor, or speeding up the construction of nuclear power plants.

To help students recognize that learning is a never-ending process and that aging is not necessarily a handicap to continued learning, the class could prepare an exhibit of books, reproductions of art work, and musical compositions produced by creative people in their senior years. Students may also invite senior community leaders, business executives, and other professionals to their classroom to explain their particular work and the reasons that age has enhanced rather than curtailed their creativity.

To help students discover how the values of society affect the production of human artifacts, they may present an exhibit of how they would spend a given amount of money to provide themselves with the greatest satisfaction. Then the class could discuss whether the priorities they established would lead to human betterment.

Do Wonder and Joy Have a Place in the Curriculum?

An important factor in learning is wonderment. Let the students' imaginations soar in the classroom. What better time to start the study of ecology than in the first grade? Help the children discover that the earth's life is a system of interdependent creatures, and we are among them. We wonder how this system works. Teach the puzzles of cosmology. Describe to the youngest minds that some things going on in the universe are unknown. Encourage students to use their imaginations to reach toward the unknown.

The humanities reflect our unceasing effort to make moral, philosophical, and spiritual sense of the world. For writers, artists, and spiritual leaders, the humanities mean a liberation from form and convention, the right to rebel and create new forms and structures in speech, writing, painting, and music. For the scientists, the humanities mean accountability as citizens for the moral consequences of the new knowledge they create.

The humanities should not be the monopoly of the intellectual elite but a part of the lives of ordinary people who need a philosophical, historical, esthetic, and moral perspective on their daily activities. For this reason, the humanities must be a part of the K-12 curriculum.

The interplay between the fear of knowledge and human aspiration comes forth dramatically in Rollo May's paper. He builds a bridge between compassion, hope, beauty, and knowledge. He quotes the last lines of John Milton's *Paradise Lost*, where Adam and Eve, eating the apple from the tree, gain access to knowledge, but simultaneously acquire anxiety, fear, loneliness, and the capacity for love.

> Some natural tears they dropped, but wiped them soon.
> The world was all before them, where to choose
> Their place of rest, and Providence their guide
> They hand in hand, with wandering steps and slow,
> Through Eden took their solitary way.

Rollo May also builds the bridge between fear and knowledge. He quotes Aeschylus who, in *Prometheus Bound*, presents the hope of creativity and the fear of the loss of knowledge:

> I found them [humankind] witless and gave them
> the use of their wits and made them masters of their minds. . . .

> For men at first had eyes but saw to no purpose:
> they had ears but did not hear. Like the shapes
> of dreams, they dragged through their long lives
> and handled all things in bewilderment and confusion. . . .

> They lived like swarming ants in holes in the ground,
> and in the sunless caves of the earth. . . . all their
> doings were indeed without intelligent calculation
> until I showed them the rising of the stars, and the
> settings, hard to observe. And further I discovered
> to them numbering, pre-eminent among the subtle devices,
> and the combining of letters as a means of remembering
> all things. . . .

> I first adjudged what things come verily true
> from dreams; and to men I gave meaning to the
> ominous cries, hard to interpret.

> . . . all arts that mortals have come from Prometheus.

In his struggle against the tyranny of Zeus, Prometheus gains the support of the chorus: "Your mind was yours, not his." But then the chorus cautions: "You regarded mortal men too highly."

Children experience the connection between questing and joy, the fundamental relationship between the sciences and the humanities. A few years ago I read an article by Albert Szent-Györgyi in *Science* magazine.[2] I rewrote the article and placed it (with Szent-Györgyi's permission, of course), in my second-grade teacher's guide to *Our Working World: Neighbors at Work*.

I included Szent-Györgyi's thoughts to tell children that they go to school to learn about the ideas of other people, to discover ideas of their own, and to use these ideas to build a better world. Here is a part of that message:

> Nature is wondrous and full of secrets. Men must work very hard and be very patient to discover Nature's secrets. But every day, scientists learn more and more of them. Well, this makes you children and your teachers wonder: how can we possibly learn all the many things that scientists are discovering? Do not worry, for Nature's most wonderful secret is that the truly important things are really simple. As scientists learn more and more, they discover that things that seem complicated and confusing at first are really all parts of a few simple big ideas. . . .
>
> All around our world are people writing stories and poems, and people reading them, and people writing music and people making music and dancing, and artists painting pictures, and people being pleased or surprised by them. All around the world people are working hard to make our world a healthier place. All around our world people are working hard to produce more food to bring to the hungry. Making our little world a better place takes a lot of work. Science helps us to do this work. Good feeling for our world helps us to do this work.
>
> There have always been men and women who tried to make our world a better place. They have done this with their study of science and history, and with their stories, poems, and plays, their music, paintings and hard work.

. . . and this is the way I try to communicate the optimum utilization of knowledge to children.

Notes

1. Kenneth Boulding, "How Scientists Study 'Getting Along,' " in Lawrence Senesh, *Our Working World: Neighbors at Work*. Resource Unit. Chicago, Science Research Associates, 1965. pp. 275–276.

2. Adapted from "Teaching and the Expanding Knowledge," Albert Szent-Györgyi. *Science*, v. 146, no. 3649, December 4, 1964, pp. 1278–1279.

PART THREE

Applying Knowledge to Decision Making

HERBERT STEINHOUSE

—— **15** ——

Closing the Gap Between Expanding Knowledge and Society Through Television in the U.S.

In the United States, uniquely, radio and television grew out of the heritage of the early diversion industries and the commercialized arts, as an integral part of the profit system. Only a few short years ago on many an American campus, broadcasting was still being dismissed as but a sophisticated update of the minstrel show, the song-and-dance man, *The Perils of Pauline,* and the five-cent Western. Few appreciated its potential as the effective medium for conveying culture and knowledge, often through "entertainment," to the greatest number in the shortest time. More than any other means known hitherto, television closes the great gap between increasingly available new knowledge and the information that individuals and societies already have on hand for survival—for coping with the realities, the dangers, and the goals of life—and for explanation, enrichment, and ennoblement.

In Canada and in most other countries, the tendency has been to give to broadcasting front-line responsibilities.[1] Canada, after all, is a nation largely created out of a network of east-to-west communications rather than economic ties. From the *voyageur* fur traders' transport canoes, through the vast-scale transcontinental telegraph and railway enterprises and nation-crossing highways, airlines, and telephone systems, to the world's longest microwave and to pioneering domestic broadcast satellites, came a viable state. Canadians are served by important broadcasting networks offering instantaneous shared experience that transcends regionalism, cultural diversity, and particularism. It is their prime source of those everyday realities and myths that help to cement the interests and broaden the outlook of any people.[2] For fifty years, in fact, Canadian public policy unswervingly supported the principle that *all* broadcasting in the country must serve as an instrument of the national purpose. In few other nations would an officially appointed commission report back to Parliament that "the communications of a nation are as vital to its life as are its defenses, and should receive at least as great a measure of national protection."[3]

American Commercial Television Today

Generally public broadcasters around the world conduct themselves in accordance with their great responsibilities, within their ideological contexts and budget constraints. How does U.S. commercial television use its extraordinary privilege of being franchised with the gift and public trust of the nation's airwaves?

At CBS's polished black rock headquarters on the Avenue of the Americas in New York City, the directors' boardroom is a transplanted banquet hall from a medieval French chateau. The senior executive floor's corridors are lined—floors, walls, and ceiling—with gorgeous llama-wool pile from the Andes. The last time I entered the building I was crushed against the wall in the lobby by executives who, having analyzed the rating sweeps, were rushing to get the Dow-Jones quotations on their company stock options. CBS, NBC, and ABC network headquarters are all preoccupied, body and soul, with share of audience, cumulative ratings, corporate strategies, their interconnections with major industrial and financial corporations, and mergers, acquisitions, and crossmedia ownerships.

Perhaps one key question is whether there is still time to close the gap between expanding knowledge and the "Knowledge Conglomerates'" main self-imposed obligation: to expand their wealth. These overvulgarized and overcommercialized merchandisers of diversions, misusing public property, generally appear even less willing to confront the challenge of television's potential than they occasionally did a generation ago.

The case for vigilant public regulation has been made forcefully in Canada and in Great Britain, time and time again. As the eloquent recommendations by Canada's Committee on Broadcasting stated back in 1965, "To the extent that an adequate program performance is given voluntarily, the broadcaster can be left relatively free from detailed controls. If adequate performance is not given, it should be compelled by regulation, or the franchise should be re-assigned to others who will perform responsibly. Without question the State has an absolute right to require from any broadcaster, to whom the use of a radio frequency or TV channel has been entrusted, that he use it with imagination, distinction and responsible regard for the public interest."[4]

The instrument of regulation and control is the CRTC—the Canadian Radio-television and Telecommunications Commission—whose prime function is to license all broadcasters and cable systems, extract overall operating commitments from them, and strive to hold them to national, regional, and local programming responsibilities and to content standards "in the public interest." Though government-appointed, the commissioners, on the whole, have proved that they can function outside the pulls and processes of partisan politics and of lobbyists' pressures. In Canada there is a dominant democratic broadcasting tradition free from most constraints; and there is pride, certainly within the publicly owned Canadian Broadcasting Corporation, in being the freest broadcaster, bar none, in the world.

U.S. broadcasters, on the other hand, have successfully fought most efforts to impose regulatory checks and obligations by using various means, fair or foul. In *Television and Society* Harry J. Skornia asked a fundamental question: "Has the United States found the proper institutional framework and control mechanisms for the . . . functions which television and radio must provide if democracy is to prevail? Are vast and powerful business corporations, which centralize control each year in fewer hands, the best trustees for the nation's . . . communications systems?"[5]

Nicholas Johnson, a former commissioner of the Federal Communications Commission, offered a sobering reply: "We have already reached the point where the media, our greatest check on other accumulations of power, may themselves be beyond the reach of any other institution. . . . Only the FCC is directly empowered to keep media ownership patterns compatible with a democracy's need for diversified sources of opinion and information. . . . But since the New Deal generation left the command posts of the FCC, this agency has lost much of its zeal for combating concentration."[6] That was true enough in 1965. It is irrefutable today.

The sweeping rejoinder of the private networks and their apologists, of course, is to equate all public controls with censorship, Big Government, and incipient socialism and to cite the holy writ of their ratings books as vindication: They only provide their audience, they say, with what the people most desire. This is the classic claim of a manufacturing industry, but self-respecting and creative broadcasters don't speak that way. In any event, set down a typical network audience research specialist in Oliver Twist's London workhouse and he could soon demonstrate that the majority of orphans in the five- to fifteen-year bracket desire little more from life than a double portion of thin gruel. "Far from being an expression of majority desire, as the networks say," wrote the well-known broadcaster Alexander Kendrick, "television programs are the imposition of a social minority on the majority . . . the minority consisting of the fifty top advertisers, the three networks and a dozen advertising agencies. It is what they think public taste is and demands that governs the nature of broadcasting."[7]

What most puzzles critical foreigners about U.S. commercial television is that it put its very purposes backwards, quite soon after the electronic dawn. The industry sometimes seems akin to a fraternity of slave-traders; its primary function is to deliver to the nation's advertisers, back at the plantation, so many million eyes and ears of the nation's buyers of consumer goods. These organs are obtained in different demographic packages: so-called total audiences or particular audiences composed primarily of, say, shopping housewives or covetous children. The network or station tries to keep the relevant eyes and ears reasonably responsive by surrounding the commercial blandishments with a given length of studio-produced or purchased program material—occasionally created, more often manufactured on an assembly line.[8] If the material can attract through distinctive qualities at least a third of the turned-on sets, so much the better. At the very least it is expected to possess "LOP potential," which, in self-deprecating network jargon, means catering to viewers who constantly change channels in search of the least objectionable program.

U.S. television is not all bad, of course. A continuing dramatic series can have various positive values and sensible moral lessons. An "entertainment" program might be honestly entertaining, humorous, well-crafted, and tension-relieving. Another might be adult enough to illuminate some personal concerns or to fight against hostilities and bigotry. There are even a few programs that regularly marry drama's showbiz techniques to public affairs content, attractively packaging information of greater or lesser significance, perhaps following the network sales departments' fairly recent discovery that people concerned about social, economic, and political matters *also* drink beer, wash their hands, and drive cars. There is often excellent coverage of major news happenings, e.g., political conventions and space shots. There are frequent mar-shallings of enviable resources to bring us a sports event, the explosion of a volcano, an election in India, a documentary on Ireland, an expensive recreation of the Japan of the shoguns, or Marco Polo's China— "occasional high-rise projects in a ghetto of high-return tenements," in the words of the respected documentary producer and former head of CBS News, Fred W. Friendly.

Nevertheless, any objective assessment of the total picture confirms that the priorities still are reversed, certainly when compared with those of broadcasting industries in most other nations, whose main systems are paid for *directly* by the public and operate, badly or well, with the primary purpose of serving that public's interests and needs.

"It is inconceivable that we should allow so great a possibility for service, for news, for entertainment, for education, and for vital commercial purposes, to be drowned in advertising chatter." Thus spoke none other than Herbert Hoover about America's infant broadcasting industry in 1922, when he was secretary of commerce. But it *was* conceivable. By 1959 Walter Lippmann could deplore that television had become "the creature, the servant and indeed the prostitute of merchandising."

Hundreds have sung the same litany, even a long line of network decision makers themselves. All have been prisoners of their institutional environment. Whatever their background and personal tastes, their choices of content, scheduling, and commercial options have been predicated mainly on a relentless compulsion to grab great audiences and increase profits and the market value of the shares, on the preponderant influence and earning requirements of each network's own five stations (historically the big profit centers of the corporation), and on the overwhelming powers of their profit-absorbed private affiliates.[9]

The last point should be stressed. Under the system, affiliates would probably abandon any network offering essentially programming of good taste and quality. They have long fought against special preemptions and carrying network-proffered programs that could cut into monthly earnings.[10] On Canada's major network the CBC programmers schedule and preempt at will, and privately owned stations contractually affiliated to a CBC English or French network must carry everything distributed within all mandatory network time periods. In any event, CBC can reach most of its farflung audiences from the Atlantic to the Pacific to the high Arctic directly, through the nearly five hundred television and almost six hundred radio transmitters currently owned and operated by the public corporation itself. In the United States, even when a network does courageously offer an exceptional program, it may find that many of its affiliates deem the program too controversial or commercially unprofitable and that viewers in a hundred cities consequently are unable to watch.

A still more basic public safeguard curiously missing in the United States is any officially imposed programming obligation in the first place. It is the local stations that have the official franchises, some mild accountability, a few caveats and regulations, and access to the airwaves. The U.S. networks, probably uniquely in the world, are not even licensed.

Therefore, firmly in control of each broadcasting system are its sales-, advertising-, and business-oriented custodians. After two generations of conditioning, the audience apparently finds the systems' distorted functioning "normal." By now viewers expect a nightly parade of clones, of video diversions from life's reality, and little that smells of social responsibility, education, uplift, or information.

The combined U.S. private networks devote under 4 percent of their total prime-time programming to current affairs. In contrast, Canada's private CTV network schedules about 8 percent, while the CBC's current-affairs programs on television compose about 24 percent of prime time. As for the total broadcast schedule, the CBC's English TV national network reports almost exactly 50 percent of its programs in the categories of "Information and Orientation" and "Arts, Letters and Sciences" and 50 percent in the "Light Entertainment" and "Sports and Outdoors" categories.

"My criticism of commercial broadcasting," declared Michael Dann, a former head of CBS programming, speaking "as one who contributed as much as anybody to this failure, is that, unlike the BBC or NHK in Japan, it did not make adults out of children."[11]

It is not, mind you, that U.S. television's critics ever suggest that the networks suddenly act as philanthropies. No one demands money-losing schedules fit only for earnest university graduates or concertgoers or amateur paleontologists. The medium is intended for mass audiences, and big audiences everywhere require diversity, with plenty of sports, light music, variety shows, comedies, and even a dose of distracting thrillers and westerns. Normally, wise and responsible broadcasting executives supply all these elements and more in the program mix, reaching for excellence within each category, respecting their own judgment and vision, and avoiding, if possible, the mediocre, the unhealthy, and the meretricious. But, normally, broadcasters also find plenty of good time slots to schedule the more serious substance that *does* educate and uplift. Today, reality on U.S. commercial television remains a scarce commodity, and that is *not* normal.

Public Television in the United States

In the 1960s there developed in the marketplace a curiosity about foreign beer—and about television programs with body and flavor. Many accepted conformities were being zestfully questioned on campuses and in major cities, and travelers were bearing witness to the maturing medium of television in other lands. Besides, at home, television sets by now had become so universal, and the sales-oriented networks had become so intrigued with the increased consumer role of the lesser-educated and adolescent viewers, that common-denominator programming was being pitched ever lower. The producers of a sponsored popular science special about the sun, I recall, argued fiercely during production over the great American audience's "average intellectual age": should they target their show at the fourteen-year-old or the twelve-year-old? A growing number of disenchanted viewers and former viewers began to think of profit-oriented television as irrelevant: as quaint an institution for today's needs as the medieval village water seller, as anachronistic as the privately owned mountain tollroad. The first Carnegie Commission surveyed the video barrenness, and in quick order its recommendations, *Public Television—A Program for Action*, were translated into legislation as the Public Broadcasting Act of 1967.

Essayist E. B. White told the Carnegie Commission what *he* expected: "I think television should . . . arouse our dreams, satisfy our hunger for beauty, take us on journeys, enable us to participate in events, present great drama and music, explore the sea and the sky and the woods and the hills. It should be our Lyceum, our Chautauqua, our Minsky's, our Camelot. It should restate and clarify the social dilemma and the political pickle." In his eloquent way White was urging a new, publicly owned television system to help close up the gap between expanding knowledge—and all the proliferating cultural availabilities—and contemporary American society.

But the Carnegie Commission's recommendations were imbued with circumspection and political pragmatism. Public television's province was defined as "all that is of human interest and importance *which is not at the moment appropriate or available for support by advertising*, and which is not arranged for formal instruction" (emphasis added). Public television, that is to say, should limit itself to leftovers: leftover subjects, leftover financing, and leftover viewers. It should behave as a discreet child in the corner and let the grown-ups get on with their important talk about money, cumulative ratings, and soap flakes.

Congress and government endorsed the report's Great Society rhetoric and humble aspirations and, amidst the military spending spree of the Vietnam War, established an even humbler structure, set of purposes, and financing that would keep the newest-born of the world's public broadcasters permanently starved, permanently dependent, and pathetically confused.

In Canada, on the other hand, where public radio is fifty years old and public television is thirty, and where the Canadian Broadcasting Corporation similarly is obliged to defer to North America's mercantile ethos and to operate in competition with private broadcasters, the CBC's marching orders from Parliament include the broad assignment to provide "a balanced service of information, enlightenment and entertainment for people of different ages, interests and tastes, covering the whole range of programming in fair proportion."[12] And if a choice between the public broadcaster and the private broadcasters of the overall system ever becomes a policy issue, it is the CBC's needs that should have priority.[13]

An early president of the CBC, A. D. Dunton, once spelled out the legalese of the official mandate this way: "Our role," he told a parliamentary committee, "is to serve Canadians in all walks of life, old and young; to bring broadcasting of pleasure and value to them; to meet in fair proportion their varying interests and tastes; in doing so, to use the vivid power of television to communicate many things that people want—varied entertainment, information, ideas, opinions, pictures and reflections of many doings and developments, of many aspects of life; to offer plenty that is diverting and relaxing, and also to offer things of beauty, of significance." The Canadian brand of public television is E. B. White's brand.

The Carnegie Commission had suggested modest and carefully insulated federal funding, building to $104 million annually, to make public television "a civilized voice in a civilized community . . . an instrument for the free communication of ideas in a free society." Congress appropriated under $5 million for 1969 to support the new Corporation for Public Broadcasting (CPB), plus television's needs, plus radio's. CBS alone was then spending twice as much just on programming in a single week.

With such unheroic beginnings, public television has passed much of its first decade in disappointment, controversy, internal disarray, and political accommodation. Its programs have too often been marked, in the prominent critic Les Brown's words, "by the intellectual prudence, the social cautions and the feigned creative vitality that were the hallmarks of commercial television in America."[14] It has rarely challenged the major networks seriously, has generally had to stand on the sidelines in the battles of audience-building news and current affairs programming, and, on the whole, has been constricted into the role of providing complementary, not alternative, television.

Its shackles have been those of not only severe financial limitations but structural and political ones as well. The CPB and Public Broadcasting Service (PBS) seem to emerge from each metamorphosis still intimately beholden to every easily offended politician, the government's carrot-and-stick budget men, and corporate supporters. To put it kindly, funding has not proved to be "insulated." Freedom of movement appears restrained, as well, by the basic localism of the organizational philosophy: the primacy of semiautonomous member stations over the national service, their freedom to reject and preempt, and their own subjugation to the conventional pieties of the conservative and less imaginative voices, and prominent sources of funding, in their respective communities.[15]

Early in 1979 a new Carnegie Commission reached the conclusion that Carnegie I's invention was not working. "We find public broadcasting's financial, organizational and creative structure fundamentally flawed," with little likelihood that public television (and radio) can "achieve programming excellence under the present circumstances." Not only was the system "sorely underfinanced," the public stations were "separate fiefdoms with little sense of a common purpose," with few stations, though all were zealously "local," producing much of note for their communities. Internal politics were "fierce and confusing, and often bizarre," and administration was "labyrinthine."[16] Carnegie II demanded more programs, more diversified programs, more freedom for programs that take risks, and a great deal more federal funding— something closer to the $5 per capita annually that Great Britain and Japan were spending on public broadcasting.

There were some short-lived advances. By fiscal 1981–1982, federal funding to the Corporation for Public Broadcasting was up to $172 million, covering about a third of the entire American public TV and radio system's operating budget. The number of TV member stations increased to 288, spread from Maine to Hawaii and even to American Samoa, all linked for efficient program delivery by domestic satellite. And the stations yielded much of their prime time to at least the principle of "common carriage," creating a nighttime national network of sorts from Sunday to Wednesday.

The programming also had improved somewhat by the end of the seventies, even if programs were often still acquired from outside the PBS family and from foreign sources. "These have been years of extraordinary achievement," PBS's President Laurence K. Grossman expansively declared, though all "in the face of great financial and political obstacles."[17]

But if "obstacles" were what the public system faced during three previous federal administrations, today it stares at a stone wall of tight-pursed antipathy. For fiscal 1983, President Reagan had asked for a budget cut of $52 million, and Congress agreed to a $35 million cut, appropriating only $137 million for the CPB to distribute. About $130 million annually is earmarked for 1984, 1985, and 1986. Congress also reduced the CPB's discretionary powers by specifying 90 percent of the annual appropriation for local stations. Moreover, appropriations are tied to matching funds from nonfederal sources, in a ratio of $1 granted for each $2 procured, further increasing the dependence on public appeals and corporations' patronage.

Admittedly, public broadcasters in virtually every capitalist nation currently are in dire straits. Funding has failed to keep pace with inflation, institutional growth, new technological needs, and employees' bargaining gains. The Italians, the French, the Indians, the Dutch, the British, the Australians, and all the rest have never been more worried about their ability to continue turning out enough quality programming. In Canada, the CBC's annual revenues have almost doubled in recent years, to some $740 million (Canadian) for 1982–1983, and still hard economies and frustration prevail in gloomy production studios. In the United States, however, the embattled public broadcasters struggle just to stay alive. They are hardly the only current victims of an administration's ideological views on public support for the arts, sciences, and humanities. But CPB is the only broadcasting system that now must splash about like a hooked trout every time hostile government spokesmen go fishing, casting out such lines as: "The wealthier and more educated . . . certainly possess the personal resources to support such stations. . . . Taypayers as a whole should not be compelled to subsidize entertainment for a select few."[18]

Far from serving only a "select few," public TV now reaches well beyond any elite. Its overall regular audience remains small, perhaps a 5 percent share, but the number of viewers who tune in at least once a week seems to have surpassed 50 percent of homes using television. PBS programming now appears in 42 million U.S. households, according to the surveys. And PBS President Grossman notes that the most dramatic increases are among those with less than a high school education, in homes with an annual income of less than $10,000, in blue-collar homes, and among those outside the labor force.[19]

And at how much cost to the national purse? For public radio and public TV, the $137 million of federal funding costs the taxpayers of the world's richest nation under half a cent for a day's programming, or less than $2 a year. (Canadian taxpayers pay 13 cents a day.) By comparison, the three U.S. commercial networks and their fifteen owned-and-operated stations in 1979 grossed an estimated $4 to $5 billion, about $59 per home, in national advertising revenues. Adding national spot and local advertising revenues, the industry gross averaged almost $135 per home for providing "free" private television.

In desperation public television also depends on advertising for all categories of its programming, revenues not from relentless commercial interruptions but from a far more dangerous source: corporate patronage. Between 1973 and 1980 business support increased sixfold; PBS itself had become the nation's second largest beneficiary of corporate donations, with $27 million granted for national programming alone. On the network schedule, neutral cultural offerings predominate over provocative social documents and issue-oriented programming because culture is less worrisome and more prestigious to the big corporations. With so much broadcast gratitude to Exxon, Gulf Oil, Mobil Oil, Atlantic Richfield, and others, some acerbic viewers now refer to PBS as the Petroleum Broadcasting Service.

As a further measure the public stations regularly bring out their begging bowls, driving even the most faithful viewers to distraction with their energetic and shameless appeals on the air for small handouts.

Some critics have harshly attributed the public network's problems to a philosophy of elitist programming and to its failure to arouse enough conviction that Americans need an alternative to commercial television.[20] But whatever PBS's inherent faults, the real blame has to be placed elsewhere: upon the inability of American society to demand a viable, unfettered, and truly public major network; upon the failure of responsible politicians, spokesmen, and lobbies to fight for one; and upon administrations that have not properly mandated and financed one as a national priority.[21]

The New Technology and the New Look

In cable TV the United States is fast catching up with Canada, the world's most heavily cabled country. About 75 percent of Canada's 7.2 million TV homes have access to cable TV. About 55 percent, or 4.3 million, subscribe. Most Canadian cable companies began as small independents, but today, after thirty years, six major ones serve over 70 percent of the subscribers. In the United States, ten companies already control 45 percent of the market, with cable-delivered television now entering almost 24 million U.S. TV homes, some 30 percent of the total; by 1985 cable could reach half of them. And satellite delivery already can link major production and distribution centers to virtually all 4,350 U.S. cable systems.

Within the cable industry also are the software merchandisers: the superstations, the film and videotape program suppliers, the pay-TV companies. Outside, not dependent on local cable distribution, are other program companies with experimental direct-to-home transmissions via either scrambled broadcast signals or satellite and modest earth station. Comsat, for example, is awaiting permission for its new Satellite Television Corporation to carry a three-channel pay service directly to homes. Alternatively, a hamlet may erect low-powered transmitters rebroadcasting incoming satellite channels, similarly dispensing with the costs of wiring a spread-out community. All are versions of "narrowcasting;" they are still fiercely competitive, but as the knowledge conglomerates and the giant communications and entertainment corporations ooze across the map to absorb, merge, and stake out the best territory, monopolies become the norm.

About seven hundred cable systems already deliver thirty or more channels where something moves on the screen.[22] Most viewers continue to get their daily bread from the four major broadcasting networks, but increasingly upper-income households, at least, are buying cake, sometimes with icing, from the narrowcasters. They are even ready to pay for freedom from commercials. "The nature of the revolution," wrote TV critic Les Brown, "is not technology . . . but people *paying* for television."

In other words, a new double system appears to be emerging: broadcasting as essentially a populist, common-denominator medium aimed at mass markets; narrowcasting as a more specialized medium that users pay for directly because they cannot see enough of the programs they like any other way. Public television hangs on precariously, somewhere in the middle.

And the private networks also have begun to work both sides of the street: on one side a carefully contrived full evening's schedule, complete with "locomotives," "lead-in," and LOP programming; on the other—competing even with themselves and their affiliated stations—individualized satellited offerings for pluralistic markets, for different regions, and for differing tastes that may have two dozen other cable choices. Thus, ABC has developed ABC Video Enterprises with separate mixes, for cable, of arts programming ("ARTS"), a service aimed at women ("DAYTIME"), and sports. ABC's Satellite News channels, co-owned with Westinghouse, will be launched shortly. CBS Cable is into cultural and performing arts series for cable systems in conjunction with Twentieth Century-Fox. NBC's parent, RCA, in partnership with the Rockefeller family's cable interests, now has, inter alia, exclusive U.S. first rights on all BBC programs safely in the domain of their joint venture: The Entertainment Channel.

A fragmented audience also can choose elsewhere. Several million cable viewers, in just about every state (and up to the high Arctic in Canada), may obtain their sports by satellite from WTBS in Atlanta, one of several new superstations, or newscasts around the clock or news, features, and talk shows from the same owner's two cable news networks. SIN, in its nonoriginal form, is the Spanish International Network, which links thirty-six U.S. cities and is expanding to one hundred, providing among other things direct access to Mexico's national network, Televisa. There are cable channels or pay-TV companies specifically devoted to children's programming; to Bible-thumping evangelism; to the very latest of Hollywood's feature films, uncut and uninterrupted; to twenty-four-hour-festivals of old films; to programs for blacks; to plays, music, and coverage of Congress. One service offers subscribers subtitled programs from Italy, and there are selections available from France, Japan, Ireland, and Great Britain. There is the Playboy Channel, and talk of channels for bridge players, philatelists, dieters, home decorators, and golfers; for university credit courses; for financial, weather, consumer, and health news; for information conveyed by books, magazines, and newspapers.[23] Meanwhile, local cable operators are poring over catalogues of ancient footage: how-to films, corporate and foreign giveaways, home movies, student productions, soft-core pornography—anything that will fill time cheaply on an empty channel.

And I am detailing only real-time on-air broadcasting or cable transmission; beyond, there is the further impact on ratings, on classic viewing patterns, and on network revenues of home video playback and of interactive TV. Many other new marvels also market archival material without commercials or let you record off-air to play programs back at your convenience.

The increased choice probably will result in still more families viewing television, live or postbroadcast; more multiset individual viewing; and more hours at the set. It will also entice still more entrepreneurs into trying to dislodge each other and the rich local station's franchised hold, and more corporations will be eager to acquire anything available. For a while, there is going to be what the Carnegie II report calls "a period of unrestrained competitive upheaval."

Public television could suffer the most immediate impact. The vigorous new narrowcasters have begun to invade its cultural constituency, grabbing at program ideas and sources, experienced producers, performers, and corporate patrons. Some higher-income supporters will now be buying their favorite viewing from a cable company; they may reconsider their willingness to help fund their local PBS station. If corporate support also starts to go elsewhere, just as federal and foundation funds shrink, both ambitious studio production and quality acquisition will grow still scarcer around the public television system.

Audiences will drop off. And if the Canadian example is pertinent, that is precisely the point at which the lobbyists go to work, labeling all public broadcasting as bureaucratic waste, an unnecessary luxury, a "governmental intrusion" into the free marketplace, and demanding that it become strictly network or modestly local or else that it serve as a production factory to supply the costlier prestige programs to private enterprise.

Acceding to the vested interests' demands would be a grievous error. Certainly the new technology will offer some of what was, or should be, U.S. public television's programming to those who can afford it. But the mass medium will still be needed.

One wonders how long even the upper-income minority will benefit from this shift in the way they wish. Caveat emptor! The recent history of all the conglomerate mergers and acquisitions points to the probability of narrow control by monopolies, of eliminating competition to maximize audiences and profits, of programs imitated and standardized, of a chilling eye on the bottom line, of diminishing infatuation with the frills of diversity, creativity, and program excellence. The new technology companies may soon represent too much financial concentration to allow for costly productions of Pinter or O'Neill or the New York Philharmonic if another rerun of the "Hello Dolly" tape, an old movie, or a cooking lesson would be better for business.[24] When a medium becomes a major industry, the law that generally prevails is Gresham's Law. Trivialization quickly replaces choice; twenty commercial radio stations broadcasting to a U.S. city has not made for twenty choices for the listener.

Nor is there much on the horizon to block such trends and to protect the consumer. Washington's favorite word at the moment is "deregulation," its favorite shibboleth not "act in the public interest" but rather "let the marketplace decide!"[25]

So one should tread warily in the thickets of the new technology's exuberant prose. Perhaps the television industry is not yet positioned, after all, for "finally moving to its mission's fulfillment: the mutation of the human condition, the beginning of the first adult society in mankind's history, the end of privilege. . . ."[26]

For the decade ahead, the countervailing winds of a strong and daring public television system appear to be more essential than ever, in the United States as elsewhere, in spite of—even because of—the vagaries of the new technology in a profit-obsessed industry. There must be at least one great national-cum-local institution with its sights firmly on broadcasting's, and narrowcasting's, audiences, fully committed only to producing, acquiring, and distributing vital, responsible, and comprehensive program schedules—*if* one is truly serious about realities, about gapclosing on a mass scale, about coping.

Notes

1. It is noteworthy, for example, that within a week after the 1981 change of government in both France and Greece, sweeping changes were begun in the national broadcasting organizations.

2. [Television already serves as] "their principal source of education, entertainment, information and opinion." Nicholas Johnson, *How To Talk Back To Your Television Set*, p. 8. Boston: Little, Brown, 1969.

3. From *The Report of The Royal Commission on Publications*, Ottawa, 1961.

4. *Report of the Committee on Broadcasting*, p. 5. Ottawa: Queen's Printer, 1965.

5. Harry J. Skornia, *Television and Society: An Inquest and Agenda for Improvement*, p. 7. New York: McGraw-Hill, 1965.

6. Nicholas Johnson, op. cit., pp. 70–71.

7. Alexander Kendrick, *Prime Time: A Biography of Edward R. Murrow*. Boston: Little, Brown, 1969.

8. "You'll find on ABC a diversity of contemporary tastes in a pluralistic society. From 'Eight is Enough' to 'The Love Boat', there is something for everyone." Fred Silverman, leading network programming executive in the 1970's of first CBS, then ABC, and finally NBC. Quoted by Sally Bedell in *Up The Tube: Prime-Time TV and the Silverman Years*. New York: Viking Press, 1981.

9. A single ratings point in the Nielsen surveys currently translates into an estimated $35 million in gross revenue.

10. On 8 October 1981, NBC declared that in the face of opposition from major affiliates it had reluctantly abandoned announced plans for expanding its evening newscast to one hour.

11. *New York Times*, 5 July 1981. Also note: "The [BBC's] system of control is full independence. . . . The aim is to give the best and the most comprehensive service of broadcasting to the public that is possible. The motive that underlies the whole operation is a vital factor: it must not be vitiated by political or commercial considerations." Sir Ian Jacob, former director-general of BBC, on "The BBC Ethos."

12. *The Broadcasting Act*, 1978 *et seq.*, Ottawa.

13. "Where any conflict arises between the objectives of the national broadcasting service and the interests of the private element, . . . paramount consideration shall be given . . . to the national broadcasting service." Ibid.

14. Les Brown, *Television: The Business Behind the Box*, p. 316. New York: Harcourt Brace Jovanovich, 1971.

15. Individual stations are not *required* to carry any PBS network program.

16. The Carnegie Commission on the Future of Public Broadcasting, *The Public Trust*. New York: Bantam Books, 1979.

17. *New York Times*, 17 May 1981.

18. Office of Management and Budget declaration. *New York Times*, 11 April 1981.

19. *New York Times*, 17 May 1981.

20. See, for example, Desmond Smith, Sunday *New York Times*, 10 May 1981.

21. "With no dedicated funding sources available, public broadcasting continues to be subject to internal and external pressures not to provide the bold, innovative services that the system was created to offer to the American people." Robert J. Blakely, *To Serve the Public Interest*, p. 211. Syracuse, N.Y.: Syracuse University Press, 1979.

22. Note, however, that more than half of the 24 million cable subscribers in the United States still receive only 6 to 12 channels, with little space yet

available for specialized program services. Meanwhile, Atlanta is building a 54-channel system, a 61-channel system is being built in California, and there is a 122-channel system being offered by a franchise-seeking group in the West San Fernando Valley. All three undertakings are Canadian enterprises.

23. According to *Cablevision* magazine, some forty basic or pay-TV services were in existence by early 1982, and forty more were about to start. A majority fail or merge; there are not yet enough cable channels.

24. "Will the new systems be more daring, more adventurous? I doubt it. We'll soon find that the things that work on the new systems are the very same ones that worked on the [private] networks, and the things that didn't work then won't work now." Bob Wood, former president of CBS Television.

25. Asked recently about the applicability of the deregulation philosophy to Canadian broadcasting, John Meisel, chairman of the Canadian Radio-television and Telecommunications Commission, declared: "Somebody must protect some kind of common, long-term public interest. One cannot rely solely on market forces because the market does not operate freely. If you let the market decide, you simply let various vested interests decide, interests that may or may not be *interested* in a sense of social responsibility, or be *motivated* by a sense of social responsibility. And since we haven't a perfect market, it would simply mean that the most powerful players would make the decisions." John Meisel was speaking to the Canadian Cable-TV Association Convention in May 1981.

26. Sylvester Pat Weaver, *Watch: Television in the Eighties*, vol. 1, no. 1 (December 1979): 22.

Bibliography

Arlen, Michael J. *The Camera Age: Essays on Television*. New York: Farrar, Straus & Giroux. 1981.

Barnouw, Erik. *Tube of Plenty: The Evolution of American Television*. New York: Oxford University Press, 1975. (A condensed and revised version of his three-volume *History of Broadcasting in the U.S.A.*, which included *A Tower in Babel* (to 1933), *The Golden Web* (1933–1953), and *The Image Empire* (1953–1973).)

_____ . *The Sponsor: Notes on a Modern Potentate*. New York: Oxford University Press, 1978.

Bedell, Sally. *Up the Tube: Prime-Time TV and the Silverman Years*. New York: Viking Press, 1981.

Bergreen, Laurence. *Look Now, Pay Later: The Rise of Network Broadcasting*. New York: Mentor, New American Library, 1980.

Blakely, Robert J. *To Serve The Public Interest: Educational Broadcasting in the US*. Syracuse, NY: Syracuse University Press, 1979.

Brown, Les. *Television: The Business Behind the Box*. New York: Harcourt Brace Jovanovich, 1971.

Canadian Broadcasting Corporation. *Annual Reports; 1979–1980; 1980–1981*. Ottawa: CBC.

————— . *The CBC's Programming Services: Applications For Renewal of Network Licenses.* Ottawa: CBC, 1978.

————— . *Touchstone For the CBC.* Ottawa: CBC, 1977.

————— . *CBC-2, Télé-2: A Proposal For National, Non-Commercial, Satellite Delivered CBC Television Services.* Ottawa: CBC, 1980.

Carnegie Commission on Educational Television. *Public Television: A Program For Action.* New York: Bantam Books, 1967.

Carnegie Commission on the Future of Public Broadcasting. *The Public Trust.* New York: Bantam Books, 1979.

Cater, Douglass (ed.). *The Future of Public Broadcasting.* New York: Praeger, 1976.

Cole, Barry (ed.). *Television Today: A Close-up View.* (Readings from *TV Guide.*) New York: Oxford University Press, 1981.

Cole, Barry, and Oettinger, Mel. *Reluctant Regulators: The FCC and the Broadcast Audience.* Reading, Mass.: Addison Wesley Publishing Co., 1978.

Compaigne, Benjamin M. (ed.). *Who Owns the Media: Concentration of Ownership in the Mass Communications Industry.* New York: Harmony Books, 1979.

Curran, Charles. *A Seamless Robe: Broadcasting; Philosophy and Practice.* London: Collins, 1980.

Friendly, Fred W. *Due To Circumstances Beyond Our Control . . .* New York: Random House, 1967.

Hallman, E. *Broadcasting in Canada.* London: Routledge and Kegan Paul, 1977.

Johnson, Nicholas. *How to Talk Back to Your Television Set.* Boston: Little, Brown, 1970.

Lichty, Lawrence W., and Topping, Malachi C. *American Broadcasting: A Sourcebook on The History of Radio and Television.* New York: Hastings House, 1978.

Metz, Robert. *CBS: Reflections in a Bloodshot Eye.* New York: Playboy Press, 1975.

Peers, Frank W. *The Public Eye: Television and the Politics of Canadian Broadcasting; 1952–1968.* Toronto: University of Toronto Press, 1979.

Sklar, Robert. *Prime-Time America.* New York: Oxford University Press, 1980.

Skornia, Harry J. *Television and Society: An Inquest and Agenda for Improvement.* New York: McGraw-Hill Book Co., 1965.

Whiteside, Thomas. *The Blockbuster Complex: Conglomerates, Show Business and Book Publishing.* Middletown, Conn.: Wesleyan University Press, 1981.

LEO BOGART

——— **16** ———

Mass Media: Knowledge as Entertainment

The theme "utilization of knowledge" carries connotations of social uplift, with "knowledge" (if it is to be equated with "truth") somehow distilled and separated from the more transient content of human intercourse. In this sense, knowledge is defined pragmatically as the body of information and interpretation most widely accepted by scholars at any given time. (This definition does not take issue with Fritz Machlup's useful theoretical distinction between knowledge and information. In practice, information is not only a prerequisite for knowledge, but often hopelessly intertwined with it. What is information for one individual is transformed into knowledge by another or by the same individual as evidence and insights accumulate.) It is generally assumed that humanity's lot could be improved if such information were more broadly shared. The problem in executing this moral imperative is that the appetite for knowledge is more limited than the means for its dissemination. Even the most widely diffused and frequently repeated facts (like the names of cabinet officers and foreign heads of state) are generally ignored if there is no motivation to absorb them.

Today in technically advanced countries the mass media represent the principal form through which knowledge is acquired. Since the advent of television, people spend more time in the course of their lives with the media than they do in family conversation, in school, or in learning at work. The knowledge conveyed by the media is certainly not more vivid or meaningful than what is acquired through direct personal experience, but it does cover a vastly greater and more assorted range. The media allow us to position ourselves in time and space in ways that could not have been envisioned by primitive peoples or by our ancestors in the scribal era before messages could be reproduced in quantity.

The moral imperative has always been strong among the producers of mass communication, especially those who are drawn to their profession by a creative impulse, a sense of social or political mission, or a desire to find expression for their own vision of the world. Yet the urge to express themselves, to pass on their private wisdom, has generally had to be tempered by the need to find and maintain an audience. This has created in the world of mass communication the continuing dilemma of how to balance the public interest and the public's interests. Early in the history of newspapers, editors learned that features and "human-interest stories" were needed to leaven the diet of straightforward news. In most mass media, most of the time, knowledge is embedded within layers of amusement, which appear to be the primary attraction for the audience. William Safire has called this "infotainment" (*New York Times Magazine*, September 13, 1981).[1]

Media are not merely organs of information; they are forms of recreation as well. Needless to say, the analytical distinctions between information and entertainment recede into unreality as one confronts the vast flow of symbols that emanate from printing presses and broadcasting transmitters. All symbolic communication, including musical tones, may fit under the heading of information. Conversely, acquiring information, even for purely utilitarian purposes, often has a recreational aspect. Certainly the tremendous popular appeal of the mass media is in their ability to let us pass time agreeably. They instruct us, alert us, orient us, inspire us, identify us, and enable us to recreate our own emotional experiences and those of others. But what the media mainly do is entertain us.

Fantasy and fiction dominate the time most people spend with media. In every mass medium, the secret of success is generally considered to lie in entertaining and fascinating the mass audience rather than in meeting the more rigorous standards of the information-seeking elite.

The pastime character of mass media became more predominant with the invention of film and of broadcasting, in which communication proceeds at a fixed pace, while in print it can be regulated to suit the reader. Although much in newspapers, magazines, and books is primarily informational, broadcasting and film must be classified as mainly entertainment. (Some 85 percent of current prime-time network TV consists of drama, variety, and comedy. However, this ratio may slowly be changing, as news is beginning to occupy more air time. News and documentary programming is considerably less expensive to produce than TV entertainment, the costs of which have escalated dramatically.) Broadcasting and film have also vastly broadened the audience for information, since they convey it with new intensity and with a sense of vicarious participation. But inasmuch as audiovisual entertainment now accounts for the lion's share of time spent with the media, it follows that far less of the total represents knowledge, even though more knowledge than ever is being communicated.[2] While information in print must be sought out, knowledge conveyed in films or broadcast programs is more likely to be picked up incidentally in the pursuit of recreation. Diffusing knowledge through this kind of incidental learning represents a different communications process than the reading tradition.

Commercial Culture

Can the information and entertainment aspects of culture be differentiated from other aspects—the layout of cities and landscapes, architecture, the design of clothing, furniture, furnishings, and artifacts? All these shapes we give to the material world represent information of a kind. They convey symbolic meanings and refract the current state of values and beliefs about the meaning of life, the value of human beings, the structure of our relations with one another. In the past it was possible to speak of "the arts," but media culture today embraces a great deal that manifestly is not art. And media abound with informational and instructional material of all kinds.

The mass media are the carriers of commercial culture, a symbolic system in which messages are constructed as a commodity for sale rather than as a form of creative expression. The tension and incongruity between what must be said and what will be read or listened to has preoccupied editors since the beginnings of printing, and it continues to preoccupy thoughtful media executives today.

To speak of commercial culture may raise the question, "Is there any other kind?" It may be argued that even in the most primitive societies artistic expression always has some utilitarian motive. If it seeks to propitiate or glorify supernatural forces, isn't this always with the end of making life easier and more comfortable here below?

Cave paintings, it has been suggested, were executed to capture and dominate the animals they depicted. Wandering bards composed their epics to cadge a free meal. Virtuosity in technique always has had a payoff of some kind. So it may legitimately be asked whether there is any such thing as pure self-expression, apart from social rewards. Can we differentiate the social approval for artistic or intellectual performance from pecuniary rewards as a manifestation and symbol of social approval? It is well understood that performers thrive on applause and praise. But it is also understood that they survive on their incomes.

Samuel Johnson uttered what James Boswell described as a "strange opinion" that "no man but a blockhead ever wrote, except for money." But Boswell was quick to add that "numerous instances to refute this will occur to all who are versed in the history of literature."[3]

Media enterprises are run for nonprofit motives more often than other ventures, since they represent powers to motivate and change public opinion, to influence the course of history.

Culture is power. Since earliest history, rulers have surrounded themselves with artists and borrowed glory from their creations. In contemporary times, totalitarian societies have placed high priority on mobilizing the arts to support the system. And in American society, the naive political illusions and ambitions of artists have matched the eagerness of politicians to obtain the support of artists better known and more admired than they are. The stars of film and television are the society's most popular and trusted personalities and its intimate companions.

What makes ours a commercial culture is its marketing orientation. A publisher looking at a manuscript does not ask, "Is it any good?" but rather "Is there a market for it?" Because its output seeks a market, a commercial culture must be continually innovative in its specific content, and it is likely to be fiercely competitive. Commercial culture is a victim of fashion and also a setter of fashion, since it must both follow and fix new styles of public acceptance and popularity.

In defining "commercial culture," we implicitly accept the differentiation of culture into subvarieties. Thus, folk culture encompasses the useful arts of everyday life whose practitioners are often assigned to their craft by tradition rather than by unusual skill.[4] Popular culture embraces the constantly changing styles that attract the widest audiences at any given moment. Because of its ephemeral nature, mass culture is generally contrasted with elite or high culture, which represents the enduring heritage of humanity's achievements.

Commercial culture is usually equated with popular or "mass" culture. But folk and elite cultures also may be subject to commercialization (or to political exploitation). Elite culture has its fashions, fads, and "movements," while popular culture is not without its enduring components (witness the persistence of nursery rhymes).

Elite culture is often described as having a "universal" quality. Yet rock and roll, Western shootouts, automobile chases, blue jeans, and Magnum seem to carry an attraction that transcends local cultural barriers and has made American commercial culture dominant throughout the world, even in relatively primitive areas. As national mass media have become increasingly dependent on foreign sources for their content, popular culture everywhere represents an amalgam of international and indigenous elements.

The organization and operation of the mass media system in the United States has enormous repercussions on the worldwide flow of ideas and values. The power of this presence would probably alarm nationalists in other countries whatever the media's content or style.

However, the formulas of Hollywood since early in the twentieth century have shown their potency in societies that differ radically from that of the United States, and much of what critics find objectionable in the advertising-supported mass media represents a derivation from the Hollywood fashion. In the prevailing criticism, two primary objections to these formulas recur: an obsession with violence and sex, and a suffusion of vulgar commercialism and materialism. The objections are interdependent, since the violence and sex are considered to be lures by which the audience is trapped into enduring the commercial persuasion that is the whole media system's support and true raison d'être.

The commercialism that arouses the most irritation is embodied in the intrusive advertising on television and radio. The same polls that show this also show that advertising, especially in print, is accepted as a useful informational component of the media.[5] (Newspapers that lose advertising lose readers.) But advertising is not merely a highly visible component of media content; it also has a pervasive structural effect. Advertising provides 59 percent of the total economic support for all media and has made possible a large variety of choices.

The need to serve the interests of advertisers creates strong incentives to build mass audiences. Since success in the media is linked to the size of the audience, there is an inevitable pressure to conform to popular taste, to fulfill the established formulas and fictional cliches that are guaranteed to produce satisfaction every time. Great works of art, literature, or drama arouse anxiety, irritation, or grief. In contrast, commercial culture thrives on trivia and the happy ending. (This is not to deny, of course, that there is room within the commercial culture for the finest form of expression, for little magazines, good music radio stations, and documentary television. But the very existence of such elite media may demonstrate how the commercial culture system works to satisfy every taste that represents a potential market.)

Is it the mass size of the audience that characterizes commercial culture? Not necessarily. Elite media, with small but important audiences, can be very profitable or influential. What counts is not just the size of the audience, but what it is willing to pay and what advertisers are willing to pay to reach it.

Techniques developed in media that carry advertising are carried over to those media that are publicly supported. Books and films use advertising techniques and marketing research. Thus, in generating their publics, they acquire the attributes of the advertising-dependent mass media.

The Interpenetration of Media

Competition is the essence of the marketplace, and competition among the various media of communication strongly shapes their character and content. Until relatively recently, this competition took place within a steadily expanding market, and therefore media enterprises did not necessarily see competitors as a threat to their sheer survival to the degree they may today. From the invention of printing to the end of the nineteenth century, a publisher's ability to generate an audience was limited only by the extent of literacy (which was continually growing) and by the public's ability to pay (which generally continued to improve as industrialization raised standards of living and technical improvements reduced publishing costs). Thus the success of any individual publisher did not automatically mean failure for his contemporaries. This is still true today in the media that do not carry advertising. A best-selling book or record or a hit movie in no way threatens the chances for other books, records, or movies.

This situation prevailed as long as the audience remained the primary economic support of publications. But when media became more and more dependent on advertising, competition was intensified because the financial base was so much more tightly limited. A newspaper, magazine, or television station that expands its advertising generally increases its share of a more or less fixed volume of advertising that has been allocated to its particular type of medium in its market. This is not to say that the demand for advertising in a particular medium is totally inelastic. In reality, media forms (billboards and radio, for example) compete with each other, and advertising competes with other forms of promotion and selling. The advent of a new medium can rapidly enlarge the total volume of advertising investments. Television did so in the 1950s, and new forms of telecommunication may well do the same in the 1980s and 1990s.

As in other fields of capitalist enterprise, competition has led to a concentration of ownership in the mass media. This tendency has been fostered by the growth of technology, which requires ever-larger capital investments, and by tax laws that encourage owners to plough profits back into the business. The need for capital has stimulated moves toward public ownership. This in turn has led to replacing family proprietorships by professional managements driven by the need to increase corporate earnings through acquisition and expansion. So we come to the familiar media conglomerate, whose corporate interests penetrate into a variety of different—and competing—forms: book, newspaper, and magazine publishing, TV, cable, and radio (Times-Mirror Company and the New York Times Company); books, magazines, a newspaper supplement, TV, radio, records, and film (CBS); and other combinations. In many cases, the conglomerate's interests extend beyond related fields (like forest products, electronics, or baseball) to totally unrelated ones (like RCA's car rental subsidiary, Hertz). Along with concentration of ownership, technological developments have led to an increased need for centralization in the diffusion system of mass media. Print media are essentially independent of this tendency toward concentration and control because the production of one in no way restricts the appearance of another. The development of inexpensive photocomposition machines and lightweight presses makes it mechanically more feasible to introduce new publications and thus helps to maintain diversity. However, the complexity and expense of distribution limits the opportunities for new print enterprises unless they acquire the necessary advertising support.

Broadcasting demands regulation, on both the international and the national scale, simply because of the scarcity of room on the radiation spectrum. Since access to the spectrum has come to confer power and wealth, control over allocations has led inevitably to criteria setting, standards of performance, evaluations, and a host of regulations that intrude government into matters of content. Wired communications have similarly been subject to public franchising and regulation. However, in the United States no public body has yet faced up to the problem of how to handle cable systems that have reached the limits of their capacity. At this point, they would inevitably become monopolistic arbiters of what is to be disseminated, functioning both as system operators and (in the language of the new technology) information providers.

The media have become increasingly interdependent, using each other as sources of subject matter and talent, with interrelated channels of production and distribution and increasingly common ownership. Hollywood was forced by the advent of television to exploit sensations that TV censors inhibited. But the resulting sensationalism of Hollywood lifted the barriers within television, thereby changing the public standards to which media managements have always said they wished to be responsive.

Television reduced yearly per capita film attendance of individuals ten years old or more from a high of 34.7 in 1946 to 5.3 in 1981 and caused major shifts in the content, style, and promotional methods of Hollywood filmmaking. But despite the initial intense antagonism between the media, Hollywood's talent and studios became increasingly essential to TV program production. Television's insatiable demand for programming material created a profitable market for film libraries. Films made for television found a secondary outlet in theatrical release. Producers, directors, actors, production crews, and other personnel worked interchangeably in both genres. Hollywood came to rely heavily on television as its main medium of promotion. Cable (particularly pay) television offered important new outlets for film.

The transformation of film distribution and the growth of the VCR have created a vast new market for pornographic films. Similarly, the shift of book distribution from bookstores to supermarkets has changed publishing practices and substance. The independent publisher is a fast-disappearing species. In the era of the "promotional book," new links have been forged from publishing to film and television.[6]

New works of fiction have been steadily reduced in number as a result of the publishing philosophy of concentrating on a limited number of "blockbuster" titles. Not a few of these are books written to marketing specifications or novelizations of film plots. Book publishers have turned to the established Hollywood formula of TV advertising and talk-show promotion.

The reduction in new fiction (with all that it implies for the richness of the nation's collective fantasy life and its level of artistic expression) parallels the virtual elimination of fiction from magazines. This in turn came about partly because of competition for the audience from televised drama and partly because advertisers turning to television reduced their support of magazines.

In our new age of interpenetrating media content (where evening TV newscasts are constructed from the reports in the afternoon papers and newspapers reproduce the texts of televised presidential addresses), media producers expect creative expressions to find their outlet through a number of modes or channels. Newspaper and magazine publishers are now actively engaged in feasibility studies of how to transform their information resources into an electronic format. The literary agent who negotiates subsidiary rights for his author clients is the forerunner of a new generation of specialists producing material that can be displayed on a cathode ray tube, printed out, illustrated with still or moving pictures, or read as an audio signal in the electronic world of the future.

All this is encompassed under the term *software*, borrowed from computer science. The word suggests that the same equipment in the home will be used interchangeably for the kinds of messages we traditionally derive from mass media and for a variety of other data processing purposes. "Software" also carries an unfortunate connotation that all is somehow grist for the mill: the outpost of the new educational extension program at the Metropolitan Museum of Art, the films of Andy Warhol, and the footage collected by Ugly George, who solicits women he encounters on the street to undress for the camera.

Old and New Media

The history of mass media shows a parallel development of two inherently contradictory tendencies. Economies of scale in production have made it possible to reach large and ever larger audiences. (It is commonplace to observe that a single radio broadcast of say, a Bach cantata, is heard by more people than heard it performed not merely during the composer's lifetime but in all the centuries before the invention of broadcasting.) And while new media develop audiences at the expense of older ones, they in no instance have superseded them altogether.

But along with generating mass audiences for identical messages, the proliferation of media vehicles and channels means a greater array of choices. Thus, paradoxically, while media make possible a greater measure of common experience, information, and symbolism than might once have been thought possible, they also create the opportunity for ever-greater individuation. No pair of identical twins reads the same books, goes to all the same movies, or watches all the same television programs. In fact (just as personalities and values are shaped by media exposure), exercising media preferences from an early age is now one of the critical forms by which individuals manifest and shape their own personalities.

Television focused attention on the "mass" aspects of the media experience. In the past two decades, since television has become a virtually universal presence, the buzzword has become "specialization," or in even newer jargon, "narrowcasting." The first shift occurred when the great mass magazines, with their tens of millions of readers, died off and the bulk of magazine circulation shifted toward special-interest publications that appealed to narrowly definable groups of readers. When television took over the prime-time entertainment functions of network radio, the number of radio stations did not decline. It multiplied into a galaxy of musical formulas, each geared to its own minor sector of public taste; while there were 2,773 radio stations on the air in 1950, there were 9,049 in 1980.

Specialization also appears to be in store for cable television, which will cover half the country by 1990. Inevitably, adding more channels—applicants for cable franchises have offered up to two hundred—whether from local producers of original programming or from remote sources via satellite, has cut into the mass audience of the three networks. Their share of prime-time viewing had fallen from over 90 percent to 78 percent of the households on the cable and to 61 percent of those with pay cable by 1981.

These developments have been followed avidly by advertisers eager to see the effects of enhanced competition on the costs of their schedules. Media specialization has been encouraged by the notion of market segmentation, which has discovered such truths as that young men use more hair oil than old men, especially bald ones; that women with many children are the best customers for meat extenders; and that the nouveaux riches are the best prospects for expensive costume jewelry. The people who run media are motivated to shape their output to attract the kinds of audiences that advertisers are willing to pay for.

A major impetus toward specialization comes from the increased quantification of marketing practice and the prevalence of statistical formulas and mathematical models in the construction of media plans. But the demand for specialization is not merely an outgrowth of marketers' requirements. It corresponds to the growth of avocational interests in a society that is more and more complex and in which individuals increasingly play a diversity of roles in their daily lives. Pursuing these individualized interests has also been made possible, at least through the mid-1970s, by rising incomes that permit the indulgence of more private curiosities and passions.

Specialized publications or channels are nonetheless "mass media." They may be operated with fewer economies of scale, and their charges to audiences and advertisers may be correspondingly greater per unit than those of their counterparts that speak to "everyone." Still they differ from individual, person-to-person communications, not merely because they are identical messages delivered to many separated people but because they have been packaged or produced in advance for consumption.

This "packaging"—taken for granted since Gutenberg's Bible—is now challenged by new forms of communication that will soon enable televiewers equipped with a few gadgets to construct their own media environment, directly accessing what will soon be encyclopedic files of current news and advertising, back files of the same, periodicals, book texts, films, and television programming from around the world.[7]

When books existed only in manuscript, scholars had to travel great distances to do collateral reading on a particular subject.[8] This limited the possibility of directly comparing texts and reflecting on their incongruities. Once printed books stocked libraries, there was an enormous rise in the level of intellectual stimulation, simply because of the vast number of ideas that could be cross-referenced and pursued simultaneously.

Computerized information systems may well represent a similar leap to a new level of potential inventiveness and scholarly productivity by making an even vaster array of stored information almost instantly accessible on command. Not only time savings but the increased possibilities of uncovering unexpected connections may prove to be major stimulants to intellectual growth. Apart from such effects on scholarship, the new technology can also have a significant impact on mass culture because of the way it will change the ordinary uses of information in daily life.

Does the opportunity of gaining immediate access to inexhaustible stores of information and entertainment mean the end of the familiar "packaged" media in publications and broadcast programming? It is hard to see how it could. The public now devotes vastly more time to media with preselected content than to those with the options of exercising personal choice: They listen to radio music much more than to records or audiocassettes, watch vastly more television than theater movies, and read far fewer books than "packaged" periodicals.

Why? There is some truth in the editors' and programmers' claim that the public values the authoritative professional judgments that now control the planning and selection of media content. But I see two other more important reasons.

The first is that packaged media require less effort and represent greater convenience than an active search for information. That is why newspapers try to run the comics, advice columns, and their editorials in predictable positions every day. Since much, if not most, media experience is a way of passing time rather than of acquiring knowledge, esthetic delight, or catharsis, the absence of exertion is an essential ingredient for a pastime. Even though UHF is universally available, its audiences are much smaller than those of VHF stations, simply because UHF requires more fussing with the dial. Television networks vie for the early-evening audience, since a large proportion of viewers stay with a particular channel once they have tuned it in to avoid expending the energy required to turn the knob. Retrieving Teletext information from a computer terminal is a cumbersome process compared with reading a periodical.

The other important reason why the public values the packaged media is that these media are usually less expensive and thus appear to offer greater value. Partly this is because of production costs; it is cheaper to print a hundred thousand copies of one newspaper than to produce the same content in a hundred thousand different assortments, although it will be technically possible to do the latter in the coming era of ink-jet printing. But packaged media are cheaper for yet another reason: Advertising pays much of the cost.

Information will account for a somewhat greater share of all media output in the future, and the growth of individualized direct access to information will gradually shift the economic burden of media from the advertiser toward the consumer, who will pay fees based on the amount of information consumed. But the great preponderance of media consumption for some time to come will be of the familiar packaged newspapers, magazines, and network television programming that we use today.

The proliferation of new media choices (at a greater cost per unit of choice) may make increasing demands on the budgets of both consumers and advertisers. Although mass communications have for many years taken a roughly constant percentage of consumer expenditures, there appears to be no logical reason why they should not have a larger share of consumers' recreational costs and advertisers' sales promotional costs. But there is no indication that time spent on new media choices will to a significant degree come from nonmedia discretionary leisure time, as television largely did. With the massive entry of women into the work force, available time after sleep, work, and household chores is actually diminishing for both women and men. Between 1973 and 1980, reported leisure time went down from 26.2 hours to 19.2. Time spent on new media will therefore have to come from existing media, largely from television. Since people watch television mainly to pass the time, the time that people spend with television is not altered by the amount or quality of programming available.

Advertising and Media Content

One of the first rules in any business is that the return on capital and the prospects for capital growth must be comparable with those afforded by alternative forms of investment. In the past, newspaper and book publishers were motivated by profit, but this goal was often mixed with other aims: power, idealism, the pleasure of craftsmanship. The corporate media managements of today are rarely oblivious to the goal of excellence, and they recognize its importance to the professional staffs on whom they rely to turn out successful products. But craftsmanship, professionalism, vanity, and pride all have their price.

From a purely managerial viewpoint, the content of media is instrumental to enhancing corporate profits and growth. I do not say "*merely* instrumental,*"* because it is generally accepted that if the content is adeptly and professionally fashioned, the possibilities of profit and growth are increased. But content is judged by its ability to generate revenue from audiences and advertisers. Its inherent informational or esthetic value is utterly irrelevant. Thus management has cast off the original purposes of communication: to convey facts, ideas, and speculations; to evoke and share sentiment, experience, and fantasy; to express uncertainty and insight—all the traditional goals of the humanities and sciences.

It is not that media managers reject these goals; many take pains to distinguish between their private tastes and their business practices, like the television producers who don't watch television. Yet the pursuit of excellence in expression often fails to meet the test of the marketplace, which, for the principal media, is that of advertising rather than of public approval. Even when media managements are interested in the nonpecuniary aspects of media, as Time, Inc., was with the political influence of the *Washington Star*, they sooner or later come to the day of reckoning. The reckoning in this case, as in those of other failed newspapers and magazines that maintained the loyalty of millions of readers to the end, represented the calculations of advertisers striving for cost efficiency by concentrating their ad budgets in the publications that dominated their markets by some arbitrary criterion of cost efficiency.

The fundamental premise of consumer marketing is embodied in the retail adage, "Give the lady what she wants." Traditional salesmanship seeks to find customers for an existing product, while marketers begin by analyzing consumer needs and desires to fashion products to satisfy unfulfilled demands. The adoption of this principle by American business has led to a great boom in market research dedicated to evaluating every stage of market potential, of consumer motivation, of product performance, and of promotional techniques.

From the very beginning of modern marketing in the 1920s, the analysis of advertising campaigns and of mass media has been a major focus of this research process. The two media that have lagged substantially behind the others in assembling information about their publics have been the motion picture and book industries, which are not dependent on advertisers. Advertisers looking at media have thought in financial management's quantitative terms. Returns on investment through alternate routes are calculated for different publication lists and broadcast schedules. Audience size, measured in terms of "gross rating points" or "impressions," has been substituted for the elusive yardstick of sales results (which can be tracked only with difficulty, expense, and a great deal of doubt and inaccuracy).

If seven out of ten network television programs fail to survive from one broadcast season to the next, if great magazines and newspapers disappear, it is because the audience numbers give negative indications. Since buyers of advertising all watch the same numbers, follow the same ground rules, and apply similar formulas, the net effect is concentrating investments where the return appears to be greatest, so that media that are successful in generating audiences are disproportionately successful in attracting advertising. But the entire procedure rests on the assumption that the effectiveness of communication somehow relates to the sheer quantity of message units transmitted and received.

Benjamin Franklin patched together his almanac to earn a living, and Tom Paine pamphleteered to advance his ideals. Both no doubt gauged their success by the number of people who were willing to buy what they had written; but *Common Sense* would have left no less of a mark on history if its sales had been half what they were. Johann Strauss is not a greater composer than Johann Sebastian Bach because his music attracted bigger crowds.

Because the economic survival of today's mass media is so closely tied to the size of their audiences, the media tend to operate by similar assumptions and to follow the same patterns in developing their content. Innovations, when not immediately successful, are quickly abandoned. When successful, they are quickly adopted by the competition.

Since people like what is familiar to them and what they feel comfortable with, changes in preference generally come slowly. Market research invariably shows a public preference for the tried and true, and if it were followed literally it would discourage any innovation altogether. But what is tried and true simply represents what was done in a prior period.

Violence on television network programming was explained as a natural response to the race for ratings, in which millions of dollars of advertising revenues hang on a single sharepoint. The record shows that a network that upgrades the intellectual or artistic level of its programming in a given time period is likely to lose audience share, and programs are scheduled with this in mind. On the other hand, if *all* the stations on the air simultaneously offered only quality programming, the public would quickly adapt to the available choices, and the aggregate level of viewing would stay the same.

Say's Law states that supply creates its own demand. Nowhere is this more evident than in the mass media, where the mere availability of "free" programming on the air, or of space in a monopoly newspaper, generates some kind of an audience.

Editors, publishers, producers, and others who run the media have it within their power to impose their standards of taste and judgment upon the public, within very broad limits of tolerance. They must, of course, be aware of who their potential and actual audiences are, and they must be alert to these audiences' predilections. Consumer research provides such data. But the proper use of that research is not to furnish directives to perpetuate the commercial culture of the moment by reaffirming existing taste. Rather, it is to help fulfill the moral imperative to advance the diffusion of knowledge, to use the media to enrich and uplift mankind, not merely divert it. The diversion itself, alas, is not always innocent.

Notes

1. For an expanded discussion of the subject, see Leo Bogart, "Television News as Entertainment," in Percy H. Tannenbaum, ed., *The Entertainment Functions of Television*, Hillsdale, N.J.: Lawrence Erlbaum Assoc., 1980.

2. In terms of economic investment, the split between print and audiovisual media is about even. In 1980, the public spent $5.5 billion to buy newspapers, $4.4 billion on consumer magazines, and $4.8 billion on books. Advertisers spent $15.5 billion in newspapers and $3.1 billion in magazines. The public spent $3.5 billion on movies and $3.7 billion on records and cassettes. They also spent $13.2 billion to purchase, maintain, and operate TV and radio sets and hi-fi equipment. Advertisers spent $15.1 billion in broadcast media.

3. James Boswell, *The Life of Samuel Johnson, LL.D.*, New York: Modern Library, 1931, p. 623.

4. See Peter Burke, *Popular Culture in Early Modern Europe*, New York: Harper & Row, 1978.

5. Rena Bartos and Theodore F. Dunn, *Advertising and Consumers: New Perspectives*, New York: American Association of Advertising Agencies, 1976.

6. See Thomas Whiteside, *The Blockbuster Complex*, Middletown, Conn.: Wesleyan University Press, 1981.

7. See Leo Bogart, "Mass Media in the Year 2000," *Gazette*, 13, no. 3, 1967.

8. See Elizabeth Eisenstein, *The Printing Press as an Agent of Change: Communications and Cultural Transformations in Early Modern Europe*, New York: Cambridge University Press, 1979.

Bibliography

Ben Bagdikian. *The Information Machines*. New York: Harper & Row, 1971.

Raymond A. Bauer. *Advertising in America: The Consumer View*. Boston: Harvard Business School, 1968.

Daniel Boorstin. *The Image: A Guide to Pseudo-Events in America*. New York: Atheneum, 1978.

Lester Brown. *Television: The Business Behind the Box*. New York: Harcourt Brace Jovanovich, 1971.

Benjamin M. Compaine, editor. *Who Owns the Media: Concentration of Ownership in the Mass Communications Industry*. White Plains: Knowledge Industry Publications, 1979.

George Comstock, Steven Chaffee, Nathan Katzman, Maxwell McCombs, and Donald Roberts. *Television and Human Behavior*. New York: Columbia University Press, 1978.

Lewis Coser, Charles Kadushin, and Walter Powell. *Books: The Commerce and Culture of Publishing.* New York: Basic Books, 1982.

Edward Jay Epstein. *News from Nowhere.* New York: Random House, 1973.

Otto Friedrich. *Decline and Fall.* New York: Harper & Row, 1970.

David Halberstam. *The Powers That Be.* New York: Knopf, 1979.

John Hohenberg. *The News Media: A Journalist Looks at His Profession.* New York: Holt, Rinehart & Winston, 1968.

Harold Mendelsohn. *Mass Entertainment.* New Haven, Conn.: College & University Press, 1966.

William Parkman Rankin. *Business Management of Consumer Magazines.* New York: Praeger, 1980.

Anthony Smith. *Goodbye Gutenberg: The Newspaper Revolution of the 1980's.* New York: Oxford University Press, 1980.

Jon G. Udell, editor. *The Economics of the American Newspaper.* New York: Hastings House, 1978.

LLOYD E. SLATER

——— **17** ———

Adapting
Technology Knowledge
to Social Needs

The Message: Many technological solutions to crucial problems of Society
are known, but few are accepted and applied because of misunderstanding,
distrust and political fear. Bridging the gap between "technologists" and
"sociologists" is an imperative if the present paralysis in using knowledge
is to be overcome.

My qualifications for participating in a gathering of concerned scholars
on the optimum utilization of knowledge rest on a background in food
technology. Hence, what follows will at least be independent, if not
scholarly, observations.

I'll start by postulating that knowledge, like food, nurtures the human
individual. Food is the fuel for physical growth and bodily function;
knowledge is the fuel for intellectual growth and human behavior. But
there is a profound difference in how these two forms of human
nourishment are utilized. Food, at least in reasonable quantity, is
ineluctably used; the organism grows, moves, excretes, reproduces, and
often manages to survive unthinkingly in a friendly environment.
Knowledge, on the other hand, simply accumulates without this automatic
metabolic outlet. The human mind can be crammed with knowledge,
but its value as a fuel is nil unless it is used, consciously or unconsciously,
in making decisions for purposeful action: for example, in solving
problems of survival, comfort, harmony, serenity, order, pleasure seeking
and so on or, of course, in teaching or entertaining others.

A human stuffed with unused knowledge is an unfulfilled, tentative
kind of being—somewhat like a perpetually pregnant organism that

never gives birth. A society loaded with knowledge that is not used is similarly vulnerable; it is a society in paralysis, drifting towards extinction. History describes many initially vigorous societies and cultures fading into oblivion. We have a new buzzword, conveniently pilfered from the physical sciences, describing this social phenomenon: *entropy*, or the inevitable degradation, without constant inputs of energy, of the organized system towards a state of inert uniformity. Our thesis here is that Knowledge (with a capital K), applied to give structure, content, and form, is the energy input that keeps society vigorous and productive.

The entropy/energy combination is a simple and compelling concept. Simple and compelling enough, in fact, to subsidize a best seller or two. But the knowledge explosion of the past century has vastly complicated the equation. The energy inputs needed to sustain society— the knowledge nutrients required for societal metabolism and behavior— have become bewilderingly rich and complex, offering gastronomic choices that can kill as well as cure.

Science and technology furnish the bulk of shelf items in today's burgeoning knowledge supermarket. As the industrial revolution added complexity to our Western world, it also intensified the need for more and more specialized knowledge "nutrients" to sustain it. Since mid-century, the dependency of industrial society on doses of essential knowledge became disturbingly apparent as its increasing inability to receive and act on crucial information led to visible and often shocking deterioration.

It would take volumes to document today's societal pathology, but just a few well-known symptoms suggest its status: environmental pollution, affluent waste, proliferation in crime, dissolution of family structure and loyalties, economic paralysis in major cities, an almost rhapsodic diversion of public monies into monumental piles of military hardware, increasing dependency on debilitating narcotics, and so on. The list seems endless.

Contemporary medicine and health care suggest one way to deal with societal pathology. Exemplary nutrition (or correct knowledge) applied right from the start, they suggest, probably would have prevented this alarming condition. But now that we are really and truly sick and don't quite know why, surely we have something in our therapeutic black bag, our technological box of tricks, to treat the symptoms?

Alvin Weinberg appropriately calls a sick society's need for doses of emergency knowledge its need for a "technological fix." Somewhere in our scientific arsenal, he suggests, exist information and technique for treating and subduing the symptoms of pollution, waste, crime, vaga-bondism, bankruptcy, hawkishness, and psychic insecurity. But certainly the thoughtful Dr. Weinberg will admit there is always the danger that, like methadone shots for addicts, the cure could yield results worse than the disease. Quite clearly the emergency use of therapeutic knowledge, the massive injection of "helpful" technology, requires unusual foresight and considerable sensitivity in application.

Here we come to the crux of our problem: the condition of decision-making paralysis on socially useful technology knowledge that apparently afflicts our society. For in our free and pluralistic system there are many who perceive the danger of the "quick fix," who inherently shudder at applying "the hair of the dog that bit us." They distrust technology and fail to see how it can cure the problems it obviously seems to have caused. They raise articulate, well-meaning voices, compelling enough to move our lawmakers and executives towards restrictive covenants and paralyzing inaction. They are the liberally educated, the social activists who have sprung up, of necessity, in our industrial system to oppose the rampant force of zealous technology that is usually coupled, they believe, with human greed.

Liberal education and humanist philosophy predate technological society by many centuries, so the social activists were there, ready to be vocal just as soon as the societal symptoms inducing protest appeared. But despite ominous signs of its gathering effect, for at least a hundred years after the start of the industrial revolution the social activists were curiously ineffective. The power and pervasiveness of new scientific knowledge and its outlet in technology were overwhelming. Despite small understanding, it was enthusiastically accepted by our business and governing institutions, ultimately invading our schools to create the dual-track educational pathway so lamented by C. P. Snow in his book *Two Cultures.*

Today, with social activists led by scientifically informed Ralph Naders and socially informed Barry Commoners, science and technology's influence on our educational and governing institutions has seriously eroded. And in the new balance of influence, with scientific knowledge now contested by politics and law, something unforeseen has emerged— a paralyzing division of Western societies' leadership into two mutually distrustful camps: those conditioned by education and culture to be enthusiastic advocates of technology, and those similarly conditioned to be innately distrustful of technology. Let us call them, for convenience, the "technologists" and the "sociologists."

Recently my friend Richard Critchfield, the California anthropologist who writes frequently about Third World villages, sent me a pithy letter on how this dichotomy seems to be paralyzing the professional development community. "Among the 'technologists,'" he wrote,

I would lump all farm scientists, administrators directly engaged in development as in AID or the World Bank, a few economists and such publicists as Herman Kahn, *The Economist*'s Norman Macrae or, in his non-scientific role, Norman Borlaug. The "sociologists" would include most academics, including most economists but not agricultural scientists, such publicists as Lester Brown or Dennis Meadows of *The Limits to Growth*, and those involved with the social side of things in the foundations and international development institutions.

The "technologists" more or less go about their business, developing new technology, especially agriculture technology, and spreading it around the world, in recent years particularly through the international agricultural research centers. Patiently slogging away, they have in the past 15 or so years quite spectacularly changed the face of the Third World. The "sociologists," on the other hand, do not themselves create change, as do the "technologists," but rather study its impact.

Critchfield then offers this juicy view of the difference in character in the "two cultures":

> The "technologists" tend to be optimistic, the "sociologists" pessimistic. The latter tend to be influenced by such academically fashionable notions as, technology is actually making the poorest people in the Third World poorer. They tend to argue that the world is running out of food, space and resources and that, if civilization is to survive (and they mean Western civilization), growth and consumption must be limited. The "sociologists" are more influenced by national moods, disinclined to take risks and characterized by some loss of nerve, will and confidence.
>
> The "technologists" tend to have more of the old "square" values, particularly the old-fashioned Protestant work ethic, while the "sociologists" put new emphasis on hedonism and self-fulfillment and new liberated attitudes towards family and society. Among the "sociologists" there is a marked development of anti-technology, anti-growth attitudes; they are influenced by "small is beautiful" and "limits to growth" arguments. The "sociologists" tend to put more of a political content in their work; they are more sympathetic toward revolutions and are apt to stress development specifically tailored to the poorest underdog in any society.

If you join me in a "whew," let me say that these remarks do not necessarily reflect the views of the management and also that I'm glad it was an anthropologist, not an engineer such as myself, making the observations.

Richard Critchfield reflects on how the "two cultures" conflict affects international development and how indisputable social concern by the "assessors" often backfires by preventing the "doers" from furnishing desirable technology and associated benefits to the poor. Jay Forrester, the superb technologist who did the computer models for *Limits to Growth* and hence is a sort of reverse image of Critchfield, adds another twist to the picture when he points out that when social scientists do relax and approve technology massively to meet human needs, the results are usually what he terms "counterintuitive." In other words, the solution, such as high-rise public housing for the poor or federally subsidized nursing homes, sometimes creates more problems in the long run than the original problem itself.

Let me briefly cite a few of my own observations on knowledge-use paralysis—situations where knowledge exists to meet crucial human needs but where its use is being withheld or delayed by cultural conflict.

First, consider the field of health care. Its escalating cost places it beyond the reach of increasing millions, yet the technology is known and available to alleviate this problem. At the heart of the solution is the computer, a remarkable tool for juggling, at ridiculously low cost, limitless bits of health information. Sick people could communicate cheaply and pleasantly with a computer that would offer them programmed solace, a status report, and treatment advice. But the notion is abhorrent to those who honestly believe (or cynically maintain) that such technology will "dehumanize" medicine. I've observed poor people in poor countries absolutely charmed and delighted when "talking" with a medical computer. After all, they ask, what is a "doctor"?

Human nutrition, closely allied with health care, also suffers from withheld technology. Take the problem of chemicals added to food and the laws that limit their application. There is a valid, scientific basis for such laws, but much of the social force behind them stems from an emotional issue as well as distrust of technology. Nature's foods, the advocates hold, should not be contaminated with artificial chemicals. Yet the fact is that nature's foods are all chemicals, and those added by humans usually are to enhance safety, shelf life, appearance, and palatability—all desirable improvements for folks far removed from the garden plot. The issue gets sticky, too, when technology such as particle irradiation (an emotional no-no to many) is legally banned for use on food on the basis that it is an "additive" and hence must be proven noncarcinogenic. Yet food irradiation may be the cheapest and most effective way to deal with the massive problem of food spoilage in developing countries. What is the tradeoff? More food for desperately malnourished people, or the impossibility of proving that nonexistent radiated particles, never retained in the food to begin with, will cause cancer in rats?

A third and final example here of knowledge caught in cultural conflict involves the question of "appropriate technology." The concept of furnishing technology suited to the economic system, infrastructure, and capabilities of local people certainly seems both logical and humane. But the recipients of such apparently well-intended assistance, upward-bound Third Worlders, have come to view appropriate technology as either the unpalatable fruit of an uneasy honeymoon between sociologists and engineers or a con job by the Western establishment. "Should we be stuck with nineteenth-century technology," they say, "on the premise that it is labor-intensive and suited to the limited skills of our people? Is this the way we are supposed to close the gap? There is no such thing as appropriate technology for us; there is only the best technology." To these feisty Third Worlders (and I'm inclined to agree with them), the appropriate technology concept is another classic example of Western do-gooders being far off target when deciding what is best for people in other cultures.

What, then, is the answer to this knowledge-use conflict, this often paralyzing cultural dichotomy that seems to have sprung full blown in Western society since the middle of the century? I'll conclude with a few thoughts, neither profoundly researched nor even modestly tested, which may suggest a way to proceed.

First, I'll propose a new motto for use with technology knowledge that may be acceptable to both cultures, to both technologists and sociologists—namely, "Let the Means Justify the Ends." This contemporary version of a well-known dialectic might just take the monkey off the back of both parties. Rather than make the means subservient to the ends and hence forgive ruthless application, it implies that technology must be assessed *before* use, for both immediate and long-range *social* impact. It suggests a hopeful, more creative role for technology knowledge.

My next, equally blithe proposition is to have the Academy of Independent Scholars commission a few of its senior semanticist members to develop a new, mutually accepted lexicon or jargon for social technology. A good deal of the cultural conflict between technologists and sociologists is surely due to the fact that they speak two separate languages. As a socially concerned technologist, I know how put off I am when reading a proposal couched in the indecipherable jargon of the social sciences. But I am certain that there is a reverse reaction when a sociologist is required to wade through a typical engineering report. Perhaps a new language for collaboration is not necessary, but in preparation for work in social technology an old copy of Rudolph Flesch's *The Art of Clear Writing* might be required reading.

A more tangible suggestion for a short-term approach to the problem would be a special training effort or program, perhaps carried out as an exercise on many campuses, to create instant, hybrid social-technologists by a process of intellectual osmosis. Using a workshop environment, I have found that it only takes two or three days for technologists and sociologists to tune into one another, and that after one week of problem solving and argument together in such an environment, a certain amount of homogenization takes place.

As a serious aside on this suggestion, I should observe that mixing sociologists with technologists in so-called multidisciplinary teams in the field rarely accomplishes this hybridization process and usually results in inadequate solutions to problems. If anything, when the team members finally break up and return to their home institutions, they are more culturally locked in than ever.

This last suggestion brings up my ultimate remark and perhaps the only one that I should have made in the first place. Specifically, let me suggest the urgent need for fundamental change in the way we educate our decision makers and problem solvers.

Occasionally, out in the tropical boondocks or deep in the inner city, one comes upon a brilliant example of technology being used to solve, with few or no losers, some truly human problems. When you look for how it happened, you will usually find not a team of specialists but a single crosscultural, Renaissance, holistic, systems-type (call it what you will) person who was the driving force behind it all.

How we can decompartmentalize our present system to yield to such a person, how we can build a new, creative synthesis between the sciences and humanities in the educative process—I'll leave these questions to the experts. That such a change must take place soon, before our society ultimately drowns in a sea of unspent and misapplied knowledge, I believe is self-evident.

VERNON RUTTAN

——— 18 ———
Accountability in Research: Examples from Agriculture

Introduction

The productivity of modern agriculture is the result of a remarkable fusion of technology and science. In the West this fusion was built on ideological foundations that, from the early Middle Ages, have valued both the improvement of material well-being and the advancement of knowledge.[1]

This fusion did not come easily. The advances in tillage equipment and cropping practices in Western Europe during the Middle Ages and well into the nineteenth century evolved entirely from husbandry and mechanics. "Science was traditionally aristocratic, speculative, intellectual in intent; technology was lower-class, empirical, action oriented."[2] This cultural distinction has persisted in the folklore, giving basic science priority over applied science long after the interdependence of science and technology had eliminated the functional and operational value of the distinction.

The power the fusion of theoretical and empirical inquiry has given to the advancement of knowledge and technology since the middle of the nineteenth century has dramatically increased their impact. It is not unrealistic to argue that agronomists, along with engineers and health scientists, have been the true revolutionaries of the twentieth century.[3]

In the 1960s and 1970s a new skepticism emerged about the benefits of advances in science and technology.[4] A view emerged that the power created by fusing science and technology—reflected in the cataclysm of war, the degradation of the environment, and the psychological cost of social change—is obviously dangerous to the modern world and to the future of man. The result has been to question seriously the significance for human welfare of scientific progress, technical change, and economic growth.

Agricultural science has not escaped these questions. Some interpret the mechanization of land preparation or harvesting as a source of poverty in rural areas rather than as a response to rising wage rates. Milling grain by wind and water power was counted as progress in twelfth-century Europe. But critics today view substituting rice mills for hand pounding as destroying opportunities for work in twentieth-century Java. There are those who regard the use of yield-increasing fertilizers as poisoning the soil rather than as a means of removing the pressure of agricultural production on marginal lands and fragile environments. The new income streams that flow from more productive farms are viewed as destroying the integrity of rural communities rather than as enabling rural people to participate in a society in which the gap between rural and urban income, lifestyles, and culture has been narrowed.

What should the agricultural scientist or science administrator make of these charges? Can they be dismissed as the mistaken or malicious rhetoric of romantics, populists, and ideologues?[5] How does one examine the role of science in society in an atmosphere that is so politically and emotionally charged?

A first step is to recognize that similar economic and social forces have generated both the drive for technical change—advancing the productive capacity of plants, animals, machines, and men—and the drive for institutional change—managing more effectively the direction of scientific and technical effort and capacity. The increased scarcity of natural resources—of land, water, and energy—continues to create a demand for technologies that can generate higher levels of output per worker, per hectare, and per kilocalorie. The increasing value a society places on the health of workers and consumers and on environmental amenities such as clean water, clean air, and clean streets continues to lead to a demand for effective social controls over the development and use of agricultural technology. These demands go beyond considerations of economic feasibility, viability, and impact. Issues of ethical and esthetic sensibility are also involved.

Responsibility for Research Results

There is a demand for greater responsibility in the way the results of science and technology are put to use.[6] Should government respond to this demand by changing the institutions that induce the generation of new knowledge and new technology? Should government assume a stronger role in the adoption and use of new technology? Should it attempt to encourage greater esthetic and moral sensitivity on the part of scientists, engineers, agronomists, and science administrators? What can be expected from such efforts?

The difficulties that face governments in responding to the demand for greater moral responsibility in producing and using new technology can best be illustrated by referring to specific examples. The recent controversy over the employment displacement created by the tomato harvester is one useful illustration and research on tobacco improvement is a second. The cases are not chosen because tomatoes and tobacco are the most significant examples that might be selected. But they do illustrate in a dramatic way the underlying principles.

Technical Change and Employment Displacement:
The Tomato Harvester Case

The introduction of machine harvesting of tomatoes has been accompanied by an especially vigorous debate. It has been viewed as the product of uniquely effective collaboration between mechanical engineers and plant scientists. It has also been vigorously attacked for displacing farm workers and small producers.[7]

In 1978 a suit on behalf of the California Agrarian Action Project and a group of farm workers was filed against the University of California regents, charging that they had allowed agribusiness corporations and their own economic interests to influence their decisions to spend public tax funds to develop agricultural machines. The plaintiffs sought to compel the university to use the funds it receives from its machinery patents to help farm workers displaced by those machines.

In December 1979, U.S. Secretary of Agriculture Bob Bergland announced that he intended to stop USDA funding for research that might put farm laborers out of work.[8] The dean of the University of California College of Agricultural and Environmental Sciences at Davis criticized Bergland for attempting to impose restrictions on the freedom of academic research. In the summer of 1980 Secretary Bergland established an Agricultural Mechanization Task Force to examine the policies of the USDA with respect to mechanization research in greater depth.

Clearly farm workers displaced by labor-saving machinery deserve a reasonable degree of protection from unemployment. This is a legitimate claim on the new income streams—the productivity dividends—resulting from the adoption of the new technology. But who among the displaced workers deserves protection? Do the displaced workers who immediately found other employment have a legitimate claim on the new income streams? What about the workers who found other employment but at lower wage rates? And what about the tomato growers in Indiana and New Jersey who lost part of their market due to the lower costs in California? Who should pay the compensation? Should it be the inventors and manufacturers of the labor-displacing equipment? Should it be the farmers who captured the initial gains from lower costs or the processors who expanded their production as a result of their ability to buy tomatoes at a lower cost? Or should it be the consumers, who ultimately gained as competitive forces passed on the lower costs of production?

The answer is implicit in the questions. The gains of productivity growth are diffused broadly, and the costs should be borne broadly. In a wealthy society such as the United States, a worker should not have to prove specific displacement—that he or she was displaced by a tomato harvester or a Toyota—in order to be eligible for such protection.

The first line of defense against the impact of displacement is an economy in which productivity is growing and employment is expanding. Society has little obligation to compensate the worker who can readily find alternative employment. The second line of defense is a program of severance payments and unemployment insurance that is effective for all workers, those who are forced to seek seasonal or casual employment as well as those in more favored industries.

A society that provides generalized protection will be in a stronger position to realize the gains from technical change and to diffuse these gains broadly than a society that insists on specific or categorial protection.[9] The failure to develop institutions to protect farm workers from the effects of seasonal employment and technological displacement has resulted in the transfer of an excessive burden of displacement costs to farm workers. This transfer in turn has induced a legal and political response that, if effective, could slow technical change and limit the gains from productivity growth.

In a society in which employment opportunities are expanding rapidly and protection from unemployment is adequately institutionalized, researchers involved in the development of a tomato or a lettuce harvester need not be excessively burdened by the moral implications of trade-offs between the economic and social costs and the benefits of mechanization. Public policy has relieved them of that burden. But who should bear the burden of responsibility in a society that is too poor to protect workers from technical displacement? Or in a wealthy society that forces the burden onto its poorest citizens?

Efficiency in the Production of a Health Hazard:
The Case of Tobacco

Tobacco is a commodity that has been the subject of moral debate and political intervention since it first became a commercial export from colonial America. In the 1950s and 1960s conclusive evidence was found of the association between cigarette smoking and lung cancer, coronary artery disease, chronic bronchitis, and emphysema. The addictive effects and part of the health hazard are due to nicotine and related alkaloids.[10] What are the moral responsibilities of agricultural researchers regarding a crop that not only induces chemical dependency but also has a high probability of shortening the life of those who use it?

One would think that, under these circumstances, efforts to develop tobacco varieties with low nicotine content would have the support of both farmers and consumers. Yet when in the early 1950s Professor W. D. Valleau of the University of Kentucky developed low-nicotine varieties of tobacco, they were bitterly attacked by Kentucky farmers because of their potential competition with burley tobacco.[11] In retrospect, we have little difficulty in supporting the objectives of Professor Valleau's research to reduce the nicotine content of burley tobaccos. Today even a marginal contribution to reducing chemical dependency and health hazards of cigarette smoking would seem to be desirable.[12] But what about the issue that underlies this judgment?

Should public funds be used to do research to reduce the costs and improve the productivity of a product that induces chemical dependency or shortens life expectancy? What are the moral responsibilities of the directors of the agricultural experiment stations in states that support tobacco research? And what about the individual scientist who devotes his life to understanding the physiology or the nutrition of the tobacco plant? Is the farmer who grows the tobacco absolved from responsibility by the fact that there is a market demand for tobacco? Are state legislatures and experiment station directors absolved by the fact that tobacco has been one of the more profitable crops for small farmers in the depressed areas of Kentucky and North Carolina? Are the scientists relieved of responsibility because they should be free to do research? What are the moral implications for the tobacco breeder, employed by either a private firm or a public research institution, of responding to market criteria when the market is most effectively enhanced by inducing chemical dependency?

As evidence has accumulated on the health hazards of smoking, there is, in the United States, a tendency to insist that the members of the legislative body that appropriates the funds, the science administrators who allocate funds, and the individual researchers in both public and private sector research institutions assume greater responsibility for the impact of their actions on the health of those who use tobacco. What moral guidelines can be drawn in a society in which the government spends billions of dollars on medical care necessitated by smoking and millions of dollars on research on tobacco-related disease and campaigns to discourage smoking, supports research to improve efficiency in tobacco production, and legislates programs to support the incomes of tobacco producers?

There are, as in the case of the tomato harvester, institutional changes that would relieve research administrators and scientists of the moral dilemma posed by tobacco research. If a public consensus were to outlaw the sale of tobacco products in the United States it is doubtful that Kentucky and North Carolina would allocate any more resources to tobacco improvement than they now allocate to marijuana research. There has not yet been sufficient convergence of opinion to take the steps necessary to limit the content of dependency-forming or carcinogenic substances in cigarettes. Moving toward complete prohibition would require a careful balancing of the desirable effects on individual health against the undesirable effects of attempts to enforce prohibition.[13]

Technology, Institutions, and Reform

There is no way that the science community can avoid sharing in the responsibility for the economic consequences of the mechanical tomato harvester, the health effects of improved tobacco, or the environmental and health effects of persistent pesticides. Even the most unregenerate adherents to traditional forms of market relationships acknowledge that the principle of caveat emptor (let the buyer beware) cannot be accepted as an appropriate guide to market practice. The fusion of science and technology, so powerful in releasing man from the constraints of the natural world, have made traditional concepts of the absolute freedom, including the freedom to conduct research, obsolete. When the freedom to know can no longer be distinguished from the freedom to do, the nature of that freedom changes.[14]

There can be no question about society's right to hold scientists, engineers, and agronomists responsible for the consequences of the technical and institutional changes set in motion by their research. When credit is claimed for increased productivity from advances in agricultural technology, responsibility cannot be evaded for altering the distribution of income between suppliers of labor, land, capital, or industrial inputs. Nor can responsibility be evaded for the impact of substances (for example, pest-control chemicals) on the environment or on the health of workers and consumers. *But it is in society's interest to let these burdens rest lightly on the shoulders of individual researchers and research managers.* If society insists it be assured that advances in agricultural technology carry minimum risk—that agricultural scientists abandon their revolutionary role—society must accept the risk of losing new incomes from technical change.

In allocating resources to agricultural research, a first consideration must be whether there are opportunities to advance knowledge or technology. The second consideration must be, given the society in which the research is conducted, whether there will be an economic demand for the knowledge or the technology generated by the research.

Both of these criteria are consistent with the motivations of the agricultural science community. The first meets the criteria of professional integrity. The second meets the need to avoid alienation or, more positively, the need to feel that exercising one's professional skill and insight has meaning for society.

The Objective of Research Management

It is in society's interest to take great care before insisting that researchers commit themselves to scientific or technical objectives that are unrealistic, given the state of scientific and technical knowledge. It was unrealistic in the 1950s to expect that utilization and marketing research could make a significant contribution to the solution of agricultural surplus problems in the United States. Allocating excessive research resources to these areas led both to a waste of resources and to an erosion of the credibility of research.

It is equally wasteful for society to ask agricultural scientists to adopt objectives inconsistent with the economic or political marketplace. It is unrealistic, for example, to insist that the California Agricultural Experiment Station focus on the needs of the 160-acre farm unless the state or the federal government is prepared to support the reversal of the trend toward large-scale agriculture. A research system cannot be asked to produce knowledge and technology that will not be used without eroding the intellectual integrity and ultimately the scientific capacity of the research system.

It might be argued that policymakers should ask researchers to "discover" society's true objectives (a social welfare function) before its objectives are "revealed" in the political or economic marketplace. This argument implies that the researcher should have the capacity not only to assess the benefits and burdens of the technical changes anticipated from a research program but, in addition, to develop a set of weights or shadow prices that reflects the value society places on the welfare of each individual or group that may potentially be benefited or burdened by the results of the research. This view requires research directors to allocate resources on the basis of a social welfare function prior to the time that function is revealed by either the economic or the political system!

What alternative do I have to suggest? Clearly, a research director must have access to the analytical capacity to gauge any potential benefits and burdens in order to enter into effective dialogue with the political system about research budgets and priorities. The research director who fails on this count stands naked before both critics and supporters. Research leading to a better understanding of the discrepancies or the disequilibrium in the economic, political, and social weighting system is essential. But the objective of such research should not be to provide research directors with the weighting systems for internal research resource allocation; the objective should be to contribute to a political dialogue resulting in institutional changes leading to convergence of the several weighting systems.[15]

Let me illustrate. Sanders has demonstrated for Brazil and Binswanger for India that biased signals from differential exchange rates and subsidies encouraged more rapid mechanization of farming operations than would have occurred if the decisions were guided by more "efficient" prices.[16] One effect was to bias the flow of benefits to larger landowners and to impose excess burden on hired laborers. The market bias also resulted in excessive allocation of research resources in the direction of mechanization.

Research managers do have a clear responsibility to inform society of the impact of pricing systems and tax structure on the choice of mechanical, chemical, and biological technologies by farmers; on the incidence of technical change on the distribution of income among laborers, landowners, and consumers; on the structure of farming and rural communities; and on the health and safety of producers and consumers. They also have a responsibility to enter into the intellectual and political dialogues necessary if society is to achieve more effective convergence between "market" and "shadow" prices and between the "individual" and "revealed" preferences of its citizens. If political processes can lead to greater consistency, individual scientists might no longer be confronted by a situation in which cigarette smoking is branded as dangerous to health and at the same time public resources are appropriated for research on tobacco.

Agricultural Technology as an Instrument of Reform

A second reason it is unwise for society to insist that the moral and esthetic consequences of technical change weigh heavily on agricultural research is that technical change is such a blunt instrument of reform. A nation's agricultural research system can be a powerful instrument for expanding its capacity to produce food and fiber, but it is a relatively weak instrument for changing income distribution in rural areas.

In thinking about the incidence of benefits and burdens of technical change, it is important to distinguish among *embodiment, augmentation, and incidence.*[17] Technology embodied in one factor of production has the capacity to augment the productivity of other factors, and the incidence of benefits and burdens may be experienced by other factors or even in other sectors. Embodiment is a characteristic of the technology itself. Augmentation and incidence are influenced by the *technology's* institutional environment.

For example, research embodied in a technology such as improved seed, available to both small and large farmers, may have a different impact on income distribution depending on the economic or institutional environment into which it is introduced. If introduced into an environment in which the supply of labor is more elastic than the supply of land, it will augment the returns per unit of land more than those per unit of labor, even though it may greatly expand the employment of labor per unit of land. If introduced into an environment in which the supply of labor is inelastic, it will augment the returns per unit of labor more than those per unit of land, even though there is little increase in employment per unit of land.

The incidence of benefits is also affected by institutional endowments and changes. If the technology is introduced into an economy with a share-tenure system, the incidence of benefits will be different than in a system in which agriculture is carried out primarily on owner-cultivated farms. If mechanical technology is introduced into a society in which capital investment is encouraged through interest and tax rate subsidies it will have a different impact than in a society in which monetary and fiscal policy are more neutral with respect to the use of capital and labor.

The research system is often criticized for failure to respond to distributional considerations, not because it is a powerful instrument for bringing about changes in the distribution of income, but because it is more vulnerable to pressure than institutions with a broader base of political support. There is a great danger that in attempting to respond to such pressure, the research system will not become a source of equitable growth but will lose its capacity to contribute to growth at all.

These considerations lead me to conclude that the primary consideration in allocating resources to agricultural research should be criteria relevant for the adoption and diffusion of the technology. These same criteria will result in the highest rates of return to the research when evaluated in economic terms.

Institutional Innovation as an Instrument of Reform

Technical change can be a powerful source of institutional change. Institutional innovation can, in turn, exert a powerful impact on the rate and direction of technical change. But technical change contributes only indirectly to institutional reform. Its incidence is uncertain and difficult to anticipate. In contrast, institutional innovations can both generate technical change in a manner consistent with resource endowments and product demand and bias the incidence of benefits and burdens in a manner consistent with social policy. Institutional innovation is both a more powerful and a more reliable instrument of reform than technical change.

Among the most effective instruments for directing the gains from technical change are changes related to the ownership of resources. The land-to-the-tiller-type land reforms employed in Japan, Korea, and Taiwan were, for example, powerful instruments for achieving greater equality in the distribution of income in rural areas. The "green revolution" seed-fertilizer technology, when introduced into an environment with reasonable equity in land ownership, like Taiwan or Korea, contributed to greater equity in income distribution. This same technology, introduced where there was a great inequality in the distribution of assets, in the Pakistan Punjab for example, has reinforced this inequality. The education of rural people is also a powerful source of institutional reform; reforms in land tenure and in market organization in Denmark were clearly facilitated by a literate rural population.

Institutional innovations are often subject to constraints in knowledge that are similar to the constraints that limit advances in technical change. I argued above that knowledge does not seriously constrain our ability to design institutional innovations to protect against the employment displacement effects of the tomato harvester or other advances in labor-saving technology. But knowledge does appear to be a serious constraint on designing the institutional innovations needed to reduce the health impact of tobacco or other forms of chemical dependency.[18]

Agricultural Research and the Future

What should society expect from agricultural science in the future? And what does agricultural science have a right to expect from society if it is to meet society's expectations?

First, society should insist that agricultural science maintain its commitment to expanding the capacity of the resources used in agricultural production. These include the original endowments of nature—soil, water, and sunlight; the agents that humans have domesticated or adopted—plants and animals and organic and mineral sources of energy; the agents they have invented—machines and chemicals; and the people engaged in agricultural production.

It is essential for the future of humanity that by the end of this century the capacity to maintain this commitment should be established in every part of the world. During the last two decades, the world has become increasingly dependent on North American agriculture. This dependence poses danger both to the developing world and to North

America. Agricultural institutions must be established to produce the knowledge and the technology to reverse the trends of the last several decades. Agricultural science in North America must remain strong enough and sufficiently cosmopolitan to both contribute to and learn from the emerging global agricultural science community.

Second, society should insist that agricultural science embrace a broader agenda that includes a concern for the effects of agricultural technology on the health and safety of agricultural producers, a concern for the nutrition and health of consumers, a concern for the impact of agricultural practices on the esthetic qualities of both natural and man-made environments, and a concern for the quality of life in rural communities. And society should insist that it consider the implications of current technical choices on the options that will be available in the future.

These concerns are not new. But they have often been viewed as peripheral to the main task of agricultural science by those responsible for the financial support of agricultural research. It is important for the future of agricultural science that these concerns be fully embraced. It is also important that the capacity to work on these problems outside the traditional establishment be maintained so that an effective dialogue can be achieved both within the research community and in the realm of public policy.

What should the agricultural science community expect from society?

First, agricultural science should expect that society gradually acquire a more sophisticated perception of the contribution of agricultural technology to the balance between humans and the natural world. The romantic view that agricultural science is engaged in a continuous assault on nature is mistaken. Society must come to understand that agricultural science can expand productive capacity only as it reveals and cooperates with the laws of nature.

We in the West are the inheritors of a tradition that views material concern as a defect in human nature. This inheritance leads to a romantic view of man's relationship to the natural world. It also leads to a view that technology alienates man from both the natural world and the natural community. But I cannot believe that a Taiwanese farmer who is able to harvest six metric tons of rice from one hectare by planting higher-yielding varieties, using chemical fertilizers to complement organic ones, and controlling weeds with herbicides feels a greater alienation from nature than his father, who harvested less than two tons of rice from the same field.

Scientists, engineers, and agronomists have a right to expect the philosophers of society to achieve greater insight into people's relationship to technology and nature. It is time to recognize that the invention, adaptation, and use of knowledge to achieve material ends does not "reduce" experience but rather expands it.

Second, it is time the general science community followed the lead of agricultural science in embracing the fusion of science and technology rather than continuing to hide behind the intellectual and class barriers that protect its privilege and its ego from contamination by engineering, agronomy, and medicine. This change will become increasingly important in the future as the close of the fossil fuel frontier joins with the close of the land frontier to drive technical change along a path that implies a much larger role for biological and information technology.

The 1970s were a decade of declining productivity growth in the United States and in several other advanced economies, dangerous trends more apparent in the industrial than in the agricultural sector. Rates of return to agricultural research have remained high. The evidence suggests that institutional linkages that have provided effective articulation between science, technology, and agriculture have continued to be productive sources of economic growth in both developed and developing countries. There is much that can be learned from this experience by those who are not blinded by outmoded status symbols or cultural constraints.

Notes

1. I would like to express my appreciation to Maury E. Bredahl, Francis C. Byrnes, Jeff Davis, David Ervin, Charles M. Hardin, J. C. Headly, Glenn L. Johnson, Keith Huston, Charles P. Lutz, Don Paarlberg, Gordon C. Rausser, Lawrence Senesh, Eldon D. Smith, and David Zilberman for comment on an earlier draft of this paper. The perspectives on accountability and responsibility in research have been strongly influenced by the work of Lynn White, Jr., Samuel C. Florman, and Glenn L. Johnson. See particularly Lynn White, Jr., *Machina Ex Deo: Essays in the Dynamism of Western Culture* (Cambridge, Mass.: MIT Press, 1968); Samuel C. Florman, *The Existential Pleasures of Engineering* (New York: St. Martin's Press, 1976); Glenn L. Johnson and Judith L. Brown, *An Evaluation of the Normative and Prescriptive Content of the Department of Energy Mid-Term Energy Forecasting System (MEFS) and the Texas National Energy Modeling Project (TNEMP)* (July 9, 1980, mimeographed).

2. Lynn White, Jr., *Machina Ex Deo,* p. 79. This same point has been emphasized by Isaac Asimov, "Pure and Impure: The Interplay of Science and Technology," *Saturday Review* 6 (June 9, 1979):22–24, 29; see also Kenneth E. Boulding, *The Impact of the Social Sciences* (New Brunswick, N.J.: Rutgers, 1966) and N. Bruce Hannay and Robert E. McGinn, "The Anatomy of Modern Technology: Prolegomenon to an Improved Public Policy for the Social Management of Technology," *Daedalus* 109 (Winter 1980):25–53. Hannay and McGinn point out that "modern technology . . . is itself obtained with the aid of

sophisticated products of modern technology—electron microscopes, computers, spectographs, and so on. 'Modern science as applied technology' is no less true and no more misleading than 'modern technology as applied science' "(p. 39).

3. It will be useful, for the sake of brevity, occasionally to use the term "agronomy" to refer to the whole body of agriculturally related science and technology and "agronomists" to refer to the community of production-oriented agricultural scientists. In the United States the term agronomy has the more narrow connotation of field-crop production and management.

4. For a useful historical perspective see Edward Shils, "Faith, Utility and the Legitimacy of Science," *Daedalus* 103 (Summer 1974):1–15.

5. For an example of romantic criticisms, see Wendell Berry, *The Unsettling of America: Culture and Agriculture* (New York: Avon Books, 1977). For a populist perspective, see Jim Hightower, *Hard Tomatoes, Hard Times* (Cambridge: Schenkman, 1973). For an ideological perspective, see Francis Moore Lappe and Joseph Collins (with Gary Fowler), *Food First: Beyond the Myth of Scarcity* (Boston: Houghton Mifflin, 1977). See also E. G. Valliantos, *Fear in the Countryside: The Control of Agricultural Resources in Poor Countries* (Cambridge, Mass: Ballinger, 1977); Susan George, *How the Other Half Dies: The Real Reasons for World Hunger* (Montclair, N.J.: Allanheld Osmun, 1977). For reviews of this literature, see Nick Eberstad, "Malthusians, Marxists, and Missionaries," *Society* 17 (September/October 1980):29–35; and Charles M. Hardin, "Feeding the World: Conflicting Views on Policy," *Agricultural History* 53 (October 1979):787–795.

6. Since the late 1960s the term "technology assessment" has been increasingly introduced into discussions about the distributional, environmental, and esthetic consequences of research and development. See, for example, National Academy of Sciences, *Technology Process of Assessment and Choice* (Washington, D.C.: Government Printing Office, July 1969). There has been considerable confusion over the objectives and methodology of technology assessment. To some it appears to be a new and more powerful methodology designed to overcome the limitations of narrower or more partial approaches to problems of technology generation and choice, but to some enthusiasts it is more of a social movement designed to incorporate advances in esthetic and moral sensitivity into technology design and management. For further discussion see Joseph F. Coates, "The Role of Formal Models of Technology Assessment," *Technological Forecasting and Social Change* 9 (1975):139–189; Vary T. Coates, *Technology Assessment in Federal Agencies: 1971–76* (Washington, D.C.: George Washington University Program of Policy Studies on Science and Technology, March 1979); Robert T. Holt, "Technology Assessment and Technology Inducement Mechanism," *American Journal of Political Science* 21 (May 1977): 283–301; Lynn White, Jr., "Technology Assessment from the Stance of a Medieval Historian," *Technological Forecasting and Social Change* 6 (1971): 359–369; C. Marchetti, "A Postmortem Technology Assessment of the Spinning Wheel: The Last Thousand Years," *Technological Forecasting and Social Change* 13 (1979):91–93.

7. See Wayne D. Rasmussen, "Advances in American Agriculture: The Mechanical Tomato Harvest as a Case Study," *Technology and Culture* 9 (October 1968):531–543; Andrew Schmitz and David Seckler, "Mechanized Agriculture

and Social Welfare: The Case of the Tomato Harvester," *American Journal of Agricultural Economics* 52 (November 1970): pp. 569–577; W. H. Friedland and A. E. Barton, *Destalking the Wily Tomato: A Case Study in Social Consequences in California Agricultural Research* (Davis: University of California Department of Applied Behavioral Research, monograph no. 2, 1975); Richard E. Just, Andrew Schmitz, and David Zilberman, "Technological Change in Agriculture," *Science* 206 (December 14, 1979):1277–1280.

8. Eliot Marshall, "Bergland Opposed on Farm Machinery Policy," *Science* 208 (May 9, 1980):578–580.

9. For a useful discussion of the constraints on the feasibility of a general policy to provide specific protection, see E. C. Pasour, Jr., "Economic Growth and Agriculture: An Evaluation of the Compensation Principle," *American Journal of Agricultural Economics* 55 (November 1973): 611–616. For a more positive view, see Gordon C. Rausser, Alain de Janvry, Andrew Schmitz, and David Zilberman, "Principle Issues in the Evaluation of Public Research in Agriculture," in George W. Norton, Walter L. Fishel, Arnold A. Paulson, and W. Burt Sundquist, eds., *Evaluation of Agricultural Research* (St. Paul: University of Minnesota Agricultural Experiment Station, miscellaneous publication 8–1981, April 1981), pp. 262–280.

10. For a definitive review of the evidence, see U.S. Public Health Service, *Smoking and Health: A Report of the Surgeon General* (Washington, D.C.: U.S. Department of Health, Education, and Welfare, Public Health Service, HEW publication no. (PHS) 79–50006, 1980).

11. Charles M. Hardin, *Freedom in Agricultural Education* (1955; New York: Arno Press, 1976), pp. 56–61.

12. Tobacco breeders have now gone well beyond Professor Valleau's limited objectives. At present it is possible to manipulate the nicotine content within a very broad range without significantly altering the yield potential. The ability to manipulate the chemical characteristics of tobacco is probably more advanced than understanding of the health implications of the several characteristics. Over the next decade or so technical and institutional changes in tobacco harvesting and marketing are likely to result in substantial labor displacement along the lines described in the tomato harvester case (Eldon D. Smith, *personal communication,* June 20, 1980).

13. It is doubtful that prohibition of tobacco use would be any more effective than the attempts that were made in the 1920s in the United States and Finland to prohibit the consumption of alcoholic beverages. It is of interest, however, that in 1980 Malaysia imposed rather severe restrictions on the advertising of alcoholic beverages and of cigarettes. The restrictions on tobacco advertising have been less severe than on alcoholic beverage advertising primarily because tobacco is produced by large numbers of small farmers.

14. This is consistent with the view expressed by Hans Mohr, "The Ethics of Science," *Interdisciplinary Science Reviews* 4 (March 1979):45–53. Mohr notes that "freedom of inquiry . . . does not necessarily imply freedom in the choice of any particular goal; it implies, however, that the results of scientific inquiry may not be influenced by a factor extrinsic to science" (p. 48).

15. The position expressed here is similar to that of Peter O. Steiner in "The Public Sector and the Public Interest," in Robert H. Haveman, ed., *The Analysis and Evaluation of Public Expenditures: The PPB System*, Subcommittee on Economy in Government, Joint Economic Committee, Congress of the United States (Washington, D.C.: Government Printing Office, 1969), pp. 13–14.

16. John H. Sanders and Vernon W. Ruttan, "Biased Choice of Technology in Brazilian Agriculture," in Vernon W. Ruttan, Hans P. Binswanger, and others, *Induced Innovation: Technology, Institutions and Development* (Baltimore: Johns Hopkins, 1978), pp. 276–296; Hans P. Binswanger, *The Economics of Tractors in South Asia* (New York: The Agricultural Development Council and Hyderabad, India: International Crops Research Institute for the Semi-Arid Tropics, 1978).

17. Hans P. Binswanger, "A Note on Embodiment, Factor Quality and Factor Augmentation," in Hans P. Binswanger, Vernon W. Ruttan, and others, eds., *Induced Innovation: Technology, Institutions and Development* (Baltimore: Johns Hopkins, 1978), pp. 159–163.

18. See for example, Jeffrey E. Harris, "Taxing Tar and Nicotine," *American Economic Review* 70 (June 1980):300–311.

ARTHUR R. KANTROWITZ

——— **19** ———

The Overutilization of Ignorance of Science and Technology in the Making of Public Policy

The Insularity of Expertise

In many vital cases technical expertise is a near monopoly of insular communities. Insularity can be a consequence of specialized training and terminology, or military and industrial secrecy, or of a community of economic interest. Moreover, real expertise requires extraordinary commitment to a narrow field and frequently involves an unshakable conviction that the field is beneficial to humanity. Commitment and conviction insulate the expert far more effectively than any external pressures.

Rapid advance of powerful technologies has always entailed unforeseeable risks and benefits. However, when the expertise needed for predicting risks and benefits is confined to an insular group with clear self-interest, exploitation of public ignorance is inevitable. General perceptions of the inevitability of this primary form of exploitation have given rise to a reaction that, in its extreme form, asserts that control of advancing technology is impossible, that further advance must be prevented, and that we must retreat to decentralized technologies in which adequate expertise (and capital equipment) is generally accessible. In spite of convincing proof that retreat would involve unacceptable sacrifices, the fantasy of returning to a simpler way of life is influential in the ivory towers of affluent societies.

If retreat is a fantasy, the insularity of expertise and the power of modern technology make effective and efficient regulation a challenging necessity. The most demanding prerequisite for the effective regulation of industrial technology is the creation of expertise external to the industry comparable to the internal expertise. Industry offers the scientifically trained recruit the opportunity to create new technology, continuing the tradition that built our technological society. Regulatory agencies offer scientific recruits an opportunity to criticize and to exert power by influencing public policy. The asymmetry of these offerings results in very different populations.

These populations have now formed two establishments, the *progress establishment*, dedicated to technological progress, and the *critical establishment*, dedicated to implementing social goals by regulation of industry. Confrontation between these establishments has been a primary fact of life in the 1970s. This confrontation occurs primarily in the media, with success determined by opinion polls, congressional votes, and election returns.

The simplicity of these criteria for success has demanded that both establishments exploit voter ignorance to the maximum. This is easily done by smothering scientific uncertainty with skillful emotional appeals. The technique of confusing scientific facts with values is exploited by both sides to sway voters whose values differ from their own. The critical establishment has so far successfully utilized scientific uncertainty to arouse fear of the unknown impacts of radiation and chemical carcinogens in the environment in order to greatly expand government regulation and its own power. Conversely, in the 1980 campaign, one of Reagan's strongest appeals was his unprovable assertion that reducing government regulation would help return the United States to the vigorous growth and prosperity that ended in the late 1960s.

The Frankness Rule

The existence of two opposed establishments seeking to impose their values on the nation could be constructive or destructive. To make the public dialogue constructive, laymen must be able to judge the validity or the attractiveness of the proposals offered. If proposition A is offered by group a and B by b, laymen can decide between A and B when descriptions by a and b differ only in areas where laymen can adequately judge. If, however, a and b use different statements of scientific fact in their descriptions, it will not generally be possible for laymen to decide for themselves between these descriptions. We thus come to the familiar dilemma: which scientist do you believe?

The scientific community prides itself on a traditional harshness in dealing with those who are not frank in confessing uncertainty and ignorance. Within the scientific community the frankness rule is enforced by encouraging vigorous discussion at scientific meetings and by sending papers submitted for publication to referees known to be expert in the field. Communication within the scientific community is an adversary process in which those claiming to add to knowledge always prepare themselves to deal with the public criticisms of competing experts who are not easily persuaded of the validity of a new significant claim.

The frankness rule applies, however, only to communications within the scientific community. Currently, when scientists speak to laymen they only need worry about the nontechnical questions that will be addressed to them by laymen. Laymen can usually deal with conflicting claims of sophisticated scientists only by examining their credentials. The bankruptcy of this practice is exhibited every time we see competing lists of Nobel Prize winners supporting opposing propositions.

This contrasts with procedures in the scientific community where (ideally at least) it is what a person says, not the person who says it, that is important. Examining the validity of factual scientific statements for logical consistency or for correspondence with observations of nature precludes bankrupt appeals to authority but requires much more expertise and time than laymen and lay officials can devote to purely scientific matters. It is my position that when statements of scientific fact are needed to rationally make public policy and the facts are apparently disputed, the scientific community has a duty to provide some kind of due process for stating what is known, what the uncertainties are, and what is currently unknown. The scientific community has its own form of due process for internal communications, as was mentioned above. What is needed is to extend these internal procedures to provide scientific information to the public in a way that both the scientific community and the public will find credible.

To achieve this end, I propose the following ethical principle, to be enforced by the scientific community:

Any scientist who addresses the public or lay officials on scientific facts bearing on public policy matters should stand ready to publicly answer the questions not only of laymen but of expert adversaries.

The science court was proposed as an experimental first step toward implementing this ethical principle. The procedures proposed have often been described, but since they have frequently been misunderstood it might be worthwhile to briefly set them forth again here. Suppose a public decision must be made between propositions A and B. The function of the science court is not to make the decision or even to recommend a decision; its only function is to find the scientific facts that bear on the decision. For this purpose the procedure leans heavily on groups a and b that are committed advocates of these propositions, asking their representatives to approve the procedures, examine the scientific judges for prejudice, and so on. These advocates are also expected to prepare a list of factual assertions they consider important for their side of the case, to accept or to challenge the factual assertions of the opposing group, to substantiate challenged factual statements, and to publicly answer the questions of the most informed experts their adversaries can find.

After this public procedure, the judges write their opinions on any factual matters that still remain controversial. The publication of the agreed-upon factual statements and the judges' opinions completes the procedure.

Experience with the Science Court

The science court as presented here was formulated by a task force of a committee advisory to President Ford.[1] This task force suggested that a public meeting be held at which opinions for and against the science court experiment could be aired. The meeting was held 19–21 September 1976 in Leesburg, Virginia, sponsored by the U.S. Department of Commerce, the National Science Foundation, and the American Association for the Advancement of Science. At this meeting the task force position was set forth by Richard Simpson, former chairman of the U.S. Consumer Products Safety Commission. Anthropologist Margaret Mead agreed to present what was intended to be an opposition view. It turned out that by the time she got to the meeting, Dr. Mead was certainly not opposed to the notion, and in a typically colorful manner she expressed her opinion: "We need a new institution. There isn't any doubt about that. The institutions we have are totally unsatisfactory. In many cases they are not only unsatisfactory, they involve a prostitution of science and a prostitution of the decision making process."

Her misgivings about the science court were consistent with an observation she has made that eventually all social innovations are corrupted; she pointed out that it would be essential that the science court be carefully protected from early corruption.

The science court was supported by numerous distinguished people. (A transcript of the proceedings is available from the U.S. Department of Commerce, National Technical Information Service, Washington, D.C., Document No. Pb-261 305.)

During the 1976 presidential campaign, the development of a science court procedure was endorsed by both President Ford and candidate

Carter. It has received numerous other endorsements, among them that of the Committee of Scientific Society Presidents, which includes chief executives of twenty-eight of the leading scientific societies of the United States.

During the 1980 presidential campaign candidate Reagan promised: "In addition, I will explore the feasibility of a 'Science Court,' to help arrange public discussions of controversial scientific issues. This will help guide the public, the Congress, and the executive branch. The purpose would be public exposure, not decision making."[2]

The development of the science court procedure to a point of general utility is a substantial undertaking, and thus far only tentative beginnings have been undertaken. Here are several examples.

One interesting case was called to my attention by Dr. John C. Bailar of the National Cancer Institute in Bethesda, Maryland. Bailar had been conducting a campaign to reduce the use of X-ray examination for detecting breast cancer in women under fifty. He reported that some of the relevant medical organizations had refused to consider the possibility that this procedure was doing more harm than good. He let it be known that he intended to pursue a science court procedure to bring out the facts in this matter, and from his experience it appears that the very possibility of a science court may have a beneficial effect on the resolution of technical disagreement. The matter was settled, at least temporarily, and guidelines restricting the mass screening of women under fifty have been issued.

For some time the claim has been made that low-frequency electromagnetic fields have deleterious physiological effects on plants, animals, and humans. These effects have been advanced as reasons for opposing powerful extremely low-frequency radio transmitters and, more recently, long-distance power transmission lines. A controversy arose in Minnesota concerning the impact of a transmission line, with a group of farmers resorting to vigorous civil disobedience to prevent its construction. Minnesota Governor Perpich offered to form a science court to provide factual scientific information helpful in resolving the dispute. He attempted to use the prestige of his office to persuade both the farmers and the utility companies to accept a resolution by a science court of the problems of health and safety. The farmers insisted on two alterations in the procedure, both of which were intended to politicize the process. First, they insisted that questions of the need for the power line be brought up before a science court along with the health and safety issues. These questions of need obviously would make the disentangling of facts and values much more difficult. Second the farmers' representatives proposed that Governor Perpich himself, rather than a panel of scientists, should sit in judgment. This measure again would obviously politicize the determination of scientific facts, and it was opposed, properly in my opinion, by the governor.

In connection with the power-line dispute Professor Allan Mazur has made an attempt to promote an exchange in the dispute over possible harmful effects from the electromagnetic fields of high-voltage transmission lines, using a science court. Specifically, in cooperation with two leading scientific advocates of the deleterious effects of electromagnetic fields, Andrew Marino and Robert Becker, Mazur[3] attempted to phrase their scientific claims in language that would be acceptable as falsifiable statements suitable for use as claims in a science court proceeding. This effort was remarkably successful. However, Mazur's efforts to induce the participation of proponents of the power line who denied the importance of the claims of Becker and Marino were unsuccessful. Obviously, he lacked the authority to force a confrontation. However, Mazur's work indicates very clearly the feasibility of translating highly partisan statements into clear statements of fact.

The third case that has been brought to my attention is an effort by the Division of Magnetic Fusion Energy of ERDA (now the Department of Energy) to evaluate a series of magnetic fusion geometries other than their two principal directions (Tokamaks and Mirror Machines). An adversary of science court–like procedure was used for arriving at judgments on the criteria for each concept, a procedure that was efficient and useful.

These three cases provide a little added insight into what needs to be done before the development of science court–like procedures can be undertaken in earnest. First, the Minnesota case illustrates the need for enough authority to make adversaries present and substantiate their cases in the presence of opposition. Governor Perpich was unable to bring about this confrontation. However, later in the dispute, the discussions of health and safety issues were muted, and the farmers stated much more simply that they did not want the power lines to cross their lands for esthetic and practical reasons.

In the breast cancer case it is clear that Dr. John Bailar, editor in chief of the *Journal of the National Cancer Institute,* had sufficient authority that his proposal to set up a science court procedure had to be taken seriously. The result was the institution of "consensus" procedures by the National Institutes of Health (described below). In the magnetic fusion energy case, a funding agency obviously had power to require the confrontation. In the power-line controversy it was perfectly clear that, while authority was lacking to force a scientific confrontation, the very threat of such a confrontation may have helped simplify that dispute.

Difficulties in Applying the Science Court to Real Controversies

Experience has revealed a number of difficulties that will have to be faced in any attempt to improve communication between the scientific community and the public:

1. There are an array of interests vested in the present "flexible" system, including politicians and industrialists who utilize confusion about the state of scientific knowledge in defending their policies, scientists whose positions depend on their willingness to disregard the frankness rule when supporting partisan policies, and institutions financially supported by doing "studies" for sponsors comfortable with their previous output.

2. Distinguished scientists who are quite prepared to answer pointed questions from their expert adversaries in scientific meetings are frequently unwilling to publicly answer the questions of the same adversaries when they make scientific statements relevant to public policy matters. This unwillingness was responsible for the dilution of the science court procedures begun by Bailar at the National Institutes of Health to the present "consensus procedures." Perhaps this unwillingness is related to the generally low regard for the way scientific matters are treated by the legal courts. In the science court it will be necessary to exhibit that ad hominem attacks will not be tolerated and that rules of procedure similar to those in a scientific meeting will be enforced.

3. Perhaps the most important difficulty in implementing the science court is one underlying the frequent observation that the procedure will be welcomed by partisans who see themselves as underdogs. Partisans who see themselves as winning with current procedures will resist the introduction of new procedures, the outcome of which is unpredictable. The impetus for improving communication between the scientific community and the public will have to come from those who are persuaded that procedural improvements are needed to adequately manage our very powerful technology.

4. It must be recognized that before the science court can attain its full utility, a considerable development would be required. Thus it will be necessary to develop procedures that not only are acceptable to all parties but will be perceived as leading to a full statement of the current knowledge. It will also be necessary to develop the profession of scientific advocate, with adequate protection for those who defend viewpoints unpopular with powerful interest groups.

Conclusion

It is remarkable that, in a time characterized by strident rhetoric in conflicts involving apparent disagreements over scientific facts, no powerful constituency for the development of an improved process has yet appeared. We have seen a proliferation of organizations claiming credibility because of who they are rather than how they proceed. Thus the National Academy of Sciences asserts that it is to be believed because it is an "elite organization." The Office of Technology Assessment is to be believed because it is an independent agency of the U.S. Congress. Public interest groups and regulatory agencies are to be believed because they exist only to protect the public interest. Industry is to be believed because of its expertise.

I believe science and technology play so large a role in our lives that, in cases where they affect public policy, we must begin the transition made centuries ago in other important areas: from a government of men to a government of laws.

Notes

1. Task Force of the Presidential Advisory Group on Anticipated Advances in Science and Technology, "The Science Court Experiment, An Interim Report," *Science* 193 (Aug. 20, 1976):653–656.

2. "Presidential Candidates Answer Science Policy Questions," *Physics Today,* vol. 33 (Oct. 1980):50.

3. A. Mazur, A. Marino, and R. Beckers, "Airing Technical Disputes: A Case Study," Address presented at the AAAS Annual Meeting, Washington, D.C., Feb. 13, 1977. See also A. Mazur, *The Dynamics of Technical Controversy* (Washington, D.C.: Communications Press, 1981).

JAMES N. DANZIGER

——— 20 ———

Power Is Knowledge: The Linkages Between the Political System and Knowledge

This essay examines the profound linkages between the political system and the knowledge system—those captured most obviously in Bacon's aphorism that knowledge is power. A close relationship between those who wield political power and those with superior knowledge has been a central element of many utopian visions of government and society from Plato's Republic to Bacon's New Atlantis to Galbraith's New Industrial State. More broadly, Mosca's observation that the power of the ruling class will increasingly depend upon its control of knowledge resources has become commonplace among observers of postindustrial societies. For many, the primary uncertainty regarding the contemporary linkage is whether the holders of knowledge will serve the dominant political class, whether the political order will become fundamentally dependent upon those with critical knowledge, or whether there will be a fusion of knowledge and political power within a technocratic elite.

While much has been written about how knowledge is converted into political power, I shall stress the transitive nature of the knowledge-power equation. From this perspective, power is knowledge, in the

Extremely helpful comments on this paper were provided by Lesley Danziger, Lawrence Senesh, and Gary Thom.

sense that political power can influence the uses and even the very nature of knowledge in a society. This will be revealed by examining the selective utilization of knowledge by those with political power and by suggesting how those who dominate the political order attempt to influence or even to control the creation and diffusion as well as the utilization of knowledge in a given society.

We can conceptualize both politics and knowledge in terms of the analytic notion of a system. Political scientists agree that "the political system" can be defined as those structures that authoritatively allocate values for a society.[1] Hence the political system makes choices (policy decisions) regarding the state's role in the distribution of individual and group wants, and most people accept these choices as binding. Actors within the political system respond to demands and supports, opportunities, and constraints in their environment, in order to maintain and enhance their own power and control and, more broadly, to serve the values of the group(s) dominant in the sociopolitical order of their society. Although a consensual definition of "the knowledge system" has not yet emerged, I follow Holzner and Fisher in defining it as those structures and processes through which public and private actors respond to demands for the creation, diffusion, and utilization of knowledge-related resources in the society.[2]

Defining the function of the political system as the authoritative allocation of values for a society suggests a prior question: Who determines what *is* valued in the society? Clearly, the political system has a profound stake in individuals' cognitive, affective, and evaluative orientations toward public and private objects. There are compelling reasons why the political system attempts to determine what activities and experiences should be known and valued by its population and which of these are *res publica*—things of the people, and hence legitimate domains of state action. Thus the essential function of the contemporary political system goes deeper than the allocation of values to an attempt to allocate *meanings* for the society. What varies from political system to political system is the content of those meanings and the extent to which the state allows other social structures (such as the churches, private corporations, interest groups, and so on) to participate in the processes through which these allocations of meanings and values are determined and through which the resulting social actions are taken.

The view that the political system attempts to allocate meanings for its population is a claim that the political system attempts to shape the very nature of knowledge in its society. To explore this claim, it is important to clarify another issue: How is knowledge to be defined? There is a bias in written analyses of the politics-knowledge linkage toward "positivist" knowledge—that is, toward the kinds of knowledge generated by and validated by a more or less strict adherence to the scientific method. Yet one need only consider the role of Sharia law for the governance of Iran or the role of Marxist ideology on policy decisions by the Soviet government or the role of astrology in Burmese politics or the role of political "savvy" for politicians like the late Mayor Richard Daley of Chicago to recognize that knowledge other than that produced by positivist science can be a crucial determinant of the beliefs, decisions, and actions of individuals whose behaviors help constitute a political system.

Clearly, there are other ways of knowing or, in the words of C. S. Peirce, of "fixing belief," in addition to the scientific method. For example, there is the method of authority, in which knowledge is derived from any source believed to hold the controlling explanation, whether the Koran, Karl Marx, or chicken entrails. In the method of introspection, knowledge might be grounded in intuition (as insight or in the Platonic sense of grasping), in reasoning from self-evident principles, or in *Verstehen*. Moreover, there is knowledge based on tenacity, whereby something is taken as known because it is strongly held to be true by a substantial majority of relevant others after competing among knowledge claims in a marketplace of alternative views. And there is practical knowledge derived from an individual's life experiences and common sense.[3] All these ways of knowing are relevant to the political system and its actions; but my emphasis will be on positivist knowledge, because the scientific method is usually viewed as especially resistant to political power and because it is afforded special standing and validity among competing knowledge claims in the political processes of most contemporary societies.

My working hypothesis is that knowledge in a society can be subject to extensive control by the political system. Most accept that knowledge based on authority or tenacity could be substantially shaped by political power; but they might question whether knowledge based on the scientific method is subject to similar influence, given the crossnational, peer, and "apolitical" standards of the scientific community. However, I accept the powerful argument of recent literature in the sociology of knowledge that all knowledge, even that based on positivist methods, is "socially constructed." In this view, all knowledge is embedded in a social and ideological context.[4] These contexts establish what is worth knowing, modes of transformation of knowledge across domains, and even truth tests.[5] Thus "versions of reality are not found in nature, but are constructed in social action . . . [and] the construction of knowledge is embedded in the structure of society."[6] Recent empirical research provides strong support for this social construction of knowledge, even in the hard sciences.[7] The political system constitutes one, and perhaps the single most crucial, social and ideological context within which the nature of knowledge in a society is constructed.

The Political System and Knowledge Creation

There are several means through which the political system can affect the nature of knowledge creation within its society. Clearly, the most direct manner in which the political system can influence knowledge creation is through providing financial or other support for research and development activities. Most nations establish governmental agencies whose functions include knowledge creation or the provision of material support for private R&D (examples of such agencies in the United States are the Department of Education and the National Science Foundation).

Due to the complex and often secretive nature of the basic and applied research activities supported by many nation-states, it is not possible to specify precisely the scale or even the nature of such activities. In most Third World nations, direct state expenditure on knowledge creation is low because these nations rely mainly on knowledge transfer from developed societies. Knowledge creation is most extensively state supported in the Soviet-bloc nations, particularly the Soviet Union. The Soviet Union acknowledged spending more than $20 billion per year on scientific research by the mid-1970s; the actual total, including military research, was possibly twice that high.[8] In the United States, available data suggest that total federal government spending on R&D by the early 1980s was more than $35 billion per year. Bernard Roth (in this volume) reveals how the nature of U.S. scientific activity is powerfully influenced by the kinds of research and development supported by these funds.

The political system also has the authority to implement a range of incentives that can stimulate or discourage the creation of knowledge. For example, a patent system encourages private-sector innovation by enabling private actors to capture the financial rewards from merchandising knowledge that they have created. The state can also distribute material incentives such as state employment opportunities and financial prizes to knowledge producers, and has an array of very effective symbolic rewards, such as Britain's Crown honors (the C.B.E. and O.B.E.) or party membership in a communist political system.

A more subtle form of state influence is its authorization of legitimate knowledge creation. In its mild form, this involves giving certain organizations like the British Medical Association the right to license, validate, or otherwise control the activities of individuals who wish to create or apply knowledge within a given domain of inquiry. Proposals for founding a science court represent a broader effort through which state power could be used to authorize "experts" to adjudicate knowledge disputes in many domains (see Chapter 19).

In its more pervasive form, the authorization of legitimate knowledge creation by the state can involve explicit prescriptions about what domains of inquiry and what types of findings will be permissible. The control of scientific inquiry in the Soviet Union and Eastern Europe and the insistence that knowledge be consistent with Marxist-Leninist ideology is well known. Such state-controlled knowledge creation has been decried as a perversion of the scientific method.[9] It can have disastrous consequences, as in the Soviet insistence upon the validity of Lysenkoist knowledge in genetics.[10] But the Soviets view state control of knowledge as beneficial:

> One fundamental advantage of Soviet science is that it is based on materialist dialectics, the supreme achievement of the human mind, offering the only correct approach to social and natural phenomena. The Communist Party's policy, aimed to develop the whole spectrum of social and natural sciences, has opened up vast possibilities for creative scientific research in the name of the noble ideals of peace and communism. . . . This has made it possible to channel scientific effort and material resources along the main lines of science and make sure that scientific work accords with the demands of socialist construction. . . .[11]

Even in societies that support "free" knowledge creation, the political system might ban certain such activities. For example, on the basis of the Nuremberg and Helsinki precedents, there are general state controls over human experimentation in most First World nations, particularly in such areas as fetal research.[12] In recent years, some local political systems in the United States have explicitly banned certain knowledge-creation activities, forbidding recombinant DNA research within their jurisdictions, and the U.S. federal government has set strict guidelines for the conduct of such research.[13] In sum, a political system can powerfully influence the scale and even the scope of knowledge creation in many ways, ranging from inducements to adjudication between knowledge claimants to the strict determination of the kinds of knowledge creation that will be tolerated.

The Political System and Knowledge Diffusion

There are diverse mechanisms by which knowledge spreads within a society. The political system can be quite effective in the "positive" diffusion mode, since it has direct or indirect control over important institutional channels that insure widespread and efficient dissemination of the knowledge it wants to diffuse. The individual's knowledge of politically relevant information is largely based on the activities of certain structures that political scientists term the "agents of political socialization." And the political system has potentially great control over several of the prime agents, especially the school system and the media.

Every political system shapes the form and content of the educational process in order to disseminate to students its preferred knowledge package about the political world and the individual's roles and responsibilities in serving the state. At a broad level, the behaviors required between teacher and student and between students are structured to reflect the patterns of social relations (including superordinate-subordinate relations and peer group interactions) judged desirable by the state. And there are extensive examples of the ways in which the state influences the knowledge base of the child through its control over the content of education, particularly by regulation of curricula and textbooks.[14]

The communications media are another agent of knowledge diffusion over which the political system is likely to assert some control. There are a few nations in which the state control of the media is so pervasive that comparisons with the Orwellian vision of "newspeak" and "doublethink" are not inappropriate. Indeed, the former director of TASS, the Soviet news agency, has observed that "news is merely agitation by means of facts." The modal pattern among contemporary nation-states is that the political system exercises considerable control over the content of the nation's press, radio, and television by direct operation, censorship, restrictive codes, and control of materials.[15] No political systems permit absolutely unfettered knowledge diffusion by the media. In Britain, for example, the media are limited by such restrictions as the Official Secrets Act, severe punishment for contempt and libel (both expansively defined), and strict prohibitions against pretrial publication in criminal cases.

The political system has other resources to insure that its knowledge package will be diffused. It can print and distribute reports and broadcast information directly to citizens. It can build knowledge networks among peer groups and facilitate the distribution of acceptable knowledge within such networks. In the United States, for example, agencies such as the Office of Science and Technology Policy have mounted major programs to transfer technology (that is, applied knowledge) to desired users; and a basic rationale for founding the National Academy of Sciences was to help transfer scientific knowledge to public agencies. More broadly the Soviet Academy of Sciences provides the political leadership a forum in which acceptable scientific knowledge can be systematically presented and an excellent structure with which to monitor the work of scientists.[16] Some political systems also assiduously use culture to disseminate knowledge. The content of Chinese dance, drama, literature, and opera during the Cultural Revolution was an extreme example of regulation and manipulation of culture.

While the political system has many opportunities to distribute knowledge that serves its needs, to influence the knowledge content of other distribution channels, and even to suppress certain knowledge it deems undesirable, no political system can totally control knowledge diffusion within its boundaries. There are a number of reasons why this is so. First, no political system has yet achieved the ideological unanimity and total efficiency necessary to establish and implement a precise political "line." Second, most political systems are partially constrained by the obligation to show some respect for the freedoms guaranteed in their constitutions. Third, even the considerable power of the political system cannot completely stifle alternative sources of knowledge from institutional, underground, or external media. Fourth, it is impossible to suppress the informal modes of knowledge diffusion within family, friendship, and peer networks. And finally, culture is able to transmit knowledge contrary to that diffused by the dominant political order, if only by metaphor and allegory.

This analysis has stressed the considerable power of the state to influence or control the content of knowledge disseminated by major institutions within a society. The will and capacity of different political systems to control knowledge diffusion varies substantially. In education, for example, the decentralized authority of relatively independent local school boards in the United States results in far less national control over curricula than is evident in East Germany or in Kenya. (It is said that the Minister of Education in the French Fourth Republic could state precisely what all students at a certain level were studying in a given subject on a particular day.) And the power to control knowledge diffusion is tempered, even in the most totalitarian political systems, by a variety of limitations on the effectiveness of the state to exclude knowledge claims contrary to its own. The existence of rebels and outsiders in all sociopolitical systems indicates that the capacity of the political system to control knowledge diffusion is limited.

The Political System and the Utilization of Knowledge

Ultimately, the political system is interested in how knowledge is utilized by individual citizens and groups as well as by political actors. Thus the state intervenes in knowledge creation and diffusion, believing its actions will affect knowledge in use which, in turn, will produce behavior supporting the state's goals. This is most obvious in areas that influence individuals' orientations toward explicitly political phenomena, such as their roles as citizens, their expectations about the actions of the state, and their beliefs about the international political environment. This use of knowledge shapes the demands and supports individuals direct toward the political system.

The state can also use its power to influence other behavior of its citizens. Illustrative examples of this are the Soviet government's insistence that Lysenkoist genetics be applied in agriculture, the Indian government's efforts to alter social behavior toward the caste of untouchable, and the U.S. policies about the "legality" of Laetrile treatments for cancer.[17] At the extreme, the political system can manipulate the entire knowledge in use of its citizens in an effort to transform their world view (weltanschauung). Two striking examples of this approach are China under Mao Tse-tung, which replaced Confucian principles with an ethic stressing sexual and age equality and "serving the people," and Turkey under Kemal Ataturk, which attempted to secularize and modernize the nation virtually overnight by mandating a civil legal code, the emancipation of women, a Latin alphabet, and other measures to supplant Islamic fundamentalism as the knowledge in use governing public behavior.

The most direct linkages between the political system and the knowledge system involve political actors using or not using knowledge to formulate and implement public policy. Given the impacts of such policies on individuals in the society, there is great interest in learning how political actors utilize knowledge and in determining what might enhance the contributions of knowledge to the policy and implementation processes. Consequently, this aspect of the politics-knowledge linkage has received the most scholarly attention.

While there is a considerable recent literature on the use of knowledge within the political system, it is characterized by important inconsistencies.[18] Some analyses define knowledge narrowly, including only specific, predictive statements based on positivist methods.[19] Others also include a vast category of ordinary knowledge "that does not owe its origin, testing, degree of verification, truth status or currency to distinctive professional (social inquiry) techniques but rather to common sense, casual empiricism, or thoughtful speculation and analysis."[20] And while the most empirical research focuses on applying knowledge to crucial actions and policy decisions, many discussions also include routine actions and problem solving guided by standard operating procedures.

In addition, there is disagreement about the role and utility of positivist knowledge in public organizations. One stream of analyses is characterized by optimism about the utility of knowledge: (1) it is found to be a driving force in political decisions and actions; (2) it is generally

valid, reliable, timely, and useful; (3) it reduces information "pathologies";
and (4) it improves the quality of policymaking and policy implementation.[21]

The spirit of the alternative analysis is captured by Carol Weiss:

> [K]nowledge, at least the sub-category of knowledge that derives from
> systematic research and analysis, is not often "utilized" in direct and
> instrumental fashion in the formulation of policy. Only occasionally does
> it supply an "answer" that policy actors employ to solve a policy problem.
> Instead, research knowledge usually affects the development and modi-
> fication of policy in diffuse ways. It provides a background of empirical
> generalizations and ideas that *creep* into policy deliberations. Its influence
> is exercised in more subtle ways than the word "utilization"—with its
> overtone of tools and implements—can capture.[22]

This view, based largely on empirical research in U.S. governments,
suggests that use of rational-scientific knowledge to determine action—
what some call "instrumental use" of knowledge—is infrequent and
perhaps even rare among public actors.[23] In most instances, instrumental
use eliminates certain options previously considered but found unsatisfactory or rationalizes a preferred policy position.[24] This research also
indicates that many actors in the political system internalize a considerable
amount of knowledge that is indirectly applied—what is termed "conceptual use." Such knowledge use influences the context within which
these actors structure decision and action, and it also constitutes part
of the loosely articulated set of "facts" and "beliefs" they employ.[25]

While the widespread conceptual use of knowledge by political actors
seems indisputable, researchers in this area are somewhat preoccupied
with explaining why there is such limited instrumental use of knowledge.
As Knott and Wildavsky observe, there are three obstacles: (1) relevant
knowledge does not exist, (2) the political actor is ignorant of knowledge
that does exist, or (3) the actor is aware of the knowledge but refuses
to use it.[26] Each of these obstacles merits further exploration.

The most common situation is the absence of clear and relevant
knowledge to inform political decisions and action. The complex social
phenomena requiring political decisions involve analytic problems that
defy explicit "if x, then y" generalizations. Rather, our knowledge is
usually limited to extremely broad tendency statements or to competing
knowledge claims. There is simply no precise knowledge to inform the
political actor about the immediate effects and spillovers of most policy
choices—for example, reducing the M1-B money supply in the United
States by n percent, occupying the Falkland Islands, or allowing "independent" trade unions in Poland. While knowledge can reduce un-

certainty in many cases by identifying some policy interventions that will not achieve desired outcomes, our "positive" knowledge is extremely limited in nearly every area of concern to the political system.[27] Moreover, as Lindblom and Cohen argue, in some cases even action based on information (rather than merely upon some form of social interaction), common sense, casual empiricism, or thoughtful speculation is often sufficient or superior to knowledge grounded in the scientific method.[28] Minimally, it is wrong to assume positivist knowledge is a sufficient or even a necessary component of effective political decision making.

A second explanation for the limited utilization of knowledge is a breakdown in the linkage between knowledge and actor. The most common form of this is the "two communities" concept—that the knowledge creator and the knowledge user have vastly different ways of thinking about an issue, including different frames of reference, theoretical levels, concepts and language, and experiential bases.[29] In this view, there is knowledge that could be relevant, but it is not packaged properly or disseminated effectively, and so political actors fail to use it. Political system actors frequently comment on their needs for more relevant information from knowledge producers, although these needs might be less real than rhetorical or imagined.

A final explanation for limited knowledge utilization holds that individuals in the political system resist acquiring and using the information available to them. It is important to suggest reasons for this resistance, arguably the greatest obstacle to knowledge utilization. First, while relevant knowledge might be attainable, the cost of creating and/or transforming it into a usable form could be judged too high relative to its expected benefits. Second, in most cases, only knowledge suggesting decisions and actions that are politically feasible and acceptable is usable. Knowledge is not likely to be utilized unless it indicates value allocations that are consistent with available resources that are within the capacity of the political system to act and that are compatible with the dominant political ideology. Third, another potential cost of knowledge is that it might expose failings in favored policies or current practices. A primary reason why there is considerable lip service to but limited use of evaluation studies in the political system is that the political benefits of a documented policy "success" are modest and brief while the political costs of policy "failure" can be devastating.[30] When political actors suspect certain knowledge might be embarrassing, they typically prefer that such knowledge not be produced or diffused.

A fourth reason for resisting knowledge use is the paradox of information in the political process: although Claude Shannon defines information as whatever reduces uncertainty, additional information can *increase* the uncertainty of political actors. As Thorstein Veblen observed,

"The outcome of any serious research can only be to make two questions grow where one question grew before." Lindblom and Cohen similarly argue that the usual effect of new knowledge on the political system ". . . is to raise new issues, stimulate new debate, and multiply the complexities of the social problem at hand."[31]

Ironically, the new information technologies, particularly computerized systems, exacerbate the tendency for increased knowledge to increase the uncertainties for political actors.[32] The remarkable capabilities of computerized information systems to keep, retrieve, restructure, and analyze data are available to any actor with access to the system and to technical expertise. It has become difficult, often impossible, for any political actor to control the access to knowledge or the uses to which such knowledge will be put. Thus the common pattern where automated information systems are well developed is for political controversies to develop into "data wars," in which major competitors support their alternatives with data and experts. And since this "knowledge" is usually inconclusive, it tends to be devalued from "truth" to political ammunition.[33]

The proliferation of knowledge, expertise, and technology has reduced the political actor's capacity to withhold or selectively utilize knowledge. But it is important to recognize that access to knowledge (particularly to experts and advanced information technologies) and the capacity to utilize it in the political process are unevenly distributed among groups and interests in the social system. While members of the political system might be uncertain about their control of knowledge resources, they enjoy a decided advantage over most other groups in the use of knowledge as a factor in the allocation of values for society. Indeed, those groups least generously treated under a society's distribution of values tend also to be the ones with least control of knowledge resources.[34] Fundamentally the selective use of knowledge in the political process, as described in this section, underscores the premise that knowledge and political power are conjoined in the struggle for relative advantage. As Holzner and Fisher observe, "Knowledge utilization always involves someone's ideal or material interests. There are always some considerations of power relations. . . ."[35]

Politics and the Optimum Utilization of Knowledge

I have argued that the political system is a major and often dominant force in shaping the knowledge system in its society. Because values are scarce relative to demands and because there is no consensus over meanings, the political system attempts to cope with ubiquitous conflict. And in such a context, knowledge becomes an important resource, with a capacity to influence the value allocation process and, even more crucially, to shape the allocation of meanings. In contrast to a Platonic utopia, contemporary political systems are not in the hands of philosopher-kings who have divested themselves of particularistic values and possessions, and there is no "true" knowledge to guide the decisions and actions of political actors. Rather, knowledge is embedded in the context of a particular political system where the participants attempt to construct a knowledge system to serve *their* values and goals rather than those of others.

Few would take exception to Pool's view that "knowledge is important to the mandarins of the future for it is by knowledge that men of power are humanized and civilized."[36] But the problem is that the knowledge associated with the political system is inextricably bound with the values and biases of the political order. Indeed, Pool's statement is actually part of his argument advocating that academics undertake contract research for the CIA. If knowledge is a powerful resource manipulated by all political systems, is it possible to develop a constructive perspective regarding the Academy of Independent Scholars' quest for an "optimum" linkage between the knowledge system and the political system?

One approach is to focus on improving the *process* by which the two systems are linked. The philosophical traditions of liberal democratic theory support the view that the political system ought to facilitate the knowledge process. That is, the political system should enact policies that (1) encourage a multiplicity of public and private knowledge creators, (2) suppress knowledge diffusion and competing knowledge claims only under extreme threats to the social order, (3) insure that its own policy decisions and actions are informed by the most compelling knowledge available, and (4) communicate its knowledge base and decision premises to all interested publics. In this process approach, one accepts that knowledge will be politicized but stresses that the political system can and should insure that the process of allocating values and meanings is open to pluralistic competition, outside scrutiny and public accountability.

Max Weber, however, provided a classic formulation of the limits of knowledge in the political process.[37] Weber observed that knowledge can help individuals clarify facts and understand the implications of their values. But the problems and issues facing the political system are preeminently clashes of ultimate values, Weber noted, and decisions resolving these essential questions are more suited to metaphysics than to the scientific method. Similarly, James Rule, in his thoughtful assessment of the use of (social scientific) knowledge by the political system, concludes that such knowledge can provide insights on how to improve social conditions, but only to the extent that social problems are grounded in ignorance rather than in value conflicts.[38]

Weber's attention to value questions and Rule's interest in what he terms "social betterment" suggest that our inquiry into the optimum linkage between politics and knowledge should include an assessment of *outcomes* as well as process. That is, we must also determine the extent to which the interactions between the political system and the knowledge system lead to decisions and actions that increase the chances for creating and sustaining a humane and satisfying social order. Focusing on the outcomes of the politics-knowledge linkage brings the inquiry into an explicitly normative domain. Indeed, in a political world of scarce resources and competition over values, the very notion of optimization leads inevitably to basic questions: Optimum for whom? Under what conditions? Although this essay can address these questions only briefly, two broad propositions seem germane.

The first is that it is unlikely the same configuration of linkages between the political system and the knowledge system will produce optimum processes and outcomes in France, India, Zaire, and everywhere else, given the quite different political cultures, stages of economic development, geopolitical situations, and other historical-cultural characteristics of countries. Thus one would need to assess the extent to which a particular politics-knowledge linkage is life-enhancing for the population of a specific political society at a given time. The second proposition is that the one who makes such an assessment should be no less than each citizen in the society. The criteria of efficiency and effectiveness can justify representative systems of political actors and knowledge elites to maintain institutional processes. But each individual in the society should actively participate in insuring that knowledge is created, diffused, and utilized in ways leading to a more humane social order.

Reality contrasts sharply with this idealized vision. Most contemporary political systems seem to produce few individuals with the capacity and will to make such reflective political choices. And there are few if any political systems within which most individuals have access to enough knowledge and political power for them to evaluate and influence their society's linkages between the political system and the knowledge system. Hence this vision would necessitate major changes in civic education in its broadest sense and, most fundamentally, changes in the structure and distribution of power in political society. It should be evident that these propositions and prescriptions are grounded in my biases and values regarding political power, knowledge, and the optimum linkage between them and that they represent some of the basic premises guiding my own attempt to influence the allocation of values and meanings. I suggest that attempts to establish optimality or even what Boulding calls "plateaus" of acceptability for humans in an actual political environment, rather than in a theoretical context, require societal debate on these premises and on proposals for their implementation.

Although I have addressed the politics-knowledge linkage from a normative perspective, it seems important to consider briefly what an "optimum" linkage might mean in the world of *realpolitik*. All contemporary societies are experiencing continual expansion of the role of the state, intensifying conflicts over the allocation of values and meanings as resources become more scarce, and the increasing domination of knowledge as the major instrumental resource for resolving problems and meeting needs. The result is profound interdependencies between the political system and the knowledge system.

The degree of effective control over the knowledge system by the political system varies considerably across polities. Some have asserted strong and single-minded control over their knowledge systems—indeed, a defining characteristic of a "totalitarian" political system is its extensive control over the knowledge system both negatively (as censorship) and positively (as propaganda).[39] Other political systems have allowed loosely organized and pluralistic knowledge systems to evolve. The pivotal issue is: Which approach is better able to adapt and prevail in an international environment dominated by a life-threatening struggle between world views in conflict over scarce resources and fundamental meanings? At this point, it is by no means clear that the more "democratic" approaches will prevail in this struggle. The outcome will provide one sort of answer, at the level of praxis, regarding the "optimum" linkage of power and knowledge.

Notes

1. Easton, David, *A Systems Analysis of Political Life.*
2. Holzner, Burkart, *Reality Construction in Society;* Holzner, Burkart, and Evelyn Fisher, "Knowledge in Use: Considerations in the Sociology of Knowledge Application."
3. Machlup, Fritz, *The Production and Distribution of Knowledge in the United States.*
4. See Berger, P., and T. Luckmann, *The Social Construction of Reality;* Habermas, Jurgen, *Legitimation Crisis;* Spector, M., and John Kitsuse, *Constructing Social Problems;* and Holzner, op cit. (Gary Thom has pointed out to me that the implications of the social construction of reality and knowledge apply to my own analysis, particularly to its positivist tone. I accept that my method of argument and analysis are within the context of social construction and that the essay is one claim on how the creation and uses of social meaning should be understood.)

5. Holzner and Fisher, op cit.

6. Gusfield, Joseph R., "Review of Knowledge Application."

7. See Mitroff, Ian, *The Subjective Side of Science: A Philosophical Inquiry into the Psychology of the Apollo Moon Scientists;* Mulkay M. J., "Sociology of the Scientific Research Community," in *Science, Technology and Society;* Mahoney, M. J., "Psychology of the Scientist: An Evaluative Review"; Latour, Bruno, and Steve Woolgar, *Laboratory Life: The Social Construction of Scientific Facts;* Knorr-Cetina, Karin, *The Manufacture of Knowledge.*

8. Golovanov, L. V., *Socialism and the Scientific and Technical Revolution.*

9. Polanyi, Michael Q., et al., "The Republic of Science: Its Political and Economic Theory."

10. Joravsky, D., *The Lysenko Affair.*

11. Golovanov, L. V., op. cit.

12. Maynard-Moody, Steven, "The Fetal Research Dispute." In *Controversy.*

13. Krimsky, Sheldon, "Regulating Recombinant DNA Research." In *Controversy.*

14. See, for example, Dawson, Richard, and Kenneth Prewitt, *Political Socialization,* pp. 143–180; and Nelkin, Dorothy, "Creation versus Evolution: The California Controversy." In *Controversy.*

15. Seymour-Ure, C., *The Political Impact of the Mass Media.*

16. Gerasov, V., "Academy of Sciences, Long Range Social Research."

17. Petersen, James C., and Gerald E. Markle, "The Laetrile Controversy." In *Controversy.*

18. Larsen, Judith K., "Knowledge Utilization: What Is It?"

19. Knott, Jack, and Aaron Wildavsky, "If Dissemination is the Solution, What is the Problem?"

20. Lindblom, Charles, and David K. Cohen, *Usable Knowledge: Social Science and Social Problem Solving.*

21. See Kerr, Donna, "Knowledge Utilization: Epistemological and Political Assumptions"; Marver, James D., *Consultants Can Help;* Simon, Herbert, *The New Science of Management Decision.*

22. Weiss, Carol, "Knowledge Creep and Decision Accretion," p. 381.

23. Rich, Robert, "Uses of Social Science Information by Federal Bureaucrats: Knowledge for Action versus Knowledge for Understanding." In *Using Social Research for Public Policy Making;* Caplan, Nathan, et al., *The Use of Social Science Knowledge in Policy Decisions at the National Level;* Scott, Robert A., and Arnold R. Shore, *Why Sociology Does Not Apply: A Study of the Use of Sociology in Public Policy;* Aaron, Henry J., *Politics and the Professors: The Great Society in Perspective;* Lynn, Lawrence (ed.), *Knowledge and Policy: The Uncertain Connection.*

24. Benveniste, Guy, *The Politics of Expertise.*

25. Caplan et al., op. cit.; Patton, Michael Q., et al., "In Search of Impact: An Analysis of the Utilization of Federal Health Evaluation Research." In *Using Social Research in Public Policy Making;* Uliassi, Pio D., "Research and Foreign Policy: A Review from Foggy Bottom." In *Using Social Research for Public Policy Making;* Weiss, Carol, op. cit.; Weiss, Carol, and Michael J. Bucuvalas, "The

Challenge of Social Research to Decision Making." In *Using Social Research in Public Policy Making*; Weiss, Carol, and Michael J. Bucuvalas, *Social Science Research and Decision Making*; Knorr, Karin, "The Gap Between Knowledge and Policy." In *Improving Policy Analysis*.

26. Knott, Jack, and Aaron Wildavsky, op. cit.

27. Ibid., pp. 549–550.

28. Lindblom, Charles, and David K. Cohen, op. cit.

29. Caplan, Nathan, "The Two-Communities Theory and Knowledge Utilization"; Feller, Irwin, et al., "Scientific and Technological Information in State Legislatures"; Danziger, James N., "Social Science Fails Again: Policy Research and Proposition 13."

30. Dutton, William et al., "Did the Policy Fail?: The Selective Use of Automated Information in the Policy-Making Process." In *Why Policies Succeed or Fail*.

31. Lindblom, Charles, and David K. Cohen, op. cit.

32. Danziger, James N., "The Use of Automated Information in Local Government: A Critical Assessment."

33. Danziger, James N., et al., *Computers and Politics: High Technology in American Local Government*; Wildavsky, Aaron, and Ellen Tenenbaum, *The Politics of Mistrust*.

34. Danziger, James N., et al., op. cit.

35. Holzner, Burkart, and Evelyn Fisher, op. cit., p. 241.

36. Pool, Ithiel, "The Necessity for Social Scientists Doing Research for Governments." In *The Rise and Fall of Project Camelot*, p. 267.

37. Cited in Gerth, H. H., and C. Wright Mills (eds.), *From Max Weber: Essays in Sociology*, pp. 129–158.

38. Rule, James B., *Insight and Social Betterment*.

39. Crick, Bernard, *Basic Forms of Government*, p. 79.

Bibliography

Aaron, Henry J. *Politics and the Professors: The Great Society in Perspective.* Washington, DC: Brookings Institution, 1978.

Benveniste, Guy. *The Politics of Expertise.* Second edition. San Francisco, CA: Boyd and Fraser, 1977.

Berger, P., and T. Luckmann. *The Social Construction of Reality.* Garden City, NY: Doubleday, 1967.

Caplan, Nathan. "The Two-Communities Theory and Knowledge Utilization." *American Behavioral Scientist* 22 (1979):459–470.

———, A. Morrison, and R. Stambaugh. *The Use of Social Science Knowledge in Policy Decisions at the National Level.* Ann Arbor, MI: University of Michigan Institute for Social Research, 1975.

Crick, Bernard. *Basic Forms of Government.* London: Macmillan, 1973.

Danziger, James N. "Social Science Fails Again: Policy Research and Proposition 13." *Journal of Contemporary Studies* 4 (1981):59–68.

_____ . "The Use of Automated Information in Local Government: A Critical Assessment." *American Behavioral Scientist* 22 (1979):363–392.

_____ . William Dutton; Rob Kling; and Kenneth L. Kraemer. *Computers and Politics: High Technology in American Local Government.* New York: Columbia University Press, 1982.

Dawson, Richard, and Kenneth Prewitt. *Political Socialization.* Boston, MA: Little, Brown, 1968.

Dutton, William; James N. Danziger; and Kenneth L. Kraemer. "Did the Policy Fail?: The Selective Use of Automated Information in the Policy-Making Process." In *Why Policies Succeed or Fail.* Helen Ingram and Dean Mann (eds.). Beverly Hills, CA: Sage Publications, 1980.

Easton, David. *A Systems Analysis of Political Life.* New York: John Wiley, 1965.

Feller, Irwin; Michael King; Donald Menzel; Robert O'Connor; Peter Wissel; and Thomas Ingersoll. "Scientific and Technological Information in State Legislatures." *American Behavioral Scientist* 22 (1979):417–436.

Gerasov, V. "Academy of Sciences, Long Range Social Research." *Obshchestvennye Nauki* 4, 1978 (as translated in JPRS 71759:100–108).

Gerth, H. H., and C. Wright Mills (eds.). *From Max Weber: Essays in Sociology.* New York: Oxford University Press, 1958.

Golovanov, L. V. *Socialism and the Scientific and Technical Revolution.* Moscow: Progress Publishers.

Gusfield, Joseph R. "Review of Knowledge Application." *Knowledge* 2 (1981): 590–596.

Habermas, Jurgen. *Legitimation Crisis.* Boston, MA: Beacon Press, 1975.

Holzner, Burkart. *Reality Construction in Society.* Cambridge, MA: Schenken, 1968.

_____ , and Evelyn Fisher. "Knowledge in Use: Considerations in the Sociology of Knowledge Application." *Knowledge* 1 (1979):219–244.

Joravsky, D. *The Lysenko Affair.* Cambridge, MA: Harvard University Press, 1970.

Kerr, Donna. "Knowledge Utilization: Epistemological and Political Assumptions." *Knowledge* 2 (1981):483–501.

Knorr, Karin. "The Gap Between Knowledge and Policy." In *Improving Policy Analysis.* Stuart Nagel (ed.) Beverly Hills, CA: Sage Publications, 1981.

Knorr-Cetina, Karin. *The Manufacture of Knowledge.* Oxford: Pergamon, 1981.

Knott, Jack, and Aaron Wildavsky. "If Dissemination Is the Solution, What Is the Problem?" *Knowledge* 1 (1980):537–578.

Krimsky, Sheldon. "Regulating Recombinant DNA Research." In *Controversy.* Dorothy Nelkin (ed.) Beverly Hills, CA: Sage Publications, 1979.

Larsen, Judith K. "Knowledge Utilization: What Is It?" *Knowledge* 1 (1980):421–442.

Latour, Bruno, and Steve Woolgar. *Laboratory Life: The Social Construction of Scientific Facts.* Beverly Hills, CA: Sage Publications, 1979.

Lindblom, Charles, and David K. Cohen. *Usable Knowledge: Social Science and Social Problem Solving.* New Haven, CT: Yale University Press, 1979.

Lynn, Lawrence (ed.). *Knowledge and Policy: The Uncertain Connection.* Washington, DC: National Academy of Sciences, 1978.

Machlup, Fritz. *The Production and Distribution of Knowledge in the United States.* Princeton, NJ: Princeton University Press, 1962.

Mahoney, M. J. "Psychology of the Scientist: An Evaluative Review." *Social Studies of Science* 9 (1979):349–375.

Marver, James D. *Consultants Can Help.* Lexington, MA: D. C. Heath, 1979.

Maynard-Moody, Steven. "The Fetal Research Dispute." In *Controversy.* Dorothy Nelkin (ed.) Beverly Hills, CA: Sage Publications, 1979.

Mitroff, Ian. *The Subjective Side of Science: A Philosophical Inquiry into the Psychology of the Apollo Moon Scientists.* Amsterdam: Elsevier, 1974.

Mosca, Gaetano. *The Ruling Class.* New York: McGraw Hill, 1939.

Mulkay, M. J. "Sociology of the Scientific Research Community." In *Science, Technology and Society.* I. Spiegel-Rosing and D. Price (eds.) Beverly Hills, CA: Sage Publications, 1977.

Nelkin, Dorothy. "Creation versus Evolution: The California Controversy." In *Controversy.* Dorothy Nelkin (ed.) Beverly Hills, CA: Sage Publications, 1979.

Patton, Michael Q., et al. "In Search of Impact: An Analysis of the Utilization of Federal Health Evaluation Research." In *Using Social Research in Public Policy Making.* Carol Weiss (ed.) Lexington, MA: D. C. Heath, 1977.

Petersen, James C., and Gerald E. Markle. "The Laetrile Controversy." In *Controversy.* Dorothy Nelkin (ed.) Beverly Hills, CA: Sage Publications, 1979.

Polanyi, Michael. "The Republic of Science: Its Political and Economic Theory." *Minerva* 1 (1962): 54–73.

Pool, Ithiel. "The Necessity for Social Scientists Doing Research for Governments." In *The Rise and Fall of Project Camelot.* Irving Horowitz (ed.) Cambridge, MA: MIT Press, 1967.

Rich, Robert. "Uses of Social Science Information by Federal Bureaucrats: Knowledge for Action versus Knowledge for Understanding." In *Using Social Research for Public Policy Making.* Carol Weiss (ed.) Lexington, MA: D. C. Heath, 1977.

Rule, James B. *Insight and Social Betterment.* New York: Oxford University Press, 1978.

Scott, Robert A., and Arnold R. Shore. *Why Sociology Does Not Apply: A Study of the Use of Sociology in Public Policy.* New York: Elsevier, 1979.

Seymour-Ure, C. *The Political Impact of the Mass Media.* Beverly Hills, CA: Sage Publications, 1974.

Simon, Herbert. *The New Science of Management Decision.* Englewood Cliffs, N.J.: Prentice-Hall, 1977.

Spector, M., and John Kitsuse. *Constructing Social Problems.* Menlo Park, CA: Benjamin/Cummings, 1977.

Uliassi, Pio D. "Research and Foreign Policy: A Review from Foggy Bottom." In *Using Social Research for Public Policy Making.* Carol Weiss (ed.) Lexington, MA: D. C. Heath, 1977.

Weiss, Carol. "Knowledge Creep and Decision Accretion." *Knowledge* 1 (1980): 381–404.

————, and Michael J. Bucuvalas. "The Challenge of Social Research to Decision Making." In *Using Social Research in Public Policy Making.* Carol Weiss (ed.) Lexington, MA: D. C. Heath, 1977.

_____ . *Social Science Research and Decision Making.* New York: Columbia University Press, 1981.

Wildavsky, Aaron, and Ellen Tenenbaum. *The Politics of Mistrust.* Beverly Hills, CA: Sage Publications, 1981.

Wilensky, Harold. *Organizational Intelligence.* New York: Basic Books, 1967.

LEONID HURWICZ

—— 21 ——
Economic Issues
in the Utilization of
Knowledge

Knowledge has many facets. It can sometimes be painful or dangerous. This essay, however, focuses on *useful* knowledge, specifically knowledge capable of increasing productivity or directly enhancing consumer welfare. It may include basic facts of science, practical technological inventions, medical procedures, consumer information about products, and information about needs, values, and preferences of various population groups. (We are not dealing with utilization of knowledge in weapons production, since it is not obvious that it qualifies as useful in our sense, or with various types of personal privacy-invading information.)

Although some knowledge is generated spontaneously or even accidentally, under contemporary circumstances it more typically results from a conscious activity like research and development or experimental innovation. Knowledge may be produced by individual study, writing, home garage inventive effort, or huge public or private organizations. Knowledge-creating activities involve people, materials, and capital. Decisions must be made to devote resources to these activities, and the decisions, in turn, require an appropriate motivation and incentives, psychological and/or material.

To take advantage of existing knowledge is not usually costless. The transmission of knowledge may require a process of education or adaptation. But very often the utilization of knowledge also requires the creation of additional new knowledge. Basic scientific knowledge, say in nuclear physics, is utilized by generating the technological knowledge to design and construct a nuclear power plant. To utilize the knowledge embodied in the discovery of a new drug, one must explore its effects on different patients and diseases, as well as its toxic effects. Thus, to a significant extent, knowledge utilization involves creating more knowledge.

Knowledge as an Economic Good

From the economist's point of view, perhaps the most important characteristic of knowledge and information (in many contexts we do not distinguish between them) is that its availability to one user does not diminish its availability to someone else. We say that, as an economic good, knowledge is *nonrival in use*.[1] "Nonrival" implies that any restriction on the availability of existing knowledge is likely to result in a resource allocation that is inefficient. (By "efficient" we mean what in the contemporary jargon would be characterized as *Pareto-optimal*; thus, "inefficient" means "not Pareto-optimal."[2]) This is so because broadening the access to existing information will typically create additional possibilities of production and consumption without significant additional costs and, given an appropriate distribution of goods and services, could raise the welfare of some (or all) individuals without hurting anyone.[3]

The Pareto-efficiency criterion is widely used in contemporary economics as an indicator of the efficiency of a resource allocation system. Inefficiency (in the Pareto sense) indicates the presence of unexploited opportunities to increase welfare. Thus any restriction on the flow of useful information typically contributes to the inefficiency of resource allocation.

In a market economy, any charges for existing information that exceed the cost of transmitting (rather than creating) that information contribute to inefficiency.[4] Assuming for the sake of simplicity that the transmission costs are negligible, efficiency requires that all existing information be made available free of charge. But this conclusion runs immediately into two difficulties.

First, making existing information more broadly available does not, by itself, guarantee no one will be made worse off. On the contrary, those who previously had the exclusive possession of the information may lose their "monopoly" advantage and see their welfare going down, perhaps because others to whom information has now been made available are in a better position to exploit it competitively. Thus broadening access to information may not lead to a uniform improvement in efficiency, that is, a Pareto-improvement—a move to a resource allocation that makes no one worse off and makes some people better off. To accomplish such an improvement, one may have to combine the broadening of access to knowledge with compensations to those who would otherwise be affected adversely. The burden of paying for the compensations can be so distributed that no one need be worse off and some will be better off.

Without such compensations, those who would suffer from broader access will oppose the move. Regulations requiring inventors to make their inventions freely available to all interested users are not likely to be adopted as the law of the land and would be difficult or impossible to enforce.

Even if such a law could be enforced, however, its implementation would create other difficulties by weakening a major incentive to produce new knowledge. Of course, some knowledge is created by accident; furthermore, some is motivated by an effort to expand the frontiers of knowledge, a goal that goes beyond the material reward. Scientific curiosity, desire for recognition, scholarly competition, response to a practical challenge, or concern for the welfare of others account for many important discoveries and inventions. But under modern conditions, a major part of knowledge-creating activity is responsive to the material rewards, as is suggested by the statistics of corporate (as distinct from individual) inventions and the research and development activities sponsored by the government.[5] It seems beyond question that both the intensity and direction of knowledge creation are affected by material incentives.

If inventors were compelled immediately to share their discoveries free of charge with all comers, there would be less inventive activity— certainly by firms, but very likely also by individuals. In fact, no such free sharing occurs or is required. Indeed, in many fields new information is regarded as a "trade secret," and every effort is made to keep it from others. The tendency toward (at least temporary) secrecy is not absent even from scientific endeavors, where a desire to be the first to solve a major problem creates inducement to keep secret various intermediate auxiliary findings.

Keeping a discovery secret may, however, prevent the inventor from reaping the full benefits, since there may be other persons or firms who are in a better position to put the discovery to advantageous use. On the other hand, publicizing the discovery might deprive the inventor of any benefits without providing some proprietary rights to the fruits of the invention.

The Role of the Patent System

This dilemma is to some extent resolved by the patent system, which reduces the disadvantages of publication while providing, for a limited time, exclusive proprietary rights. The system does not, however, eliminate the disadvantages completely, because the publication of the invention in the form of a patent does leave room for the development of imitative patents and may stimulate alternative approaches to the problem.

The rights the patent provides may be used to give the inventor either a temporary monopoly or an opportunity to profit by licensing someone else to utilize the patent. The possibility of patenting an invention strengthens the incentives for creating and publishing new knowledge.

Once the patent or copyright has been obtained, it is an obstacle to the free use of existing knowledge and may contribute to the inefficiency of resource allocation when the patent is exploited monopolistically or made available for licensing subject to fees.[6] Dangers inherent in the patenting of improved grain seeds have also been claimed.[7]

Patents are not always effective in preventing imitation because of the practice of "inventing around patents." But this effort involves a good deal of social waste.[8]

Monopolistic exploitation of patents is not the only way of acquiring monopoly over technologically relevant knowledge. Sometimes patents are acquired to block competition, but then not exploited.[9] A whole firm may be acquired to weaken or eliminate competition. For instance, in July 1980 a federal jury ruled that the Johnson and Johnson Company had bought a small firm to suppress the marketing of an electronic pain-killing device because it would compete with drugs (especially Tylenol) produced by Johnson and Johnson. The company was planning to appeal.

In contrast, there are situations where it is difficult or impossible to enforce proprietary rights. The best example is the impossibility of protecting literary property since the advent of low-cost copying techniques. Photocopying may seriously cut into the potential sales of books and periodicals. Here the obstacles to free propagation of knowledge are minimized. In effect, access to published knowledge is free of charge, but the incentives and even the financial feasibility for making knowledge available in the form of books and journal articles are seriously weakened.[10] This is a classic example of the *free rider* phenomenon in the area of public goods. (By a "public good" we mean one that is nonrival in use and such that no one can be deprived of access to its services.)

Similar problems may arise when results of technological research are difficult or impossible to appropriate. For instance, the question has been raised of whether the drug companies would have an incentive to undertake research on the alleged anticlotting properties of garlic. While this question may have no merit, it illustrates how inappropriability and free ridership may discourage investing in creating socially useful knowledge if it cannot be held exclusively.

We thus face a genuine dilemma. Where access to knowledge is free, the market incentives for and financial feasibility of creating and transmitting knowledge are weakened. The price of free access is risking that the creation and transmission of new knowledge may fall below socially desirable levels. (We use terms such as "social desirability" as equivalent to Pareto-optimality, or at least consider the absence of Pareto-optimality as socially undesirable. Other interpretations are also possible.) On the other hand, where knowledge and information are appropriable, the supply incentives are strengthened but the rate of utilization of knowledge will go below optimal levels, creating another kind of social dilemma.

The potential for underutilization of existing knowledge is not the only problem when knowledge is appropriable. Even though appropriability provides and strengthens incentives for research and development, market imperfections may warp the directions of knowledge creation and utilization. Other things being equal, areas protected by a monopoly will be more attractive, though perhaps not more desirable socially. Also, a monopoly can more easily afford significant research and development expenditures. On the other hand, monopolies have sometimes been weakened by inventions that might not have been made without the incentive provided by the patent system.

Reform Proposals and Alternatives

Is there a way out of the dilemma? Can one eliminate restrictions on access to knowledge without weakening the incentives for creating and transmitting knowledge? To accomplish this, it would be necessary to sever the link between the actual rate of utilization of knowledge by a given firm or individual and the financing of knowledge creation and transmission. This would amount to changing from "user fees" (such as licensing fees to holders of patents or copyrights) to taxes, i.e., once access to knowledge and information is opened without restriction, the burden of financing the creation and transmission of knowledge would not be based on the actual degree to which the knowledge was used; this regime would lead toward efficient utilization of knowledge once that knowledge existed.

But how should society determine the overall level of financing knowledge-creating activities, and how should these activities be aimed at socially desirable objectives? Here again is the classic issue of the supply of public goods. In recent years, much progress has been made in understanding this issue, but, in my opinion, we are far from having found adequate answers.

In practice, societies have resorted to various forms of public financing to support the creation and transmission of knowledge. On the transmission side, we have the public subsidization of the education system, including colleges, universities, libraries, and public radio and TV broadcasting. These institutions primarily transmit knowledge that is already in the public domain. Without public subsidization, would existing knowledge continue to be transmitted to successive generations to the same extent? Only if private incentives were strong enough to maintain the desire for education and if real incomes of middle- and lower-income groups were high enough to make the desire into effective demand.

As for the creation of knowledge, governments are directly subsidizing a variety of research and development activities. In our time, government subsidies are particularly evident in the military areas, but they exist in many other fields as well—agriculture, the many subjects being studied by the National Science Foundation, energy, space, the environment, and so forth. But such support goes quite far back in history; the support of the tyrant of Syracuse for Archimedes is an early example. Kings and academies have offered prizes for specific inventions and problem solutions for many centuries. To the extent that such support guides the direction of development, judgments (possibly imperfect) of scientific peers, administrators, or politicians are substituted for those (possibly imperfect) of the market. These public subsidization systems in mixed economies, such as that of the United States, constitute a supplement to the market mechanism supported by the patent system.

But a more radical proposal was made in the mid-1940s by Michael Polanyi.[11] Starting from the proposition that "the full benefit of knowledge is only reaped when its circulation is free," Polanyi saw patents as "not infrequently being used . . . for the consolidation of . . . purely restrictive monopoly." Considering that "any proprietary management of useful knowledge is . . . both irrational and open to grave abuses," he urged that the government grant patent holders the right to be rewarded from the public purse rather than making them earn their rewards commercially and that it "supplement the licenses of right by government rewards to patentees on a level ample enough to give general satisfaction to inventors and their financial promoters."[12] Polanyi expressed the hope that under this system, "most patents would gradually be transformed by consent—with only occasional compulsion to assist the process— into the proposed type of license of right." How would the patentees' rewards, to be paid by the government, be determined? According to Polanyi, the licensing party would have to supply to the patentholder information concerning the economic benefits created by the invention; additional information might be obtained by the patentholder from users of products made under the patent. The annual government reward to the patentholder would be a fixed fraction ("perhaps one tenth to one third") of the economic value of the invention during the previous year.[13]

Polanyi was aware of the dangers of corruption and arbitrariness in this assessment procedure. To avoid these dangers, he suggested that the valuation must be based only on "data endorsable by accountants' certificate."[14] But it is doubtful, in my opinion, that his proposed remedy is adequate. His assessment process calls for estimating the increment in a license holder's profits ascribable to a particular invention. Such an estimate involves more than accounting; it requires determining the profits that would have been made had the invention not been available to the firm. Clearly, such an estimate is extremely difficult to make without a strong element of subjectivity.[15]

The matter deserves further analysis on our part because it goes to the heart of the dilemma we are concerned with. For it should be noted that when license fees are determined by private bargaining between the parties, the assessment of benefits attributable to an invention must be made *before* the license holder has used the invention. This *ex ante* estimate is bound to be even more difficult and more subjective than the *ex post* estimate required by Polanyi's proposal. But there is an important difference. Under the *ex ante* bargaining process, prospective license holders pay the license fee so they will not tend to overestimate the potential benefits of the license. In the Polanyi *ex post* scheme, license holders are in a relatively better position to make estimates, but they have little incentive to avoid overestimating the benefits. In fact, the relationship of license holder and patentholder may encourage generosity in benefit estimation, if not actual collusion; in the economist's jargon, the Polanyi assessment system is not incentive-compatible.[16] In fact, even if the benefits could be assessed correctly (or at least in an unbiased manner), it is questionable whether setting the awards equal to a fixed fraction of benefits would promote efficient resource allocation within the invention-procuring sector of the economy or between it and other sectors.

I have focused on the Polanyi proposal because I regard it as a serious and highly ingenious attempt to analyze the deficiencies of the existing system and to construct a superior alternative. As it turns out, Polanyi's proposal, while avoiding the inefficiencies on the user side by the "licensing of right," runs into difficulties in the case of determining rewards to be given to the inventors. But these difficulties, in my opinion, are not merely a defect of this particular proposal. They are inherent in the problem of designing an efficient and incentive-compatible mechanism for resource allocation in the presence of nonrival (public) goods. The measure of benefits ascribable to an invention (needed in Polanyi's assessment process) is closely related to the measure of willingness to pay used in the public goods literature, and the Polanyi procedure itself has important elements in common with the so-called demand-revealing mechanisms.[17] These mechanisms, it has been shown, can only reveal the willingness to pay and optimally set the supply of public good by sacrificing other aspects of efficiency of the system. Furthermore, in order that a demand-revealing process be incentive compatible, it would, I believe, have to be operated on an *ex ante* basis. But *"ex ante"* here does not mean merely before a license for an existing patent has been granted, because a major purpose of a demand-revealing mechanism is to determine the level of resources to be used for the public good. In our problem, (*"ex ante"*) means determining the level and direction of inventive activity for the country as a whole long before one can know in any detail what inventions will be made, much less knowing who would benefit from these inventions and to what extent.

Such uncertainty concerning the outcomes is an additional difficulty not present in standard problems of the public good. But, of course, the same uncertainty must be faced under the existing regime. The decision to invest resources in the expectation of creating new knowledge may be made by an individual whose time and effort are the resources in question. If this individual is an inventor, and if he or she is motivated to make an invention that will result in a profitable patent, it is this individual who estimates the potential demand for the invention "output" as well as the probability of success in making the invention. Also, the individual is assuming the risk that these expectations will prove incorrect. If the decision to invest in research and development is made by an organization—a corporation or government agency—the estimation of potential patent profits and of the probability of success may be made by administrators, and the risk of failure will be assumed by the organization. Ultimately, failures may also affect the careers of the decision makers. Thus, in either case, the decision makers close to the invention, research, and development process have a strong incentive to make correct estimates. They may also possess more information to make better estimates than "outsiders," but this need not always be the case.

These facts speak in favor of a decentralized system of decision making, either the type now in existence, with private financing and only voluntary licensing, or a Polanyi-type scheme with public financing and compulsory licensing, if the difficulties in the assessment process could be overcome. It is not easy to visualize a successfully operating demand-revealing mechanism in this area, however. Such a mechanism would require the pooling and reconciling of conflicting estimates of prospective benefits and probabilities of success by researchers, firms undertaking the development work, and prospective users. The mechanisms would also have to take into account the conflicting interests of the participants in the estimation process and the biases likely to arise because of those interests. Some of these difficulties are already known from the experience of arms or space development contracts where delays, cost overruns, and other snags are familiar phenomena.

The Polanyi proposal is a scheme calling for mandatory ("of right") patent licensing. The possible economic effects of some form of compulsory licensing were studied in a recent monograph. Its author, F. M. Scherer, stresses that situations differ widely: "Some innovations will be forthcoming only with strong expectations of exclusivity, some with none. Most fall in between."[18] Ideally, therefore, he would favor "a flexible policy—one that can be 'fine-tuned' to individual circumstances."[19] He is persuaded that "technical progress would not grind to a halt if a uniform policy of compulsory licensing at 'reasonable' royalties . . . were implemented."[20] Of course, not grinding to a halt is hardly an ambitious criterion by which to judge a reform program, but Scherer clearly thinks that social benefits might outweigh social losses under a properly designed compulsory licensing system. Such a system might, for instance, create a presumption in favor of compulsory licensing five years after the date of patent application, but the presumption could be waived by an appropriate tribunal in cases where stronger patent rights are essential to maintain incentive.[21] Clearly, this system would call for special administrative and judicial machinery. From past experience it is known that the concept of "reasonable" royalties is subject to contradictory interpretations.[22] In any case, to decide on reasonable levels of royalties and on the need to waive the compulsory licensing presumption, the administrative bodies would face the task of acquiring and assessing complex and often subjective data. The costs and imperfections in operating the system would have to be taken into account in forming a judgment about its "net" advantages as compared with alternatives.

When there is a well-defined area in which new knowledge and new technologies are desired, the situation is very much simplified. Simon Ramo gives an example based on the assumption that the United States has decided to stimulate synthetic fuel development from coal or shale. He proposes that the government announce its demand (quantity, quality, delivery schedule of the synthetic fuel to be supplied) and call for bids from private firms, possibly subject to a ceiling price. If bids come forth that satisfy the prescribed conditions, the government agency would award contracts to the low bidders but retain at least two sources. Ramo stresses that "the government is not at all involved in the technology, an area where it has the least contribution to make. . . . It merely creates a guaranteed minimum market for the output of the private sector."[23]

Note that such a solution retains the private incentives toward relevant knowledge creation and development while permitting the knowledge to be made freely available. Financing is by taxation rather than user fees. Government subsidizes the possible excess of the bid cost of synthetic fuel over the market price of imported or domestic oil. However, the bid system assumes that national needs are known and are defined in terms of specified quantities and qualities of certain goods. When needs are not so clearly defined, this approach cannot be used.

Some Recent Developments

The universities have traditionally constituted a major area of openness where research results have been freely and rapidly communicated through professional journals, conferences, and other means. Presumably because of nonmonetary rewards such as fame and professional advancement, there has seemed to be sufficient stimulus for both the production of new knowledge and its rapid and open dissemination to all interested. But cuts in research funds threaten this traditional openness. The paucity of unrestricted research funds from federal and foundation sources has led some universities to seek increased sponsorship from private corporations.

Paul E. Gray, the president of MIT, envisages the possibility that such privately sponsored research may sometimes require the granting of limited-term exclusive patent licenses to the sponsors and expresses a willingness to delay publication to allow the preparation of patent applications.[24] Similar pressures toward secrecy of research results, possibly for a longer term may come when more university research is sponsored by defense agencies. These steps toward secrecy could assume greater importance in an era of curtailment of basic science research funds to agencies such as the National Science Foundation.

Another source of pressure toward restricted access to knowledge is the potential for private profit inherent in such recent scientific advances as genetic engineering. This potential was greatly enhanced by the 1980 U.S. Supreme Court decision permitting the patenting of new forms of life. In some cases, university scientists have left the more open university environment to establish their own private companies. Not long ago a proposal was made that Harvard University itself enter the field in its corporate capacity, a proposal that Harvard ultimately rejected.[25] There have also been media reports about prizes of up to 10,000 Swiss francs offered to students and research assistants at a Swiss school of higher learning for accomplishing certain laboratory research tasks quickly and in secrecy.

Another step toward restricting the flow of existing knowledge was reported by U.S. Representative George Brown at a recent symposium. A bill signed by the president in December 1980 permits small business and nonprofit institutions to keep rights to patents arising from federally funded projects. Extension of this to larger business awaits action in the 97th Congress.[26]

On the opposite side of the ledger, the results of the laboratory experiments and other scientific data available at the Fermi National Accelerator Laboratory became "public property" due to the Stevenson-Wydler Technology Innovation Act, passed by Congress in October 1980.[27] It requires the Fermi Laboratory and some five hundred other federally funded research agencies to make their scientific advances available to industry. Here again, the implicit assumption is that scientific research does not require the financial incentives provided to industrial researchers through the existence of patents.

Conclusion

This chapter focused on measures to make existing knowledge more widely available, but we must recognize that such measures might weaken the incentive to produce new knowledge. However, there is a widespread opinion that the current drop in growth of U.S. industrial productivity is due at least in part to low levels of R&D expenditures that result in inadequate technological innovation.

In considering measures to improve access to existing knowledge, one would, therefore, want to avoid further aggravating these difficulties. This requirement intensifies the need for techniques that widen accessibility without weakening incentives for creativity. Government subsidization of R&D activities, although unpopular in the present political climate, satisfies these requirements. However, except in areas where peer judgment seems a good guide, e.g., basic research, there is a danger of inefficient direction or incorrect level of resource allocation. A partial remedy may be found in arrangements whereby subsidies are matched by contributions from the direct beneficiaries.

In any case, underinvestment in the development and transmission of knowledge seems to be at present both more likely and more damaging than overinvestment. If this diagnosis is accepted, it suggests principles to be used in choosing among the various policies designed to cure the existing ills in the area of knowledge creation and utilization. All these policies are bound to have serious disadvantages because useful knowledge as an economic good has troublesome features—nonrivalness in use and *ex ante* uncertainties as to productivity of effort and usefulness of results. These features make it unrealistic to aim at levels of efficiency attainable in more conventional economic areas. We will have to accept second-best solutions, but we need not and should not give up the goal of improving the utilization of existing knowledge.

Notes

1. The term "nonrival in consumption" is used in, e.g., E. K. Browning and J. M. Browning, *Public Finance and the Price System* (New York: Macmillan, 1979). We say "nonrival *in use*" because we refer to the use of knowledge in production as well as in consumption.

2. Pareto-optimal is defined as follows: Given two feasible resource allocations, say A and B, A is said to be *Pareto-superior* to B if no one is worse off and some individuals are better off under A than under B. A feasible resource allocation A is said to be *Pareto-optimal* if no feasible resource allocation is Pareto-superior to A.

3. In technical terms, making existing knowledge more widely available typically will push outward the production possibility frontier.

4. See K. J. Arrow, "Economic Welfare and the Allocation of Resources for Invention," in R. R. Nelson, ed., *The Rate and Direction of Inventive Activity: Economic and Social Factors* (Princeton, N.J.: Princeton University Press, 1962), pp. 14–15.

5. See W. D. Nordhaus, *Invention, Growth, and Welfare* (Cambridge, Mass.: MIT Press, 1969), p. 17.

6. In fact, even aside from licensing fees, technology transfer is difficult. See "Business Can Now Buy Ideas from Federally Funded Labs," *Wall Street Journal*, Oct. 6, 1981, p. 25. This difficulty may be due to high cost of development, lack of effective communication, or business suspicions of research. "What do a bunch of scientists at a federal lab know about the real world?", the article asks.

7. See "High-tech Seeds Have Changed the World. Patent Them, Though, and You May Lose the Crucial Element: Nature's Diversity," *Christian Science Monitor*, Aug. 19, 1981.

8. See *New York Times*, Aug. 26, 1981, p. 27. F. M. Scherer (in a private communication) comments that allocative inefficiencies of monopolization may be mitigated by price discrimination. He also points out that the waste involved in "inventing around patents" may, in some cases, be compensated for by making available a greater variety of products.

9. In this connection, it is interesting to note that, according to the *New York Times*, Oct. 31, 1981, p. 34, the United States is objecting to a proposed revision of the Paris Convention for the Protection of Industrial Property by Patents and Trademarks. The proposal "involves sanctions that a government

can apply against the individual holding the patent for failure to 'practice' or make some commercial use of his or her invention. The provisions tentatively adopted without U.S. approval would permit more severe sanctions."

10. See *New York Times*, Aug. 23, 1981, p. E9, mentioning a British plan to store journal articles on optical disks, creating the possibility of competing with the publishers of journals at one-tenth the cost.

11. Michael Polanyi, "Patent Reform," *Review of Economic Studies* 11 (1944): 61–76.

12. Under a license of right in the United Kingdom, the patent holder undertakes to grant a license to any person wishing to apply the invention either at agreed-upon terms or, in the absence of agreements, on terms fixed by the comptroller of patents. Ibid., pp. 66–67.

13. CBS news reported on July 25, 1981, that in the United Kingdom authors are paid a penny every time one of their books is borrowed from a public library. In the literary property area, this is close in spirit to the Polanyi idea.

14. Polanyi, "Patent Reform," p. 68.

15. Polanyi himself raises a related issue when he says that the patent law "aims at a purpose which cannot be rationally achieved. It tries to parcel up a stream of creative thought. . . . But the growth of human knowledge cannot be divided up into such sharply circumscribed phases. . . ." (Ibid., p. 70.) He does not seem to notice that the impact of inventions is also hard to separate from the effects of other phenomena. See also F. M. Scherer, *Industrial Market Structure and Economic Performance*, 2d ed. (Chicago: Rand McNally, 1980), p. 458, for a discussion of the award system and its drawbacks, with references to experience in the United States and in the Soviet Union.

16. See L. Hurwicz, "On Informationally Decentralized Systems," in C. B. McGuire and R. Radner, eds., *Decision and Organization* (Amsterdam: North-Holland Pub. Co., 1972), Chap. 14.

17. See J. Green and J.-J. Laffont, *Incentives in Public Decision-Making* (Amsterdam: North-Holland Pub. Co., 1979); T. Groves and M. Loeb, "Incentives and Public Inputs," *Journal of Public Economics* 4 (1975): 211–226; and E. H. Clarke, "Multipart Pricing of Public Goods," *Public Choice* 11 (1971): 19–33.

18. F. M. Scherer, "The Economic Effects of Compulsory Patent Licensing," Monograph Series in Finance and Economics, no. 1977–2 (New York: N.Y.U. Graduate School of Business Administration, Center for the Study of Financial Institutions, 1977).

19. Ibid., p. 85.

20. The pharmaceutical industry, however, might be adversely affected, according to survey data quoted in the study.

21. Scherer, "Economic Effects," p. 86.

22. Ibid., pp. 43–50.

23. Simon Ramo, "The U.S. Technology Slip: A New Political Issue," in W. Hoadley, ed., *The Economy and The President: 1980 and Beyond* (Englewood Cliffs, N.J.: Prentice-Hall, 1980), pp. 156–176.

24. The following statements made by President Gray were quoted in "Academic Research: M.I.T. Wants Closer Ties With Business," *New York Times*, Sept. 27, 1981.

Under the agreement with Exxon, M.I.T. has the right to file patents on all technology developed as a result of the research. M.I.T., however, will grant Exxon . . . nonexclusive licenses. That is, M.I.T. may issue licenses to third parties, with Exxon sharing in any royalties. . . .
These licenses provide no royalties to M.I.T.

We much prefer non-exclusive licenses, like the one with Exxon, but we also recognize that limited term exclusive licenses may sometimes be necessary as a commercial incentive to a company, particularly when there are large costs and risks associated with commercialization.

As for the question of openness and confidentiality, . . . while we cannot freeze information, we *are* willing to delay publication for a reasonable period of time to allow the preparation of patent applications and to insure that information proprietary to the sponsor is not inadvertently included in publication [emphasis in the original].

One agreement is a 10-year research contract between the Exxon Research and Engineering Co. and M.I.T. providing support for research of mutual interest in the field of combustion, . . . to generate the scientific and engineering base to develop the more efficient and safe burning of fossil fuels.

No royalties to M.I.T., because (the patents) have been developed as a result of research sponsored and thus paid for up front by the corporation.

25. Here are excerpts from Harvard University President Derek C. Bok's article in *Harvard Magazine* (May–June 1981):23–25, "Business and the Academy: Can the Universities Enter the Marketplace Without Subverting Their Commitment to Learning and Discovery?"

This brief review has revealed several responsible steps that universities can take to assist in the application of scientific knowledge while attracting added financial support for academic science. Consulting arrangements, industry-associate programs, patent licensing, research agreements with individual firms or groups of companies—all these afford useful opportunities to stimulate technological innovation. While each of these alternatives can be abused in ways that will harm the university or the public, all can be administered in a manner that will bring the dangers within acceptable levels of risk.

The same cannot be said of efforts to join the university with its professors to launch new entrepreneurial ventures. In such enterprises the risks are much harder to control, and there are few benefits to society or the academy that cannot be achieved in other ways. Instead of helping its professors to launch new companies, therefore, the university would do better to seize the initiative by asking the faculty to consider this new phenomenon in order to fashion appropriate safeguards that will maintain its academic standards and preserve its intellectual values.

ISSUE: Whether Harvard University should play a leading role in founding a genetic-engineering company. [Harvard's decision: *not* to proceed.]

26. From the January 13, 1981, Symposium on Reindustrialization or New Industrialization, Manufacturing Studies Board, Assembly of Engineering, National Research Council.

27. Laurel Sorenson, "Business now can buy ideas from federally funded labs," *Wall Street Journal*, October 6, 1981, p. 29.

BERNARD ROTH

—————— **22** ——————

The Impact of the Arms Race on the Creation and Utilization of Knowledge

The world that we have made as a result of thinking we have done thus far creates problems that we cannot solve at the level we created them at.
—Albert Einstein

Introduction

The arms race has been a fact of life in the United States for over thirty years. This means everyone under sixty completed the first levels of professional or vocational training during the Cold War or the world war that directly preceded it. For all of us, the arms race is not only a fact of life, it is one of life's major fabrics, one of the contexts in which our lives take place. To document its influence on the creation and utilization of knowledge would be an encyclopedic undertaking; what is intended here is a broad-brush picture pointing at some of the major issues.

My own experience has been mainly with the universities, the practice of engineering, and the question of productivity. Accordingly, my views are weighted toward these areas.

The Arms Race

Implicit in Dwight D. Eisenhower's oft-quoted warning about the union of military and industrial interests is the notion that something was changing in U.S. society. What began during the war as an uneasy cohabitation among the military, industrial, and scientific establishments was turning into a munificent, if not blissful, ménage à trois. Today, this may seem the natural order of things, but in fact it was something quite new for the United States. Vannevar Bush, an early prominent backer of the new order, disparagingly described the situation before World War II:

> Certainly this country failed to make much progress in the application of science to military matters. Congress cut appropriations, while the Army and Navy applied what they received principally to other things than improving their methods. Industry was not interested and took military contracts with reluctance. The reluctance was justified, for the business was unattractive, and the head of any company that developed weapons was likely to be called a merchant of death. Science turned its full attention elsewhere. Technical men in industry were developing some of the most bizarre gadgetry the world had seen, but not for war. In this country it was not merely that the people turned aside from the paraphernalia for war. Civilians felt that this was a subject for attention only by military men; and military men decidedly thought so too.[1]

After World War II, under the banner of defense against imminent Soviet aggression, the United States headed into the Cold War with the arms race as one of its major tactics. What made the arms race different from other peacetime military buildups was its dimensions, which went beyond training troops and manufacturing and stockpiling weapons. This race was to be run in a squirrel's cage, on a track without a finish line; as the wheel went round and round, U.S. society was being rapidly transformed. Only by examining some of these changes can we start to grasp the profound impact of the arms race.

Research and Development (R&D)

For the United States, a basic strategy of the arms race called for the creation of knowledge, the utilization of this knowledge, and, in many cases, the concealment of these developments. The vehicle for this process has been the research and development (R&D) contract. These contracts are made by one of the federal agencies and some research laboratory, think tank, or other private or governmental institution. The network of such institutions has grown dramatically since World War II.

Today there are well over ten thousand industrial and research facilities cleared by the Department of Defense (DOD) for secret military work. There are special R&D government laboratories, the quasigovernmental Federal Contract Research Centers (FCRC), and many university laboratories. They constitute the R&D industry, which has been aptly described as "a vast, powerful, and well-financed empire within the nation, complete with its own priorities, powers, and pecking order. Atop this empire is a diverse group of institutions called think tanks, which as agents of applied research and policy study have a fateful impact on the nation."[2]

Calculating exactly how well this empire is financed depends on which part of the federal budget one counts as supporting the generation of knowledge. According to Frank Press, former director of the Office of Science and Technology Policy (OSTP), fiscal year 1981 obligations for R&D were $35.359 billion.[3] The five largest items were:

Defense-military functions	$16.555 billion
NASA	$5.398 billion
Energy	$5.056 billion
Health and human services	$3.916 billion
National Science Foundation	$0.992 billion

These five areas account for over 90 percent of all federally supported R&D. Of the total, 46 percent is directly labeled as military R&D. The actual amount for the arms race should include at least another $5 billion of the NASA and energy money, bringing the arms race share to over 60 percent of the 1981 R&D totals. Although many analyses do not take into account the overlap of DOD, NASA, and energy spending, this consolidation is certainly justified. (Harvey Brooks, former dean of engineering and applied physics at Harvard University, lumped all of the NASA and Atomic Energy Commission R&D funds with the DOD and concluded that in 1970 a total of 84 percent of all federal research and development dollars went to the defense establishment.[4])

Even these numbers probably still underestimate the actual expenditure. The portion of NASA and energy funds included is probably conservative, and at least another billion dollars for R&D is reimbursed to companies in the form of overhead charges on procurement contracts.

It is interesting to contrast these enormous sums and the riskfree forms of present-day R&D contracts with the first industrial-military R&D contract ever awarded.[5] It was for $12,500 in 1937. Westinghouse took this contract in the hope of getting follow-up production business "knowing, *of course*, that initially there would be a loss on the R&D."[6]

The total cost of the arms race far exceeds the amount allocated for R&D. In 1981, for example, the R&D total accounted for less than 10 percent of the Defense Department's procurement, research, development, test, and evaluation and construction obligations. All of this is exclusive of other branches of government, which also spend vast sums on the arms race. For our purposes, however, the R&D expenditures are of greatest interest, since these are the ones that are supposed to finance the creation of knowledge. The huge amounts mentioned for 1980 are typical—if we correct for inflation—of the orders of magnitude we have been averaging for the last thirty years. The obvious question is, What has been the impact of this enormous expenditure for the production of knowledge?[7]

Although the most direct result of military R&D is the creation of new weapons and military information, there has always been debate as to which knowledge should be developed into actual hardware systems. The B1 bomber, the neutron bomb, the MX deployment, and the high-tech-big-bucks weaponry philosophy are only the most recent issues in this debate.[8] Moreover, the resolution of this debate constantly feeds back to and greatly influences the arms race that created it in the first place.[9] As in any feedback system, one of the crucial questions is stability. There are widespread fears that the arms race is basically unstable.[10] Even the most sanguine admit that we are dangerously close to instability at times.

Technology Transfer

One direct result of military R&D is the creation of new civilian products and knowledge. The spin-off of military research to the civilian sector is usually studied under the heading of technology transfer. There are several oft-quoted examples used to show that military R&D has "contributed immeasurably to the nation's industrial and economic growth."[11] The list includes jet engines and aircraft, radar, titanium, communication and navigation satellites, and integrated circuits.

It is certainly true that commercial products have been either created or helped to develop by money spent on the arms race. However, although the list keeps growing, most students of the subject find the amount of technology transfer is disappointing.[12] This problem received a lot of attention in the early 1960s, but no real improvement seems to have resulted.

In early 1969, a detailed study of NASA concluded that "numerous federal programs presently exist to transfer technical information to various segments of the economy, but aside from the Department of Agriculture program it appears that little thought or effort has gone into providing for interpersonal transfer of technology at the local level or to means of motivating the use of this new technology. Most of the programs to date are expanded technical library programs. . . . it does not appear that they form a significant part in actually motivating the adaption of new technology across institutional lines."[13]

In 1975 another study concluded that "government expenditures concentrated according to specific mission-oriented needs for DOD, NASA and AEC. For NASA three fourths of items proposed for commercial application were in electronic, electric, and mechanical fields. Forcing of these fields inflated expenditures and increased the rate of obsolescence, both reducing the value of technology awaiting innovation. DOD items have additional disadvantages of duplication from three services, multiple approaches, and commercial non-applicability of defense-oriented items. For industrial sectors, government-generated technology for other than whole systems did not compete well with company technology or with traditional commercial sources of new technology. Industrial innovators heavily discounted new Federal technology."[14]

The Department of Commerce estimated that ten man-years of industrial R&D are needed to produce a commercial patent but that it takes a thousand man-years to produce such a patent from in-house or contract R&D work from DOD or NASA.[15]

In the 1960s the Defense Department conducted Project Hindsight, its own study of technology transfer. This study considered the origins of the knowledge most useful in developing weapons systems. Considering time spans of twenty years or less, it found that 90 percent of the significant improvements in cost or effectiveness resulted from work directly addressed to a specific defense problem, while only 0.3 percent of these came from undirected science.[16] At the time there was some fear that this report might be used to undercut support of the basic sciences from mission-oriented agencies; but the report was very vulnerable to criticism, and nothing came of it. It did, however, make the rather obvious point that, in the short term at least, the best way to solve problems and generate knowledge in a given area is to work in that area.

In summary, if we look at the impact of the arms race on the creation of knowledge we may conclude that the new knowledge is first and foremost directly applicable to the arms race itself. There have been (using James Burke's term) "connections" that have brought new products and knowledge into the civilian sector. However, military R&D does not seem to be an efficient vehicle for this knowledge generation.

How about the area of information? This is where most observers give the defense sector high marks. According to Hough, "Important information science developments have resulted from federal programs, some with unique forms. In 1966 DOD and AEC operated 36 major information analysis centers on subjects of national technical interest. DOD departments (Army, Navy and Air Force) also operated specialized centers. The Nuclear Data Center of AEC, for example, contributed to the shell model of the nucleus."[17]

The government indexing services run by NASA and the Defense Documentation Center are today important sources of information—especially in matters related to the arms race.

Secrecy

At the same time that it was generating information at a prodigious rate, the arms race was promoting a secrecy system without parallel in our previous history. Using four major secrecy classifications (Top Secret, Secret, Confidential, and Restricted) and some variants (such as Eyes Only), government agencies and private companies have buried or severely restricted access to vast amounts of information. The quantity of classified material is mind-boggling. In 1974 the DOD reported that in a review of documents twenty-five or more years old, the archivist of the United States had declassified 50 million pages and the military had declassified 110,000 linear feet, over 20 miles of paper; this represented only one-quarter of their total classified holdings from that period.[18] In addition to the government's direct holdings, there are over ten thousand industrial facilities and research centers cleared by DOD for custody of classified information, and these institutions also hold millions of classified documents.

In an information-based society such as ours, whoever controls information controls power and wealth. The secrecy system provides the Pentagon with control over private industries and research centers. Secrecy has been used to give insiders the advantage in policy debates or financial competitions. The rationale for the secrecy network is the need to guard national security. However, as Arthur M. Cox's recent critique points out, this is indeed a myth.[19]

In reaction to the executive branch's abuses in withholding information, Congress passed the Freedom of Information Act in 1966. Interestingly one of its purposes was to make government information more available to members of Congress. This law has provided a counterweight to secrecy and is a small light shining into the vast darkness of secrecy. Though there already are broad exemptions, there are ongoing attempts to further dilute this law; recently 152 private organizations formed a coalition to oppose new exemptions being considered by the Reagan administration.

In science there is a tradition of open discussion and consequently some resistance to secrecy on esthetic as well as strictly functional grounds. Edward Teller's 1974 congressional testimony emphasizes the functional aspects:

Our policy of secrecy in science and technology has created the illusion we are in possession of valuable information which is not available to other nations, and in particular, not available to our chief competitor, the Soviet Union. In the field of nuclear explosives where we used to have a great advantage, secrecy did not perpetuate the advantage. In the field of electronics and the art of high-speed computers a great national advantage was brought about without the aid of secrecy. That technological secrecy amounts to security is, in my opinion, indeed an illusion.[20]

Secrecy actually impedes the creation and utilization of knowledge: Teller points out, "The spirit of modern science is antithetical to the spirit of the diligent researches performed for almost 2000 years by alchemists. When the secrecy and the mutual isolation of the alchemists was replaced by the novel code of openness, this brought about the dawn of modern chemistry."[21]

Within the scientific community there have been groups that have continually sought to lessen Cold War tensions using openness and collegiality. The *Bulletin of the Atomic Scientists* and the *Pugwash Symposia* are notable examples of their work. In spite of such protests and strong recommendations from within the system, a wastefully excessive classification system continues to exist.[22] Ironically, one justification for the massive military R&D effort is to avoid "technological surprises"; yet the secrecy system itself promotes the possibility of surprise.

Another, perhaps the most insidious, aspect of the secrecy system is its impact on the individuals involved. Certainly some people enjoy the whole ritual of secrecy and even gain a sense of personal importance from participating in it. Yet for others it is a debilitating experience. There are social, psychological, and physical side effects resulting from the fragmenting experience of not being allowed to discuss one's work with family or friends.

The security system does much to curtail the exercise of civil liberties. It is widely believed that any behavior that deviates from accepted political or social orthodoxy is punished by denying or revoking security clearance. Many individuals who do not actually need government clearance in their work find that their employers require it of them. For some, professional survival hinges on a clearance. The threats implicit in the system inhibit free expression and the creation of knowledge.

Universities

During the Vietnam War there were significant debates about DOD support of university research, and secrecy was a major issue. However, beyond the question of secrecy and the immediate desire to stop the war in Vietnam was a basic moral and political question: What is the proper role of the university in the arms race?

This question is still not resolved. The universities remain participants in the arms race, and the debate continues. The impact of the defense establishment on the universities in the early days of the Cold War was a profound one. What happened at that time transformed our leading universities and, through them, engineering and the applied sciences.

The schools that have become the leading Ph.D.-producing universities were a key element in this transformation. Building on wartime experiences with scientists, the Office of Naval Research (ONR) became a major supporter of university research and Ph.D. production in engineering, mathematics, and several of the sciences. This well-managed program had, as it does to this day, a good reputation among academics. Other funded research programs followed, and the leading schools all participated.

Once they obtained contracts, faculties needed students to do the research; the result was an expansion of graduate programs. More funds meant a university could also hire additional faculty, who in turn raised funds and attracted still more graduate students. In this way MIT, for example, was able to quadruple its faculty, increase its graduate student population by almost six times, and multiply its sponsored research funding over nine thousand times between 1938 and 1970.

The early infusion of money into the leading engineering and science departments had a tremendous influence on post–World War II science and engineering. This funding paved the road to financial success, suggested areas of research, revolutionized the content of curricula, shifted the power bases within and between universities, and created the "academic jet set."

The system was a tremendous success. There was a ready market for its "products," and the competition for the research money was not too onerous. In engineering, for example, the Cold War products were engineers highly trained in mathematics and basic science and eager to work in a specialized area. The defense industry with its cost-plus budgets for large R&D departments was eager to absorb these tailormade specialists. Those with Ph.D.s who wanted teaching careers found plenty of opportunity; their universities expanded; schools lower down on the pecking order anxiously sought Ph.D. holders in order to modernize their image and, they hoped, to get a crack at government R&D money.

Whereas in 1935 only 100 Ph.D.s were earned in engineering, by 1968 the "production rate" had reached 3,000 per year. For the first time it became necessary to have a Ph.D. in order to teach undergraduate engineering.[23] Sputnik provided the death blow to the old guard on engineering faculties, successfully pushing technical education into an alliance with the rapidly growing applied sciences and the high-tech military research establishment.

The DOD funds had a leverage effect. Even without continued DOD funding, Ph.D.s followed careers rather close to their own training. This is not surprising, once one is trained in a given direction it is only natural to keep going in that direction. Thomas Kuhn has pointed out that scientific specialists, "to an extent unparalleled in most other fields . . . have undergone similar educations and professional initiations; in the process they have absorbed the same technical literature and drawn many of the same lessons from it. Usually the boundaries of that standard literature mark the limits of a scientific subject matter. . . . the members of a scientific community see themselves as uniquely responsible for the pursuit of a set of shared goals, including the training of their successors."[24]

Universities expanded quickly, some relying heavily on so-called soft money, which increased both the individual's and the institution's dependence on the military. At Stanford University, for example, all engineering school faculty were for many years expected to raise at least 20 percent of their salary from research contracts. Many had to do more since the administration expected a 25 percent schoolwide average.

This situation pressured researchers to get their research funded—even those who could manage quite well with no government funding. It caused a skewing toward fundable research and, as we have seen, toward the defense establishment. Although in recent years the National Science Foundation has provided strong alternatives, the game was already defined before NSF was born.

The universities have put themselves under the gun. They have learned to charge various parts of their normal expenses to research overhead and to direct research costs wherever possible. When they lose research funding, other parts of the institution are also jeopardized. (For example, in 1969 MIT fiscal policy was based on an estimated $7 million annually coming to the institution from two of its defense laboratories.[25])

During the Vietnam War, student activists, with some faculty support, led several unsuccessful campaigns to convert university-owned defense laboratories to more socially productive work. The results of these efforts were the divestment of some laboratories and some restrictions against secret research on campuses.

One basic issue was the DOD's motivation for funding research. By spending or withdrawing its money in certain areas, the DOD could make or break a research field. What criteria did it use to decide to fund a given research project—scientific or mission criteria?

The Mansfield Amendment to the fiscal year 1970 military appropriation required that DOD only fund research with a "direct and apparent relationship to a specific military function or operation." This law required the DOD to use mission criteria. Many faculty took no responsibility for the mission aspects of their work. Some claimed not to know what it was; others felt it was irrelevant, as they would do the same work regardless of sponsor. All DOD R&D, however, fulfilled some mission requirement listed in the classified *Technical Objectives Document*.

A detailed study of the situation at Stanford University concluded that "the Department of Defense designs its R&D programs intelligently so that they meet projected military needs."[26] Although military spokespeople have said the same thing for years, some faculty continued to deny this perception.[27] The Stanford report quotes the chief scientist of the Army Research Office, when asked about faculty perceptions regarding the use of their work, as responding "Basic research, like beauty, is in the eye of the beholder."

Although the universities got less than 2 percent of the military R&D budget, the military gained tremendous leverage. This was accomplished by spending most of the money at the most influential universities and limiting support to certain selected fields. The net result was that the defense dollars had a disproportionately large influence on the leading engineering and science departments of this country compared to the rest of the economy.

Where do we stand today? A whopping number of research contracts from the U.S. Defense Department is headed for universities in the country, and they will welcome the business. (Stanford's President Donald Kennedy said that he would be happy to see more government research on campus as long as the university's rules on open information are followed and as long as classified research is avoided.[28])

A rapprochement has been orchestrated between the DOD and the universities. According to science analyst Daniel S. Greenberg, the reason is that "the Pentagon needed good science and the universities needed more money." He further points out that

The figures and trends are striking. Over the past three years, Department of Defense spending for basic research in universities has increased by 70 percent, to a total of about $265 million. When all types of military research-and-development are put together they amount to over $500 million. When you exclude the health-research money that government spends in medical schools, the Defense Department accounts for 25 percent of all federal research-and-development funds in academe. The military role in campus R&D is now three-fourths the size of the National Science Foundation's—and gaining fast.

Greenberg closes his analysis with a question about the future: "What few academic scientists are talking about, however, is what happens if present trends give Defense the mainstay role in academic science, and today's sensitive management is succeeded by one with less devotion to the traditions of academic science."[29]

It seems the pendulum has swung back to the 1950s; the DOD is again one of the major funders of on-campus research. Yet researchers can never regain their lost innocence; the warnings sounded in the 1960s and 1970s are still valid.[30] A recent letter to *Science* argued that "(1) the universities should decrease rather than increase their dependence on federal funding, (2) it is inappropriate for the DOD to fund nonmilitary research, and (3) it is immoral to increase defense spending and "narrow-minded and self-serving for the universities to take their begging bowls to the Pentagon."[31]

Export Restrictions

The relationship between the military and the academic community is not tranquil. There is a smoldering controversy about basic research in cryptography. The latest problem arose when the National Science Foundation was apparently directed by the National Security Agency (NSA) to withdraw funds for part of an academic research project. It seems the NSA was attempting to gain control over cryptography and remove it from the public sector.[32] A panel advising NSF concluded that "the controversy over cryptological research is 'just the tip of the iceberg' and that similar controversies will soon affect other fields."[33] They recommended that funding decisions be separated from security and other considerations.

Another recent controversy focuses around research on very high-speed integrated circuits (VHSIC). Although basic research in this area is funded by DOD, work at Stanford, MIT, Caltech, and other universities is being done under unclassified contracts. Yet in December 1980 the DOD sent a memorandum to all VHSIC program directors advising them that under the authority of the International Traffic in Arms Regulation (ITAR) and the Export Administration Regulation (EAR), DOD was henceforth requiring that:

1. Experimental devices made under this program were subject to the Commodity Controls of EAR and therefore could not be shown outside this country without permission from the Department of Commerce.

2. Any reports containing the "results of basic research and process or utilization technology" (as distinguished from basic science) should be clearly marked: "This document contains technical data subject to control under the International Traffic in Arms Regulations. Disclosure to foreign nationals, except under certain restricted conditions, is not authorized. Contact the office below prior to any such disclosure."

3. "In the case of basic research supported by the VHSIC program, although such research and its results are not generally controlled, it is the preference of the Program Office that only U.S. citizens and immigrant aliens who have declared their intention of becoming citizens participate. Where this preference cannot be accommodated, the contractor should be directed to the Program Office for resolution. This does not apply to contractors operating under a technical assistance agreement approved by the Department of State."[34]

Since about half of all engineering students today are foreign nationals, these rules would prevent many faculty and students from continuing their education and research programs. Several universities stated that these research programs will be seriously disrupted or even terminated if such restrictions hold.[35]

A letter signed by the presidents of Stanford, Caltech, MIT, Cornell, and the University of California stated: "Unfortunately, these initiatives appear to be only the first of many such actions to follow."[36] The letter points out that "the new construction of these regulations appears to contemplate government restrictions of research publications and of discourse among scholars . . ." and that furthermore, "Such restrictions would conflict with the fundamental precepts that define the role and operations of this nation's universities."

This controversy is simply the latest clash in a series of incidents involving the government's efforts to control access to certain broad areas of knowledge. In 1976 the Defense Science Board analyzed the transfer of technology as it relates to U.S. national security and issued the Bucy Report[37] in response. Secretary of Defense Harold Brown issued a policy statement defining DOD's role in the control of exports of "critical U.S. technology and related products."[38] He defines critical technology as "classified and unclassified nuclear and non-nuclear unpublished data, whose acquisition by a potential adversary could make a significant contribution, which would prove detrimental to the national security of the United States, to the military potential of such country . . . Irrespective of whether such technology is acquired directly from the United States or indirectly through another recipient, or whether the declared intended end use by the recipient is a military or non-military use." He then explains that the "data" he is talking about is "information of any kind that can be used, or adapted for use, in the design, production, manufacture, utilization, testing, maintenance or reconstruction of articles or materials." The application of these incredibly sweeping guidelines led in January 1979 to a list of fifteen broad areas of applied science and engineering in which the critical technologies are to be found and controlled.

It is not yet widely recognized, but these regulations coupled with those of ITAR and EAR in fact give the military the power to restrict wide areas of knowledge. Any activity in these areas—which include one called "miscellaneous"—can be restricted even if it involves unclassified work done in the civilian sector without government support.

So far there have been two main areas of restrictions. One is publication. The DOD has long had a "conditions of release" clause in research contracts that requires all information generated under the contract be reviewed and approved by the government before it can be released to the public. During the last twelve years this clause has been used sparingly at universities, although it is fairly standard in industry and research laboratories. Now, however, it seems to be coming into vogue. Recently, the Public Cryptography Study Group agreed to a system of prior review of publications by the National Security Agency.[39]

Secretary Brown's new "critical technology" guidelines have been used to incorporate prior-notice provisions in university contracts by the Defense Advanced Research Projects Agency (DARPA) and other DOD agencies. There has been controversy about a similar clause at the University of Wisconsin's Mathematics Research Center.[40]

The second area is restrictions applied to Eastern Europeans and other foreign nationals. Using the same export laws as in the VHSIC case, combined with the critical technologies areas list generated by the DOD, the State Department screens all visiting scholars from Eastern Europe. Anyone whose work is related to a "critical" area is automatically rejected from participating in the International Research Exchange Board (IREX) program.

Last year Eastern European scientists were prevented from attending an open meeting organized by the American Vacuum Society. Other foreign nationals at the meeting were required to sign a pledge that they would not reveal information from the sessions to citizens of communist countries, including the People's Republic of China. There was a similar restriction at another "open" conference.[41] Other scientific visits have also been canceled because of these regulations, and foreigners have been denied access to software systems. State Department restrictions are placed on Eastern European scientists visiting U.S. universities. In addition to the usual travel restrictions, some visitors are now denied "access (visual, oral or documentary) to production, research or other activity funded by DOD contracts or grants, classified or unclassified. . . ."

Intelligence agencies have long been interested in scholars. Some researchers have been agents; other have been used to gather information and as advisers. The CIA, FBI, and other agencies have a history of campus involvements. These covert operations, as well as the Cold War, have reduced the possibilities for scientific field work in certain areas of the world.[42] The new export restrictions will most assuredly make matters worse.

Infrastructure

The arms race has created its own industry and an entire subculture within U.S. society. The military is actually the largest industry in the country. Three million uniformed people and civilians work for the military. It spends millions each year just on moving people among stations. It owns hundreds of thousands of dwellings (370,000 in 1970) and builds from 5 to 10 thousand replacement units each year. Its vast health care program includes over 200 hospitals.[43] It runs the largest in-service technical training programs in the country, is a major source of scientific and technical education, and maintains the Defense Documentation Center (DDC), which contains an exhaustive collection of reports on weapons and other DOD matters. Clearly, it has its own very considerable infrastructure. In addition, because of its large share of the federal budget, it has an important impact on the civilian sector of U.S. society. What have been its effects on the commercial technological base?

The impact of the arms race on the scientific and engineering disciplines was recently assessed by F. Karl Willenbrock, the former director of the Institute for Applied Technology of the National Bureau of Standards:

> Most members of these disciplines are only partially aware of the tremendous influence that federal R&D policies have on the health of their disciplines. Considering the engineering disciplines, for example, it is evident that, in the post–World War II era, those engineering fields in which the most able faculty and students are to be found are those in which there has been a high level and consistent patterns of federal R&D funding. It is in these fields, such as electronics, aerospace, and computers,

that the greatest technological advances have been made. In other fields, such as building and constructions technology, the rate of progress has been much slower. . . . for example, when decreases were made in the funding for the defense- and space-related industries in the early 1970's, there were, for the first time since World War II, numbers of unemployed scientists and engineers. University enrollments in the physical sciences and engineering dropped sharply at that time. Now there is a significant shortage of technical personnel in these fields. . . .[44]

This skewing effect as well as the shortage of technical people continues. Part of the problem is resource allocation. It has turned out that the arms race and its budget priorities work directly against the generation of knowledge and, even more importantly, against the national goals of maximizing employment, purchasing power, production, economic dispersion, equitable development, and a healthy physical environment. The reasons for this are as follows.

1. The increase in knowledge in the form of technological change or advance is by far the most important factor in economic growth.[45] However, analyzing the costs of typical weapons systems shows the following distributions:[46]

Early-stage R&D	3%
Full-scale development	12%
Production	35%
Operation and support	50%

Most new knowledge comes from the first two of these steps, so for a typical system only 15 percent of the money produces the type of knowledge that can lead to economic growth. Thus, even within the arms system itself, the current money allocation does not maximize knowledge creation, and this is one reason the military has a poor reputation in this regard.[47]

2. Procurement funds as well as R&D grants are awarded so that relatively few contractors get most of the funds; therefore, most of the scientific talent is concentrated in only a few large corporations. Those defense contractors with civilian operations have an inside track in spinning off commercial products. However, defense distorts a company's perspective: Those who produce advanced military miracles often muddle commercial ventures.

3. For most companies in advanced science and technology, the DOD is their largest customer, and their staff scientists and engineers work on advanced military projects. Many of these people would rather use their talents in more socially productive ways, yet they are not well

trained for anything but military-type high technology. After years of boom or bust in military work, many engineers turn to other pursuits—some voluntarily, others because their employment is terminated. The departure of scientists and engineers further depletes the technological infrastructure.

4. Military spending uses up a large portion of new fixed capital formation, which hurts the civilian sectors' ability to produce new knowledge. From 1956 through 1970, military spending consumed an average of 8.3 percent of the U.S. gross national product. Since then it has declined steadily each year to 5.2 percent in 1979 and 1980. Now it is climbing back up to 6 percent. In contrast, Japan spends less than 1 percent of its GNP on defense.[48]

5. Defense technology focuses on special economic sectors that tend to be costly and inaccessible to the other sectors. With capital-intensive military, industry, and employment decreases, the civilian economy is drained. In fact, some analysts assert that manufacturing, transportation, education, and other parts of our civilian infrastructure are in trouble because of the arms race. In recent years there has been a strong negative correlation between military spending and growth of GNP.

Conclusion

Judging from current events, the flow of knowledge will become more restricted as our world trade position declines and military buildup escalates to trillion-dollar levels. The defense establishment will continue to be a major financier for selected segments of our civilian educational, research, and production efforts, thereby defining the types of knowledge our society supports.

The knowledge the arms race creates is primarily useful for continuing the arms race. Throughout the Cold War, the knowledge necessary to perpetuate the arms race has been much more sought after than the knowledge needed to end it. This subversion of values is the greatest impact the arms race has had on the optimum utilization of knowledge.

Notes

1. Vannevar Bush, *Modern Arms and Free Men*, paperback edition (Cambridge, Mass.: MIT Press, 1968), p. 19.

2. Paul Dickson, "The Empire of Think Tanks," *The Progressive*, Nov. 1971, p. 37.

3. These figures come from his testimony on the Research and Development Authorization Estimates Act, hearings before the Committee on Science and Technology, U.S. House of Representatives, May 30, 1980, p. 21.

4. Harvey Brooks, "Impact of the Defense Establishment on Science and Education," National Science Policy (H. Con. Res. 666), hearings before the Subcommittee on Science, Research and Development, Committee on Science and Astronautics, U.S. House of Representatives, 91–2, 1970, p. 931.

5. According to Dr. H. A. Zahl, the first industry-military R&D contract was awarded by the U.S. Signal Corps for work on radar. H. A. Zahl, "The Invention of the R&D Contract," *Signal*, Feb. 1970, pp. 34–37.

6. Ibid., p. 34 (italics added).

7. There are those who feel these sums are far from sufficient. Today's complaints are almost identical to the ones voiced in 1970 by C. W. Borkland, the editor of *Government Executive*, in his "Defense R&D: The Trend is Ominous," *Government Executive*, vol. 2 (July 1970), pp. 44–48. Borkland laments the decline in real funding due to inflation and blames this on "misinformation about the content and misunderstanding about the strong national security necessity and powerful economic and social value of Defense R&D."

8. See James Fallows, *National Defense* (New York: Random House, 1981).

9. See *Impact of New Technologies on the Arms Race*, edited by B.T. Field et al. (Cambridge, Mass.: MIT Press, 1971).

10. See Herbert York, *Race to Oblivion* (New York: Simon and Schuster, 1970).

11. Donald M. MacArthur, "Defense Technology: Benefits to Industrial Progress," *Defense Industry Bulletin*, Aug. 1970, p. 1.

12. Food pouches and outdoor supplies are described as some of the most recent spinoffs in Bern Keating, "Uncle Sam's Workshop," *Science*, April 3, 1981, pp. 37–42. For more comprehensive descriptions of spinoffs see Bush, op. cit.; MacArthur, op. cit.; and the two studies referred to in notes 13 and 14.

13. Samuel I. Doctors, *The Role of Federal Agencies in Technology Transfer* (Cambridge, Mass.: MIT Press, 1969), p. 164.

14. Granville W. Hough, *Technology Diffusion* (Mt. Airy, Md.: Lomand Systems, Inc., 1975), p. 233.

15. Ibid., p. 47.

16. "Project Hindsight," *Science*, June 23, 1967, p. 1577. There was also a follow-up study called TRACES with slightly different conclusions.

17. Hough, op. cit., p. 52.

18. Arthur Macy Cox, *The Myths of National Security* (Boston: Beacon Press, 1975), pp. 73–74.

19. Ibid.

20. Quoted in ibid., pp. 70–71.

21. Quoted in ibid., p. 71; *Christian Science Monitor*, Nov. 1, 1978, reports Teller stated that secrecy is slowing our fusion research.

22. A 1973 study, *U.S. Military R&D Management*, Special Report Series, no. 14 (Washington, D.C.: Georgetown University Press) Center for Strategic and International Studies, concludes the "DOD should radically reduce the secrecy in R&D technology."

23. Brooks, op. cit., p. 947.

24. Thomas S. Kuhn, *The Structure of Scientific Revolutions*, second edition, (Chicago: University of Chicago Press, 1970), p. 177.

25. Dorothy Nelkin, *The University and Military Research* (Ithaca, N.Y.: Cornell University Press, 1972), p. 139.

26. Stanton A. Glantz and Norm V. Albers, "Department of Defense R&D in the University," *Science*, Nov. 22, 1974, pp. 706–711.

27. MacArthur, op. cit., p. 12.

28. *Peninsula Times Tribune*, Palo Alto, California, September 20, 1981, p. 1; see also John Walsh, "DOD Funds More Research in Universities," *Science*, May 28, 1981, p. 1004.

29. Daniel S. Greenberg, "The New Harmony Between Campuses and the Pentagon," *Chronicle of Higher Education*, Feb. 23, 1981, p. 25.

30. Martin Brown, *The Social Responsibility of the Scientist* (New York: Free Press, 1971). See especially the articles by S. Klaw, C. Schwartz, O. Chamberlain, and S. Lang, pp. 2–81.

31. Colleen J. G. Clark and John R. Clark, "University Research and DOD," *Science*, vol. 212, June 26, 1981, p. 1446.

32. John Noble Wilford, "Science Foundations Aid Denied For Sensitive Research on Codes," *New York Times*, Aug. 27, 1980. See also Martin E. Hellman, "Protecting Assets by Cryptography," *Christian Science Monitor*, Mar. 11, 1981.

33. John Walsh, "Shunning Cryptocensorship," *Science*, vol. 212, June 12, 1981, p. 1250.

34. Memorandum from Larry W. Sumney, Director, VHSIC Program Office, Office of the Under Secretary of Defense, to VHSIC program directors, Dec. 12, 1980.

35. Memorandum from John C. Crowley, Office of Federal Relations, Association of American Universities, to Thomas A. Bartlett and Newton O. Cattel, Dec. 22, 1980.

36. Reprinted in *Campus Report*, Stanford University, Apr. 15, 1981, p. 8. The letter, dated Feb. 27, 1981, was addressed to Malcolm Baldridge, Alexander M. Haig, Jr., and Caspar Weinberger. It was signed by Donald Kennedy, Marvin L. Goldberger, Paul E. Gray, Frank H. T. Rhodes, and David S. Saxon. For an analysis of this situation see Gina Bari Kolata, "Attempts to Safeguard Technology Draw Fire," *Science*, vol. 212, May 1, 1981, pp. 523–526.

37. "An Analysis of Export Control of U.S. Technology—A DOD Perspective," Report of the Defense Science Board Task Force on Export of U.S. Technology, Office of the Director of Defense Research and Engineering, February 4, 1976.

38. Harold Brown, "Interim DOD Policy Statement on Export Control of United States Technology," Aug. 24, 1977.

39. "Policy on Cryptography Proposals," *Science*, Oct. 23, 1980, p. 511.

40. "Math Center Protests Army Contract Terms," *Science*, vol. 208, June 6, 1980, pp. 1122–1123.

41. David Dickson, "Universities complain at Pentagon policy," *Nature*, vol. 290, April 9, 1981, p. 435. See also Walter Sullivan, "State Dept. Bars Soviet Scientists Invited to Two Technical Parleys," *New York Times*, Feb. 22, 1980.

42. George Alexander, "Tensions of World Curb Researchers," *Los Angeles Times*, Mar. 18, 1981.

43. MacArthur, op. cit., p. 2.

44. *Testimony on Research and Development in the Federal Budget,* hearings before the Committee on Science and Technology, U.S. House of Representatives, 96-1, Apr. 1979, pp. 153–154.

45. Ibid., p. 310.

46. Boston Study Group, *Price of Defense* (New York: Times Books, 1979), p. 234.

47. *Testimony on Research and Development,* op. cit., p. 266, and also *Technology Transfer and Utilization,* Academy of Engineers Report C0110–74 (Washington, D.C.: National Academy of Engineering, 1974).

48. Seymour Melman, "Puff Piece for A War Economy," *The Nation,* May 9, 1981, pp. 566–569. See also Seymour Melman, *The Permanent War Economy* (New York: Simon and Schuster, 1974).

DONALD A. SCHÖN

─────── **23** ───────

Education for Reflection-in-Action: An Alternative to the Positivist Epistemology of Practice

The Crisis of Confidence in Professional Knowledge

Although our society has become so thoroughly dependent on professionals that the conduct of business, industry, government, education, and everyday life would be unthinkable without them, there are signs of a growing crisis of confidence in the professions. In many well-publicized scandals, professionals have been found willing to use their special positions for private gain. Professionally designed solutions to public problems have had unanticipated consequences, sometimes worse than the problems they were intended to solve. The public has shown an increasing readiness to call for external regulation of professional practice, and laymen have been turning to the courts for defense against professional incompetence or venality. As the public has begun to doubt professional ethics and expertise, the professional's traditional claims to privileged social position and autonomy of practice have also come into question.[1] And in recent years, professionals themselves have shown signs of a loss of confidence in professional knowledge.

───────────────

The material in this chapter is condensed and recast from that in my book *The Reflective Practitioner* (New York: Basic Books, 1982).

In 1963, the editors of *Daedalus* introduced a special volume on the professions with the sentence, "Everywhere in American life the professions are triumphant."[2] They noted the apparently limitless demand for professional services, the "shortages" of teachers and physicians, the difficulty of coordinating the proliferating technical specializations, and the problems of managing the burgeoning mass of technical data. The essays in the volume, by doctors, lawyers, scientists, educators, military men, and politicians, articulated variations on the themes of professional triumph, overload, and growth. There were only two discordant voices: the representative of the clergy complained of declining influence and the "problem of relevance," and the city planner commented ruefully on his profession's lagging understanding of the changing ills of urban areas.[3]

Less than a decade later, the discordant notes had become the dominant ones, and the theme of professional triumph had virtually disappeared. In 1972, a colloquium on professional education was held at the Massachusetts Institute of Technology. Participants included distinguished representatives of the fields of medicine, engineering, architecture, planning, psychiatry, law, divinity, education, and management. These individuals disagreed about many things, but they held one sentiment in common—a profound uneasiness about their own professions. They questioned whether professionals would effectively police themselves and asked whether they were really instruments of individual well-being and social reform or were more interested in preserving their own status and privilege, caught up in the very problems they might have been expected to solve. They even expressed doubts about the relevance and remedial power of professional expertise.

It is perhaps not very difficult to account for this dramatic shift over a single decade. Between 1963 and 1972 there had been a disturbing sequence of events, painful for professionals and the lay public alike. A professionally instrumented war had been disastrous. Social movements for peace and civil rights had begun to see the professions as elitist servants of established interests. The much-proclaimed shortages of scientists, teachers, and physicians seemed to have evaporated. Professionals seemed powerless to relieve the rapidly shifting "crises" of the cities, poverty, environmental pollution, and energy. There were also the scandals of Medicare and, at the end of the decade, Watergate. All of these factors created doubts about professional strategies of diagnosis and cure, pointing up instead the overwhelming complexity of the phenomena with which professionals were trying to cope and raising questions about the adequacy of existing theories and techniques for relieving the most urgent sources of societal distress.

The participants in the MIT colloquium analyzed their predicament in terms of four main factors. First, they believed there had been a shift in the nature of social reality, which had created problems of a complexity and uncertainty ill suited to the traditional division of labor. A noted engineer observed that "education no longer fits the niche, or the niche no longer fits education." The dean of a medical school spoke of the complexity of a huge health care system, only marginally influenceable by the actions of the medical profession. The dean of a school of management referred to the puzzle of educating managers to judge and act under conditions of uncertainty.

Second, they were troubled by the irreducible residue of "art" that was deemed indispensable to professional practice, even in the fields of science and engineering. They doubted if this indispensable art could be codified and taught. As one participant said, "If it's invariant and known, it can be taught; but it isn't invariant."

Third, professional education tended to focus on problem solving, but the most important issues for professional practice were those of problem *finding*. "Our interest," as one participant put it, "is not only how to pour the concrete for the highway, but what highway makes sense? When it comes to designing a ship, the question we have to ask is, which ship makes sense in terms of the problems of transportation?" Representatives of schools of architecture, planning, social work, and psychiatry also spoke of the pluralism of the schools, the conflicting views of the competences to be acquired, the problems to be solved, and the nature of their professions. A leading professor of psychiatry described his field as a "babble of voices."

Fourth, there were calls for liberating the professions from the tyranny of the professional schools and the universities. "American universities are products of the late nineteenth and early twentieth centuries," one participant observed. "The question is, how do you break them up in some way, at least get some group of young people who are free of them? How do you make them free to do something new and different?"

The ten years since the 1972 colloquium have reinforced its conclusions. In 1982, no profession would celebrate itself in triumphant tones. In spite of the continuing eagerness of the young to embark on apparently secure and remunerative professional careers, professionals still are criticized, and criticize themselves, for failing to live up to their own norms and adapt to a changing social reality. There is widespread recognition of the absence of a stable institutional framework of purpose and knowledge within which professionals can confidently exercise their skills.

Nevertheless, there is something puzzling about the ways in which participants in the 1972 colloquium accounted for the troubles of the professions. Professionals do sometimes find ways of coping effectively, even wisely, with situations of complexity and uncertainty. If the element of art in professional practice is not invariant, known, and teachable, it does appear occasionally to be learnable. Problem setting is an activity in which some professionals engage consciously and skillfully. And some students and practitioners of the professions do seem to make thoughtful choices from among the multiple views of professional identity.

Why, then, should leading professionals and educators have been so troubled by the phenomena of complexity, uncertainty, instability, art, and pluralism? It was not, I think, because they were unaware that practitioners sometimes display artistry and cope with uncertainty. I suspect it was rather that they found it difficult to account for the processes by which they do so.

Complexity and uncertainty are not dissolved by applying specialized knowledge to well-defined tasks; on the contrary, tasks are defined by restructuring complex and uncertain situations. The irreducible element of art in practice cannot be reduced to the exercise of known technique. Problem finding has no place in a body of professional knowledge concerned exclusively with problem solving. One cannot rely on professional expertise in order to choose among competing paradigms of professional practice. The underlying model of professional knowledge is unable to account for processes professionals see as central to their competence.

The Dominant Model of Professional Knowledge

The epistemology of professional practice, which is built into the very structure of professional schools and research institutions, has been clearly set forth in two recent essays that treat professional practice as an application of research-based knowledge to the solution of problems of instrumental choice.

Edgar Schein, in his *Professional Education*, proposes a threefold division of professional knowledge:

1. An *underlying discipline* or *basic science* component upon which the practice rests or from which it is developed;
2. An *applied science* or *"engineering"* component from which many of the day-to-day diagnostic procedures and problem solutions are derived;
3. A *skills and attitudinal* component that concerns the actual performance of services to the client, using the underlying basic and applied knowledge.[4]

In Schein's view, these components constitute a hierarchy of application, justification, and status. The application of basic science yields engineering, and engineering provides the models, rules, and techniques applicable to the instrumental choices of everyday practice. The actual performance of services "rests on" applied science, which rests, in turn, on the foundation of basic science. In the epistemological pecking order, basic science is highest in methodological rigor and purity; its practitioners tend to be superior in status to those who practice applied science, problem solving, or service delivery.

Nathan Glazer argues that the schools of such professions as social work, education, divinity, and town planning are caught in a hopeless predicament.[5] Educators in these "minor" professions, beguiled by the success of the "major" professions of law, medicine, and business, have tried to substitute a grounding in scientific knowledge for their traditional reliance on experienced practice. In this spirit, they have placed their schools within the universities. Glazer believes, however, that their aspirations are doomed to failure because the "minor" professions lack the essential conditions of the "major" ones: stable institutional contexts of practice, fixed and unambiguous ends that "settle men's minds," and a basis in systematic scientific knowledge.[6] They cannot apply scientific knowledge to instrumental problems, and they are, therefore, unable to produce a rigorous curriculum of professional education.

> Can these fields [education, city planning, social work, and divinity] settle on a fixed form of training, a fixed content of professional knowledge, and follow the models of medicine, law and business? I suspect not because the discipline of a fixed and unambiguous end in a fixed institutional setting is not given to them. And *thus* [italics added] the base of knowledge which is unambiguously indicated as relevant for professional education is also not given.[7]

Glazer and Schein share an epistemology of professional practice that I call positivist because it is rooted historically in the positivist philosophy, which so powerfully shaped both the modern university and the modern conception of the proper relationship between valid theory and rigorous practice.[8] The positivist epistemology of practice still underlies the curriculum that follows the hierarchy of professional knowledge: first, the relevant basic science, then the relevant applied science, and finally, a practicum in which students learn to apply classroom knowledge to the problems of practice. The dominant conception of the proper relations between research and practice is still very much what Thorstein Veblen propounded some seventy years ago.[9]

The university and the research institute are devoted to the production of new knowledge in the protected setting of the scholar's study or in the carefully controlled environment of the scientific laboratory. They are kept separate from the relatively unprotected and uncontrollable context of practitioners whose purpose is the useful application of knowledge. Research and practice are in a relationship of exchange: Researchers are supposed to give practitioners theories and techniques for solving day-to-day problems, and practitioners are supposed, in return, to give researchers new problems to work on and practical tests of the utility of their results.

The positivist epistemology of practice depends critically on separating research from practice, but it also depends on separating ends from means and knowing from doing.

Rigorous professional practice is conceived as essentially technical, using described, tested, replicable techniques of problem diagnosis and solution. According to this view, professional problem solving can be objective, consensual, cumulative, and convergent. But for practice to be technical, it must be oriented to clear and fixed ends, like Glazer's examples of profit, health, and success in litigation. Technical means, on the other hand, are considered to be variable; their appropriateness varies with the situation. It is the business of applied science to provide a rigorous basis for selecting the means best suited to established ends. Means and ends are conceived as separately defined and determined, so the solution of means-ends (instrumental) problems can be seen as a technical activity.

If professional practice is thought to be technical and science-based, then it must also be seen as consisting of a kind of knowing—problem solving, judging, or deciding. The practitioner is supposed to use research-based theory and technique to *decide* on the strategies best suited to solving instrumental problems. When rigorous practice is equated with rigorous deciding, the actual "doing" comes to be seen as simply implementing technically sound decisions.

It is not hard to understand why those committed, explicitly or implicitly, to this model of technical rationality should be troubled by uncertainty, complexity, instability, professional pluralism, and the irreducible element of art in practice. Each of these phenomena transcends the dichotomies of technical rationality. In the conversion of uncertain situations to technical problems, on which technical rationality depends, ends and means are *reciprocally* determined. Artistry is in the doing as well as in the knowing. And conflicts of professional paradigms affect research as well as practice; they cannot be resolved for practice by research.

The Dilemma of Rigor or Relevance

The positivist epistemology of practice contributes to an urgent and essential dilemma that I call the dilemma of rigor or relevance. In the dominant view of professional rigor, which prevails in universities and is embedded in the institutions of professional education and research, rigorous practice depends on "well-formed" problems of choice of strategy amenable to solutions from research-based theory and technique.[10] But real problems do not come well formed. They tend to present themselves, on the contrary, as messy, indeterminate situations. A civil engineer's question of what road to build, for example, cannot be solved by an application of locational techniques or by decision theory. The engineer confronts a complex, ill-defined situation, and usually one in which geographic, financial, economic, and political factors are all mixed up together. A well-formed problem must be constructed from the materials of the problematic situation, and the problem of problem setting is not a well-formed problem.[11]

A practitioner sets a problem by choosing what to treat as the "things" of the situation, deciding what to attend to and what to ignore. This choice frames the "things" in an appreciative context that sets a direction for action. A vague worry about hunger or malnourishment may be framed, for example, as a problem of selecting an optimal diet. But situations of malnourishment may be framed in many different ways.[12] The debates of economists, environmental scientists, nutrition scientists, agronomists, planners, engineers, and political scientists over the nature of malnourishment have given rise to a multiplicity of problem settings worthy of *Rashomon*. Indeed, the practice of malnourishment planning is largely taken up with constructing the problem to be solved.

When practitioners succeed in converting a problematic situation to a well-formed problem or in resolving a conflict over the proper framing of a practitioner's role in a situation, they engage in a kind of inquiry that cannot be subsumed under a model of technical problem solving. It is through the work of naming and framing that the exercise of technical rationality becomes possible.

Similarly, the artistic processes by which practitioners make sense of unique cases, and the art they sometimes bring to everyday practice, do not meet the prevailing criteria of rigorous practice. Competent practitioners recognize phenomena like the families of symptoms associated with a disease, the peculiarities of a building site, or the irregularities of materials, for which they cannot give a complete, or often even a reasonably accurate, description. They make judgments of quality for which they cannot state adequate criteria and display skills for which they cannot describe procedures or rules.

It is the centrality of problem setting and of such artistic processes as these, together with the prevailing, institutionalized commitment to the positivist epistemology of practice, that create the dilemma of rigor or relevance. By defining rigor only in terms of technical rationality, we exclude much of what competent practitioners actually do, including the skillful performances on which technical problem solving depends. Indeed, we exclude the most important components of competent practice.

In the varied topography of professional practice, there is a high, hard ground that overlooks a swamp. On the high ground, manageable problems lend themselves to solution through research-based theory and technique. In the swampy lowland, problems are messy, confusing, and incapable of technical solution. The irony is that the problems of the high ground tend to be relatively unimportant, however great their technical interest may be, while in the swamp lie the problems of greatest human concern. Practitioners are confronted with the choice of remaining on the high ground and solving relatively unimportant problems according to rigorous standards or descending into the swamp of important problems and nonrigorous inquiry.

In medicine, engineering, and agronomy, three of Glazer's major or near-major professions, there are areas in which problems are clearly defined, goals are relatively fixed, and phenomena lend themselves to available theory and technique. Here practitioners can function effectively as technical experts. But when one or more of these conditions is lacking, competent performance is no longer a matter of exclusively technical expertise. Medical technologies like kidney dialysis or tomography have created demands that stretch the nation's willingness to invest in medical care. How should physicians behave? How should they try to influence or accommodate to health policy? Engineering solutions that seem powerful and elegant when judged from a relatively narrow perspective may have a wider range of consequences that degrade the environment, generate unacceptable risk, or put excessive demands on scarce resources. How should engineers take these factors into account? When agronomists recommend efficient methods of soil cultivation that favor large land-holdings, they may undermine the small family farms on which peasant economies depend. How should the practice of agronomy take such considerations into account? These are not problems, properly speaking, but problematic situations from which problems must be constructed. Practitioners must approach them through kinds of inquiry that are, according to the dominant model of technical rationality, unrigorous.

The doctrine of technical rationality, promulgated and maintained in the universities and especially in the professional schools, infects the young professional in training with a hunger for technique. Many students of urban planning, for example, are impatient with anything other than "hard skills." In schools of management, students often chafe under the discipline of endless case analyses; they want to learn the techniques and algorithms that are, as they see it, the key to high starting salaries. Yet professionals who really tried to confine their practice to the rigorous application of research-based technique would find not only that they could not work on the most important problems but that they could not practice in the real world at all.

Nearly all professional practitioners experience some version of the dilemma of rigor or relevance, and they may respond to it in several ways. They may choose the swampy lowland, deliberately immersing themselves in confusing but crucially important situations. When asked to describe their methods of inquiry, they speak of experience, trial and error, intuition, and muddling through. When teachers, social workers, or planners operate in this vein, they tend to be afflicted with a nagging sense of inferiority to those who present themselves as models of technical rigor. When physicians or engineers do so, they may be troubled by the discrepancy between the technical rigor of the "hard" zones of their practice and the apparent sloppiness of the "soft" ones.

Those who opt for the high ground confine themselves to a narrowly technical practice and pay a price for doing so. Operations research, systems analysis, policy analysis, and management science are examples of practices built around formal, analytic models. In the early years of the development of these professions, following World War II, there was a climate of optimism about the power of formal modeling for the solutions of real-world problems. In subsequent decades, however, there has been a growing recognition of the limits of these techniques, especially in situations of high complexity and uncertainty.[13] Some practitioners have responded by confining themselves to the limited class of problems, for example, to inventory control. Others have continued to develop formal models for problems of high complexity and uncertainty, quite undeterred by the troubles incurred whenever a serious attempt is made to put their models into practice. They may become researchers pursuing evolving questions of modeling theory and technique, increasingly divergent from the context of actual practice. Or they may try to cut the situations of practice to fit their models. This procrustean strategy is a further response to the dilemma of rigor or relevance.

The procrustean response makes use of a variety of strategies. Some practitioners may employ selective inattention, blocking out the phenomena that do not fit their models.[14] Educators may preserve their confidence in competence testing, for example, by simply ignoring the kinds of understanding and skill that competence testing fails to detect. Others may use catch-all or junk categories to explain away discrepant data, as when physicians or therapists use the term "patient resistance" to dismiss the cases in which an indicated treatment fails to cure.[15] Or practitioners may try to be effective by exerting unilateral control over the practice situation, for example, by removing "rebellious" or "slow-learning" children from the classroom.

All such responses to the dilemma of rigor or relevance protect the positivist epistemology of practice. Those who confine themselves to the limited range of technical problems or cut the situations of practice to fit available models and techniques seek a world in which technical rationality works. Those who choose the swamp tend to pay homage to the prevailing models of rigor; what they know how to do, they have no way of describing as rigorous.

Writers about the professions tend to follow similar paths. Both Glazer and Schein recognize, for example, that professional practice manifests uncertainty, instability, and uniqueness, but they try to square their recognition of these phenomena with their underlying epistemology of practice. Glazer localizes uncertainty and instability in the "minor" professions, of which he despairs. Schein treats applied and basic science as increasingly "convergent" while locating the "divergent" phenomena of uncertainty, complexity, and uniqueness in the concrete situations of practice. He believes that practitioners match convergent knowledge to divergent practice by the exercise of "divergent skills."[16] About these, however, he can say very little; for in his mainstream view of professional knowledge, if divergent skills fall into the category of theory or technique, they belong on another level of the hierarchy of knowledge. And if divergent skills are neither theory nor technique, how can they be described? They are a kind of junk category that protects an underlying model of technical rationality.

Yet the epistemology of practice embedded in our universities and research institutions, in habits of thought about professional knowledge, and in the dilemma of rigor or relevance has lost its hold on the field that nurtured it. Philosophers of science no longer want to be called positivists.[17] There is a rebirth of interest in the ancient topics of craft, artistry, and myth, the fate of which positivism seemed once to have finally sealed. Positivism and its epistemology of practice now seem to rest on a particular *view* of science that has been largely discredited.

It is timely, then, to reconsider the question of professional knowledge. Perhaps there is an epistemology of practice that takes full account of the competence practitioners sometimes display in situations of complexity, uncertainty, and uniqueness. Perhaps there is a way of looking at problem setting and intuitive artistry that renders these activities describable and proves them susceptible to a different kind of rigor. The following section describes my approach to the development of such a view.

Reflection-in-Action

When we go about the spontaneous, intuitive performance of the actions of everyday life, we show ourselves to be knowledgeable in a special way. Often, we cannot say what it is that we know. When we try to describe it, we are at a loss. Our knowing is ordinarily tacit, implicit in our patterns of action and in our feel for the stuff with which we are dealing; our knowing is *in* our action. Similarly, the workaday life of the professional practitioner reveals in its recognition, judgments, and skills a pattern of tacit knowing-in-action.

Once we put aside the model of technical rationality, which categorizes intelligent practice as an *application* of knowledge to instrumental decisions, there is nothing strange about the idea that a kind of knowing is inherent in intelligent action. Common sense admits the category of know-how, and it does not stretch common sense very much to say that the know-how is *in* the action—that, for example, a tightrope walker's know-how lies in and is revealed by the way she takes her trip across the wire, or that a major-league pitcher's know-how is in his way of pitching to a batter's weakness, changing his pace, or distributing his energy over the course of a game. Nothing in common sense makes us say that know-how consists of rules or plans in the mind prior to action. Although we sometimes think before acting, it is also true that in much of the spontaneous behavior of skillful practice we reveal a kind of knowing that does not stem from prior intellectual operation.

As Gilbert Ryle has put it,

> What distinguishes sensible from silly operations is not their parentage but their procedure, and this holds no less for intellectual than for practical performances. "Intelligent" cannot be defined in terms of "intellectual" or "knowing *how*" in terms of "knowing *that*"; "thinking what I am doing" does not connote "both thinking what to do and doing it". When I do something intelligently . . . I am doing one thing and not two. My performance has a special procedure or manner, not special antecedents.[18]

And Andrew Harrison has recently put the same thought in this pithy phrase: when someone acts intelligently, he "acts his mind."[19]

Over the years, several writers have been struck by the fact that skillful action often reveals a "knowing more than we can say." Chester Barnard wrote of the "non-logical processes" that are not capable of being expressed in words or as reasoning, that are only made known by a judgment, decision, or action. His examples included anyone's judgment of distance in ball-throwing, a high school student's solving quadratic equations, and a practiced accountant's taking "a balance sheet of considerable complexity and within minutes or even seconds [getting] a significant set of facts from it."[20] Michael Polanyi, who invented the phrase "tacit knowing," drew examples from the recognition of faces and from the use of tools, where, for example, the feeling of a probe in our hand becomes transparent to a "sense of its point touching the objects we are exploring."[21] Geoffrey Vickers pointed out that not only in artistic judgments but in all of our ordinary judgments of quality, we "can recognize and describe deviations from a norm very much more clearly than we can describe the norm itself."[22]

In examples like these, knowing has the following properties:

1. There are actions, recognitions, and judgments that we know how to carry out spontaneously; we do not have to think about them prior to or during their performance.
2. We are often unaware of having learned to do these things; we simply find ourselves doing them.
3. In some cases, we were once aware of the understandings that were subsequently internalized. In others, we may never have been aware of them. In both situations, however, we are usually unable to describe the knowing which our action reveals.

It is in this sense that I speak of knowing-*in*-action, the characteristic mode of ordinary practical knowledge.

If common sense recognizes knowing-in-action, it also recognizes that we sometimes think about what we are doing. Phrases like "thinking on your feet," "keeping your wits about you," and "learning by doing" suggest not only that we can think about doing something but that we can think about doing something while doing it. Some of the most interesting examples of this process occur in the midst of a performance.

When good jazz musicians improvise together, they manifest a "feel for" their material and make on-the-spot adjustments to what they hear. Listening to one another and to themselves, they feel where the music is going and adjust their playing accordingly. They can do this because, first of all, their collective musical invention uses a metric, melodic, and harmonic schema familiar to all the participants that gives a predictable order to the piece. In addition, each musician has a repertoire of musical figures that can be delivered at appropriate moments. Improvisation consists in varying, combining, and recombining a set of figures within the schema that gives bounds and coherence to the performance. As the musicians feel the direction of the music developing out of their interwoven contributions, they make new sense of it and adjust their performance to the new sense they have made. They are reflecting-in-action on their collective music and their individual contributions to it, thinking what they are doing, and, in the process, evolving their way of doing it. Of course, we need not suppose they reflect-in-action with the medium of words. More likely, they reflect through a "feel for the music" not unlike a pitcher's "feel for the ball."

Much reflection-in-action hinges on the experience of surprise. When intuitive, spontaneous performance yields nothing more than the expected results, we tend not to think about it. Sometimes, however, intuitive performance leads to surprises that may be pleasing and promising or unwanted. In either case, we may respond to surprise by reflection-in-action. Like a baseball pitcher, we may reflect on our "winning habits;" or, like a jazz musician, on our sense of the music we have been making; or, like a designer, on the misfit we have unintentionally created. In such processes, reflection tends to focus interactively on the outcomes of action, the action itself, and the intuitive knowing implicit in the action.

Professional practitioners, such as physicians, managers, and teachers, also reflect-in-action, and the character of their reflection indicates how professional practice is both different from and similar to other kinds of action.

When we speak of a lawyer's practice, we refer to the kinds of activities performed, the kinds of clients served, the kinds of cases handled. When we speak of practicing the piano, we refer to the repetitive and experimental processes by which someone tries to become more proficient on that instrument. The two senses of "practice" are distinct but related to each other in an interesting way. Professional practice also includes a necessary element of repetition. Professional practitioners are specialists who encounter certain types of situations again and again, building, in the process, a repertoire of expectations, examples, images, and techniques. Experiencing many variations on a relatively small number of types of cases, professionals are able to "practice," and their knowing-in-practice tends to become increasingly tacit, spontaneous, and automatic, thereby conferring on them and their clients the benefits of specialization. On the other hand, this specialization can lead to a parochial narrowness of vision or it can induce a kind of overlearning that takes the form of a tacit pattern of error to which the practitioner becomes selectively inattentive.

Reflection can serve as a corrective to overlearning. Through reflection, practitioners can become aware of and criticize the tacit understandings that have grown up around the repetitive experiences of a specialized practice, and they can experience and make new sense of situations of uncertainty and uniqueness. This inquiry may be retrospective reflection *on* past practice, undertaken either in a spirit of idle speculation or in a deliberate effort to prepare for future cases. Or it may be reflection on practice while in the midst of it, that is, during an interval of time, whatever its length, in which an action can still make a difference to the situation.

The possible objects of this reflection are as varied as the kinds of phenomena and the knowing-in-practice a professional brings to them: the feeling for a situation that has led to a particular course of action, the way a problem has been framed, or the role the professional has carved out within a larger institutional context. In all of these modes, reflection-in-action is central to the art through which practitioners sometimes cope with the "divergent" situations of practice.

When the phenomenon at hand eludes the ordinary categories of knowledge-in-practice, presenting itself as unique or unstable, a practitioner may recognize and criticize his or her initial understanding of the phenomenon, construct a new description of it, and test the new description by an on-the-spot experiment. Sometimes the practitioner arrives at a new theory of the phenomenon by articulating a feeling about it.

Stuck in a problematic situation that cannot readily be converted to a manageable problem, practitioners may construct new ways of setting the problem, new frames to try to impose on the situation. Confronted with demands that seem incompatible or inconsistent, they may respond by reflecting on the appreciations that they and others have brought to the situation. A dilemma may be attributed to the way the problem was set or even to the way the professional's role was framed. The practitioner may then find a way of integrating, or choosing among, the values at stake in the situation.

The following examples, both drawn from the field of education, seem to me to be very good prototypes of an important kind of reflection in and on professional practice.

In his mid-thirties, sometime between writing *The Cossacks* and *War and Peace*, Lev Nikolayevitch Tolstoy became interested in education. He started a school for peasant children on his estate at Yasnaya Polyana, visited Europe to learn the latest educational methods, and published an educational journal, also called *Yasnaya Polyana*. Before he was done (his new novel eventually replaced his interest in education) he had built some seventy schools, had created an informal teacher-training program, and had written an exemplary piece of educational evaluation.

For the most part, the methods of the European schools filled him with disgust, yet he was entranced by Rousseau's writings on education. His own school anticipated John Dewey's approach to learning by doing and bore the stamp of his conviction that good teaching required "not a method but an art." In an essay, "On Teaching the Rudiments," he described his notion of art in the teaching of reading:

> Every individual must, in order to acquire the art of reading in the shortest possible time, be taught quite apart from any other, and therefore there must be a separate method for each. That which forms an insuperable difficulty to one does not in the least keep back another, and vice versa. One pupil has a good memory, and it is easier for him to memorize the syllables than to comprehend the vowellessness of the consonants; another reflects calmly and will comprehend a most rational sound method; another has a fine instinct, and he grasps the law of word combinations by reading whole words at a time.
>
> The best teacher will be he who has at his tongue's end the explanation of what it is that is bothering the pupil. These explanations give the teacher the knowledge of the greatest possible number of methods, the ability of inventing new methods and, above all, not a blind adherence to one method but the conviction that all methods are one-sided, and that the best method would be the one which would answer best to all the possible difficulties incurred by a pupil, that is, not a method but an art and talent.
>
> Every teacher must . . . by regarding every imperfection in the pupil's comprehension, not as a defect of the pupil, but as a defect of his own instruction, endeavor to develop in himself the ability of discovering new methods. . . .[23]

An artful teacher sees a child's difficulty in learning to read not as a defect in the child "but as a defect of his own instruction"; so the teacher must do a piece of on-the-spot experimental research to find an explanation of "what it is that is bothering the pupil" and a method that answers to the pupil's difficulties. The teacher cannot assume that the repertoire of explanations, even though they are "at his tongue's end," will suffice, but must be ready to invent new methods for *this* pupil and "develop the ability of discovering" them.

Over the last two years, researchers at MIT have undertaken a program of in-service education for teachers organized around the idea of on-the-spot reflection and experiment, very much as in Tolstoy's art of teaching. In this Teacher Project,[24] a small group of teachers have explored their own intuitive thinking about apparently simple tasks in such domains as mathematics, physics, music, and astronomy. The teachers have made some important discoveries. They have allowed themselves to become confused about subjects they are supposed to "know"; and as they have tried to work their way out of their confusions, they have also begun to think differently about learning and teaching.

Early in the project, a critical event occurred. The teachers were asked to observe and react to a videotape of two boys playing a simple game. The boys sat at a table, separated from one another by an opaque screen. In front of one boy, blocks of various colors, shapes, and sizes were arranged in a pattern. In front of the other, similar blocks were lying on the table in no particular order. The first boy was to tell the second one how to reproduce the pattern. After the first few instructions, however, it became clear that the second boy had gone astray. In fact, the two boys had lost touch with one another, though neither of them knew it.

In their initial reactions to the videotape, the teachers spoke of a "communications problem." They said that the instruction giver had "well-developed verbal skills" and that the receiver was "unable to follow directions." Then one researcher pointed out that, although the blocks contained no green squares—all squares were orange and only triangles were green—she had heard the first boy tell the second to "take a green square." When the teachers watched the videotape again, they were astonished. That small mistake had set off a chain of false moves. The second had put a green thing, a triangle, where the first boy's pattern had an orange square, and from then on, all the instructions became impossible to follow. Under the circumstances, the second boy seemed to have displayed considerable ingenuity in attempting to reconcile the instructions with the pattern before him.

At this point, the teachers reversed their views. They now could see why the second boy behaved as he did. He no longer seemed stupid; he had, indeed, "followed instructions." As one teacher put it, they were now "giving him reason." They saw reasons for his behavior; his errors, which they had previously seen as the result of an inability to follow directions, they now found reasonable.

Later on in the project, as the teachers increasingly challenged themselves to discover the meaning of a child's puzzling behavior, they often spoke of "giving him reason."

In examples such as these, something falls outside the range of ordinary expectations. Tolstoy thought of each of his pupils as an individual with unique ways of learning and imperfections. The teachers were astonished by the sense behind a student's mistake. In both instances, the practitioners experienced surprise, puzzlement, or confusion in an uncertain or unique situation and reflected on the current phenomena and on prior understandings. They carried out experiments to generate both a new understanding of the phenomena and a change in the situation.

Someone reflecting-in-action becomes a researcher in the context of practice, not depending on established theory and technique, but constructing a new theory about the unique case. To such a researcher, means and ends are not separate but are defined interactively in framing a problematic situation. Thinking is not separate from doing; because the experimenting is a kind of action, implementation is built into the inquiry. Thus, reflection-in-action can proceed even in situations of uncertainty or uniqueness because it is not bound by the dichotomies of technical rationality.

Although reflection-in-action is an extraordinary process, it is not a rare event; indeed, for some it is the core of practice. Nevertheless, because professionalism is still mainly identified with technical expertise, reflection-in-action is not generally accepted—even by those who do it—as a legitimate form of professional knowing.

Many practitioners, locked into a view of themselves as technical experts, find nothing in the world of practice to occasion reflection. They have become too skillful at the techniques of selective inattention, junk categories, and situational control, techniques that preserve the constancy of their knowledge-in-practice. For them, uncertainty is a threat; its admission is a sign of weakness. Others, more inclined toward and adept at reflection-in-action, nevertheless feel profoundly uneasy because they cannot say what they know how to do, cannot justify its quality or rigor.

For these reasons, the study of reflection-in-action is critically important. The dilemma of rigor or relevance may be dissolved by developing an epistemology of practice that places technical problem solving within a broader context of reflective inquiry and shows how reflection-in-action may be rigorous in its own right. We may thereby increase the legitimacy of reflection-in-action, encourage its wider use, and foster the kinds of rigor appropriate to it.

Notes

1. Everett Hughes, "The Study of Occupations," in Robert K. Merton and Leonard Broom, eds., *Sociology Today*, Basic Books, New York, 1959.

2. Kenneth Lynn, Introduction to "The Professions," *Daedalus*, special issue, vol. 92, no. 4, Fall, 1963, p. 649.

3. James Gustafson, "The Clergy in the United States," *Daedalus*, vol. 92, no. 4, Fall, 1963, p. 724; and William Alonso, "Cities and City Planners," *Daedalus*, vol. 92, no. 4, Fall, 1963, p. 838.

4. Edgar Schein, *Professional Education*, McGraw-Hill, New York, 1973, p. 43.

5. Nathan Glazer, "The Schools of the Minor Professions," *Minerva*, Vol. 12, no. 3, July, 1974.

6. Ibid., p. 363.

7. Ibid.

8. For a discussion of positivism and its influence on prevailing epistemological views, see Jergen Habermas, *Knowledge and Human Interests*, Beacon Press, Boston, 1968. And for a discussion of the influence of positivist doctrines on the shaping of the modern university, see Edward Shils, "The Order of Learning in the United States from 1865 to 1920: the Ascendancy of the Universities," *Minerva*, Vol. 16, no. 2, Summer, 1978.

9. Thorstein Veblen, *The Higher Learning in America* (1918), A. M. Kelley, New York, 1965.

10. I have taken this term from Herbert Simon, who gives a particularly useful example of a well-formed problem in his *The Sciences of the Artificial*, MIT Press, Cambridge, Mass., 1972.

11. Martin Rein and I have written about problem setting in "Problem-Setting in Policy Research," in Carol Weiss, ed., *Using Social Research in Public Policy Making*, D. C. Heath, Lexington, Mass., 1977.

12. For an example of multiple views of the malnourishment problem see Alan Berg, Nevin S. Scrimshaw, and David L. Call, eds., *Nutrition, National Development, and Planning*, MIT Press, Cambridge, Mass., 1973.

13. See Russell Ackoff, "The Future of Operational Research is Past," *Journal of Operational Research Soc.*, Vol. 30, no. 2, 1979, pp. 93–104.

14. I have taken this phrase from the work of the psychiatrist Harry Stack Sullivan.

15. The term is Clifford Geertz's. See his *The Interpretation of Cultures: Selected Essays by Clifford Geertz*, Basic Books, New York, 1973.

16. Schein, op. cit., p. 44.

17. As Richard Bernstein has written (*The Restructuring of Social and Political Theory*, Harcourt, Brace, Jovanovich, New York, 1976), "There is not a single major thesis advanced by either nineteenth-century Positivists or the Vienna Circle that has not been devastatingly criticized when measured by the Positivists' own standards for philosophical argument. The original formulations of the analytic-synthetic dichotomy and the verifiability criterion on meaning have been abandoned. It has been effectively shown that the Positivists' understanding of the natural sciences and the formal disciplines is grossly oversimplified. Whatever one's final judgment about the current disputes in the post-empiricist philosophy and history of science . . . there is rational agreement about the inadequacy of the original Positivist understanding of science, knowledge and meaning."

18. Gilbert Ryle, "On Knowing How and Knowing That," in his *The Concept of Mind*, Hutcheson, London, 1949, p. 32.

19. Andrew Harrison, *Making and Thinking*, Hackett, Indianapolis, 1978.

20. Chester Barnard, *The Functions of the Executive* (1938), Harvard University Press, Cambridge, Mass., 1968, p. 306.

21. Michael Polanyi, *The Tacit Dimension*, Doubleday, New York, 1967, p. 12.

22. Geoffrey Vickers, unpublished memorandum, MIT, 1978.

23. Leo Tolstoy, "On Teaching the Rudiments," in *Tolstoy on Education*, Leo Wiener, ed., University of Chicago Press, Chicago, 1967, pp. 58–59.

24. The staff of the Teacher Project consisted of Jeanne Bamberger, Eleanor Duckworth, and Margaret Lampert. My description of the incident of "giving the child reason" is adapted from a project memorandum by Lampert, 1981.

W. N. HUBBARD, JR.

——— **24** ———

The Creation and Utilization
of Knowledge in
the Business Community

A business is generally concerned with obtaining or creating only knowledge demonstrably useful in performing the work for which the particular business exists. In seeking such knowledge, a business is extremely pragmatic, just as ready to accept folk knowledge as scholarly knowledge. It is as interested in acquiring the noncognitive, or experiential, knowledge as knowledge derived from systematic or scientific inquiry. It is, in a word, eclectic in its approach and, to the casual observer, may even appear uncritical or, in some cases, unappreciative of the elegance of exact explanation and the beauty of succinct descriptions of orderliness—most especially when these are expressed in mathematical terms.

This appearance is misleading. Scholarly knowledge is generally disciplinary and is derived from inquiry, using a reductionist strategy to obtain less complex and more precise hypotheses. The utility of scholarly knowledge depends upon highly selective organization into a frame of reference created by a natural problem of great complexity and imprecision. In the business setting, inquiry that leads to decisions for action is made in response to this larger problem itself, utilizing a variety of types of knowledge. It is a situation somewhat analogous to the physician's dealing with the whole entity of a person's illness, utilizing, as appropriate, the scholarly knowledge of the many sciences basic to clinical medicine and an experiential and idiosyncratic knowledge of the patient.

The concept of "business" is itself an analytical construct without precise definition and is used in such an enormous variety of contexts

333

that it is difficult to describe the characteristics covered by the term. There is the defense industry, which is an inextricable complex with government. There is the communications business, including the constitutionally protected function of the mass media. There is the doctor business, which originates in the high value attributed to personal health. There is the publicly supported education industry, which, along with agriculture, has a special place in the peculiar history of the evolution of institutions called universities in this country. There are the businesses of energy, of transportation, of housing, of entertainment, and of recreation. There is a major business devoted to cosmetics, to odor suppressors and enhancers. There is an enormous business devoted to serving the self-destructive abuse of alcohol, automobiles, and tobacco. There are local and multinational businesses. There are financial businesses dealing only in money and its surrogates. There are low-technology businesses, such as the manufacture of clothing, and high-technology businesses, such as the manufacture of pharmaceuticals. There are many criminal businesses that rival in size all but the largest legitimate firms. There are, of course, schools of business that deal with the generalizations that apply to this enormous variety of enterprises; but even there, specialization is now the order of the day. I am representing the senior management of a highly specialized business and I will focus on a high-technology international manufacturing and distributing corporation that receives no government grants and contracts for its production and is in competition with its counterparts. My comments are therefore intrinsically limited in their application.

How Business Uses Knowledge

The acquisition and utilization of knowledge in such a business setting results from three broad streams of countervailing forces.

Managing People

First, there is the need to make *efficient* use of available resources in order to produce current earnings. The most important and the most difficult resource to manage is people. The classic social tension between the individuals that compose a group and the group itself is reflected by persons in the corporate business setting. By far the largest single direct operating expense in a business is the support of persons employed. The productivity of the enterprise depends in the first instance on the capacity of the people working to make effective use of corporate resources. Physical facilities and equipment, along with the materials that move through them and the information that is processed by them, all require particular and efficient utilization if the end product of the enterprise is to be competitive in terms of quality, availability, and cost. The independent initiative of an individual is the essential ingredient of adaptive change. The ability to recognize and reward individual achievement is essential if such effort is to be reinforced so that advancement reflects personal merit. Each person has to be recognized if work tasks are to be self-fulfilling for all. Finally, those people who are naturally interactive in their work should—as a group—have some acknowledged responsibility for the quality and efficiency of their efforts. These precepts are characteristic of personnel practices that have gained increasingly general acceptance over the last twenty years.

Set against this is the need for predictable, stable relationships in a business organization that is made up of tens or even hundreds of thousands of people distributed over wide geographic areas. Different national, cultural, and political environments require their own distinct patterns of personnel management. From the union-dominated atmosphere of Great Britain to the company affiliation of Japan, from the countries of North America to those of Middle and South America, variety defeats standardized practice. To maintain order, a centralized authority is necessary for policy, reporting procedure, financial accounting standards, and commitment to quality and standards of business practice. Without any central authority, advantages of common purpose and efficiencies inherent in a large scale will be lost as size increases.

The social and behavioral sciences have contributed mightily to the validation of the precepts of respect for the individual and the working group as the foundation of effective management of human resources. Industrial engineering, financial analysis, accounting practice, and the history of corporations that have prospered or failed over two or three generations give eloquent and irrefutable confirmation of the necessity of central authority.

The problems of managing human resources arise in the inevitable tensions generated by the opposing poles of central authority and individual self-fulfillment. There is, in my view, no stable and symmetrical balance to be found, but rather a dynamic ebb and flow of adaptation that substitutes for equilibrium.

Managing Money

Second, there is that resource, money, which has to be acquired and managed efficiently if the people, plant, and materials are to exist, adapt, and grow. There is a very large body of knowledge derived from the need to use fiscal and material resources efficiently—indeed, to optimize their use. Here, too, the knowledge pertaining to the short term (months or a few years) as contrasted with the long term (many years or a few decades) creates a field of tension that is complicated by changing political attitudes toward profits.

The knowledge of the efficient use of resources that is valid within one disciplinary field cannot be transposed intact to apply to a large natural problem. Just as surely, the necessary decision for action on a problem should be taken with as little uncertainty as possible, so systematic knowledge is required in the problem's analysis. Relevant knowledge may either enhance or diminish the success of decision making. Unhappily, most knowledge has little relevance to a given problem, and zealously assembling the largest array of knowledge may confuse or delay a timely decision. The danger is in choosing one or the other extreme of accumulating knowledge rather than seeking the best available accommodation within the highly unstable field between the poles.

The second directing force is the need to survive over the long term. The administration of the modern corporation tends to assume there will be an indefinite, if not permanent, corporate life span. To have such a long-term survival, a corporate entity must adapt positively to changes in the general society, but more particularly to changes in those segments that contain the market for the goods or services being produced. For such survival, a corporation must be innovative to avoid the syndrome of the business optimized for "buggy whip" production. (Although this analogy has broad circulation, I am not entirely sure what the immediate innovative successor to the buggy whip was supposed to be; but clearly a new product of some kind was necessary.) In practice, innovation is moving away from the inventor model of a Thomas Alva Edison to the more sophisticated model of innovation through the use of scientific methods and knowledge to create a marketable technology.

Long-term corporate survival also implies continuing access to the financial resources required for maintaining solvency while accommodating to broad swings in the economic environment. For instance, the strengthening of the value of the U.S. dollar compared with the currencies of other developed nations is currently being reflected in a drastic decline in the dollar income of U.S.-based companies with a large part of their business in those other developed countries.

In the United States during the late 1950s and early 1960s, the preferred method of obtaining capital was through equity financing, that is, selling the company through stock to public owners. Since the late 1960s and the early 1970s, equity financing has declined to a tiny fraction of its former magnitude, except for utility companies, which have little choice. Twenty years ago, long-term borrowing through bonds dominated the market. More recently, the uncertainty created by inflation has so increased long-term interest rates that bonds maturing in twenty to thirty years have almost vanished and the current value of such bonds has fallen dramatically, discouraging potential buyers even further. Short-term borrowing has become much more important, as have bonds or loans maturing in less than ten years—which are playing the role of "long-term" debt.

These shifts in financing have inevitably increased the importance of current cash flow, with interest costs growing as a cost of doing business. Fewer and fewer businesses can finance capital investment needs from current retained earnings. To maintain a stock price in excess of the corporate assets (that is, book value) and to maintain access to the most favorable vehicle for borrowing, current earnings assume predominant importance. Rapid payback of investment and the possibility of near-term rather than long-term growth become increasingly important in decision making. The largest firms thereby gradually lose their international competitiveness for lack of capital investment, while entrepreneurial small businesses find scant opportunity for financing growth at interest costs that allow them to expand to participate in international markets.

The capacity for adaptation, innovation, and accommodation to economic contingencies demands resources that could also be utilized in optimizing current earnings. There is, therefore, a direct competition between simple maximization of current earnings through the most "efficient" use of resources on the one hand and long-term survival of the corporation through adaptation and innovation on the other.

Managing Growth

The third force to be conjured with is the need for continuing growth, both in sales and in earnings. Like any large, complex system, a business corporate entity is a high-entropy phenomenon. The natural tendency of businesses is to dissolve. Yet even so simple a matter as providing employees with upward mobility suggests a constantly growing, rather than a shrinking or even a static, business. Access to money markets for growth depends heavily upon the perception financial analysts have of the corporation's vigor. Therefore, such matters as growing market share and stable earnings margin become prerequisites for ready access to financial markets. Fundamental to such growth is wider acceptance of the goods or services that are produced, a result that implies increasing funds for marketing. Growth requires resources that are invested near term for a future benefit. These same dollars could be utilized for enhancing current earnings.

The process of growth is, in and of itself, energy-consuming, so one must choose the relative emphasis to be placed on current earnings or on growth. The feasible rate of growth is determined by the size of the available market. Since most market opportunities are also open to competitors, prompt action to take advantage of a market potential is essential. Such action may well require very large current investments in facilities, materials, and people—creating a negative cash flow, or at least reduced earnings, during the growth phase. The corporation must acquire large sums to maintain growth itself, and the return on such investment comes at some uncertain future time.

Funds used to support growth could also have been used to support research or to accumulate fiscal assets that would allow adaptation and accommodation to business cycles. Resources to sustain growth must inevitably be allocated in competition with the function of optimizing near-term earnings or the function of long-term survival. The body of knowledge that surrounds each of these three general countervailing forces—current earnings, long-term survival, and growth—is a fair description of the knowledge used in a business enterprise.

The Executive's Role

It is not entirely clear what the body of knowledge used in business actually consists of. Indeed, it is very probable that the role of the executive is to deal with high degrees of uncertainty in realms where knowledge is insufficient. In the obverse, where knowledge in one or more segment of the three realms mentioned above is adequate, the task of decision making is either automated or assigned to the lowest competent level. The executive, rather, is confronted with the simultaneous, interdependent, multivariant, and rapidly changing state of those elements of a business that represent a kind of *problematique* or complexity that cannot readily be described in an orderly way. Dealing with such a system means entering the realm of noncognitive skills and experiential value judgments.

The executive at this level of decision making generally depends on the work of others to make intentions effective. The willingness and fidelity of this *following* will define the degree to which the executive is a leader. Over time, persuasion and performance are more important than position and power in maintaining the executive's leadership position. In a real way, the executive is *permitted* to exercise his or her position by those who deem their own interest to be enhanced thereby. Even so, the changing external conditions surrounding the corporation may require new kinds of relevant expertise, so circumstantial obsolescence may bring the executive's competence to an end. Rarely will an executive have the exact knowledge or the precise experience most relevant to immediate problems; rather, it is when this knowledge and experience do *not* suffice and the inevitable tensions of a large organization *fail* to provide a comfortable compromise that the role of the executive is necessary to defeat entropy.

This same complexity creates a strong incentive toward a reductionist strategy in knowledge management not unlike the one adopted by scientists confronted with complex phenomena. Professional specialists now abound in business. The obverse trend, an increasingly popular one, is to use so-called statistical models of the system in which the significant variables are given relative weights and the outcome is the result of an orderly manipulation of their interdependencies. Suffice it to say that the success of a reductionist strategy in predicting the behavior of an integrated complex system is limited. In like manner, the linear concepts built into almost all statistical models are defeated by the nonlinear character of the actual system itself. Nevertheless, countervailing functions of current earnings, long-term survival, and growth do create a field, albeit a field of tension, within which useful knowledge is constantly sought and consumed.

Motivation for Research

Business is unlikely to seek out knowledge simply because it increases understanding. Rather, the incentive in business for acquiring knowledge and using it effectively is to make an efficient use of current resources, thereby achieving the short-term success that allows the investments necessary for long-term survival and growth in a competitive environment. Business may very well pursue lines of inquiry in its research programs that are as basic to understanding and as innovative as those of any cloistered academic. Academics, on the other hand, are growing more and more sensitive to the commercial value of their basic understanding, even though their initial motivation may be much more personal and even, sometimes, abstract. The potential utility of any knowledge is the prime and exclusive motivation for its creation by industry. In point of fact, however, much of the knowledge created by industry turns out not to be useful and becomes part of the general store of information that serves to enhance understanding. Most innovative technologies fail, and those that succeed are ephemeral. Nevertheless, the process continues.

The fundamental incentive to undertake research is the opportunity for a period of monopolistic use, during which relatively high earnings margins are available. The patent system establishes this period in the case of substances and processes, and copyright law gives much longer protection to composers and authors. Presently, the patent system is threatened by regulatory procedures that consume much of the patent's life, leaving a very short effective period. Also threatening is the frequency with which courts disallow patents issued by the Patent Office.

As high technology derived from electronic, communications, and molecular biology creates the feasibility of enormous new markets, the nationalism and mercantilism of prior centuries is being reincarnated. Open worldwide trade is essential if the huge investments in new technology are to remain the realm of private enterprise. In both Europe and Asia, the role of private corporate enterprise is being blended with the political and nationalistic aims of government. The multinational corporation, the only kind capable of modern, worldwide dissemination of innovation, is increasingly submerged by these political functions. The loss of free trade in high technology among those traditional allies, the democratic nations of the world, is an imminent hazard.

Since their growth and long-term survival depend on research, discovery, innovation, and dissemination, the private corporations will continue to commit themselves to creating knowledge. However, the number of such corporations will increase very little, and the size needed to support an adequate research effort will increase hugely. Since many of the urgent problems of "Spaceship Earth" require technology derived from improved knowledge as a component of their solution, and since innovation has been concentrated in democratic countries at least nominally committed to the market as the preferred means of resource allocation, the present risks and disincentives to corporate research deserve sympathetic efforts aimed at preserving this operative system.

The search for new methodologies or new sensing devices and the exploration of new realms of feasibility are areas of participative concern for business. All these cases, however, are motivated by the application or utilization of the new knowledge rather than by the improved power to acquire knowledge or the expanded understanding it brings. Business is eclectic in its approach to sources of knowledge, and because it must satisfy a need for a "good" or a "service" in order to exchange a "value" with the consumer, it turns out that business is the principal means by which the development and distribution of knowledge without other direct utility are socially validated. Indeed, it may be that the most important contribution business makes over time is to make visible the social utility of improved human understanding. In this, it is both a compatriot of and a competitor with those who deal with knowledge in other settings.

Business is the principal source of funds that move through taxes, philanthropy, or grants to support so-called nonprofit institutions. Business is the interface that adapts general knowledge to social needs. The creation and utilization of knowledge in business therefore represents the institutional characteristics of that particular entity. As a human enterprise, business shares the common characteristics of all human social institutions. To the extent that these interinstitutional differences are valid, it is proper that knowledge is created and utilized differently within that institution we call business than it is in other settings. I have tried to allude to some of these differences. I will leave others to discuss the impediments to transfer of knowledge across the borders of social institutions as an inevitable result of these institutions' differentiation. Whether it is possible, or even desirable, to increase the flow of knowledge at the cost of obfuscating the differential character of the specific social institution that utilizes knowledge is a question that I leave open for response.

EDMUND D. PELLEGRINO

——— **25** ———

Optimizing the Uses of Medical Knowledge

Introduction

> *The arts that promise to keep our bodies and souls in health promise a great deal; but, withal, there are none that less keep their promise.*
> —Montaigne, *Essays* III, 13 (1533–1592)

> *. . . We could be free of an infinitude of maladies both of mind and body, and even possibly of the infirmities of age, if we had sufficient knowledge of their causes and all the remedies which nature has provided us.*
> —Descartes, *Discourse on Method*, Part VI (1596–1650)

Montaigne's petulant skepticism about things medical was justified. The physicians of his time mixed a few astute observations with large measures of diagnostic fancy, artfully deceptive prognoses, and ineffective and dangerous polypharmacy. The sick were well advised to heed Montaigne's advice that they heal themselves.

Descartes, born a few years after Montaigne's death, experienced little that was different in the medical knowledge of his time. His optimism stemmed rather from his philosophical conviction that the body could be understood as a mechanism and repaired the same way. Harvey, his contemporary, showed the way by unraveling the mysteries of blood circulation and the pumping mechanisms of the heart.

Today both Frenchmen, the optimist and the pessimist, would be astounded—as would Harvey—at how much of the promise of medicine has been fulfilled. No branch of human knowledge has expanded more rapidly or with more beneficent results. Today's skepticism has different sources—expectations that exceed even the unprecedented wonders of contemporary medicine, disaffection with the decline in personal attention, confusion over the interpretation of conflicting medical advice, and fear that a triumphant but misdirected technology might inundate ethics.

In contrast with the medicine of Montaigne and Descartes' times, today we know that the methods of experimental science do yield effective and reliable medical knowledge. We know specific treatments can be directed effectively at specific causes. We can extract the active agents from those remedies "nature has provided us" or synthesize our own molecules to act on specific membranes, enzymes, or subcellular organelles.

We are in the age of specific and radical cure and prevention. Polypharmacy, disorderly diagnosis, and ill-informed prognoses persist, but not because we lack the intellectual tools to eradicate them. We know the rules of probabilistic logic and how they apply in diagnosis and the evaluation of therapy as well as the norms of classical and modal logic.

What we are not sure of today is how to use medical knowledge wisely. How do we choose those things that can enhance individual and social good without subjugating ethics to technology? We oscillate between adulating medicine's technical brilliance and rejecting it in a sincere and romanticized but distorted version of humanism.

The questions that would arrest Montaigne and Descartes, were they our contemporaries, relate to the humane use of medical knowledge— the questions of means, ends, purposes, and the relationships among them.

Medicine cannot answer those questions for itself since it lacks a coherent theory in which to ground its responses; its instruments of inquiry are not suited to philosophical questions. Further, a medical education does not prepare physicians for philosophical discourse; it is more likely to inhibit it.

The educated public as well as the physician need a grasp of what medical knowledge may be, together with the norms and mechanisms that should guide its humane and wise use. Without this grasp, we oscillate between Montaigne's pessimism and Descartes' optimism— between medicine as salvation and medicine as nemesis. The same difficulties surround the wise use of all the powerful means contemporary technology puts before us. But the immediacy, effectiveness, and ubiquity of medicine make it the paradigm of the humane use of human knowledge.

This essay will not recount the multitudinous marvels of modern medicine; they are exuberantly exhibited in the public media. We now accept as commonplace what a few years ago we would have found literally unimaginable. This essay aims, rather, at examining three questions: What is the nature of medicine and medical knowledge? In what ways can it be useful to human societies? How can we assure some measure of wisdom in its uses?

The Nature of Medicine and Medical Knowledge

Before we can think about how to use medical knowledge optimally we must be clear about what kind of knowledge it is. The epistemology of medicine has only recently become a topic of serious philosophical interest.[1] To be sure, debates have flourished for centuries about whether to regard medicine as craft, science, art, or one of the humanities. But these debates oversimplify the anatomy of medical knowledge, which is really a mosaic of several different kinds of knowledge gained through several different modes of inquiry and using different rules of evidence and conditions of proof and demonstration.[2]

Even before we can examine the morphology of medical knowledge we must have some clear conception of what medicine itself is. What about medicine differentiates it from other human activities? Does medicine embrace everything that has some remote connection with human well-being, as some would have it? Or is medicine to be confined only to the application of sure methods of technology and science? If these extremes are too broad and too narrow, where between them would we locate medicine?

We cannot distinguish medicine solely by its object of study; for that object is humanity, which every human science studies. But medicine, too, examines the person from a distinctive point of view, that of well- and mal-functioning. It does so with a practical end in view: healing, restoring the balance we call health, whether the balance is disturbed by "disease" as defined by the physician or "illness" as defined by the patient's subjective experiential state. Its end in the clinical encounter is a *right* and *good* healing action for a particular patient. That end is what the patient expects, what society ordains, and what the physician is obliged to provide unless the patient or society declare otherwise.

A right action, in this view, is an action that conforms best with the available scientific information and technology adjusted to the particular needs of *this* patient. It is not a general statement of the scientific principles of diagnosis, prognosis, or therapeutics applicable to *cases* like this. It is rather a statement of how those principles are optimized in choosing an action in the context of age, sex, occupation, severity— all those particular things that make this patient an individual, not just an example of the workings of a scientific law or mechanism. The only morally defensible use of medical knowledge, therefore, is its optimal use.

The peculiar epistemological difficulties in using the general laws of medical scientific knowledge to make particular clinical decisions are well formulated by MacIntyre and Gorowitz in their analysis of the inherent fallibility of medicine.[3] Making a "right" decision in any clinical encounter is a more complex and less certain affair than applying a general law of science to an instance of that law in operation.

What is more, a right healing action is not synonymous with a good healing action. Competence is clearly a necessary—but not a sufficient—condition of a good decision. One can think, for example, of technically right decisions (such as transfusion) that are wrong for a Jehovah's Witness. One can also think of wrong decisions (such as not transfusing when blood is indicated) that are good decisions to the Jehovah's Witness.

To be good, a medical decision should be in the "best interest" of the patient. That interest is not limited to bodily integrity, survival, or even cure of life-threatening illness. What is good for *this* patient is always difficult to define in general terms but includes several elements at a minimum. A good decision enhances the fulfillment and expression of *this* patient's person and life experience. It helps the patient to pursue all freely chosen goals and enhances the humanity of the person who is the patient. It restores precisely those distinctly human capacities that illness erodes—the capacity to make one's own choices without coercion or manipulation, based on a knowledge of the alternatives and in keeping with the patient's evaluation of those alternatives. A good decision is one that is "worthwhile" as defined by the patient's vision of the balance between the aspirations and the reality illness forces upon the patient's life.

A good decision therefore modulates technical rightness with the meanings of the experience of illness for this patient, seen against the patient's meanings of life, suffering, death, and the patient's relationships with God and with other people. A good decision matches as many points as possible in the pattern of this patient's autobiography—the experience of living in a body across time—a pattern shared at some points and asynchronous at others with the patterns of other people's autobiographies. That pattern, even in the most chaotic lives, has meanings the physician can discern only dimly since the experience of another's life and illness is not wholly penetrable. Yet without some penetration of those meanings a good clinical decision is not possible.

To be both right and good the medical decision must be a balanced composite of objectivity and compassion; the physician must stand back, analyze, classify, move from possibly beneficial to most probably beneficial treatments, from statistical and stochastic prognostics to prognostics for *this* patient.

The intellectual challenge is of the most formidable kind. It must take account of Aristotle's and Aquinas's regard for abstractive cognition of general laws. But at the same time, these laws must be seen as instances in particular and concrete—in what is real for *this* person. Essences and particularity must somehow be reconciled.[4] That challenge is one never wholly confronted or fully resolvable. It is nonetheless the challenge of all human decisions that lead to praxis, that move beyond speculative philosophy or scientific theory to influence the lives of people. It is, therefore, the challenge of all knowledge to be used in the practical order, whether in law, medicine, engineering, the ministry, teaching, or politics.

This is ultimately what defines medicine itself as that human activity that eventuates in a right and good healing action for a particular patient or for society. Medicine qua medicine therefore comes into existence only when medical knowledge is used to make right and good healing decisions. In the use of medical knowledge, "optimal" means both right and good.

Medicine is a true *techné* in Plato's sense of knowledge of how to do a thing that is incomplete, as knowledge, until it is used. It is also a model of ethical activity because it must be used for the good of those it serves. In the Aristotelian-Thomist view, medicine qua medicine is primarily a knowledge of right action (a *recta ratio agibilium*) and not primarily a knowledge of making things (*recta ratio factibilium*) or the science, art, or knowledge of the nature of things (*recta ratio speculabilium*). Indeed, medicine is, in Aristotle's sense, a virtue, an exercise in prudence: Selecting the right and best action in a particular circumstance is what the "optimal" use of medical knowledge entails.[5]

To achieve this end medicine uses knowledge of many different kinds; the morphology of medical decisions is a mosaic of several kinds of knowledge. To arrive at a diagnosis, the physician uses scientific knowledge and methods—observation, experiment, measurement, and empirical test—and uses logic that is modal but also statistical and stochastic. The same is true with prognostics and therapeutics. When the "facts" are in, when no more information can be added by observation or test, the process becomes an exercise in dialectics, examining alternative diagnoses, therapies, and outcomes in an orderly and rigorous way.

These different kinds of knowledge converge on a choice, an optimization of outcomes defined by what is "best" for this patient. To make the right decision a good decision, the knowledge of ethics and ethical discourse is crucial. Moreover, the process of decision making must itself be morally conducted (obtaining consent, telling the truth, dealing with conflicts of value, enhancing the moral agency of physician and patient). The end toward which medical decision tends—to what *ought* to be done—is as much an exercise in moral judgment as in scientific.

Once an optimal decision has been made it must be carried out efficiently, competently, and safely. Here medicine does function as an "art," a perfection in executing the acts themselves as well as in executing those activities that lead to the decision, like examining, taking histories, and performing tests.[6]

Medical knowledge, then, is a composite of whatever knowledge is needed to arrive at a right and good healing action and of executing that action with perfection. That knowledge is drawn from all the human sciences—physical, social, and biological—channeled to a specific end and modulated at every stage by the moral imperatives of that end.

Unfortunately what the public and the media, and some clinicians and educators, regard as medical knowledge is too often synonymous only with the newest breakthrough in the laboratory, operating room, or clinic. It is true that the problem of the use of medical knowledge arises largely because of the unprecedented explosion in factual knowledge. But if that knowledge is to be used wisely and optimally, then we must appreciate the varieties of medical knowledge, how they relate to each other, and how each contributes to optimal use of the others.

The view I am advancing leaves little room for reductionist theories of medicine and medical knowledge. Medicine cannot be encompassed in any one model: as a craft, technology, branch of sociology or biology, or as a science with physics as the paradigm. These and other models—ethnomedical, biosocial, molecular, and epidemiological—all have only partial validity because of what each makes comprehensible or what can be studied by their methods. But none by itself constitutes the whole of medicine qua medicine.

This point is fundamental to any consideration of the optimal use of medical knowledge. The sciences can tell us what is true about humankind and its diseases according to its own canons of proof; technology can tell us whether we can solve a particular problem successfully; ethics tells us whether we ought to use that knowledge and for what purpose. Only medicine considers all these questions for *this* person or *this* society as they bear on healing. In fact medicine qua medicine comes into existence only in the clinical encounter when patient and physician decide together what ought to be done. It is the healing action that defines the physician, not the knowledge of biological science, which the biologist has, or the ability to use a drug, which the pharmacologist knows, or the technical proficiency to do operations, which others can master.

The Social Uses of Medical Knowledge

Although I have emphasized how medical knowledge can be used to cure, contain, or prevent illness and disease in individuals, there are two additional uses of medicine. One is social: to enhance the health of human groups; the other, cultural: to shape and to criticize the kind of culture and society in which we live.

Social and public health medicine aim at decisions and actions in the interest and good of society, which implies some definition and valuation of what is "good" for society. If that task is difficult for the individual, how much more complex must it be for a society made up of disparate and often conflicting interests where the "common good" is extremely difficult to discern.

On some things there is more or less agreement, such as immunization against infectious and contagious disorders, sanitation, or sewage treatment. On many others—smoking, diet, nutrition, recreational use of drugs, seat belts, alcoholism, mental health, occupational and environmental hazards—there is far less agreement.

For one thing the results of the widescale societal applications of medical knowledge are uncertain. For another, there are widely differing values about what constitutes a "quality" existence. Smokers aver the risks are worth running, nonsmokers do not; drinkers and nondrinkers, hunters and gun controllers, ecologists and nature exploiters, all differ sharply on what is important for the "good" life.

Yet these conflicts cannot eliminate the prime function of social medicine, to assist in the selection of actions that will advance the good of the whole society, defined in terms of a society's social and political value systems and aspirations. Social, like individual, health is never absolute but rather a minute-to-minute changing balance struck between aspirations and realities. Social illness debilitates society as it does the individual. Healing is likewise more than eliminating obvious pathology.

Decisions to apply medical knowledge on a societal scale cannot be made by the profession alone. Since there are so many interests, it is much more difficult to obtain "consent" than with the individual patient. Yet the same kind of participation in decisions is mandatory.

It is also essential to delimit the pretensions of medical knowledge and society's expectations of the doctor. All social pathology is not remediable by medical means. Crime, violence, racism, familial strife, and war have all been placed at the doorstep of medicine at one time or another. It is essential to define medicine's limits as an instrument of social good and recognize the limited help medical knowledge can offer for such complex social phenomena.

Increasingly, individual and social uses of medical knowledge are coming into conflict with each other. The cumulative effects of individual medical acts have already changed the shape of our society: the effects of life-prolonging treatments and the cure of infectious diseases on the age of the population, or the economic impact of high technology on the allocation of society's resources. Where does medicine's first responsibility lie? Is the physician primarily an instrument of social and economic policy, as in totalitarian regimes, or primarily the agent of the individual patient? I have argued elsewhere that the first responsibility of the physician must be to the one he professes to help, not primarily to society. Yet the physician cannot deny a responsibility for the social consequences of the medical acts taken. This is one of the more difficult of the many exquisite moral questions that surround the optimal use of medical knowledge.

A third way medical knowledge can be used is as a source of criticism of the humaneness of society and culture. The detailed phenomenological knowledge medicine gains in studying health and illness gives it a comprehensive view of the sciences of humanity. Its viewpoint does not absorb the whole of sociology, psychology, biology, or anthropology, nor can medicine be totally subsumed by them. But medicine must unify the data of these human sciences in its decisions and actions; in doing so it works toward a synthesis of what we know about human nature.

Medicine can offer a powerful critique of the kind of society we are fabricating, helping us discern its humaneness—the degree to which it enhances human potentiality, well-being, and even happiness.[7] Any rational critique of our mores must call upon medical observations about the effects of noise pollution, environmental despoliation, recreational drug use, the dissolution of family ties, jet lag, and a hundred other manifestations of our contemporary lifestyle.

Medicine itself must also be the subject of serious social criticism since it continues to be among the most powerful forces shaping human society and its values. Each new technological advance challenges traditional cultural and social values. The actualities of safe abortion, contraception, in vitro fertilization, amniocentesis, and gene recombination have already modified what society considers morally defensible or socially desirable. The optimal use of these techniques and those we cannot yet even imagine constitutes an urgent moral challenge.

Medical knowledge, therefore, is simultaneously a source of criticism and control of the kind of life we wish to live. To use it wisely, we cannot permit ethics to be submerged in our avidity to implement every new technical advance simply because we have it. As we examine each value question critically, we grow in our appreciation of what it is to be human, humane, and civilized. Perhaps we may even gain some perception of the need to shape our society consciously toward humane ends. Medical knowledge is indispensable both to shaping those ends and to critiquing the quality of our performance in attaining them.

In such a delicate act of social cybernetics, we need mechanisms that enable individuals and societies to maintain a creative tension between medical knowledge and human values. We can turn briefly to an outline of some of those mechanisms.

How to Use Medical Knowledge Optimally

If medical knowledge has the socially useful purposes we propose, then how can we assure its optimal use? Optimization implies some norm by which to judge, some set of values that serve as benchmarks of performance. Each of us individually possesses a more or less orderly value set against which to judge whether an action, medical or otherwise, is "worthwhile," as well as norms of what we conceive a good society to be. In a pluralistic society, however, these individual values vary widely and contradict each other. We cannot expect common agreement on what the ultimate norms will be, even though we may hold, as I do, that some norms are more rational than others and deserve universal approbation.

In a pluralistic society, therefore, we cannot proceed deductively from some irrefrangible and transcending values except in a few instances. Our own society holds to democratic values—protecting the rights of individuals, freedom of speech and choice, and participation in government, for example. These values could be abrogated only by profoundly changing the kind of society we aspire to be. In the use of medical knowledge few would overtly wish to sacrifice these values. Indeed, if they did, they would do so in the name of freedom, the rights of individuals, and the good of society.

In a pluralistic and democratic society, then, we cannot think of predetermined optima, but rather of "negotiated" optima, of best solutions where there are conflicting interpretations of what is good. Our emphasis is on process, once we accept the ends of medicine and medical knowledge. These ends have universality while the choices in individual instances may not.

We seek mechanisms to preserve the commonly held values on a democratic society, consistent with the ends of medical knowledge. These are irreducible minima. Within these boundaries, what is "optimal" will emerge from a process of dialectic and negotiation between patients and physicians and between medicine and society.

We will look at two uses of medical knowledge, in clinical and social medicine. We can hardly set rules for a medical criticism of society since the essence of criticism is that it be free to focus on any social or cultural practice or idea that seems irrational, imprudent, intemperate, or inconsistent. The only conditions a critique must meet are those of rational discourse. If the critique results in *action*, then the process of choosing will fall under either of the two categories discussed below.

Negotiated Optima in the Clinical Decision

The clinical encounter between one who is ill and one who professes to heal is at the heart of the optimal use of medical knowledge. Yet the conditions that assure optimal decisions are just beginning to emerge. For the greatest part of medicine's history the physician decided *for* the patient, a choice perceived as optimal by both physicians and patients. With the democratization of society, the education of patients, and the manifest power of medical decisions, this assumption is no longer optimal, either morally or in terms of the ends of medicine as we have defined them.

The optimal use of clinical knowledge depends on certain conditions, some intrinsic to making it right and others to making it good. For a right decision, the physician must be competent, that is, possessing accurate scientific and empirical knowledge and capable of reasoning correctly from that knowledge.

Optimal utilization of this medical knowledge demands a clear perception of what the physician knows, with what degree of certainty and uncertainty; of what is simply not known, and of the distinction between them. To a surprising degree these obvious requirements are too frequently absent. I have outlined elsewhere the ways in which the interests of the patient modulate every step in the medical reasoning process.

Granting that the scientific facts are secure, the most crucial element is a morally sound consent process. Optimally, physician and patient should reach a negotiated optimum together. Each recognizes the other's values, recognizes the points of difference, and decides whether accommodation is possible without compromising principle. Patient and physician are each owed the exercise of their own moral agency. The physician is obliged to educate, advise, and assist, but does not make the decision *for* the patient unless expressly asked to do so or in an emergency when morally valid consent is not possible.

In sum, the right decision becomes a good decision and optimal on both counts when subjected to negotiation based on disclosure of the facts and free of coercion, manipulation, and fear. Thus the technical and moral authority of the physician, for so long combined, must now be separated, allowing the patient's concept of what is good to interact with the physician's. Optimal use of medical knowledge in the clinical setting rests therefore on optimization, not only scientifically but morally. This requires a degree of patient participation and a sophisticated concept of consent not found in traditional professional moral codes. Accommodating this need calls for the most profound alteration of the patient-physician interaction: from a physician-dominated to a physician-facilitated decision-making process.

Optimizing the Social Uses of Medical Knowledge

When we turn to the best use of medical knowledge for society as a whole, we enter the realm of public decisionmaking. Neither the individual physician nor the profession as a corporate body has any special expertise in human values. What is good or worthwhile for a whole society—the allocation of resources among medical techniques or between medical and other social goods like security, environment, housing, and welfare—is not to be determined by physicians alone.

Rather, physicians as physicians are experts whose factual and technical testimony is essential but not sufficient for optimization. Medicine can and should detail accurately what can be done, what alternatives are available, what each may cost, and what dangers to society are inherent in the application of any particular medical knowledge. Only social, public, and legislative action in a democratic society can determine, when the facts are in, whether a certain piece of medical knowledge ought to be applied.

We lack social mechanisms for collectively making important public decisions that depend upon technical expertise. In the optimal uses of medical and other technical knowledge, the central problem is to use expert knowledge for the good of all without surrendering value choices to the expert. A subtle moral tyranny is possible in a technocracy that is as dangerous as the cruder moral tyranny of political despots.

As Stephen Toulmin points out, it is difficult to separate fact and value from each other. I agree with Toulmin that ethics and science must be "reconnected" in some dynamic way. The crucial question is, as he says, "What the proper scope and limits of professional autonomy are and at what points scientists cross the lines separating legitimate professional issues from matters of proper public concern whether political or ethical."[8]

To recognize the need for better connections between scientific and ethical knowledge is, however, not to reduce them to one category of knowledge. There is a realm of knowledge governed by the methods of inquiry, rules of evidence, and modes of knowing best suited to empirical statements, and another realm quite different, best suited to moral and ethical statements.

What is needed is some sort of two-part process. In one, the questions are factual: What in fact do we know? How certain is that knowledge? What is the evidence? In the other, the questions are moral: What value choices are involved? What kind of society do we want? What is it to be human? What are humans for? How do we enhance our lives as humans?[9]

Although it is difficult, it is not impossible to focus on these two domains of knowledge separately. By refining the questions and assigning them to different types of panels, one can achieve a functional separation with practical utility. One panel could be heavily weighted with scientific expertise, the other with moral and ethical expertise. The separate products of these two deliberative bodies could then become the input for discussion and decision by whatever deliberative bodies (usually legislatures) are constituted to decide what ought to be done in the interests of a democratic society.

The negotiated optima, then, in the social uses of medicine arise from a three-way partitioned dialectic among scientists qua scientists, ethicists qua ethicists, and political bodies and decision makers. Through an orderly, critical, and discriminating interaction of these bodies some rationality can be injected into social decisions.

Such a process would forestall some of the wild oscillations in public policy regarding alterations in the American diet to reduce atherosclerosis, the use of exercise to prevent coronary disease, the "safe" levels of chemical toxins in food and environment, the advisability of chemical modifications of learning or social behavior, and a host of other contemporary applications of medical knowledge. The decisions will rarely enjoy the status of metaphysical truth but will at least result from some orderly process subject to change with experience.

Negotiating optima in this way will certainly transfer knowledge between domains. Public policy makers and ethicists need to comprehend the differing kinds of evidence used to establish epidemiological and experimental knowledge. Scientists and policy makers need to appreciate that ethics can be a rigorous pursuit, not just an exercise in ideological and emotional excesses. Scientists and ethicists need to comprehend the complexity of political and social decisions and recognize that the fact-value dialectic must eventually result in a decision to act. An action, unlike a false scientific or ethical conclusion, is not easily retrievable.

The irretrievability of human actions that influence human lives is what imposes moral obligations on all who possess, exploit, or seek medical knowledge. The problems I have sketched in the use of medical knowledge are similar wherever knowledge is used for practical ends—

law, engineering, teaching, or the ministry. The responsible professional of today and tomorrow, therefore, needs as much familiarity with ethics as with the technical foundations of his or her own expertise.

This challenge will become more urgent when, as will surely be the case, access to all sorts of technical knowledge is greatly expanded. The new generation of personal computers will make it possible for patients, for example, to have access to most of what is known about their illness—very likely more than is known to any but the most highly specialized consultant. How will the healing relationship be conducted?

Some might imagine the physician will no longer be necessary and will be replaced as a source of factual information by the personal computer. But in another sense, the physician becomes even more indispensable in an era of information expansion. With all the factual knowledge available, patients must still know whether to use it in *their own* cases, whether it is worthwhile, and how to reconcile the inevitable conflicts in factual data. We will need the objectivity of observation and of diagnostic thinking to be sure whether *this* patient belongs or does not belong in *this* disease category. But more than that, *this* patient needs help in discerning what is the *right* and *good* healing action to take in the face of the particularities, uncertainties, urgencies, and anxieties that make the climate of each clinical decision so complex and so unique.

The physician will still be needed as the advocate, interpreter, partner, helper, carer, the one with the critical faculties to decide, with the patient, to what end and to what purpose *this* medical knowledge will be put. The same will be the case for engineers, lawyers, and those who make public policy decisions. Universally available facts will accentuate, not eliminate, the need for ethical, moral, and value judgments by individuals and society. How we educate the professionals and the public of the future to use knowledge optimally, without being over-shadowed by it, remains the paramount and the exciting challenge for universities and schools.

Notes

1. Wartofsky, Marx, "Medicine and knowledge" (editorial), *The Journal of Medicine and Philosophy*, Vol. 3, no. 4, December 19, 1978, pp. 265–272. The whole of this issue is dedicated to an inquiry into the nature of medical knowledge.

2. Pellegrino, Edmund D., "The anatomy of clinical judgment," in *Philosophy and Medicine*, ed. H. Engelhardt, S. Spicker, and B. Towers (Boston: D. Reidel Pub. Co., 1979), pp. 169–194.

3. Gorovitz, Samuel and MacIntyre, Alasdair, "Toward a theory of medical fallibility," *The Journal of Medicine and Philosophy,* vol. 1, no. 1 (March 1976):51–71; Minogue, Brendan, "Error, malpractice, and the problem of universals," *The Journal of Medicine and Philosophy,* vol. 7, no. 3 (August 1982):239–250; Brody, Howard, "Commentary on error, malpractice, and the problem of universals," *The Journal of Medicine and Philosophy,* vol. 7, no. 3 (August 1982):251–257.

4. John Duns Scotus saw the need for a principle of individuality by which an essence becomes a particular individual, ". . . this composite being composed of this matter and this form." Frederick Copleston, *A History of Philosophy,* Vol. 2 (Westminster, Md.: Newman Press, 1960), p. 517.

5. See Pellegrino, Edmund D., "Anatomy of clinical judgment," pp. 190–191. The application of this classical distinction to medicine is illustrated.

6. Ibid.

7. Vickers, Geoffrey, "Medicine's contribution to culture," *Medicine and Culture,* ed. F. N. L. Poynter, (London: Wellcome Institute of the History of Medicine, 1969), pp. 5–6.

8. Toulmin, Stephen, "Science and ethics: can they be reconnected," *University of Chicago Magazine,* Winter 1981, p. 6.

9. The idea of the separation of facts and values is given practical significance in the suggestion of a science court to establish some consensus on factual foundations for public decisions. Arthur R. Kantrowitz, "Controlling technology democratically," *American Scientist,* Sept.-Oct. 1975, pp. 505–509. See also Chapter 19 in this volume.

Germino rightly condemns the positivist interpretation of the fact-value dichotomy. See Dante Germino, "The fact-value dichotomy as an intellectual prison," *Modern Age,* Vol. 23, no. 2, Spring 1979, pp. 140–144. The distinction I am using is not between subjective and objective beliefs but between what is ascertainable by science and what by ethics.

Bibliography

Pellegrino, E. "The Anatomy of Clinical Judgment: Some Notes on Right Reason and Right Action." *Philosophy and Medicine.* ed. Engelhardt, H.; Spicker, S.; and Towers, B. Vol. 6. (The Netherlands: Reidel, 1979), pp. 169–194.

————— . "Being Ill and Being Healthy: Some Reflections on the Grounding of Medical Morality." *Bulletin of the New York Academy of Medicine.* Vol. 57, no. 1, Jan.-Feb. 1981, pp. 70–79.

————— . "Graduate Education in the Humanities: The Need for Reaffirmation, Connection, and Justification" (occasional paper). Washington, D.C.: The Council of Graduate Schools in the U.S., 1982.

————— . "Health Promotion as Public Policy: The Need for Moral Groundings" (editorial). *Preventive Medicine.* Vol. 10, no. 3, May 1981, pp. 371–378.

————— . *Humanism and the Physician.* Knoxville: Univ. of Tennessee Press, 1979.

————— . "Medical Economics and Medical Morality: The Conflict of Canons." *The Ministry of Healing.* The Catholic Health Association of the U.S., 1981, pp. 91–102.

————. "Religion and Sources of Medical Morality and Healing." *New York State Journal of Medicine.* December 1981, pp. 1859–1864.

————. "Toward a Reconstruction of Medical Morality: The Primacy of the Act of Profession and the Fact of Illness." *The Journal of Medicine and Philosophy.* Vol. 4, no. 1, March 1979, pp. 32–56.

Pellegrino, E. D., and Thomasma, D. *A Philosophical Basis of Medical Practice, Toward a Philosophy and Ethic of the Healing Professions.* Oxford: Oxford Univ. Press, 1981.

————. "Toward an Axiology for Medicine: A Response to Kazem Sadegh-zaden." *Metamedicine.* Vol. 2, June 1981, pp. 331–342.

DONNA H. KERR

—————— 26 ——————

Mediating Structures in the Utilization of Knowledge

Proponents of minimal, laissez faire government perpetuate a myth that knowledge will be utilized if only two necessary and sufficient conditions are met: individuals must be educated, and they must be left alone to put their knowledge to use. The preceding essays illuminate the fictitious nature of that idea. If truth be known, governments (no matter what their ideologies), institutions, and their policies and practices all shape the utilization of knowledge. Only if we develop analytic understandings of just how various structures for collective action mediate the use of knowledge can we hope to comprehend what is required for knowledge utilization at its best.

In "Power Is Knowledge: The Linkages Between the Political System and Knowledge" (Chapter 20), Danziger argues persuasively that political systems can and do shape knowledge utilization, a finding that should both please and concern us. First, the good news: If political systems can make such a difference, then it is possible for humans to devise ways of shaping and using power that favor some understandings and values over others. Thus there is hope that collectively we can choose (1) how we shall conceive of knowledge and (2) what values we shall honor and promote as we utilize that knowledge.

Now, the bad news: It is *not* a foregone conclusion *either* that our richest and best conception of knowledge will prevail in action *or* that the values we embrace will be brought to bear as that knowledge is utilized. Put another way, institutional arrangements in large part shape our decisions and actions; if those arrangements favor conceptions of knowledge we find indefensible while promoting values that are antithetical to our beliefs, what passes as knowledge utilization in the actual political order (which is not always the one professed) will probably offend our sensibilities. For example, adherents of liberal (small "l," in the Enlightenment sense) democracy would shudder at even the remote prospect of a country's being run, in effect if not in name, by the military. The problem in that situation would be not the lack of knowledge utilization but rather the nature of knowledge utilization. As the controlling institution, the military would give decisive weight to a narrow technical conception of knowledge that would be blind to the full epistemological spectrum and would promote values the liberal democrat does not embrace.

In my opinion, the growth of the military's power in the conduct of a society's affairs clearly exemplifies both a misconception of knowledge and its misutilization. But one need not turn to institutions that purposely build capacities for life's destruction to find cases of unacceptable knowledge utilization. Indeed, a society whose government functions in a highly liberal democratic fashion, without threats to its integrity from any military system, could still fall short of well-conceived, desirable knowledge utilization. Lower-level institutions and practices within a society could be (and all too commonly are) based on misconceptions of knowledge and on values antithetical to liberal democracy. Not only, then, can and do political systems shape knowledge utilization, but also those seemingly subpolitical-system institutions—structures that a government may, by choice or default, fail to govern—can promote or subvert knowledge utilization.

While Danziger shows how the political system affects knowledge utilization, Hurwicz, Schön, Slater, Ruttan, and Pellegrino demonstrate ways in which a society's "subsystems" or institutions can hinder or aid the acceptable use of a defensible conception of knowledge. The variety and range of institutions and the practices they analyze suggest that such subsystems, though commonly escaping our closest scrutiny, may have even greater bearing on knowledge utilization than the political stripes of governments.

In "Economic Issues in the Utilization of Knowledge" (Chapter 21), Hurwicz examines the patent system, which, he concludes, should be reformed to widen accessibility to new knowledge without weakening incentives to create further new knowledge. Hurwicz appeals to the Pareto-efficiency criterion to argue for openness and accessibility of information and a free flow of knowledge; but the case for reform could also be made by appealing to those same values of openness and accessibility of information and knowledge as standards of liberal democracy (see Mill's *On Liberty*). Whichever way one constructs the case, however, the conclusion is the same: The patent system, as a vehicle for promoting the creation and utilization of knowledge, favors particular political values. Given the system's present exclusively free-market support for the generation of knowledge, it promotes secrecy rather than an openness that would foster broader knowledge utilization.

In "Education for Reflection-in-Action" (Chapter 23), Schön calls for a reform of the conception of knowledge inherent in professionalism. His objection to professional knowledge as technical rationality is basically epistemic, but there is an additional political moral to be drawn. First, those who treat professional knowledge as technical rationality miscast the conditions under which and to which the professional must respond. Schön would have us abandon the assumption that professionals solve prepackaged problems in favor of the view that out of unstructured "messes," the professional creates problems to solve. The model of reflection-in-action includes not just know-how but also awarenesses and a richness of vision and values as elements of professional knowledge. The political point is that values are integral to a professional's framing of problems. Thus, the institution of professionalism as it has evolved unavoidably treats laypersons as children whom the professional tells not only how to solve their problems but also what their problems are. In doing so, professionalism violates both our best understandings of the complexity of knowledge as applied in practice and the liberal value of the participation of people (in this case, clients) in decisions affecting their own destinies.

Slater, in "Adapting Technology Knowledge to Social Needs" (Chapter 17), remarks on the historically rooted schism in our research institutions between those who generate technical, how-to knowledge and those who focus on, among other things, what constitutes a sound conception of knowledge and what values particular actions promote. Slater offers that standoffs on such issues as whether to preserve food by irradiation derive from the inability of the two groups of knowledge producers to talk to one another. In effect, he argues that if technical knowledge is to be utilized and if, at the same time, the epistemic and value demands of defensible, desirable knowledge utilization are to be heeded, we shall have to revise both the fashion in which our research institutions define problems and generate solutions and the way we educate for problem solving.

In "Accountability in Research: Examples from Agriculture" (Chapter 18), Ruttan urges changing the way in which research institutions are grafted onto society. In particular, if liberal-democratic values are to be protected and promoted in the use of research, decisions about what to do in light of technical knowledge must be a responsibility shared by all and not the burden solely of the research technologists.

Pellegrino's "Optimizing the Use of Medical Knowledge" (Chapter 25) presents a view of medical practice as properly including, in addition to technical, probabilistic, goal-directed knowledge, an overriding regard for each individual patient's beliefs and values. As a professional practice, medicine could blatantly violate the liberal value of individuals' deciding for themselves. In the case of public health, Pellegrino would enhance the quality of medical practice by increasing the participation of those with expertise in moral and ethical questions.

In sum, these papers indicate the ways in which professionalism and other of society's subsystems have the capacity to operate independently of our most sophisticated understandings of knowledge and the professed values of the political system. Professionalism and research are neither epistemically nor value neutral. If we wish to promote knowledge utilization at its best, we shall have to reform professionalism, as the institution that generates and uses specialized knowledge, and the research system, as the institution that expends scarce resources in the selective generation of knowledge. In this set of papers, a link, a third type of mediating structure, is missing. We shall also need to reform bureaucracy, the dominant institution for organizing work, through which knowledge must be used if it is to have broad application in the society.

About the Contributors

ALBERT L. AYARS is superintendent of schools in Norfolk, Virginia. Born in Washington in 1917, he received his Ph.D. from Washington State University; he has been involved in school administration and educational development since 1942. He has served in an advisory or consulting capacity to many groups and institutions, both in the United States and abroad, and has been visiting professor at a number of universities.

In addition to numerous educational filmstrips, booklets, and resource and teaching units, he has written several well-known texts in the education field. Among these are *Administering the People's Schools* (1957), *The Teenager and Alcohol* (1970), and *The Teenager and the Law* (1978).

MARY CATHERINE BATESON is currently dean of the faculty and professor of anthropology at Amherst College in Massachusetts. Born in New York, she received her Ph.D. from Harvard in linguistics and Middle Eastern studies. She has taught or conducted research at the University of Northern Iran, Ateneo de Manila University, Northeastern University, Harvard University, Brandeis, and the Massachusetts Institute of Technology.

Her published articles deal with mother-infant communication, linguistic development, and Iranian value systems. She is author of *Arabic Language Handbook* (1967), *Structural Continuity in Poetry: A Linguistic Study of Five Early Arabic Odes* (1970), and *Our Own Metaphor: A Personal Account of a Conference on Conscious Purpose and Human Adaptation* (1971) and coeditor with T. A. Sebeok and A. S. Hayes of *Approaches to Semiotics: Anthropology, Education, Linguistics, Psychiatry, Psychology* (1964).

ROBERT D. BEAM is an assistant professor of economics in the Division of Business and Economics at the University of Wisconsin–Superior.

Born in Illinois in 1945, he received his Ph.D. at the University of Cincinnati in 1979.

He is currently director of the Center for Economic Education at the University of Wisconsin–Superior and was a recipient of the 1980–1981 Special Merit award for teaching excellence at that institution. He has previously held faculty positions at Berea College and Miami University.

His research interests include unified social science, general systems theory, organizational theory, and macroeconomic analysis. He is the author of "Testing the Integrated Social Science Hypothesis: An Economic Approach" and *The Logic of Organization* (with Alfred Kuhn; 1982).

LEO BOGART is executive vice president and general manager of the Newspaper Advertising Bureau, which he joined in 1960. He holds a Ph.D. in sociology from the University of Chicago. He has been president of the American Association for Public Opinion Research and received its award for distinguished contributions to public opinion research. He was in the first group elected to the American Marketing Association's Hall of Fame; he received the first Market Research Council award, the Sidney Goldish award, and a number of Media/Scope awards.

Bogart has been president of the Radio and Television Research Council, the World Association for Public Opinion Research, and the Market Research Council. He is a fellow of the American Psychological Association. He is author of *Press and Public* (1981), *Premises for Propaganda* (1976), *Silent Politics* (1972), *The Age of Television* (1972), *Strategy in Advertising* (1967), and several other books, along with over eighty articles.

PAUL BOHANNAN is now dean of the Division of Social Sciences and Communications at the University of Southern California, Los Angeles. At the time this book was written, he was professor of anthropology at the University of California, Santa Barbara. Born in Nebraska in 1920, he went to Oxford as a Rhodes Scholar and took his D.Phil. there in 1951. He has taught at Oxford, Princeton, and Northwestern.

His field work was done among the Tiv of Nigeria, the Wanga of Kenya, and several groups of people living in the United States— divorcées, stepfamilies, and old men living in the center-city hotels of San Diego. He has written books on Africa, the history of anthropology, and divorce as well as a textbook on social anthropology and a regular column for *Science 82*. He was president of the American Anthropological Association during 1978–1979.

KENNETH E. BOULDING is Distinguished Professor Emeritus of Economics and is affiliated with the Institute of Behavioral Science at the University of Colorado, Boulder. Born in England in 1910, he was educated at Oxford (B.A. and M.A.) and was a Commonwealth fellow at the University of Chicago. He also holds honorary degrees from a number of universities.

He is a well-known author of articles and books whose works include *The Image* (1956), *The Meaning of the Twentieth Century* (1964), *Beyond Economics* (1968), *Stable Peace* (1978), *Ecodynamics* (1978), and *Evolutionary Economics* (1981).

Prior to joining the University of Colorado in 1968, he held academic positions at several universities, including the University of Michigan, McGill, Iowa State, and Colgate, in addition to visiting appointments at the University of Texas–Austin, Dartmouth, and Ohio State, among others. He has received several awards, including the American Council of Learned Societies Prize for Distinguished Scholarship/Humanities and the Frank E. Seidman Distinguished Award in Political Economy. He has been president of several organizations, including the AAAS and the American Economic Association.

JAMES N. DANZIGER is professor of political science in the School of Social Sciences and Research Scientist at the Public Policy Research Organization at the University of California, Irvine. Born in California in 1945, he received his Ph.D. from Stanford. He is associate editor of the journal *Knowledge: Creation, Diffusion and Utilization.*

He is author of *Making Budgets: Public Resource Allocation* (1978) and coauthor of *Computers and Politics: High Technology in American Local Governments* (1982). He also has written numerous articles in books and professional journals. He was a Marshall Scholar at the University of Sussex and Ford Foundation Foreign Area Fellowship Program fellow (Western Europe). He received the Distinguished Teaching Award from the University of California, Irvine, in 1979; the Leonard D. White Award of the American Political Science Association in 1974; and the Marshall E. Dimock Award of the American Society for Public Administration in 1979.

HERMAN T. EPSTEIN is professor of biology at Brandeis University. Born in Maine in 1920, he received his Ph.D. in physics in 1949 from the University of Michigan–Ann Arbor. He utilizes his extensive research in brain growth to generate working hypotheses concerning child development, the underachieving school child, schooling strategies, and the possible relevance of these implications to separate education for boys and girls.

He was a National Science Foundation fellow (1959), Commonwealth fellow (1963), Guggenheim fellow (1969), and visiting professor at Hebrew and Tel Aviv universities. Epstein was also a member of the "think tank" that created the Medical School at Ben Gurion University of the Negev, with its special orientation in public medicine.

DAVID HAWKINS is Philip A. Danielson Distinguished Professor of Philosophy at the University of Colorado, Boulder. Born in Texas in 1913, he was educated at Stanford and the University of California, receiving his Ph.D. from Berkeley in 1940. For the last twenty years he has been involved in practical and theoretical work affecting elementary school education. Most recently he has been director of the Mountain View Center, offering advisory help to preschool and elementary school teachers.

Retiring in 1982, he has received a five-year MacArthur fellowship and plans continued work in education, relating mainly to science and math teaching. He is author of *The Language of Nature* (1964), *The Informed Vision* (1973), and *The Science and Ethics of Equality* (1976).

W. N. HUBBARD, JR., has been president of The Upjohn Company in Kalamazoo, Michigan, since 1974 and has held executive positions with Upjohn since 1968. Born in North Carolina in 1919, he was educated at Columbia University and the University of North Carolina School of Medicine. He received his M.D. from the New York University School of Medicine in 1944. He has been actively involved with the National Science Board of the National Science Foundation, the Board of Science and Technology for International Development of the National Academy of Sciences, the National Library of Medicine, and others. He is a member of the board of trustees at Columbia University.

He also has served in both faculty and administrative positions at the New York University College of Medicine and the University of Michigan Medical School. He is author of numerous books and articles; his works have appeared in such scholarly journals as the *Journal of Clinical Investigation* and the *Journal of Medical Education*.

LEONID HURWICZ is Regents' Professor of Economics at the University of Minnesota. Born in 1917, he received his law degree from Warsaw University in Poland and emigrated to the United States in 1940. He did graduate work at the London School of Economics, Massachusetts Institute of Technology, Harvard, and the University of Chicago.

He has published articles on welfare economics, theory of games, economic planning with special emphasis on incentives, and design of economic systems. He has been president of the Econometric Society, a Guggenheim fellow, and Fulbright Professor at Bangalore University in India; he has also served as visiting professor at Stanford; Harvard; the University of California, Berkeley; and the Indian Statistical Institute at New Delhi. He is a distinguished fellow of the American Economic Association, a fellow of the Econometric Society, and a member of the Academy of Independent Scholars, American Academy of Arts and Sciences, and National Academy of Sciences.

ELIZABETH WRIGHT INGRAHAM is founder and president of the Wright-Ingraham Institute in Colorado Springs, Colorado. The Institute was established in 1971 as an educational and research institution to promote, encourage, direct, and develop opportunities for conserving, preserving, and using human and natural resources. She is also in private practice as an architect and is a member of the State Board of Examiners of Architects (1979–1984).

Born in Oak Park, Illinois, in 1922, Ingraham was educated at the University of California, Berkeley, and at the Illinois Institute of Technology. She was a founder of Summer Crossroads, a posteducational program for foreign exchange students, and has been active as a member of the Front Range Project in Colorado. She was a visiting professor at the Environmental Design College at the University of Colorado, Boulder, in 1980–1981.

ARTHUR R. KANTROWITZ is a professor and senior lecturer in engineering sciences at the Thayer School of Engineering at Dartmouth, a post he has held since 1979. Prior to assuming that position he served as director and chairman of the Avco-Everett Research Lab in Massachusetts and held an academic post at Cornell. Born in New York in 1913, he received his Ph.D. in physics from Columbia University in 1947.

He has written numerous articles for professional journals and served as a member of the Presidential Advisory Group on Anticipated Advances in Science and Technology (1975–1976). He is a recipient of the Theodore Roosevelt Distinguished Service Medal and is a member of several organizations, including the National Academy of Sciences and the National Academy of Engineering. During 1980 he served as honorary professor at the Huazhong Institute of Technology in China and in 1979 received the Owl Alumni Award for distinguished service from the School of General Studies at Columbia.

DONNA H. KERR is special assistant to the director of the Institute for Advanced Study at Princeton University. At the time this book was written, she was associate dean for graduate studies and research in the College of Education, founder and director of the Institute for the Study of Educational Policy, and professor of philosophy of education at the University of Washington–Seattle. She received her Ph.D. from Columbia University in 1973.

Kerr is on the editorial boards of such journals as *Knowledge: Creation, Diffusion, and Utilization* and *Educational Theory.* A Spencer fellow of the National Academy of Education, she is author of *Barriers to Integrity: Modern Modes of Knowledge Utilization* (Westview; forthcoming), *Educational Policy: Analysis, Structure, and Justification* (1976) and numerous articles in books and professional journals, such as *Policy Sciences, Knowledge,* and *Studies in Philosophy and Education.*

DIANE McGUINNESS is a research associate in the Neuropsychology Laboratories and lecturer in the Department of Human Biology at Stanford University. She has also held academic positions at the University of California, Santa Cruz, and Hatfield Polytechnic in Hertfordshire, England. Born in California in 1938, she received her Ph.D. from University College, London, in 1974.

She is a recipient of the Goldsmiths of London fellowship and the Medical Research Council scholarship and is a member of the American Psychological Association, the Society for Research on Music Education, and the British Psychological Society. She has published numerous articles, specializing in the role of sex differences in perceptual processes.

The late FRITZ MACHLUP was an economist with strong transdisciplinary interests. Born in Austria in 1902, he came to the United States in 1933. He served as president of the American Association of University Professors, the American Economic Association, and the International Economic Association. Among his many books published since 1925 are *The Economics of Sellers' Competition* (1952), *Production and Distribution of Knowledge in the United States* (1962), *Remaking the International Monetary System* (1968), *Methodology of Economics and Other Social Sciences* (1978), and the first two volumes of a projected ten-volume series on *Knowledge: Its Creation, Distribution and Economic Significance*—Volume 1 on *Knowledge and Knowledge Production* (1980) and Volume 2 on *The Branches of Learning* (1982).

He taught at Harvard, Buffalo, Johns Hopkins, Princeton, and, for the last twelve years of his life, New York University. He was elected a member of the American Philosophical Society and a fellow of the American Academy of Arts and Sciences and the AAAS. He received six honorary degrees, two of them from universities in Europe.

ROLLO MAY is a psychoanalyst and author; he was in private practice in New York until 1975 and is now located in Tiburon, California. He has held academic positions at various colleges and universities, including Yale, Harvard, Princeton, the University of California, and the American College in Saloniki, Greece, and has lectured at universities worldwide.

Born in Ohio in 1909, he received a Master of Divinity degree from Union Theological Seminary before receiving his Ph.D. from Columbia in 1949. He received his psychoanalytic training at the William Alanson White Institute of Psychology, Psychoanalysis and Psychiatry in 1952.

Among his best-known books are *The Meaning of Anxiety* (1950), *Man's Search for Himself* (1953), *Psychology and the Human Dilemma* (1966), *Love and Will* (1969), *Power and Innocence* (1972), *The Courage To Create* (1975), and *Freedom and Destiny* (1982).

JOSEPH D. NOVAK is professor of science education at Cornell University. His research centers on the problem-solving ability of students, working with information-processing models and Ausubel's assimilation theory of cognitive learning. Recent work includes research with learning-to-learn strategies of concept mapping and Gowin's Epistemological Vee mapping.

He has specialized in secondary school science and mathematics teaching and has been active in curriculum development at both the school and university levels. He was a faculty member at the University of Minnesota, Kansas State Teachers College, and Purdue before joining Cornell in 1967.

Novak is past president of the Association of Midwestern College Biology Teachers and the National Association for Research in Science Teaching and is active in the AAAS and other professional societies. He is author of numerous books and articles. Born in Minneapolis in 1930, he received his Ph.D. from the University of Minnesota in 1958.

EDMUND D. PELLEGRINO is the first John Carroll University Professor of Medicine and Medical Humanities at Georgetown University Medical School. When this book was written, he was president of the Catholic University of America. His interests join the fields of medicine and the humanities, and he founded *The Journal of Medicine and Philosophy* to explore issues posed by these two disciplines. He is author of *Humanism and the Physician* (1979) and *The Philosophical Basis of Medical Practice* (1981), both of which reflect his interest in combining classical and modern forms of education.

In addition to numerous honorary degrees, he has received the Presidential Medal from St. John's University, the Encyclopaedia Britannica Achievement in Life award, and an award from the American Medical Association for his work in the allied health field.

Prior to joining Catholic University, he held positions at the University of Tennessee, SUNY–Stony Brook, and the Yale–New Haven Medical Center. Born in New Jersey in 1920, he was educated at St. John's University in Brooklyn and received his M.D. from New York University.

KARL H. PRIBRAM is head of the Neuropsychology Laboratories and professor of neuroscience in the Departments of Psychology and Psychiatry and Behavioral Sciences at Stanford University. His career over the past three decades has been devoted to brain research at Yerkes Laboratories of Primate Biology, Yale, and Stanford. He has a lifetime research career award from the National Institutes of Health. Born in Vienna in 1919, he received his M.D. degree from the University of Chicago and is certified in neurological surgery.

His books include *Plans and the Structure of Behavior* (with George Miller and Eugene Galanter), *Languages of the Brain* (1971), and *Freud's Project Re-assessed* (with Merton Gill; 1976). He is editor of *Brain and Behavior* (four volumes), *The Biology of Learning, The Biology of Memory* (with Donald Broadbent; 1970), *Psychophysiology of the Frontal Lobes* (with Alexander R. Luria; 1973), and *The Hippocampus* (with Robert Isaacson). He also has written numerous research publications, reviews, and theoretical contributions.

BERNARD ROTH is a professor in the Department of Mechanical Engineering at Stanford University. His research specialities are kinematics, robotics, computer-aided design, applied mathematics, and analytical methods in design.

Born in New York in 1933, he received his Ph.D. from Columbia University in 1962. He held positions as design engineer in the private sector before holding academic posts at City College of New York, Columbia, and Stanford. He is author of numerous articles in scholarly journals and of *Theoretical Kinematics* (with O. Bottema). He has been a visiting professor at Technological University of Delft (Netherlands), University of the Negev (Israel), and Chiao Tung University (Shanghai) and has participated in the USA-India NSF Scientific Exchange as well as the USA-USSR Inter-Academy Exchange. He is president of the International Federation for the Theory of Machines and Mechanisms and has held major positions with the American Society of Mechanical Engineers.

VERNON RUTTAN is a professor in the Department of Agricultural and Applied Economics and the Department of Economics at the

University of Minnesota. His research areas are the economics of technical change, resource economics, and agricultural development.

He is past president and fellow of the American Agricultural Economics Association and president of the Agricultural Development Council. He has served on the Council of Economic Advisors and the Rockefeller Foundation; he has held faculty positions at Purdue and Minnesota and visiting appointments at the University of California and the University of the Philippines. He is active in consulting and research on international agricultural problems.

In addition to numerous journal articles, he is the author of several books: *Agricultural Development: An International Perspective* (with Yujiro Hayami; 1971), *Induced Innovation: Technology, Institutions, and Development* (with Hans Binswanger; 1978), and *Agricultural Research Policy* (1982). Born in Michigan in 1924, he received his Ph.D. from the University of Chicago in 1952.

DONALD A. SCHÖN is Ford Professor of Urban Affairs and Education at the Massachusetts Institute of Technology. He is a student of creativity and the cultivation of technical innovation, educational reform, and organizational learning.

He headed the new product group at Arthur D. Little, Inc.; served as first director of the Institute for Applied Technology at the National Bureau of Standards; and helped found the nonprofit Organization for Social and Technical Innovation, which was concerned with community and neighborhood development, housing, health, and education systems. He has written many articles and books, including *Beyond the Stable State* (1971), *Theory and Practice: Increasing Professional Effectiveness* (with Chris Argyris; 1974), *Organizational Learning: A Theory of Action Perspective* (with Chris Argyris; 1978), and *The Reflective Practitioner* (in press).

Before joining MIT in 1972, he taught at UCLA, Kansas City, and the Kennedy School of Government at Harvard. He was chosen as the 1970 Reith lecturer for the British Broadcasting Corporation. Born in 1930, he holds a Ph.D. from Harvard University.

LAWRENCE SENESH is copresident and founding member of the Academy of Independent Scholars and holds the rank of Professor Emeritus of Economics at the University of Colorado, Boulder. Prior to joining the University of Colorado in 1969, he held academic positions at Purdue and the University of Denver. He is also one of the founders of the Social Science Education Consortium in Boulder and is known as the person who established the "organic curriculum," which is based on the hypothesis that the analytical structure of the social sciences can be related to the experience of youth with increasing depth and complexity. He was awarded an honorary Doctor of Letters degree from Purdue University in 1977 for his work in this area.

Senesh has served as adviser or consultant to a number of groups and has published many articles. He is the author of a series of books for elementary school children entitled *Our Working World*. Born in Hungary in 1910, he emigrated to the United States in 1940. He attended the London School of Economics and holds a Diploma of Economics from the University of Berlin and a law degree from the University of Budapest.

LLOYD E. SLATER is manager of the Food and Climate Forum, an activity of the Aspen Institute for Humanistic Studies. Trained in biochemistry and food engineering, he has divided his career between technical journalism and research-and-development management, particularly in the application of technology to societal problems. He is executive director of the Academy of Independent Scholars.

He has been editor and publisher of *Food Engineering International*, executive director of Puerto Rico's Institute of Social Technology, and associate director of research at the Case Institute of Technology. He is author of numerous publications on climatic impact, food engineering, automatic control technology, and biomedical engineering, including the books *Instrument and Control Engineering* (1952), *Bio-Telemetry* (1962), and *Climate's Impact on Food Supplies* (1981). Born in New York in 1919, he was educated at Cornell and the Polytechnic Institute of Brooklyn.

HERBERT STEINHOUSE is a senior executive with the Canadian Broadcasting Corporation in Montreal, Canada. He became a foreign correspondent in Paris and Western Europe after serving with the Royal Canadian Air Force during World War II and with the Displaced Persons Operations of UNRRA in Germany and Austria in 1945–1946.

He has been a broadcaster with the United Nations in Southeast Asia; an editor-producer with UNESCO; and a journalist with the CBC in Europe, North Africa, and Asia. He has been with the Canadian Broadcasting Corporation since the mid-1950s as public affairs producer, program director, and in various executive functions.

He is author of a political novel on France and Algeria entitled *Ten Years After* (U.S. title: *The Time of the Juggernaut*; 1958). Born in Montreal in 1922, he was educated at McGill and has an M.A. in international relations from the New School for Social Research in New York City.

Fritz Machlup (right) holds the attention of a guest from the National Education Association

Lawrence Senesh (left) shares a joke with Lloyd Slater

Herbert Steinhouse (left) and Bernard Roth

Kenneth Boulding (right) makes a point with Donald Schön

Both Victor Davidson (left) and Rollo May display skepticism

Donna Kerr's emphasis is judiciously noted by Henry Koffler (right)

Edmund Pellegrino

David Hawkins, flanked by Albert Ayars,
summarizes his position

Diane McGuinness

Henry Epstein

Paul Bohannan

Rollo May

Index

The Academy of Independent Scholars

The Academy of Independent Scholars provides a creative environment for senior academicians and senior leaders in business, labor, and civic organizations whose talents are wasted because of involuntary retirement or whose lifelong independence has isolated them from the network of creative scholarship. Scholars active in later life are an enormous asset to society; yet this asset is often shockingly wasted because of the absence of an appropriate working environment and other support. To remedy this situation, thirty scholars—building on their shared commitment—came to the Wingspread Conference Center in Racine, Wisconsin, in January 1979 to found the Academy of Independent Scholars. At present the academy is committed to three working areas:

1. identifying the needs of its members who lack institutional affiliation and attempting to help them continue their creative work;
2. promoting the optimum utilization of knowledge for human betterment;
3. encouraging interdisciplinary dialogue on national and global topics.

Lawrence Senesh

Academy of Independent Scholars Forum Series

Human knowledge is the ultimate source of all human artifacts, organization, and society and is closely bound up with human welfare. The growth of knowledge has given us many benefits: It has made us richer, extended our lifespan, and increased our comforts. But much existing knowledge is intentionally or unintentionally ignored or mis-applied in private and public decision making. If the misuse of knowledge continues, it could lead to tragic global consequences: nuclear holocaust and environmental disaster. Recognizing the consequences of under-utilization and misuse of knowledge, the Academy of Independent Scholars has launched a series of multidisciplinary forums that will explore the conditions necessary for the optimum utilization of knowledge for human betterment. This volume is the first in the Academy Forum Series. It reports on the symposium on the optimum utilization of knowledge held at the University of Massachusetts, Amherst, November 5–8, 1981.

L. S.

Academy of Independent Scholars Forum Series

The Optimum Utilization of Knowledge:
Making Knowledge Serve Human Betterment
edited by Kenneth E. Boulding and Lawrence Senesh

We all have more knowledge than we use; even so, say the editors of this book, ignorance often governs our actions. Society continues to find ways to misuse knowledge—from manipulating information to gain political power to restricting what ideas are explored on university campuses. Thus, when some of the best minds in the country met to focus on the optimum utilization of knowledge, it was not an idle academic inquiry.

In these proceedings from that conference, which was sponsored by the Academy of Independent Scholars, the contributors examine several of the key aspects of learning: the importance of knowledge in decision making, the role of our educational system and other systems in producing and disseminating knowledge, and the relationship between knowledge and the physiological, psychological, and cultural bases of the learning process. The misuse of knowledge—or the overuse of ignorance—the authors note, could threaten the existence of the entire planet, if the kind of thinking exemplified by the nuclear arms race prevails.

Kenneth E. Boulding is Distinguished Professor Emeritus of Economics at the University of Colorado, Boulder. He is a well-known author and past president of several organizations, including the American Association for the Advancement of Science and the American Economic Association. **Lawrence Senesh,** Professor Emeritus of Economics at the University of Colorado, Boulder, is copresident and founding member (with Kenneth Boulding) of the Academy of Independent Scholars. He is also one of the founders of the Social Science Education Consortium. The academy was established in 1979 to provide a creative environment for retired scholars and for those whose independent scholarship does not fit the conventional niches of their institutions.